MURDER AND MARTIAL JUSTICE

TRUE CRIME HISTORY SERIES

Twilight of Innocence: The Disappearance of Beverly Potts
James Jessen Badal

Tracks to Murder
Jonathan Goodman

Terrorism for Self-Glorification: The Herostratos Syndrome
Albert Borowitz

Ripperology: A Study of the World's First Serial Killer and a Literary Phenomenon
Robin Odell

The Good-bye Door: The Incredible True Story of America's First Female Serial Killer to Die in the Chair
Diana Britt Franklin

Murder on Several Occasions
Jonathan Goodman

The Murder of Mary Bean and Other Stories
Elizabeth A. De Wolfe

Lethal Witness: Sir Bernard Spilsbury, Honorary Pathologist
Andrew Rose

Murder of a Journalist: The True Story of the Death of Donald Ring Mellett
Thomas Crowl

Musical Mysteries: From Mozart to John Lennon
Albert Borowitz

The Adventuress: Murder, Blackmail, and Confidence Games in the Gilded Age
Virginia A. McConnell

Queen Victoria's Stalker: The Strange Case of the Boy Jones
Jan Bondeson

Born to Lose: Stanley B. Hoss and the Crime Spree That Gipped a Nation
James G. Hollock

Murder and Martial Justice: Spying and Retribution in World War II America
Meredith Lentz Adams

MURDER AND MARTIAL JUSTICE

Spying and Retribution In World War II America

MEREDITH LENTZ ADAMS

The Kent State University Press Kent, Ohio

Library of Congress Catalog Card Number 2011000670
ISBN 978-1-60635-075-1
Maufactured in the United States of America

Library of Congress Cataloging-in-Publication Data
Adams, Meredith Lentz, 1938–
Murder and martial justice : spying and retribution in World War II America / Meredith Lentz Adams.
p. cm. — (True crime history series)
Includes bibliographical references and index.
ISBN 978-1-60635-075-1 (hardcover : alk. paper)
1. World War, 1939–1945—Prisoners and prisons, American. 2. Prisoners of war—United States—History—20th century. 3. Prisoners of war—Germany—History—20th century. 4. Germans—United States—History—20th century. 5. Spies—United States—History—20th century. 6. Murder—United States—History—20th century. 7. Retribution—History—20th century. 8. Prisoners of war—Abuse of—United States—History—20th century. 9. Torture—Government policy—United States—History—20th century. 10. Executions and executioners—United States—History—20th century. I. Title.
D805.U5A33 2011
940.54'87430973—dc22

2011000670

British Library Cataloging-in-Publication data are available.

15 14 13 12 11 5 4 3 2 1

Contents

Acknowledgments

First I would like to thank the three people who made this book possible: Ken Knox, who brought the subject to my attention and generously shared his documents; Margie von der Heide, department secretary, who arranged for me to have some two-or-three day teaching schedules before I retired; and my colleague and husband David B. Adams, who uttered the magic words, "Honey, let's eat out."

Thanks to Matt Mancini, an outstanding chairman of the history department at Southwest Missouri State University (now Missouri State), who gave me unstinting encouragement. I also thank Al Rose, Bill Piston, and Phyllis Shaw for reading all or part of my manuscript, and Lyle Polly and Eleanor Link who checked my French translations for accuracy and elegance.

The archivists at the National Archives gave wonderful help, as did those at the Yale University Library. Special thanks to Pam Morrison and BW&A Books, Inc. in Durham, North Carolina. And my children contributed, eventually, an empty nest. My special thanks to Mariya, for computer help, and to Jessica, who never got to play soccer but gave me grandchildren anyway.

This book is dedicated to my teachers, particularly Miss Sarah Frances Cunningham of Newton Academy School in Asheville, North Carolina; Phyllis Abbott Peacock at Broughton High School in Raleigh (writing teacher extraordinaire); Richard Painter, Vera Largent, Jordan Kurland, Eugene Pfaff, and Richard Bardolf at the Woman's College of the University of North Carolina (now UNC-Greensboro); and Oliver H. Radkey and R. John Rath at the University of Texas, Austin.

Abbreviations

ASF	Army Service Forces
AW	Articles of War
B-CMR	Beyer Five court-martial (Beyer, Seidel, Demer, Schomer, Scholz)
BR	Board Report: "Report of Board of Officers Appointed to Inquire into and Determine the Responsibility for the Death of Prisoner of War Werner Drechsler
DB/USDB	U.S. Disciplinary Barracks (Fort Leavenworth, Kansas)
D-CMR	Werner Drechsler court-martial (Helmuth Fischer, Fritz Franke, Guenther Kuelsen, Heinrich Ludwig, Bernhard Reyak, Otto Stengel, and Rolf Wizuy)
DEF	Disarmed Enemy Forces
G-1	U.S. Army Personnel
G-2	U.S. Army Intelligence
IRC	International Red Cross
JAG/JAGO	Judge Advocate General/Judge Advocate General's Office
JCS	Joint Chiefs of Staff
M-CMR	Edgar Menschner court-martial
NA, RG	National Archives of the United States, Record Group
ONI	Office of Naval Intelligence
PMG/PMGO	Provost Marshal General, Provost Marshal General's Office
PWD	Prisoner of War Operations Division, War Department
SAC	Special Agent in Charge, FBI
SEP	Surrendered Enemy Prisoners
SP	stool pigeon or special prisoner
SWPD	Special War Problems Division, State Department

Introduction

This book deals with four murder cases during World War II, for which fifteen German war prisoners held in camps on American soil were sentenced to death, and fourteen hanged. It emphasizes one case that best illustrates how the War Department interpreted, observed, and violated the Geneva Convention of 1929. It also deals with the War Department's consequent diplomatic and public relations problems and with its attempts to control the prison camps. At present, the Pentagon defends itself against the charge of abusing war prisoners, but during the war it was charged with mollycoddling them. Whatever abuses occurred in wartime could be kept secret. The four crimes, trials, and executions thus received little or no publicity. The bodies of fourteen Germans lay in complete obscurity among the unclaimed corpses of disgraced American ex-soldiers in a small prison cemetery, about a mile from the Disciplinary Barracks at Fort Leavenworth, Kansas (DB).

How, then, did they come to be remembered? Richard Whittingham discovered the neglected cemetery by chance while he was serving as a news writer for the DB's public information office in the 1960s. Curiosity piqued, he found "a small file . . . kept in a locked cabinet along with other files on subjects about which the army was reluctant to provide information." It would take him more than six years, in those days before the Freedom of Information Act, before his curiosity was satisfied. He published his book, *Martial Justice: The Last Mass Execution in the United States*, in 1971.[1] Whittingham succeeded in telling a fascinating story based on interviews and archival research. Unfortunately, he provided no footnotes.

John Hammond Moore became interested in one of the four murder cases while researching *The Faustball Tunnel: German Prisoners of War in America and Their Great Escape (1978)*; which occurred at a camp for naval prisoners at Papago Park, Arizona.[2] Arnold Krammer's *Nazi Prisoners of War in America*, an invaluable general history published in 1979, also mentioned the camp murders in a chapter devoted to the War Department's struggle to maintain control of the prisoner of war camps.[3] None of these three authors intended to delve into the Pentagon politics behind the four murder trials or into the diplomatic problems they produced.

To my knowledge, the only German book that tells of the Papago Park case, *Die Gefangenen: Leben und Überleben deutscher Soldaten hinter Stacheldraht*, written by Paul Carell and Günter Böddeker in 1980, relied entirely on the books by Moore and Whittingham for information.[4]

In 1980 someone else discovered and explored the cemetery at Fort Leavenworth. A corrections officer, Sgt. Kenneth Knox, came across it on a Sunday bicycle ride with his wife. He sensed that "something was not right here." The place was "dirty and unkempt." The headstones, hidden in weeds, contained names and death dates but no military rank, since American soldiers convicted of crimes had been dishonorably discharged. But "along the back fence, we noticed another row of headstones separated from the rest by at least a hundred feet." These markers had German names, German ranks, and only three death dates within six weeks of each other, after the war had ended.[5]

Sgt. Knox began asking questions. At the local newspaper morgue he learned that "Nazi extremists" had been hanged for "trying to control the prisoner of war camps." He queried the National Archives, which denied having any information. Then an officer suggested that he use the words "Freedom of Information Act request."

This time, he received a large package of documents that raised more questions than they answered. They revealed that fourteen war prisoners had been executed for killing four snitches, fellow prisoners who had spied on them on behalf of their own country's enemy. "I could hardly believe what I was reading. . . . Why was each document stamped in large letters, 'SECRET'? Why were the documents so inconsistent with the newspaper articles? Why were so many of the documents from such high level military and civilian personnel?" At the nearby Truman Library he obtained copies of the execution orders. A letter to the Roosevelt Library gained him case summaries signed by Secretary of War Stimson. Then he "hit the jackpot" when "the Judge Advocate General of the United States Army" sent him three trial transcripts.

Knox was not only intrigued by what he was finding but also morally offended. "These soldiers had done what any other soldier in any army anywhere in the world would have done," namely, silenced "a traitor in their own ranks." Furthermore, some of them had been tortured into confessing their deeds. Then, to add insult to injury, they were "labeled murderers" and "buried in the most disgraceful place that any soldier can be buried," among criminals whose very grave sites symbolized their dishonor. In veterans' cemeteries, the graves "faced east and west so that the sun rises and sets over the body. At the Disciplinary Barracks, prisoners' graves faced north and south. No clergy member is allowed to bless the ground." And he heard rumors at the DB "that these German soldiers are buried face down."[6]

During a three-year tour in Germany, Sgt. Knox found that no one in the prisoners' own country "had any knowledge of the executions." After being reassigned to Fort Leavenworth, he took his documents out of storage and kept on asking questions. He developed such a reputation as the expert on the prisoner cemetery that the commandant invited him to lunch with a visiting federal judge from Kansas City. "For forty-five minutes the judge listened with interest. I failed to realize that the commandant was becoming very angry. He couldn't believe that Military Intelligence would torture prisoners of war." The next day he told Knox that "[he] had embarrassed [his] uniform and the United States Army." After six months of being assigned "one rotten detail after another," Knox retired from a twenty-two-year career.

Sgt. Knox strongly felt that these fourteen Germans should be reinterred in an honorable place. He wanted to tell their story, but the task overwhelmed him. One of his co-workers remarked that one of his former professors might be interested in helping. I was. A telephone call from a complete stranger had me hooked. What he had in mind was a quick narrative. What he got was a historian addicted to footnotes, who was held back by a busy teaching schedule and a young family, and who finally finished the manuscript in retirement.

As I read through the mass of documents Sgt. Knox shared with me, I saw wider issues. The stories of these fourteen war prisoners (and the fifteenth, who escaped hanging) stretched from internment camps in Kansas, Arkansas, South Carolina, and Arizona to the Pentagon, through the State Department to Switzerland and Berlin. To tell the story properly, I had to scour the National Archives.

Working in the National Archives is great fun. I found letters, reports, memos, policy papers, lists, transcripts of telephone calls, and stray documents carelessly left in unlikely places, until patterns emerged and the writers assumed personalities. Sometimes the best evidence is silence or, better still, attempts to cover up embarrassing incidents. Secrecy is impossible as long as mammoth bureaucracies need to communicate within and among themselves. Items expunged in one place turn up in another agency's files.

It was necessary to hack through bureaucratic jungles. Within the War Department, the Provost Marshal General's Office (PMGO) had physical custody of war prisoners. The Adjutant General's Office operated G-2, Military Intelligence, which interrogated them for vital information, although the Office of Naval Intelligence (ONI) had first go at submariners. Since the Geneva Convention placed war prisoners under the laws of the Detaining Power, and the Laws of War were the province of the Judge Advocate General's Office, that agency tried those who committed crimes.

The War Department would have preferred to exercise these jurisdictions alone; but unfortunately, diplomatic relations were the responsibility of the State Department. The Geneva Convention Relative to the Treatment of Prisoners of War (1929) set up a system of Protecting Powers. Switzerland protected German interests in the United States as well as American interests in Germany. Such protection involved inspecting POW camps, a task shared by the International Red Cross (IRC). Protecting Powers also provided communication between the Detaining Powers and their enemies and negotiated with both belligerent parties to defend the prisoners' rights under the convention. The State Department could not deal with these matters without consulting the Pentagon.

For convenience, the State Department set up a subbureaucracy, the Special War Problems Division (SWPD), to communicate with the Protecting Powers on the one hand and with the War Department's Prisoner of War Operations Division on the other. The PWD was an agency of the Provost Marshall General's Office, which had physical custody of war prisoners.[7] The State Department's SWPD was usually little more than a conduit for the War Department's communications with the Protecting Powers. The PWD, after consulting other pertinent Pentagon bureaucracies, would compose messages, which the SWPD would eventually recast in proper diplomatic language for the Swiss Legation. Communications took longer and longer to move from Washington to the Swiss foreign ministry, from there to the German Legation in Bern or the Swiss Legation in Berlin, and back again. The lag was due partly to wartime conditions and partly to the War Department's indifference or increasing refusal to cooperate.

That great humanitarian treaty, the Geneva Convention, presented serious problems for the Pentagon. On the whole, the United States was "almost obsessed" with abiding by its terms, "often far in excess of any agreed-upon requirements."[8] Indeed, according to one Pentagon publication, "War Department negotiations with the Swiss Legation were governed by the desire not to give any cause to the German Government to believe we had violated in any way our obligations under the Geneva Convention."[9]

This was a prudent attitude, in view of the fact that the convention's terms were in effect reciprocal. If the United States violated any Geneva right of one of the 372,000 Germans eventually imprisoned on American soil, such a violation would allow Hitler to do the same to his 90,000 GI prisoners. Reciprocity provided incentive to obey international law. It also meant that when the War Department did violate the convention, it had to keep that fact well hidden.

There were prudent reasons for violating Geneva. For example, under its terms prisoners were only obliged to reveal their names, ranks, and serial numbers.[10] Any belligerent state needs more information than that. Therefore, even before Pearl Harbor, G-2 and the ONI began to plan two (necessarily top secret) interrogation camps. Germany did the same thing, but that was beside the point. In view of Hitler's reputation, no one doubted that he would still take vicious reprisals for any American infraction. Furthermore, no one in Washington relished the idea of America, defender of freedom, being cast in the role of international scofflaw.

On the other hand, abiding by the convention also had its public relations hazards. Geneva laid down rules about the prisoners' diet and their right to recreation. Irate American citizens, print and radio commentators, and politicians kept telling scandalous tales of Nazi prisoners playing in their camps, gorging on rationed food while Americans died overseas. This criticism gave rise to the "coddling crisis," a perennial public relations headache for the Pentagon.

There was another matter that the War Department needed to keep secret to avoid bad publicity at home and abroad: its fear that POW camps in America were dominated by a tight network of Nazi fanatics who terrorized good, cooperative Germans whenever they showed any interest in democracy. This "Gestapo element," the Pentagon feared, conspired to suppress "good" Germans not only by threatening reprisals against their families back home but also by means of "kangaroo courts," forced suicides, and lynchings—a situation the War Department labeled "terrorism." Unless this "Gestapo element" was stopped, "terrorists" would make the United States appear contemptibly weak, would sabotage a vital camp labor program worth millions of dollars, and would preserve Nazi influence to the extent that it would re-infect postwar Germany. Furthermore, Geneva commanded that war prisoners be kept safe.[11] If the United States could not prevent murder and mayhem in its camps, how would Hitler retaliate against the GIs that he held?

The use of the term "terrorism" is not anachronistic but contemporary. The War Department believed that a "reign of terror" existed in the camps. It declared, so to speak, a "war on terrorism" in an effort to wrest control from the Nazis as soon as possible, before D-Day brought hordes of new prisoners into the country. Subsequent chapters will show how, throughout the war, the PMGO produced various schemes for segregating good Germans from bad ones. The four POW murder cases intensified these efforts and led to another anti-terror tactic: justice, American style. Terrorists must be tried and punished.

The four murder victims were not just held to be anti-Nazi by their fellow prisoners. They were considered traitors, sometimes with good reason. In the first, or "Beyer" case, a man at Camp Tonkawa, Oklahoma, had tried to give his American captors information about good bombing targets in a city that was the hometown of many fellow inmates. He was lynched in November 1943. The Eighth Service Command court-martialed five German petty officers for hauling him before a "kangaroo court" and then inciting a mob that battered him to death. A few days before the trial, a colonel informed Eighth Service Command's POW personnel that even though "trials are difficult and tedious and take a long time, . . . the Provost Marshal General and the Judge Advocate General have both said, 'Go ahead and try them.' We laid the case of these five men at Tonkawa before the War Department, and were told to go all out on this trial. We are doing just that. . . .We are using this Tonkawa case as a test case."[12]

The third of the four POW murder cases involved a lynching at Papago Park, Arizona. The victim, a U-boat sailor named Werner Drechsler, had served U.S. Naval Intelligence for nearly seven months at the secret interrogation camp at Fort Hunt, Virginia, near Washington. Drechsler had posed as an ordinary prisoner while drawing his cellmates into indiscreet conversation. He may have "extracted considerable information,"[13] but he was clumsy. Before long every German war prisoner in America knew about the traitor at "Washington."

When his handlers dispensed with Drechsler's services and sent him off to a regular internment camp, Naval Intelligence asked Army's G-2, via the Adjutant General's Office, to ask the Provost Marshal General's Office to place their former snitch in a camp where he would never meet other naval personnel. And so he was, for a few weeks. Unfortunately, the PMGO shortly began segregating naval prisoners from other German personnel. Some inattentive functionary dispatched Drechsler to the new naval camp at Papago Park. Six and a half hours after his arrival, he was dead.

Drechsler's killers were not part of that alleged Gestapo terrorist network so feared by the War Department. They were Drechsler's victims, or friends of victims. As we shall see, they were motivated by personal resentment and patriotic rage against this informer. He offended their sense of military honor. As one of them put it, no traitor had "a right to continue to live among us." According to another, the whole camp thought that "American authorities also have to take a part of the blame, because they had knowledge that Drechsler was a traitor and sent him to our camp in spite of that fact." In addition, his killers were convinced that the enemy intended Drechsler to keep on spying, endangering the lives of German submariners and even of their own families at home. "We had to prevent him from doing further harm." They feared that he would use his influence to eliminate them, the witnesses of his treason, if they did not get him first.[14] They did.

Drechsler's murder would be brutally investigated. The general in charge of the Ninth Service Command was personally offended by such a crime on his turf. The board of investigators he appointed was well aware of its commander's outrage. In Washington, G-2 demanded to know how the "Gestapo element" at Papago Park had breached the secrecy of military intelligence. How had it known when Drechsler would arrive, and how had it identified him? Bureaucrats in the PMG's Office wanted the killers punished in order to teach honest POWs that they could resist the Gestapo, a lesson that would allegedly improve discipline, aid the labor program, and reassure Berlin that the United States was protecting its war prisoners as Geneva commanded.

This set of aims created a bizarre situation in which the life of Werner Drechsler would be avenged by violating the Geneva rights of his suspected killers. Since the frustrated investigators found no physical evidence linking anyone to the crime, they took their likeliest suspects to the second secret interrogation camp at Byron Hot Springs, California, where experts tortured them into confessing (see chapter 10). Then they were brought to trial.

But how were Drechsler's murderers to be convicted on the sole basis of involuntary, hence illegal, confessions? How was the Adjutant General's Office to deal with the fact that the witnesses and suspects in Drechsler's murder case had certain legal rights guaranteed by international treaty and by the American Laws of War, both of which gave them Fifth Amendment protection against self-incrimination? In addition, Geneva gave them the right to a defense counsel and a translator of their own choosing, decreed that they be tried in exactly the same way as soldiers of the Detaining Power, and allowed the Protecting Power to send an observer to their trial. POWs also had the right to appeal (or at least, under the Laws of War, to beg for mercy).[15]

I will show how Ninth Service Command's military justice staff concocted a trial designed to condemn these seven men by means of inadmissible evidence, while seeming to comply with both American and international law and while covering up the misdeeds of command personnel and suppressing military intelligence secrets such as the motive for the crime. The trial itself was so secret that the prosecutor would record the verdict and the sentences—death by hanging—into the trial record by hand, so that not even the typists would know.

Such secrecy would seem to undermine the notion of using American justice to abash the "Gestapo elements" and encourage the resistance of good prisoners, but this notion persisted. As a legal expert in the Judge Advocate General's Office remarked when the death sentences were being reviewed, the defendants' cold-blooded crime was "the very sort of fanatical terrorism that must be suppressed in prisoner of war camps." Unless such murderers were severely punished, he said, the United States would stand in violation of Article 2 of the Geneva Convention, which bound the Custodial Power "to protect prisoners against violence."[16] He overlooked the violence exerted against the seven tortured defendants.

Those who planned this trial nearly succeeded in all their intentions but there was trouble to come. Their hand-chosen, incompetent defense counsel still managed to insert some compromising material into the trial record. That record would be the basis for two automatic reviews of the sentences. Furthermore, the Geneva Convention granted the condemned men certain "inconvenient" rights. They were to be given copies of the trial record. Geneva's Article 42 granted war prisoners the right to complain to their Protecting Power. Article 66 obliged the Detaining Power to make, as soon as possible, a full report to the government of any prisoner placed on trial, giving "details of the prisoner's offense and the decisive reasons for the verdict against him." In these four murder trials, the War Department interpreted "as soon as possible" to mean "after the President had confirmed the death sentences." Even then, the War Department's idea of "details" was very skimpy as well as tardy.

Consequently, beginning with the first, or "Beyer," trial, the German government reasonably demanded more information about why and how its nationals had been sentenced to hang. The Beyer case was sensitive enough, since any POW condemned for eliminating a traitor to his country could be considered a hero back home. Furthermore, releasing details of the Beyer trial would set a precedent that would oblige the Pentagon to hand over the record of the far more sensitive trial of Drechsler's killers, with its compromising contents. Therefore, the War Department steadfastly fought against releasing anything but the slightest information about any of the four POW murder trials, which by September 1944 had condemned fifteen Germans to death.[17]

The German government consequently accused the United States of violating the Geneva Convention and in time began threatening retaliation. The State Department remained puzzled and disturbed by the War Department's refusal to allow Berlin to see the trial transcripts. After all, Geneva required that the defendants be given copies. Why not their government?

In early October 1944, President Roosevelt confirmed the death sentences of the "Beyer Five." Since Geneva's Article 66 required a three-month wait between confirmation and execution of a death sentence, a death clock began to tick. The German government demanded that these hangings be postponed, pending its receipt of the full details about the trial which the convention required and which, owing to the differences between German and American court procedures, could only be obtained from the trial records. The Swiss minister endorsed the German request but the War Department refused to consider it.[18]

In this book I will describe the growing diplomatic crisis and its predictable outcome: the Third Reich fabricated death sentences against five American prisoners, then offered to exchange them for the Beyer five. Both the State Department and the Swiss government supported this proposal. The War Department kept sabotaging it, partly from a righteous intent to bring "Nazi terrorists" to justice and partly to keep the Papago Park trial record suppressed. Therefore, predictably, Germany proceeded to condemn more and more GIs to death for trivial reasons. The Pentagon remained unmoved. Gambling with American lives, it dragged its heels, calculating that Germany would surrender before any GI had to mount the gallows.

Upon winning this bet, the War Department soon hanged fourteen Germans, and then promptly took full public credit for using good American justice to win its "war on terrorism" in the camps. A few months later, the Pentagon quietly decided to save time and money by ignoring all crimes that war prisoners had merely perpetrated on one another.

Why does this story need to be told today? There are several reasons. Far too little has been written about war prisoners in a conflict that produced millions of them. Almost nothing has been written about how the War Department interpreted and violated the Geneva Convention, or how its multiple bureaucracies interacted with each other, or how it cooperated with, deceived, or defied the State Department and the government of Switzerland. Too little has been written about how the ideal rules of the Geneva Convention actually operated under real wartime conditions. To my knowledge, there are as yet no studies of Switzerland's wartime role as Protecting Power.

The story of these obscure German POWs should be told because it casts light on these issues—and because it is a good yarn. Their story is also timely, to my horror. Today Americans are faced with moral decisions about torturing war prisoners taken in another, more dangerous war on terrorism. If nothing else, the story of these executed Germans can show how violating international laws concerning cruel and degrading treatment can sabotage attempts to mete out justice.

There have been proposals to try some of the "civilian" al Quaeda captives in Cuba before a secret military tribunal, which in 2003 the lawyer for an Australian national called "an American kangaroo court." Amnesty International has spoken of such trials as "another retrograde step for human rights in the U.S.-led 'war against terrorism' . . . [which] will further undermine the U.S.A.'s claims to be a country that champions the rule of law."[19]

Even worse, in the wake of 9/11, various people have begun to justify the torture of terrorists. High officials have said that American interrogation techniques—such as the use of "pressure points" (forcing prisoners to pose in extremely awkward positions for hours, which produces intolerable pain), sleep deprivation, and so on—do not amount to torture. These methods were used against German prisoners in World War II. Their torturers called it "Dachou [*sic*] treatment."

The United States government acted badly in the 1940s when it was regulated by a then-respected international treaty, when it feared enemy reprisals, and when it was scrutinized by the Swiss government, the Red Cross, and the YMCA. Today it seems limited by nothing except politics and public opinion. I hope that this book will add to the national debate.

The story of a few obscure German war prisoners must be retold today to remind us that any government can do shameful things. Hypocrisy, unattractive in individuals, can be lethal in governments. Abstractions like "justice" can unjustly crush individual human beings. History needs to be written from below as well as from above. The story told in this book may put a human and individual face on public affairs—and on affairs hidden from public view.

I have documented this account so that others can check the records for themselves. I have tried to be honest, evenhanded, and thorough, as any historian must. However, I do not believe that practicing the science and art of historical research requires that I pose as a moral eunuch, as long as I state my opinions plainly for the reader to accept or reject. Having been raised during

World War II and the Cold War, I have been well programmed to expect the United States to adhere to higher standards than other countries, or at least to believe that if it in fact does not do so, then it ought to be made to do so. Furthermore, I feel bound by the words of St. Paul: "Remember those who are in prison, as though you were in prison with them; those who are being tortured, as though you yourselves were being tortured" (Hebrews 13:3).

CHAPTER 1

Spying and Terrorism

The Geneva Convention required a war prisoner to give his name, rank, and number, nothing more. Any belligerent needs more information than that. American authorities had to extract information from their unwilling "guests" while maintaining the strictest secrecy for fear of reprisals against its own soldiers. Those "guests," of course, resisted when they could, driven by motives of natural patriotism and bitter resentment against the tricks of enemy interrogators.

If secrecy posed a problem, so did the fact that the two American interrogation centers were bureaucratic hybrids shared by Army and Naval Intelligence (G-2 and ONI), which finished plans for them shortly after Pearl Harbor. One of them was located at Fort Hunt, Virginia, a wooded eighty-acre tract twenty miles south of Washington. This former Spanish War fortress, World War I command post, and Civilian Conservation Corps camp began receiving "guests" in August 1942. The second camp, at Byron Hot Springs, California, was located on the grounds of an elegant spa bankrupted by the Depression. Its new function began in early 1943.[1] A "minuscule, though critically important" percentage of war prisoners would pass through these camps, about six hundred a month in batches of thirty to forty.[2]

The Provost Marshal General (PMG) had custody of all POWs and all camps except these two, for which his office merely handled supply and housekeeping—although he did choose their post commanders. Two chiefs of intelligence from G-2 (Military Intelligence, an agency of the Adjutant General's Office) controlled camp operations and handled liaison with the post commander, the FBI, and the Office of Naval Intelligence.[3] This arrangement meant that G-2 doled out ONI's share of rooms, microphones, recording devices, and transcribers. At least ONI got first crack at naval prisoners and dealt with them according to its own rules.[4]

Inevitably, this time-share arrangement caused conflicts. For example, prisoners were never supposed to see anyone but their interrogators and roommates. They were even fed in their rooms, which were bugged. ONI agents complained that G-2 hogged the recording devices, arbitrarily placed naval prisoners in unsuitable quarters with unsuitable companions, and allowed them to mingle in large batches.[5]

Cmdr. John Riheldaffer, head of ONI's Special Activities (interrogation) Branch, had to play peacekeeper and turf protector with his counterpart, Col. Catesby ap C. Jones, chief of G-2's prisoner of war operations (covertly named the Captured Personnel and Material Branch, a subsection of the General Staff's Military Intelligence Service).[6] On one occasion, Riheldaffer wrote Jones that since their problems were caused by "excess zeal" on both sides, he was sure that "frank discussion" and their war-winning "spirit of cooperation" would lead to complete agreement "based on certain fundamentals" (such as ONI's paramount interest in all naval prisoners) and would overcome an accumulation of minor incidents (which he reviewed in detail).[7]

The Geneva Convention was another source of interagency conflict since the very existence of these two camps, not to mention the way they operated, violated "a dozen or so" of its articles.[8] For example, Articles 8 and 77 obligated the Detaining Power to report a prisoner's name to the International Red Cross (IRC) "in the shortest period possible" and to allow him free access to the IRC and his Protecting Power (Switzerland, if he were German or Italian, Spain if Japanese). Nevertheless, the PMG's office laid down the rule that "no information will be released as to numbers, nationality, arm of service, source, or destination" of any prisoner, "until further orders from higher authority."[9] Only after a prisoner was settled into a regular internment camp would his name, rank, and serial number be released and only then would he be able to exercise his Geneva rights. (The Germans also played this trick.)[10]

Military Intelligence found a useful loophole: since prisoners in transit were in legal limbo, the secret intelligence centers were attached to two ordinary transit camps. Thousands of prisoners moving in and out of Fort Meade, Maryland, and Angel Island, California, thus provided candidates and camouflage for Fort Hunt and Byron Hot Springs.

The Vice Chief of Naval Operations, who established the rules for the treatment of naval "guests" under interrogation, had no problem with this loose interpretation of the Geneva Convention. He declared that "our first interest is obtaining all information of value to us and any humanitarian considerations must be subordinated to this."[11] G-2 apparently agreed. However, Provost Marshal General Allen W. Gullion detested this stretching of international law. Having helped revise the Geneva Convention in 1929, he had a very proprietary attitude toward it.[12] As the physical custodian of all war prisoners, he felt responsible for its "rigid enforcement."[13]

Gullion also set the policy of placing boat crews together in the same internment camps, an arrangement that caused ONI to insist that whole crews be kept "in transit" and under wraps until every member had yielded his last morsel of intelligence. Since ONI's space at Fort Hunt was limited, partial crews had to be "parked" at regular camps until every man had been interrogated. This practice allowed German sailors to mingle with prisoners who had already been questioned and with other unreported crews waiting their turn at Fort Hunt. They passed along all sorts of cautionary information about enemy interrogation practices.

Gullion complained bitterly to the secretary of war about this situation. The German government usually knew when its U-boats were sunk, he said. Unless it received timely word of survivors, it complained to the Swiss government and the IRC, whereupon the secretary of state would chide the War Department for flouting the Geneva Convention. Then, adding insult to injury, ONI's Cmdr. Riheldaffer requested G-2 to instruct PMG Gullion that in spite of what Geneva said, he was "not to furnish any information regarding Naval prisoners of war to any agency" until the Navy permitted it. Gullion angrily asked Secretary of War Stimson to overrule Riheldaffer and obey the convention.[14] He also asked the Adjutant General, who was responsible for G-2, to clarify the absolute contradiction between the PMG's standing order to comply with Geneva and his standing order not to report naval prisoners. The AG had merely repeated the secrecy order.[15]

Two months later, Gullion was fuming again. G-2's assistant chief of staff had criticized both his stand on Geneva and his alleged failure to segregate submarine crews passing through Fort Hunt. He had always "most zealously observed the letter and spirit of the Treaty," Gullion snarled, unless he had received orders to the contrary—though he had "at all times" counseled compliance. He had "remarked on how the Army would appear to the State Department, the Protecting Powers, and to the International Red Cross should we not strictly" obey all Geneva's provisions. "I have also pointed out the practical results by way of retaliation which deviation on our part would entail" for captured American boys.[16]

As for his alleged failure to segregate prisoners, Gullion said, that matter was entirely under G-2's control. Was it his fault that G-2 operatives at Fort

Hunt had "proceeded to mingle the crews indiscriminately" after they had been interrogated, in order to eavesdrop on their conversations? As a result, crews from two different internment camps had shared information with fellow inmates about Fort Hunt, and if that information reached Germany, it would place the United States in the "distinctly embarrassing position" of being accused by the Nazis of failing to comply with "the letter of the Geneva Convention." Gullion demanded that this matter "be brought to the attention of the Secretary of War."[17]

The Provost Marshal General lost this round. On September 7, the Army Chief of Staff, General George C. Marshal, ordered the commander in the office of Chief of Naval Operations that "hereafter, as a matter of procedure," no survivors from hostile submarines would be reported to anyone until fully interrogated and interned in a permanent camp. Marshal justified his decision by calling it "the German interpretation of the Geneva Convention."[18]

Two weeks later, Gullion had the satisfaction of warning G-2's assistant chief of staff that the Swiss Legation was about to inspect the POW camp at Fort Devens, Massachusetts. The inspector might encounter three of those U-boat crews that had mingled with other prisoners at Fort Hunt, including a partial crew whose existence had not yet been reported. If so, the Protecting Power might learn that "the United States was violating Articles 8 and 36 of the Geneva Convention."[19] Those unreported crewmen were quickly shuffled to another camp. A month later, the PMG's office was still trying to get permission to give their names to the IRC.[20]

In February 1943, Germany demanded information about survivors of the U-94, which had been sunk in early September 1942. The Swiss Legation asked the State Department for "assurance" that captured POWs would be "reported within the shortest possible period in accordance with the Geneva Convention." As it always did, State asked the War Department how to reply. Someone in the chief of staff's office, after consulting ONI and G-2, drafted a letter claiming that "problems of transportation from overseas" had made the delay "to a large extent, unavoidable."[21]

General Gullion vented his wrath to a friend: First, G-2 had taken particular pains to mingle certain submarine crews and then "blamed it on us." Now the Navy wanted to do "just as the Germans do": leave "these submarine people" unreported "until they reach a permanent camp," even if that meant "a ninety day delay." General Marshal himself had ordered him to go along with that. Even worse, G-2's reply to the State Department had been "a damned lie!"

> I believe in obeying orders but it goes against the grain for me to violate that treaty and lie about it, when the State Department and the Swiss Government will know we're lying. And I don't believe the Secretary of War knows about it and I doubt very much if Marshal knows it and I certainly don't believe that [Secretary of War] Stimson would ever . . . tell a lie. Damned if I believe he would. Moreover, I don't know whether it is true that we're following the same interpretation [of Geneva] as the Germans. [Assistant PMG Colonel] Babe Bryan tells me that his information is that the Germans are making immediate reports. . . . I've got to have a conference on this thing.[22]

The next day, Gullion sent the Chief of Administrative Services, who was both his superior and the Adjutant General's, a more moderate protest: The PMG wished it "clearly understood" that he had "loyally complied" with all orders, "in spirit and in letter," including the dubious command to delay reporting captured U-boat crews; but unless directly ordered to do so, he refused to give the State Department a message "which is not strictly in accord with the facts as I see them."[23]

None of these problems was resolved. ONI agents complained that even when G-2 allotted them enough space at Fort Hunt, poor soundproofing forced them to leave every other room empty. Even so, "guests" still tapped on the walls and shouted from poorly covered windows, through which they could see American personnel and other prisoners.[24] Lt. Cmdr. Harry T. Gheradi, the top ONI agent at Fort Hunt, complained that the interrogators had no control over maintenance men from the PMG's office, who had intimate contact with the prisoners "at all hours of the day and night." Furthermore, G-2 still sometimes disregarded ONI's policies. "Any errors whatsoever" in such matters as room assignment, Gheradi complained, could prejudice the "important and delicate" interrogation process. If the prisoners ever realized how much information their enemy was obtaining and clammed up during direct questioning, then the "lack of the proper center for working by less direct means will become a serious embarrassment."[25] By "less direct," Gheradi meant using stool pigeons, informers also called Special Prisoners or SPs.

In July Gheradi complained to Riheldaffer again about Fort Hunt's "inadequate and unsuitable facilities." When ONI had a crush of "guests," G-2 might allot ten rooms, about half of the facilities. ONI had to reserve four for SPs, who worked most effectively with only two roommates. That left six rooms, with a theoretical capacity of eighteen, although enlisted men had to be segregated from officers and if possible petty officers. Some space had to be reserved for solitary confinement and necessary room changes.[26]

Politicking for more space, Gheradi told Admiral Ernest J. King, Chief of Naval Operations, about the "very valuable intelligence" he was obtaining on such weapons as "the new German homing torpedo." If interrogators could get these "surprisingly good results" in spite of "highly adverse conditions," surely better facilities would produce more. Gheradi had "a strong impression" that the only thing preventing this was PMG Gullion's refusal to approve money for more buildings and staff.[27]

Commander Riheldaffer later complained to the Army's chief of Captured Personnel and Material Branch that twenty-three survivors from a freshly captured U-boat, properly segregated in the "incoming building" at Fort Meade transit camp, had been fed by prisoner mess attendants, who gave them "a full description" of what to expect at Fort Hunt. This gaffe had not only cheated Naval Intelligence of important information but had also shaken the morale "of our co-belligerents, who might consequently withhold 'much valuable assistance.' Such a violation of the Army's own instructions was "entirely inexcusable . . . at this late date."[28]

If overcrowding, bureaucratic confusion and infighting could compromise secrecy, so obviously could the "guests." It was relatively easy to keep secrets from Americans. Even military top brass used euphemisms such as P.O. Box 1142 for Fort Hunt and P.O. Box 651 for Byron Hot Springs. Hundreds of civilians working at Fort Meade knew nothing of Fort Hunt's existence. The prisoners, of course, both knew and resisted. Just two months after Fort Hunt opened, an ONI agent reported that his "guests" had already spotted most of the microphones in the ceiling. (They not only made a brownish tinge on the sound-proofed ceiling tiles. They were also about two feet wide.) Consequently, his agents were mainly picking up complaints, jokes, and diatribes on Nazi invincibility.[29] According to Moore, several crews "made life interesting" by developing a "blatant, screw-the-Yanks approach: shrieking, shouting, farting and (those listening thought) occasionally masturbating as well . . . as close to the microphones as possible."[30]

No one could control what prisoners told each other after they left Fort Hunt. At their first stop, the Fort Meade transit camp, they began to compare notes about the place they knew only as "Washington" or "Sing Sing Lager." They continued to spread the word after arriving at their internment camps. In December 1943, Navy censors intercepted a letter containing "information of extremely great value to the German High Command . . . which could only have been obtained by a prolonged conversation" between someone who had been through Fort Hunt and the writer, who had not. Cmdr. Riheldaffer asked his G-2 counterpart to warn PMG Gullion again about "the vital importance of proper segregation of officer, petty officer and enlisted men."[31]

In the internment camps, angry prisoners sometimes organized discussions of "interrogation techniques . . . (just in case anyone might end up there)."[32] They particularly resented the use of stool pigeons. One POW told an agent that some paratroopers had warned him to be careful if he were sent to "Washington," because he would "probably be interrogated by one of our own kind." Therefore, when he took his turn at Fort Hunt he had merely told his overly-inquisitive room mate—Werner Drechsler—"the very opposite of what was true."[33]

This prisoner grapevine also operated out of Byron Hot Springs. Five German SPs at that facility soon realized that "several thousand" Germans "knew exactly what game was played in a camp near Frisco [San Francisco] and that 5 prisoners named so and so and with assumed names so and so were working for America." They "became uneasy," imagining that venal Red Cross agents were spreading tales of them "in almost all camps of the U.S." and even in Germany. One of the SPs reminded his employers that "we have not only risked our own life, but also the lives of our families."[34]

Naturally prisoners spread the word about traitors trying to trick them into betraying military secrets that endangered their country and kin. They also complained to their Protecting Power. The first "guest" at Fort Hunt wrote the Swiss Legation that he had been drugged.[35] Another told officers investigating Werner Drechsler's death that "we were not questioned as prisoners of war. We were threatened and interrogated like common saboteurs. We were told that we would be shot as saboteurs."[36] Another was told: "We'll send you to a bad camp if you won't talk. . . . How do we know you are not a saboteur? You know what happens to them. . . . They get the electric chair!"[37] Such complaints sound like "normal" bullying by interrogators, but if reported to Berlin they might alert Hitler's military intelligence experts to the existence of illegal American interrogation camps.

How often did frustrated interrogators at these facilities resort to torture? No one knows; but, as we shall see, some agents were trained and ready to use it on the prisoners suspected of murdering Werner Drechsler. However, most prisoners merely faced intensive questioning and eavesdropping. According to Moore, "about 90% of all information of any value came not from the interrogation sessions per se, but from 'judicious mixing' of prisoners and recording their informal conversations."[38] (The mere mention of an unknown place called Peenemunde led to its bombing, once the Allies realized that this was where Hitler's rockets were made.)[39]

What was "judicious mixing?" G-2 wanted to mix prisoners together while ONI insisted on isolating them in small batches with SPs. Sooner or later, even the most cautious prisoner might alleviate his boredom by talking shop with a sympathetic roommate. SPs were especially useful as long as hope or fear of Hitler's victory made prisoners uncooperative.

What induced these SPs to turn traitor? They were meagerly recompensed at the whim of their handlers. SPs who provided information were sometimes rewarded with trips to town and restaurant meals. According to a Fort Hunt document from December 1943, if an ONI agent wished to reward an SP by taking him outside the stockade, he merely had to sign for him, stay with him, and take full responsibility.[40] The next month, Cmdr. Riheldaffer had to address certain abuses. His directive for the "handling of co-operative Ps/W" made it clearly understood that "all forms of entertainment and special treatment are to be regarded as a reward for services . . . and the degree of favorable treatment shall be in direct ratio to value received." There were to be three degrees: "exercise and entertainment" in and around Fort Hunt, excursions away from it, such as to Washington, and "special excursions or entertainment."[41]

On the lowest level, to be granted at the "discretion of the Section Head, under the direction of the Watch Officer on duty," the "entertainment" had to be "within reasonable limits" and at the lowest possible expense, such as "walks . . . within the post and near by," to a maximum of "four hours. For ordinary exercise, two hours should suffice." (Geneva Article 56 mandated at least two hours even for prisoners undergoing punishment.) The branch head must pre-approve the other levels, which might include a six-hour trip and "not more than one regular meal in town." No more than two (male only) ONI agents could go along. "Taxicabs will NOT be used to or from the Interrogation Center." When the agent submitted his expense account, he must include "a statement as to the information secured" from his SP.[42]

Cmdr. Riheldaffer composed more rules for a German naval lieutenant named Coreth, who seems to have been interrogating prisoners while wearing an American uniform (to disguise the fact that he was a turncoat). The commander ruled that Coreth was never to wear this uniform outside of Fort Hunt, not even to walk in its neighborhood. He was not to enter the officers' mess or officers' club on his own. He must sit with the Navy or Army officer who accompanied him "and only at tables reserved for junior officers." He was "under no circumstances . . . to be included in special parties at the Officers' Club except by special invitation on the part of the host and by permission of" the post commander. "It is expected that officers will henceforth utilize some discretion" in handling Fort Hunt's star traitor.[43]

Coreth was also much better paid than the other five to seven SPs at Fort Hunt.[44] An ONI agent received $110.00 a week in cash for all of them. Out of this, he was to pay Coreth's weekly salary of $12.50 and his mess bill of $7.50. He was to pay $10.00 a week to an SP named Kelly until some arrears had been covered, then $5.00 a week after that. For the SPs' "expenses incurred on the post" he was to reserve $41.10. He might save any remainder or use it to entertain successful SPs.[45]

None of the German and Japanese SPs at Byron Hot Springs were as extravagantly rewarded as Coreth, but they could earn excursions. An ONI agent there reported to Cmdr. Riheldaffer that he had taken "two guests into San Francisco for the ride and a dinner. . . . Everything went along smoothly. We found a restaurant at Fisherman's Wharf where we would not be conspicuous. No comments were made by anyone." He added: "If we know what we want, such attention will pay dividends exactly as it does at 1142" (Fort Hunt).[46]

The five-German SP team at Byron Hot Springs (willing workers from anti-Nazi families) labored at first under close Army supervision wearing PW clothing. After proving themselves, they worked independently wearing American sergeants' uniforms; yet for a long time they received the same $3.00 per month in canteen coupons as any POW. Later, however, they were promised $25.00 a month.[47] They were also trusted to take recreational trips into San Francisco in civilian clothes, without any guards.

There were other SPs operating inside ordinary POW internment camps. Their reports went to a Capt. Peters (actually the Central Censorship Bureau in New York City), who forwarded them unopened to Fort Hunt.[48] Such information aided the PMG's office in its prolonged efforts to counteract Nazi influence in the camps by means of various segregation schemes. (The only other ways it perceived to fight what the Pentagon feared was organized terrorism were spying and punishment. Geneva forbade "re-education.")

Speaking of segregation, Geneva required only that officers be separated from enlisted men and NCOs. In 1943, the PMG's office added four more categories: anti-Nazi army and navy and ordinary army and navy. At first, only the PMG's office could assign political labels. By March 1943 it allowed the ten regional Service Commands to establish special camps for ardent Nazis and other troublemakers, but only the PMG's office could classify a prisoner as anti-Nazi and move him to a protected camp.[49]

Naturally there was Nazi influence among these German POWs—but who was a Nazi? The ill-trained, mostly non-German-speaking American camp personnel could hardly distinguish ordinary patriotic Germans from true-believing fascist fanatics. Often, any troublemaker of whatever political coloration, even a liberal or a communist, was labeled "Nazi."

To compound the problem, Articles 43 and 44 of the Geneva Convention set up a system of prisoner spokesmen. The senior POW officer ordinarily became camp spokesman, acting as intermediary between the prisoners and camp authorities, the IRC, and the Protecting Power. In the camp's individual compounds, the spokesman was normally the ranking petty officer. Being soldiers, American camp personnel channeled their control through the prisoners' own military hierarchy.[50] In this way, Nazis could end up in effective control and, if they maintained good camp discipline, win the label "good Germans."[51] Unless there was undue trouble, or until the Army began to make maximum use of POW labor, camp commandants usually felt no great urgency to weed out Nazis.

Nevertheless, whenever any sort of violence broke out among these bored, ill-assorted captives, the War Department reacted with great alarm. In fact, the Pentagon suspected a sudden, camp-controlling "wave" of Nazi terrorism, "well and extensively planned" by Gestapo agents and SA and SS men, working through kangaroo courts, lynchings, and forced suicides of "good" (meaning cooperative) prisoners.[52] Arnold Krammer has written the best description of what he calls the War Department's exaggerated, even hysterical fears of "politically motivated terrorism" in "Wrestling for the Tiller," chapter 5 of his book.

According to Krammer, the wave of political murders and forced suicides began in October 1943 and ended in February 1944. In a magazine article, the Provost Marshal General said it ended in March or April.[53] In public, of course, the War Department minimized the duration of this terrorist "wave." This vagueness about the timetable of a concerted Nazi "reign of terror" leads one to ask: was there actually any such organized terrorist network? Based on my research, I doubt it.

Once prisoners were transferred to internment camps, they obeyed officers and petty officers, who knew that maintaining military discipline was vital to prisoner morale. Nazi Party members also worked to maintain their influence (which American guards might or might not be able to distinguish from ordinary military bullying). But for an organized multicamp terrorist network to succeed, uncensored prisoner communication between camps was necessary and such communication was quite unlikely (at least until late in the war, when the Pentagon established a central clearing house for all POW mail at one of the most Nazified camps.)[54] Even within camps, contact "through the wire" between compounds was difficult.

Vague estimates of the toll of this "wave" of terror provide another reason for doubting its existence. According to one French historian, 167 anti-Nazi prisoners were lynched in American camps by war's end. Krammer says incidents "occurred at nearly 200 camps" (out of 511) while rightly pointing out that ordinary day-to-day intimidations were uncountable. According to the PMG's office, there were 477 deaths among 371,683 German war prisoners on American soil, including those from natural causes, accidents, and trigger-happy guards. Of these, only 72 were suicides, 4 murders, and 3 homicides. The PMG himself said that "only five murders and two forced suicides could be attributed to Nazi methods," adding that this suicide rate was lower than that for American civilians. Col. Tollefson, director of the POW Operations Division in the PMG's office, wrote that the "wave" produced only 14 hangings, 1 life sentence, and 1 twenty-year sentence, that there were "only five cases" with sufficient evidence for a murder trial, and that "only one person in each of these cases had been murdered." (One case was still pending.) According to a veteran of the State Department's Special War Problems Division, there were 2 murders only, and not more than 10 severe beatings.[55] Of course, government officials minimized the toll when addressing the public; but all in all, this seems a modest murder rate for an organized reign of terror.

Unlikely or not, War Department officials nevertheless believed that a terrorist network existed and they were determined to destroy it. The officers who investigated Werner Drechsler's lynching would search avidly for Gestapo conspiracy, without success. The War Department obsessed about Nazi conspiracy for several reasons. For one thing, POWs were a vital asset in a labor-starved economy. If Nazis controlled the camps, they could sabotage a program that saved irreplaceable resources, generated millions of dollars in profits, and released American personnel for combat. Furthermore, it seemed crucial to break Nazi power in the camps before D-Day (June 6, 1944) brought floods of new prisoners. Reports of flabby camp control would also allegedly cause the German government to sneer at American power.

The fact that Nazi fanaticism was a well-documented phenomenon also helps explain the obsession. And there were, indeed, some Gestapo agents in the camps. But American military authorities tended to believe that all German soldiers had been brainwashed to follow their fanatical leaders. Petty officers, allegedly ultrafanatical, had charge of the enlisted men's barracks and commanded their labor details. As early as May 1943, Col. Catesby ap C. Jones, chief of G-2's POW branch, warned the Assistant PMG in charge of war prisoners, Gen. B. M. Bryan, about the malign influence of NCOs. He quoted a "reliable" prisoner: "The superiors (Nazi officers and Feldwebels [sergeants]) suppress even the slightest suspicion of independent thinking. When anyone starts to complain, they call the paratroopers together and point this man out. . . . If those Feldwebels were taken away from the enlisted men," this prisoner was convinced, many of their underlings would break from the Nazi fold and "[corporals] would quickly find their way back to the men."[56]

The next month, the Adjutant General sent a confidential circular to the directors of intelligence in seven of the ten Service Commands.[57] He ordered that an intelligence officer be appointed in each POW camp, warning that if high-ranking NCOs and Gestapo agents were permitted to associate with enlisted men, these fanatics would soon use "intimidation, violence, or Nazification" (i.e., terrorism) to dry up possible sources of information from the many prisoners who were "social democrats, Communists, Poles, Czechs, Luxembergers and others who are bitterly opposed to the Nazi regime." The intelligence officers must "detect these confirmed Nazis" and report them to G-2's POW division, whose chief would arrange to transfer them to a segregated camp. G-2 planned to send someone to each camp in the "near future" to help carry out these provisions.[58]

This enormous 511-camp project would proceed very slowly, even though the War Department continued to believe that prisoner segregation was the key to eliminating Nazi terror and even though it was always conscious of the fact that the Geneva Convention obliged Custodial Powers to protect war prisoners from insult and harm.

The PMG's office assumed that Nazis were behind every instance of camp violence, however petty. Some were not so petty. A forced suicide at Camp Concordia, Kansas, in mid-October 1943 came to be regarded as the first foul act in the alleged "reign of terror." Col. Catesby ap C. Jones of G-2 informed the PMG's office, quoting a prisoner there, that Capt. Felix Tropschuh had killed himself because he had "betrayed the escape plan of a German officer in North Africa." The camp leader had found Tropschuh's diary and had read out some compromising entries at a roll call. The officers gave the traitor a choice: hang himself or be beaten to death. An officer "wrote the statement, 'I commit suicide voluntarily' on a piece of paper and had the man sign it." Other prisoners in the officers' compound shouted through the windows, "Hasn't he been hung yet? Hurry up, or we'll come in and help you." The informant was "very much revolted by Tropschuh's cowardice"—those inside had to help "the man to hang himself a little by pulling on his legs." Col. Jones added that a prisoners' "court-martial board," meeting after Tropschuh was dead, ruled that he "had deserved to die under German law," a maneuver that "helped to relieve the conscience of the participants" and also gave an odor of legality to lynch law. The camp authorities originally accepted Tropschuh's death as a suicide, then transferred two officer ringleaders to another camp.[59] According to Krammer's account, the "camp Gestapo" forced Tropschuh to kill himself after expelling him "from the German community of fellowship."[60] (This term, "*Volksgemeinschaft*," would recur during the investigation of Werner Drechsler's murder.)

Less than a month later, on November 4, Corp. Johann Kunze was lynched at Camp Tonkawa, Oklahoma, in the Eighth Service Command. Kunze's company spokesman had called a meeting (another "kangaroo court") to compare the handwriting on an "alleged traitorous note" with a letter Kunze had written his wife. The note suggested good bombing sites over Hamburg, the home town of quite a few of his fellow prisoners. According to the terse notice which the War Department gave the State Department to deliver to the Swiss Legation on January 12, 1944, "certain prisoners" had "commenced to beat" Kunze to death after calling him a traitor. They "will be court-martialed for riot and murder."[61]

That same month, at an Eighth Service Command conference on war prisoners, the commanding general said, "We are using this Tonkawa case as a test case." His staff had consulted the War Department, which had ordered it "to go all out on this trial." An ambitious officer, Lt. Col. Leon Jaworski (of later Watergate fame), told the command's POW officials that they were to respond immediately to any violence in the camps and to "SPARE NOTHING IN THE INVESTIGATION."[62] Jaworski launched a hasty, ill-prepared prosecution. Before the month was out, five petty officers were condemned to death: the company spokesman, Feldwebel Walter Beyer, and four other sergeants—Berthold Seidel, Hans Demme, Willi Scholz, and Hans Schomer—the "Beyer Five." This trial would provide a model for the other three.

The National Archives reveal several more incidents of "Nazi conspiracy" in the Eighth Service Command, complete with paper trails from one level of authority to another (which I expected to find in the Drechsler case also, but could not).[63] One incident was particularly embarrassing. On Christmas Eve in 1943, the prisoner Hugo Krauss died at Camp Hearne, Texas. This son of naturalized German-American citizens, who had been drafted into Hitler's army while visiting relatives, worked for the Camp Hearne administration as a translator. He managed to antagonize his fellow prisoners in so many ways that they were convinced he was spying on them for the Americans. Krauss also informed camp officials that some NCOs were trying to discourage their men from performing labor, "in order to undermine the American war effort." After these NCOs were removed from camp, Krauss was so badly beaten that he died a few days later.[64]

The War Department was severely embarrassed when Krauss's American father wrote his congressman demanding an investigation and when New York newspapers got hold of the story.[65] The War Department was even more red-faced when it could not find the culprits. The prisoners refused to talk. Some even said that the traitor "got what was coming to him, that it was the duty of all German soldiers to exterminate traitors and that they would gladly have participated had they known about it."[66]

As a consequence, the Adjutant General warned all Service Commands that POW petty officers sometimes "engaged in organized intimidation of other prisoners," extorted part of their wages, and undermined their willingness to work. NCOs who failed "to show an actively cooperative attitude toward the camp authorities, or who, in the opinion of the camp commander, in any manner adversely influence[d] the conduct of other prisoners" were to be segregated.[67] This circular went out on February 6, 1944, the month before Werner Drechsler's murder.

Meanwhile, another incident increased official fears of organized Gestapo terror. On March 3, the commandant at Camp Rosewell, New Mexico, told his Service Commander that the POW Emil Roehm had been so severely beaten and slashed that he could not speak. His assailants might have mistaken him for another man, "identity as yet unknown," who had been "tried by a Prisoner of War court, at Tonkawa Oklahoma, and sentenced to commit suicide." When this unknown prisoner had been transferred to Rosewell, the camp's "Gestapo group attempted to put into effect an execution by reason of failure of the condemned to commit suicide." The commandant had not yet verified this tale, but he was sure that "a well defined and general conspiracy" in Roehm's compound was attempting to make it appear that Roehm had inflicted those injuries on himself. The commandant also believed that the assault "was in the nature of a 'feeler' to determine the attitude of camp authorities" and would be a prelude to more terror "if not promptly and severely dealt with."[68]

On March 8 the director of the Eighth Service Command's Security and Intelligence Division told the PMG that Roehm had been attacked by "certain prisoners of war believed to be . . . leaders in work stoppage, and other non-cooperative events." On March 17 the PMG ordered the Commanding General to make a "thorough investigation" to find the attackers, who should be prosecuted "for violation of any appropriate Article of War."[69]

To complicate matters, the AG's February 6 circular calling for the segregation of petty officers had an unexpected result: it harmed the productivity of the labor gangs they had been commanding. The PMG's POW division began drafting a telegram telling Service Commanders how to square this circle. It quoted a long analysis for the Deputy Chief of Staff for Service Commands, dated March 15: "the key problem in effective segregation of Nazis and non-Nazis" was not isolating all NCOs but carefully screening out individuals "who openly exhibit cooperative attitudes while maintaining a rigid underground Nazi control of other noncommissioned officers and enlisted men." Perhaps, since "the mere presence" of NCOs "may influence the enlisted men," they should be segregated during the screening process. Though it might not be worthwhile to transfer troublemakers temporarily to separate camps, in view of the expense and the scarcity of guards, the idea should be given a trial.

Segregation and screening plans were hard to implement. Few camp officials even spoke German. Someone in the PMG's office also pointed out that very few were qualified to screen prisoners, something that had to be done right the first time because the process itself could "reasonably be expected to sharpen the conflict between the Nazis and non-Nazis." The job called for "experienced, qualified military intelligence officers."[70] These were very scarce. Since the continuing "wave" of terror made the task seem increasingly urgent, the PMG's office would keep tinkering with segregation schemes.

Meanwhile, the secret intelligence camps on both coasts continued to use SPs, who in turn continued to enrage the "guests." The story of the five SPs at Byron Hot Springs provides a foil for that of the unfortunate Werner Drechsler.

CHAPTER 2

Six Stool Pigeons

One agent, summarizing Fort Hunt's wartime intelligence work, said this about the POW informer (stool pigeon, Special Prisoner, or SP): He must be chosen with "utmost care." He must be "thoroughly reliable, a quality normally not to be expected of men who are willing to perform this degrading function."[1] Handlers did not respect their SPs. In order to recruit them or get more work from them, agents often made false promises. The careers of five SPs at Byron Hot Springs are a case in point.

Nearly every German passing through Byron Hot Springs between January and November 1943 was interrogated by a very successful SP team of four soldiers and a sailor. This quintet left several unique personal and collective accounts of their work. Marcel Barthel was a citizen of Luxembourg, son of an American mother, whose family had fled to France when Hitler overran their small country. He enlisted in the Wehrmacht but deserted to the British on the El Alamein front in October 1942, intending to contact his government in exile "in order to direct my strength and my life toward the destruction of the Nazis."[2]

Karl Linke, a communist veteran of anti-Nazi street brawls, had enlisted in the French Foreign Legion. Five years later, when the Vichy government had to hand over all German legionnaires, he suffered a six-month "re-education" sentence at Dachau before being assigned to Rommel's Afrika Korps.[3]

To follow Linke's narrative, he met Barthel in a POW camp in Suez. Both wanted "to sacrifice everything for the victory of the Allies"; but before they could enlist with the Free French forces, they were shipped with five hundred others to the United States for internment. Since they made no secret of their anti-Nazi intentions, the transport officer had to protect them. When they landed at Angel Island in San Francisco harbor, the rest of the convoy went on to Camp Chaffee, Arkansas, while Linke and Bartel "were removed. . . in a closed vehicle" on January 7, 1943, and taken "to a separate camp."[4]

According to Barthel, upon arriving at Byron Hot Springs, they were deprived of everything but their clothes and interrogated for about a week. "We had absolutely no reason to conceal anything; on the contrary, we were both ready and glad to help the Allies." After that, they were isolated in small cells without belongings, cigarettes, or even reading matter, with only twenty minutes a day for exercise. "It was getting tedious." In late January two Navy officers told them they had to prove they weren't spies. Barthel said that his government in exile would vouch for him. He knew "most of the Ministers personally." He asked to speak to them. The interrogators promised him "everything possible . . . with respect to that, but nothing was done."

Then, on February 9, a Capt. Boesch "told us that he had been sent specially from Washington to test us and that he would do everything to help us. He made a good impression on us." To meet him halfway, "we made sketches of all the military objects with which we were acquainted, especially factories, electric power plants and barracks." Then "we were given back all the things that had been taken from us, and we were well satisfied." Next, Capt. Boesch mentioned that he had two other prisoners who "were a little Nazi." Would Linke and Barthel help him? "We agreed at once." They had been looking for an opportunity to prove they were not spies, "as our words apparently were not believed."[5]

After "hard psychological combat" they recruited Herbert Vogler, with Boesch helping "somewhat" by giving "his personal word of honor" that Vogler would be rewarded with "good work on a farm" and, after the war, the opportunity to earn a good living in the United States. Vogler trusted his promises "fully and entirely." Only much later "did he learn to recognize the tricks and gave up the idea of the farm. . . . But we all believed in a livelihood, or at least recognition."[6]

By the end of March, the three had won over two more recruits. Albert Mueller, a U-boat sailor, had been a carpenter in Magdeburg. When the Nazis pressured him to join the party, his father, a democrat, advised him to join the Navy (the German armed forces being officially nonpolitical). Mueller had arrived, wounded, on the same boat as Linke and Barthel. In a San Francisco hospital, he said, Capt. Boesch "asked me if I wanted to go with him to a small camp." After Mueller had given the Americans "all the information that [he]had," Boesch promised him that if he would "help him a bit," he could have "civilian clothes and the privilege of going to the city whenever I wanted to." Mueller did not believe that, since Barthel, Linke, and Vogler were not so rewarded. "I thought he only wanted to take advantage of me and then send me to a Nazi prisoner of war camp." Boesch told him "that the American Navy would not permit this" and that he needed Mueller's services. "I was very happy about this and I pledged to help America . . . fight Nazism until it was conquered, which I did with all powers within me."[7]

The fifth man, Anton Petratschek, was German-born, to Czech parents. The Nazis imprisoned and deported his father, an active labor unionist, and drafted Anton. After he was captured at El Alamein, he was offered a chance to join the Czech Brigade in England; but before he could make up his mind he was shipped overseas and parked with the rest of his convoy in Camp Chaffee for six weeks, until there was room at the Byron Hot Springs interrogation camp. There, Capt. Boesch reunited him with Linke and Barthel, whom he had met in Egypt.[8]

Barthel described their routine: The captain and a lieutenant would visit each new prisoner, asking only his name, place of birth, military unit, and whether he considered himself Nazi or anti-Nazi. Then one of the five SPs took over. "We squeezed him from all sides, like a lemon, formulating our questions and remarks in such a way that the P/W had to declare everything that he knew, down to the smallest detail." They took pride in their craft, Barthel added. "It cost us terribly hard battles of words and mental work," but out of every hundred of these men "there were only 5 who could not be broken" and turned against "the insane Nazi way of looking at things."[9] The Byron Hot Springs' commandant, Col. Kent, was soon referring to the five as "my pets."[10]

American officers were "only very seldom" successful at interrogation, Barthel said, "in most cases" turning over "the P/Ws to us as hopeless. Of course, everyone was greatly astonished when we came up with perfect results." Furthermore, "we worked entirely independently," though "we frequently needed the Captain for 5 minutes, to confirm our words and statements." American NCOs from G-2's German Interrogation Division translated their reports verbatim, "without the slightest thing having to be changed" before the reports "were sent to Washington." All Capt. Boesch had to do, Barthel said, was to sign his name to them. It pleased the five to see them excerpted in intelligence service circulars written for "higher officers." Boesch "always told us that Washington was fully and entirely informed of our work and that we were getting all recognition for it—we would therefore have the fullest confidence and protection of the American Government."

In time, however, these five realized that Capt. Boesch, not they, "got all the credit from Washington." (According to Moore, this was because the

G-2 interrogation summaries identified them only as "PWs X, Y, Z, etc." and described them only as "more or less loyal to the U.S.") Boesch also began to bully them. According to Barthel, he was "never satisfied with the best results." Boesch had less military knowledge than a "simple infantryman," but he believed "that he must always be right" and everyone else was "very stupid." He made "the wildest promises, but we saw through his gross lies only too often, and unfortunately we made the mistake of letting him see that."[11]

If they were busy, Boesch even deprived them of their twenty-minute walk. When they were not, he shut them in their cells with nothing to read. Out of boredom, they offered to cut the grass and tend the flowers. At first he refused. Then, while they made a large garden and constructed "nice paths," he began to drive and scold them. Soon the five were interrogating prisoners all morning, gardening all afternoon, and interrogating again from 7:00 to 11:00 at night, sometimes until 1:30 in the morning. "Our good nature was soon sweated away . . . and after a trying discussion with the Captain we asked him to send us to a camp, because we could no longer stand his eternal dissatisfaction." But the captain "knew how to hold us with interesting promises," which Col. Kent confirmed; and they finally received a few privileges: "We could take a bath, shave, wash our clothing and use the toilet whenever we wanted to, without having to ask permission of the guard, as formerly. That was an immense relief for us,"[12] though Boesch still bullied and drove them.

In late April 1943 a Col. Jones, "Chief of the Information Bureau in Washington," visited Byron Hot Springs (probably Col. Catesby ap C. Jones of G-2). According to Barthel, he "had been told about our work in the garden, but about our main work with the P/Ws he knew only a little." When they asked him for a transfer to another camp, he told them their "work was considered very highly in Washington," but if they insisted on leaving he promised "that we would always get full protection from America, even in the future." He promised to "see to it that we got into a very good camp and that we would have absolute protection from Nazis and other P/Ws . . . .We came to a very good understanding with him, and expected our departure."

The next day Capt. Boesch and Col. Kent made it clear they could not leave. Boesch also promised "the following favors: We should receive civilian clothing, could then go to San Francisco frequently, would get $25 extra pay monthly, besides our $3 as prisoners of war, and we could move freely outside the camp." The commandant, Col. Kent, hinted at future rewards "concerning which they could not talk to us" yet.[13]

Three days later, Capt. Boesch "told us that our pay had already come, $25, direct from Washington by telegram; he had bought clothes for us at once"; but since new clothes were so expensive, he had already spent all that and more. When they tried on their "new" suits, they saw that "the sleeves had been lengthened, one pair of trousers was raveled out at the bottom and the lining was still dirty and full of sweat." Even the shoes were old.[14] They swallowed their anger to avoid discord and also because by then they had grasped how dangerous their work was. After they had finished with their five hundred shipmates, they adopted assumed names. "Our astonishment was great," said Barthel, when they began to encounter prisoners from other camps who "knew all about us 5 nevertheless," even their real names, and "exactly what game was played in a camp near Frisco."

The "great crash" came on May 6, 1943. In "an extremely harsh, dictatorial tone . . . [which] roused in us hated memories of Germany and the Gestapo," the Capt. gave them their options: either they would continue working there, "blindly obeying all his orders"—which he said came from Washington—or "he would personally do everything to destroy [them]" by sending them to another camp. His actual words were, "You cannot expect the least protection from America. There is a report on you in which you are designated as criminals." If the Nazis in the new camp do not murder you, "after the war you will be turned over to Germany at once—what will happen there, you know, for any German government will then condemn you to death without ceremony."[15]

Col. Kent refused to speak to them, sending a written order to obey Boesch. However, they still had their privileges. "We frequently went into the city [San Francisco] in civilian clothing. The results of our work were the same as before; perfect," said Barthel. But then they received a blow to their professional pride. When a contingent of German generals arrived, the five were packed off to another camp for a "vacation." When they returned, they were disgusted to learn that these generals had given the American interrogators nothing, while gaining "a clear idea of the camp, even its name."[16] By mid-July, the five were back at work. This time they wore American sergeants' uniforms when they interrogated German officers. "Our results rose at once by 100%."

Their morale never recovered. They also began to fear that dishonest Red Cross workers had told the German government about their work. Since they had never once heard from their families, they feared for their safety. Believing that America would recognize that they had "sacrificed everything" to help destroy Nazism, they asked Col. Kent for permission to join the U.S. Army. The commandant seemed pleased with their request, even showing them a letter recommending it; but the prospect panicked Capt. Boesch. According to Barthel, Boesch was hoping their work would gain him a promotion. "He kept looking for some ground for rendering us harmless to his plans and for pushing us into destruction."[17] Boesch tried to sow discord between them and the American interrogators. When that did not work, he threatened to have Linke, Barthel, and Vogler sent off to rot in another camp—intolerable blackmail. "We all knew that a prisoner camp would mean the same thing for us as death."[18]

Because they no longer trusted Col. Kent, Barthel and Linke conceived an astonishing plan to defend themselves: They would appeal to the FBI "because it is also secret," and it had "a different headquarters." On November 8, in civilian clothes, the two simply walked about twenty-five miles "without the slightest difficulty" to the nearest bureau office in Pittsburgh, California. They gave the agent "a full report" and asked for protection for their lives. "The FBI agreed with us a great deal and promised us real help. We ourselves now believed that we had a dependable protection from America and returned to our camp without concern," having "kept everything so secret that not even the police or the civilian population knew what was up."[19]

The agent must have submitted a report (although FBI headquarters in Washington informed me that it had no knowledge of one). The escapade is mentioned obliquely in two documents reluctantly provided by the San Francisco division. About a month and a half after Barthel and Linke had walked to the Pittsburgh office, an agent in Stockton wrote on January 11, 1944, that the prisoners who broke out of Byron Hot Springs "several months ago have been moved from the camp and no trouble of any kind has been had since that time. . . . Col. Kent is still very friendly and thinks a great deal of the FBI."[20] A second memo, dated March 5, mentions an escape "by two prisoners about two months ago" and quotes Col. Kent as saying "that since the former trouble no more 'stoolies' have been used at the camp and that he does not contemplate using any again."[21]

Linke and Barthel had not even been missed until they had returned to camp. Then their trouble began. "On orders from Washington," their "American uniforms, civilian clothing and everything else" were taken away. They faced a board of inquiry. "Sworn . . . to tell the truth," they told "three neutral captains" everything that they had experienced in the camp during "the 10 months, from January to November 1943." Their statements and the FBI report were to be sent to Washington. Capt. Boesch, not waiting to be reprimanded, requested his discharge from the army. Col. Kent maliciously told the five that they "would therefore have to bear the blame entirely alone." He told his former pets that he would "do everything possible for [them]," but that Washington had taken everything out of his hands. He ordered them "to be locked up singly, not allowed to work."[22]

According to John Hammond Moore, "when the Pentagon learned what had happened, a blistering rebuke was dispatched westward. How could anyone, the Director of Military Intelligence asked, treat men who had been so cooperative so shabbily?" He also demanded to know how these prisoners had learned the real names of American intelligence personnel and the true name and location of "P.O. Box 651."[23] Actually, they knew a great deal more than that. As Barthel put it, they were "acquainted with all possible, *permitted and unpermitted* methods that help to fulfill the purpose" of the Byron Hot Springs interrogation camp.[24]

Someone decided to bury this knowledge, literally. On December 5, Barthel said, they were "very suddenly and without the least explanation" taken in closed vehicles to the Oakland train station. At first they "naturally assumed" they were bound eastward, to have their case examined. When the guard officer told them they were headed for Nebraska, they concluded that "because death awaited us in any P/W camp," then possibly "Washington was agreed that we were to be absolutely destroyed." They planned to "jump through the window at some railroad station where there were many people, in order to rouse public notice," preferring "to be shot by an American than to be murdered secretly in a camp by Nazi Germans."

When they found the train windows escape-proof, they decided to tell their story to the guard officer. "He did not believe in our fears," Barthel thought, but he "gave us his word to speak with the camp commandant about us, whereupon we gave him our word of honor that we would not cause any trouble on the trip."[25] Thanks to this honest officer, and to the commandant at Camp Indianola, they were not thrown into the general prison population when they arrived in the middle of the night on December 7, but held safely in the camp's stockade.[26]

According to Indianola's executive officer and stockade commander, a Maj. Erwin, "this headquarters had no information pertaining to the character and special case of these prisoners." All he knew was that the five had been sent "pursuant to Special Order #91 (Secret), dated 4 December 1943," from the transit camp at Angel Island, California. He later received a letter from Col. Kent, calling these men dangerous (and according to Moore, "treacherous" and "untrustworthy")—a last kick at his former pets. Nevertheless, Maj. Erwin listened when these five prisoners "began telling the story of the work they had done as interrogators at a secret processing camp in California." Since "it would be impossible for them to live together with the other prisoners," they asked him to keep them in the stockade and send a report of their case to Washington.

Maj. Erwin allowed them to write a fifteen-page description of their work and problems, which he sent to the Provost Marshal General's Office on December 16 with his own report: since Indianola had no facilities for segregating small groups, he had moved the five into a ward of the station hospital, which no one could enter without a special pass. He was guarding them round the clock because of Col. Kent's letter. On January 14, 1944, Assistant PMG Bryan ordered him to keep them under careful observation and to report if they seemed to be in danger.[27]

There was danger. When they were temporarily assigned to a side camp,[28] its officer reported that the 120 prisoners in their compound knew about their work and "openly expressed their intentions to do away with them" if they ever got the chance. "They have even threatened to poison these men if food was furnished them from their mess."[29]

Barthel gave the American officers at Indianola credit for doing "everything possible to help us and to avoid serious incidents."[30] Back at the main camp, they were placed in a spare compound with twenty-five anti-Nazis until those were transferred to Fort Campbell, Kentucky. The Pentagon had ordered the five to be kept there in Nebraska. By then so many new prisoners were arriving that the administration needed their space and their guards, so they were moved back to a hospital ward—this time unguarded—and given work in the officers' mess.[31]

Still, as time passed without any indication that Washington had received their pleas, they became increasingly anxious. Then they read a newspaper article: "ROOSEVELT SETS UP WAR REFUGEE BOARD."[32] The president had asked the secretaries of state, treasury, and war to ensure that the government was taking "all measures within its power to rescue the victims of enemy oppression who are in imminent danger of death," in cooperation with "the United Nations and other foreign governments." Barthel the Luxembourger and Petratschek the Czech assumed that they were eligible for rescue.

Barthel wrote another collective appeal and somehow smuggled it out of camp and into the regular mail. It arrived on Secretary of State Cordell Hull's desk, together with a personal plea from Barthel, the newspaper clipping, and a copy of the long statement that the five had written on December 11.

Barthel described how they had worked "together with the Military-Intelligence-Service . . . to get all informations which are necessary to beat the Axis" and how, although the War Department knew they did a good job "in a secret Information-camp: 'Byron-hot-Springs,'" they had been shipped out "to a regular P/W camp no regarding our own protests." They were endangered victims of fascism. "Dear Sirs we beg you to check our story. . . . Please give us protection against all Nazis and German prisoners. We risced [*sic*] all we have to help the Allies and now we beg you to give us an opportunity to keep on fighting the Axis" as soldiers in the American army, on any front. "This is our 4th report about our doings [which] . . . have never been forwarded or answered, so when we found this slip in the news-paper we got the idea to address you and ask you for help and protection." Barthel begged for an answer "as soon as possible because anything may happen in the meantime." He also asked that his story be relayed to the Luxembourg government in exile.[33]

Secretary Hull merely sent everything to Assistant PMG Bryan.[34] Weeks later, Bryan asked G-2's assistant chief of staff for advice. Was it possible for these prisoners to be "released for combat duty with the Allied forces"? Eventually, on March 30, Col. Catesby ap C. Jones replied: "No steps have been taken to release Luxembourgers for service in any army of the United Nations. In the event such action is taken, . . . [Barthel] should be given consideration." Jones recommended that all five be kept at Indianola or sent where they would not be recognized. On April 5, the PMG's Office sent orders to the Seventh Service Command: these prisoners were not to be moved "without the prior notification to and approval by this office."[35] (For the continuing adventures of this quintet, see chapter 8.)

Eighteen days earlier, Werner Drechsler had been murdered at a POW camp in Arizona. This twenty-three-year-old seaman first class had served on the mine-laying and supply vessel U-118, also called the *Czygan* (its captain's name). He and two others had remained in a Norfolk, Virginia, hospital while the other thirteen survivors were taken to Fort Hunt for interrogation.[36]

Drechsler's captors tagged him as a prospective collaborator.[37] On June 29, 1943, someone at the Norfolk naval base informed the PMG's Office that "one German male prisoner of war" was sufficiently recovered from a shrapnel wound on his right knee to be immediately transferred to Army jurisdiction. Then he added that the Commandant of the Fifth Naval District considered it "impractical to phrase this document in such a manner as would permit classification other than secret." An Army colonel picked Drechsler up the next day and took him to Fort Hunt.[38]

First, he had to be interrogated. An ONI agent described Drechsler in January 1944 as "intelligent, an individual of immense conceit and vanity, very cooperative if flattered enough." A POW would tell the board investigating Drechsler's death: "An American naval officer in Washington" (Fort Hunt) "told me that Drechsler talked quite a lot. The officer didn't say he was a traitor, but he said that he talked."[39] Indeed, Drechsler gave about eighty pages of information so detailed that his description of the submarine base at Bordeaux, France, even pinpointed the official brothels.[40] Soon he was sharing rooms with other German sailors, encouraging them to speak indiscreetly and reporting to ONI behind their backs.

Drechsler himself left no record of his motives or experience, leaving one to rely upon the testimony of his captors, his angry ex-roommates, and the scant surviving information from Fort Hunt: "berthing lists" of daily room assignments[41] and the logbooks in which all Naval Intelligence personnel signed in and out.[42] On his second day, Drechsler spent over half an hour with ONI's Lt. Cmdr. Gheradi. Thereafter, he was interrogated, "visited," and taken on walks almost daily, usually by one particular lieutenant; but he was also visited by ten other lieutenants and four other yeomen and ensigns. An Agent Alberti of the FBI interrogated him four times.

Drechsler was certainly not well rewarded for his work. The first time he was "taken out" was on July 20, 1943. Ten days later he had a longer excursion. In late August, he was treated to a seven-hour drive. Perhaps he deserved no more. The list of his roommates that ONI gave the officers investigating his death contains only nineteen names, including his own boatmate Hans Wosnitzka, who also became an SP.[43] Drechsler also managed to make many of his cellmates suspicious enough to spread rumors about him.[44]

One of his future killers caught a glimpse of Drechsler through an improperly blacked out window, and other prisoners claimed to have seen him walking around in civilian clothes, accompanied by American officers.[45] The only surviving officer of the U-118 heard that Drechsler—or was it Wosznitska?—had shown pictures of himself with American girls.[46] Some of his victims, comparing notes later at Fort Meade transit camp, decided that the same man had "represented himself to some as having a wife and child and to some that he was single, and to some he represented himself as a noncommissioned officer and to some as a radio man." He had even told one person he was engaged to a popular German movie star![47] Drechsler may have called himself "Nimmer," "Limmer," "Niemer," or "Leimi," but the victims of his deception all remembered being urged to talk by a man with a prominent scar on his right knee. Furthermore, he had told them all that he had served aboard the U-118, the *Czygan*! Some knew he had been a torpedo man. Some knew his true hometown, Chemnitz.

Drechsler's surviving crew—except for himself and Wosznitska—were interned together at Stringtown, Oklahoma. Since crews were kept together, they began to worry when neither man joined them. They knew that both had remained behind in Norfolk. Three of them had caught a glimpse of Drechsler at Fort Hunt.[48] Then, after about two months, the U-118 crew began to hear painful rumors. As one of them later told interrogators, newly arriving men said "that there was one in Washington giving away information," a person who "questioned German prisoners and then would turn around and betray them and give the information to the Americans . . . . It was talked all over Stringtown." Another new man said that "a Chemnitz boy" at the interrogation camp "was a traitor."[49] From the newcomers' descriptions, the U-118 survivors reluctantly recognized both their absent men.

Of course, the newcomers at Stringtown soon learned exactly who had betrayed them. As Rolf Wizuy, a future assassin, put it, "I said that this 'Leimi' was from the U-boat *Czygan* and they said that was the man who was missing." Drechsler's absence did not prove his treason, but "we took it for granted because this man was missing for a long time."[50]

Drechsler's crew tried to give him the benefit of the doubt. As one of them put it, "You can't say a person is a traitor 'til you are absolutely sure."[51] His closest friend, Seaman Polowzyk, would add: "No one from our crew could say he was a bad fellow because he was a good kid. No one from our crew knew for sure that he was a traitor . . . . They only heard that he was."[52]

The U-118's only surviving officer, Chief Warrant Officer Gross, took pains to be exact. No one told him what Drechsler actually said to the Americans, but only that Drechsler had reportedly told his roommates "things that he wasn't even supposed to tell [another German sailor] and even after some of these men told him to keep quiet he would still keep talking," in spite of the microphones at "Washington." Drechsler would say to the others: "Did you tell them [the Americans]?"— "Well, I did." He reportedly told about military secrets, even some things "that were not yet even installed on our own submarine." Gross said his crew "knew that Drechsler was a very smart man and what he talked about and the way he expressed himself," and no other person fit those descriptions of the "traitor in Washington."[53] No one from the U-118 would tell investigators who had given them this information about Drechsler.

Drechsler's absence seemed even more suspicious when, toward the end of 1943, the Army began to move its 6,286 naval prisoners into segregated camps. According to Moore, the Navy had demanded this because it was "never completely happy with Army supervision of Naval POWs," and it feared that Army censors "were inadvertently letting nautical secrets get back to Germany."[54] In January 1944, sailors from Stringtown were shunted to the new, poorly administered camp at Papago Park, Arizona, where trainloads of prisoners were thrown together with no attempt at political segregation.

In the new camp, Drechsler's crew kept asking questions and newcomers kept describing the "traitor at Washington."[55] One sailor who arrived about three weeks before Drechsler would tell investigators how he had been approached by men from both the U-118 and the U-boat *Graf*, who "asked me if 'Limmer' was truly a traitor and I had to answer then because I knew 'Limmer' personally."[56] At Papago Park, therefore, hundreds more German POWs learned Drechsler's true name. The U-118 crew shared a compound with eleven of his former victims.

Drechsler would not arrive at Papago Park until mid-March. He had served his nation's enemy at Fort Hunt from June 30, 1943, until January 8, 1944. On December 17, Naval Intelligence officially "turned him over to the Army" (and asked for his removal to a permanent camp).[57] ONI had begun thinning out its SPs because the Battle of the Atlantic was being won and most new prisoners were soldiers from Italy. But were there other reasons for dismissing Drechsler? The Fort Hunt logbook shows him in the Fort Meade hospital from October 2 until November 5, apparently being treated for a severe neck wound. His official record mentions only the shrapnel wound on his knee; and its full face and side photographs, taken at the Norfolk hospital after capture, show no neck injury. A POW who had roomed with him shortly after his return from the hospital would say he recognized Drechsler's corpse by the scar on its neck.[58] One of the killers, Otto Stengel, said that Drechsler had shown him a wound on his neck "from a shot," which had reopened.[59] When another killer, Rolf Wizuy, confronted his former roommate, he jeered: "Show me your right knee where you are wounded . . . show me your wound in your neck resulting from a splinter."[60] He must have sustained this injury while working at Fort Hunt. Was he attacked by an angry roommate?

When Naval Intelligence decided to dismiss Drechsler, it had to settle his account. On November 22, the adjutant at Fort Meade transit camp wrote to the director of the POW Division of the PMG's Office asking for information "in order to prepare initial payroll."[61] (Had he never been paid?) He would leave the interrogation center with $38.00 in his account.[62] At least $18.00 of this had accrued from the $3.00 monthly allowance every POW received.

When ONI had asked the Army to assign Drechsler to a permanent camp on December 17, at least it recognized the fact that Drechsler's life might be in danger. (Traitors were not welcome even in the small camp for anti-Nazi naval prisoners at Camp Blanding, Florida. Its commandant, who reported that his POWs were "all loyal Germans who resented traitorous talk," had to remove two former SPs in March 1944 after a third had been badly beaten.)[63]

Since the Army had physical custody of all POWs in regular camps, ONI could only ask G-2 (an agency of the Advocate General's Office) to ask the Provost Marshal General's Office to shield Drechsler from contact with other naval prisoners. The AG's Office routinely forwarded such requests to the PMG's Office, which also had the sole authority to assign a prisoner to anti-Nazi status and to so inform the headquarters of the Service Command in which that prisoner's permanent camp was located.[64]

On December 18, 1943, G-2's Col. Catesby ap C. Jones wrote the PMG's Office a variation on the standard notification of transfer:

1. It is requested that Prisoner of War, Werner DRECHSLER, Mechaniker-obergefreiter, 5G-61NA, be transferred to Jefferson Barracks, Missouri and Prisoner of War, Rudolf BRENDEL, Funkgefreiter, 1G-300NA, be transferred to Camp Blanding, Florida.
2. It is further requested that these Ps/W be shipped to Ft. Meade [from Fort Hunt] only when they will be shipped out immediately from there to respective camps . . . without being held at the Holding Enclosure [where alumni of Fort Hunt awaited assignment and transportation to regular camps]. Please notify us when the transfer can be made.
3. These Prisoners of War are classified as Anti-Nazi and are Naval Prisoners.[65]

On December 20 Col. Jones wrote again: The Navy had "special reasons for making this request" for Drechsler's transfer to Missouri. A note in the margin of Jones's memo says: "In telephone conversation of 22 Dec. '43 . . . it was agreed to disregard paragraph 2." Instead of being rushed through Meade, did Drechsler work there as an SP, perhaps among newly arrived prisoners? This would explain the gap between his leaving Fort Hunt on January 8 and his arrival in Missouri on February 4, 1944. A penciled note on the back of this document says "placed in Ft. Leonard Wood."[66]

To arrange for Drechsler's transfer, the assistant director of the PMG's POW Division sent a standard communication[67] to the Commanding General of the Third Service Command, in which Meade and Hunt were located. The first two paragraphs requested Drechsler's transfer, "under guard," from Fort Hunt "to the custody of the Commanding General, Seventh Service Command, at Prisoner of War Camp, Fort Leonard Wood, Missouri"; that general had "been informed of the transfer. It is requested that you inform him, in advance, the approximate time and date of arrival."

So far, this was routine. The next paragraph was unique: The transfer of a German naval prisoner to a camp "designated for the internment of German Army prisoners of war, is an exception to the segregation policies outlined in War Department secret letter, dated 18 February 1943 . . . [and is] authorized at the specific direction of the Office of the Assistant Chief of Staff, G-2."[68] In other words, Drechsler was sent to mingle with Army prisoners—mainly Rommel's Afrika Korps veterans, notoriously pro-Hitler. (Was Drechsler perhaps to serve as a camp SP?)

Since the U.S. Army trashed its World War II prison camp records to make room for Korean War material, one can only wonder how much weight Drechsler's exceptional status carried at Fort Leonard Wood. The Pentagon might make policies, but minor camp functionaries usually carried them out—people who had no notion that the interrogation camps even existed. At any rate, Drechsler did not remain in Missouri long. About a week after his arrival, Seventh Service Command received an order to ship all its naval prisoners to the new camp at Papago Park, Arizona, in the Ninth Service Command.

One cannot say for sure why Drechsler was included in this exodus. Since the Army also dumped most Service Command records, a researcher must rely on duplicate copies in other War Department files, such as those of the Property Branch of the PMGO's Enemy Information Bureau, which contain a document indicating that Drechsler might have been saved. A telegram from Fort Leonard Wood, sent on March 1 to Seventh Service Command Headquarters in Omaha, Nebraska, and to the PMG's Office, reveals that six prisoners at Fort Leonard Wood had protested the transfer, claiming to have been Army personnel, not Navy, when captured. Provost Marshal General Gullion himself replied the next day: They should be assigned army serial numbers, and remain where they were.[69]

Why was there no mention, on either end, of Drechsler's "exceptional" status? Perhaps some indifferent camp bureaucrat ignored it. But even if Drechsler had spoken up, a U-boat sailor like himself could not claim Army status. Apparently, Drechsler was not deliberately sent into harm's way as was the quintet ejected from Byron Hot Springs. Nevertheless, those SPs remained in comparative safety at Camp Indianola, Nebraska, which was also in the Seventh Service Command. One of them, Albert Mueller, was also a sailor. The fact that Mueller was saved shows that Drechsler could also have been protected.

Indianola's commandant, Lt. Col. Frederick E. Whitten, must have known Mueller personally since the five worked in the officer's mess. When Whitten received orders on March 3 to ship his naval prisoners to Papago Park, he noticed that this new camp had no separate compound for anti-Nazis. The next day, he notified command headquarters that Mueller might be in "actual danger" there, since he and his companions had been "employed on special work by the Military Intelligence Service," interrogating "a number of German prisoners of war, including Navy personnel, to whom their identity and the nature of their work is known." Whitten also cited the orders he had received on January 14, 1944, from Assistant PMG Bryan: to keep the five at Indianola because they would be safer among newly captured prisoners, to observe the situation carefully, and to report any "actual danger" at once. Whitten suggested that Mueller should remain in Nebraska, particularly in view of the fact that headquarters itself had telegraphed him on February 24 that these five segregated prisoners "had been recommended for assignment to German mail" (censorship?). Col. Whitten's good letter got results. Someone at Command Headquarters in Omaha stamped it "immediate action" and forwarded it to Washington on March 6.[70] Two days later, someone in Seventh Service Command's Security and Intelligence Division also telephoned the PMG's POW Division about the matter. Col. Whitten's letter went to the PMG himself. On March 11, nearly instantly in bureaucratic time, Omaha received orders to keep these five at Indianola "until their transfer is requested by this office, by name."[71]

Albert Mueller's salvation makes Werner Drechsler's fate all the more shocking. On March 7, after only thirty-five days in Missouri, he was placed on a slow train collecting naval prisoners bound for Papago Park. He would arrive there on March 12 in a herd of 350 strangers. Unlike the five companions in Nebraska, he had no support group. His disaster was compounded by his isolation, his ego, and perhaps his inexperience. Having been insulated at Fort Hunt, playing a friendly cellmate to newly captured prisoners, did he even realize that he had become notorious? He was also younger than the other five, much more passive, and astonishingly lacking in common sense. Perhaps Drechsler had been warned never to speak about the secret camp at which he had worked. Whatever the reason, he had no sympathetic officer to speak for him.

With luck, Drechsler might have gone straight from the train depot at Tempe, Arizona, to the Papago Park post hospital. While the others lined up for a long walk to camp, he displayed his knee to an ambulance driver and claimed to have "just gotten out of the hospital." But there was no sick call on Sunday, March 12. The driver followed his orders, which were to deliver this prisoner to Compound 4, where his boatmates were interned.[72] One of them recognized him as soon as he walked through the compound gates—wearing an Afrika Korps uniform![73] Soon the whole camp knew that the "traitor from Washington" was there among them. Having an injury too slight to win him refuge in the post hospital, yet bad enough so that he might escape the compound at sick call on Monday, was ill luck indeed. The situation gave his enemies a motive to deal with him at once.

Since there was no room for him in the barracks where his crew lived, Drechsler was assigned to bunk with fifty-seven other newcomers, strangers all. Six and a half hours later, he was dead.

As for the five at Indianola, some weeks later their hopes soared when a major on a G-2 screening team reassured them "that all details of their former work and their entire case was known to Washington."[74] Later, discouraged again as time passed without further word of their fate, they would act on their own behalf again, more outrageously than before.

CHAPTER 3

"Hang Him One Head Higher"

Papago Park, where Werner Drechsler died, is now the Phoenix zoo and botanical garden. But during the war, "at least for the 3,500 sailors and 120 officers surrounded on all sides by barbed wire" and desert,[1] it was a hell of brownish-pink lava. One ensign marveled, "There was nothing, absolutely; not a house, nor tree, nor plant for dozens of kilometers all around. Not a drop of rain, 120 degrees in the shade, and in the rubble of the desert all the scorpions and rattlesnakes you could want."[2] Inside the wire, there were shortages of everything but prisoners. In January 1944, when the naval prisoners from Stringtown, Oklahoma, arrived in the still-unfinished camp, it contained around 1,600 men. They kept coming by the trainload. Nazis and anti-Nazis were dumped together. In March, an inspector from the PMG's Office called Papago Park "a very difficult" place, with "numerous political agitators" stirring up "strong opposition to all cooperation with camp authorities."[3]

The Americans blamed *Fregattenkapitän* Juergen Wattenberg, the camp spokesman, for this situation. He often told prisoners that the Führer expected them to make trouble. He and the chief quartermaster from his boat, Franz Hox, the spokesman for Compound 4, encouraged prisoners to use their Geneva right to complain to the Red Cross and the Protecting Power. On February 19, Hox wrote that when the 507 men in his compound arrived, there had been only sixty-eight tubes of toothpaste and sixty bars of soap on hand for the entire camp. The classrooms had no furniture. Furthermore, the American officer in charge of the compound refused to discuss any issue or allow Hox access to the commandant. The chief of the Swiss Legation's Division of German Interests stiffly requested the State Department to remind the Provost Marshall General that according to Geneva Article 42 "prisoners of war have the right to inform military authorities of their requests."[4]

Capt. Wattenberg complained effectively about every breach of the prisoners' Geneva rights. The camp's commandant, Col. A. H. Means, was obliged to write an explanation to the Swiss and to his superior, Maj. Gen. McCoach of Ninth Service Command. McCoach also received—and resented—a smart reprimand for lax conditions at Papago Park.[5]

Wattenberg had a long history of matching wits with his captors. Early in the war, he had walked away from a camp in Argentina, where more than a thousand Germans had been interned after the scuttling of the *Graf Spee* to prevent its capture. Next, he had commanded a U-boat, which the Americans sank in September 1942. While he was being interrogated at Fort Hunt, the Royal Navy asked ONI to grill him about "escape possibilities in the Argentine." He gave so little information that ONI was reduced to sending its ally excerpts from the Argentine Congressional Record.[6]

Wattenberg was sent to Camp Crossville, Tennessee, where he became spokesman because of his rank. Soon, he issued a noncooperation order. If any officer so much as spoke to an American, he demanded a detailed report. An anti-Nazi officer turned informant because he feared a plot to haul him before a kangaroo court, hang him, and destroy his body in a Mayday bonfire. The Germans called him crazy, but a G-2 report described this officer as a member of the German *Abwehr* (Army intelligence) and an almost entirely reliable source. According to him, the "officer-ringleader" (Wattenberg) not only urged "a constant spirit of rebellion," but he had actually arranged for an uncooperative subordinate to be killed by American guards, then had made a martyr of him and told everyone how to testify when the death was investigated. The informer also named other troublemakers, especially NCOs, who acted as camp Gestapo, communicating with the officers through their orderlies.[7]

Another Crossville prisoner, a doctor, offered information about Wattenberg in exchange for protection and a chance to continue his research in endocrinology. According to him, "about 30 percent" of Crossville's prisoners were Nazis. The other 70 percent, he said, were terrorized anti-Nazis.[8]

After naval prisoners were segregated into special camps, the notorious Wattenberg became spokesman at Papago Park. He had nothing to do with Drechsler's lynching there, but he fit the War Department's image of a Nazi terrorist ringleader so well that he distracted the board of officers investigating the incident. (Months later he would organize the largest, most impudent POW escape on American soil.)[9]

The new naval camp at Papago Park was built to a standard pattern. There were several compounds for POW enlisted men and NCOs, one for their officers, one for American personnel, and one containing administrative buildings and the guardhouse. Tall double rows of barbed wire fence separated compounds from each other and from the post hospital.

Compound 4 contained the usual five rows of barracks, each ending in a latrine and a two-room wash house with showers, sinks, and laundry tubs. Each row formed a company or squad of around two hundred men, with up to fifty per building, wedged together on canvas cots. Squad 2 housed the NCOs and the enlisted men from Drechsler's boat, the U-118 or *Czygan*. Since their building was full, Drechsler was assigned to squad 5, the last barrack in the last row. He tried to claim a place beside a man who had shared his ambulance ride, only to be shouldered aside by his buddies. He landed in the second cot from the end, where a door opened onto a soccer field.

For almost three of the remaining six and a half hours of his life, Drechsler might have felt quite anonymous among the crowd of new prisoners entering Compound 4 around 3:30. An NCO from Drechsler's boat, riding back from a Sunday movie in a truck with other wounded men, spotted him at once. When the able-bodied prisoners arrived on foot, the news spread as they lined up for roll call, ate supper, and watched soccer games. "More people came into the [NCO] barracks and said that: 'Drechsler is here in camp.'"[10] Soon everyone but the Americans knew.[11]

Drechsler and his former crew mates ignored each other,[12] but Compound 4 also contained eleven of his angry ex-roommates. Siegfried Elser and another NCO, Friedrich Murza, began searching for him, as did seamen Peter Duer, Heinz Taubert, and Lothar Mandelkow, all without success.[13] Heinrich Ludwig and Rolf Wizuy were tied to their jobs in the officers' mess, but Wizuy's "boat comrades" Guenther Kuelsen, Helmuth Fischer, and Bernhard Reyak began stalking Drechsler on his behalf. Fischer had his own grudge, because he had been spied upon in "Washington" by another SP. Kuelsen, possibly the first to find Drechsler, spoke to him and heard him say that he would be leaving for the hospital the next day. Realizing that Drechsler would have to be dealt with that night, Kuelsen went looking for his friends.[14]

Meanwhile, Drechsler made the acquaintance of Otto Stengel, a dedicated gossip who had come out to cadge news from the newcomers. When Stengel overheard someone say he was from Chemnitz, he offered to take him to meet a man from his hometown. The newcomer refused.[15] "From that moment," Stengel said later, "I knew I was talking to the traitor."[16] In another dramatic version, he said that he only realized his identity after he told his acquaintance, Heinz Richter, that someone else from Chemnitz was in camp. Bystanders started telling Richter that if he spoke to this fellow he'd "get a bad reputation."[17] In yet another version, Stengel said he himself pointed the newcomer out to Richter, who "asked me the name of the man and I answered: 'Yes! it is Drechsler.'" Bystanders shouted: "You have a fine buddy!" "Why?" "He is a traitor. It is possible that he will get the Holy Ghost tonight or that he won't live until morning." Heinz Richter then remarked, "I don't want to see him."[18] Two bystanders would later be compelled to admit that Stengel himself had predicted that "the traitor should be hung." Someone else said he told Stengel he "should leave his hands out of it because it was none of his business" and he didn't know Drechsler.[19] Whatever happened, Stengel the gossip now had a fine phrase with which to astonish others: "Do you know what's going to happen tonight?" he began asking. "No." "Someone shall get the Holy Ghost and possibly will not survive the next morning." "Who?" "Who do you think but the traitor?"[20]

Stengel defined "Holy Ghost" as "self-education among buddies." If anyone did something which caused others to suffer, "then some comrades get together" and throw a blanket on top of the offender; "and when he is covered . . . he gets a couple of hits on his behind in a way that he will have to see the doctor sometime." Helmuth Fischer, Wizuy's friend, said the phrase meant someone "should get kicked in the ass and that well."[21] Drechsler might have escaped with just such a beating had he not carried on self-destructively foolish conversations with the first strangers he encountered.

According to Otto Stengel, when he reported the news to his barracks mates they commissioned him to go out again, "because I am, so to speak, the source of information . . . all the men come to me with the news because I took care of their laundry."[22] He found Drechsler again and asked, as PWs usually did, how long he had been a prisoner and what camp he had come from. Drechsler replied (said Stengel): "From a better camp than the one we are in now. We had different cots, almost everyone had a radio, it was so good that I left the hospital on my own responsibility." He showed Stengel the wound on his neck.[23]

In another of Stengel's versions of the encounter, Drechsler asked him what he thought of the war. When Stengel said that Germany would of course win, Drechsler scoffed at him: in his last camp, he had learned about American victory from a German-language newspaper. When Stengel dismissed that as enemy propaganda, both "became mad."[24] Stengel would tell his interrogators: "That paper insults our own Government, Dr. Goebbels, Hermann Göring, and even our Führer Adolf Hitler. (You can believe me, my blood was boiling.)"[25] He said to Drechsler: "My friend, you had better watch out, otherwise something is going to happen. I am a German and I don't allow you talking like that." Drechsler laughed and went away, "saying they would talk again." Deeply offended, Stengel returned to his barracks "in a very excited state."[26] "My hatred against Drechsler was pretty intense, because he had insulted Adolf Hitler and my Government in the worst possible way. A thing like that hadn't happened to me up to that time . . . after two years, being a prisoner of war."[27]

Stengel would be the only one of Drechsler's seven assassins to mention Hitler or to claim a political motive. The others would act from anger at being betrayed or, in the case of Wizuy's three friends, from simple comradeship. But all of them felt that they were protecting their families, homes, and fellow submariners by preventing this spy from doing more harm.

Meanwhile, Guenther Kuelsen had found his boatmates Bernhard Reyak and Helmuth Fischer. Along with another of Drechsler's ex-roommates, an NCO named Guenther Bleise, they located the traitor. As Fischer later remarked, Drechsler's "way of speaking was not to get sympathy from us."[28] First, Drechsler said that his last camp had been so "wonderful, he'd had a chance 'to become Camp Speaker.'" (This was a ridiculous notion. The post usually went to the senior officer!) Drechsler bragged again that "they listened to German news there and [he] asked in the same sentence whether we had German news at Papago Park, too. We told him 'No' and he thought we were very far behind with things."[29] (Asking about illegal shortwave radios was suicidal.) Then, according to Wizuy, Drechsler also asked Kuelsen "for a large number of names who were known to be missing from individual boat crews and who were suspected of being 'traitors,' claiming he knew about 'officers who deserted.'"[30] What could they conclude but that Drechsler was still spying?

Kuelsen, Reyak, Fischer, and a fourth buddy, Fritz Franke, told these things to their friend Rolf Wizuy when he got off work. Wizuy was "dumbfounded" to hear about his former roommate, Fischer said. They went at once to confront him.[31] According to Wizuy, he greeted Drechsler as "Obermaat Leime and he started to sweat" and stutter. He protested that he was only a corporal named Drechsler, and he had never seen Wizuy before, even when Wizuy "reminded him of different talks and Washington" and, as Franke recalled, when he described Drechsler's wounds and challenged him to show them off.[32] Wizuy said: "I got very mad at him because he lied to my face."[33] Kuelsen was disgusted. How could Drechsler deny knowing Wizuy, after he had so kindly brought Wizuy an ice bag after his appendicitis operation at "Washington"?[34] At this point, Drechsler realized he was in serious trouble.

Kuelsen recalled that he "became quiet and embarrassed" when "some more buddies recognized him." Reyak said he "got unsteady and disappeared with the words that he wanted to go to bed."[35]

According to Fischer, the friends' next step was to tell the NCO who was Drechsler's company leader "that he had received a traitor among his new men. This Master Sergeant was very much shocked over the news and mentioned that it was a very serious matter."[36] (Otto Stengel would see this master sergeant during the first attack on Drechsler, shooing onlookers away from the building, then walking off.)[37]

Meanwhile, the compound's petty officers had already discussed the situation among themselves. Obermaat (chief boatswain's mate) Murza had described how "Nimmer" had spied on him at "Washington." They had wondered "why Drechsler was sent to Papago Park. . . . We said it took a lot of nerve to send him to this camp," but no one had said anything about punishment.[38]

Obermaat Werner Reinl, Drechsler's senior surviving NCO, felt that while he had no authority, his rank obliged him at least to gather more facts. After supper, Reinl asked Heinrich Ludwig and Guenther Bleise to name other men who had been with Drechsler. Ludwig thought of two. The NCOs advised Reinl to ask around in the barracks. According to Ludwig, Reinl also asked him to do nothing until he could report to the compound spokesman, Obersteuermann (chief quartermaster) Franz Hox, the highest available German authority. "We should think this over," Reinl said. "We should not act in too much of a haste."[39]

After Reinl had collected "ten or twelve" other names, he located Hox. Had the *Obersteuermann* heard that Drechsler was in camp? There were rumors that he was a traitor. "As I am the senior noncommissioned officer from the *Czygan*, I don't want to say anything because I haven't been with Drechsler lately" and cannot prove whether he is a traitor or not. Reinl handed the spokesman his list of names and said: "'Perhaps you can call these men together and ask them whether there is anything to this rumor' and [Hox] answered: 'What should I do in this matter?'" A bit later, Reinl (or the translator) said Hox's reply was: "I cannot do anything about it." Duty done, Reinl began to watch the Sunday soccer game. He spotted Drechsler at a distance, but returned to his own barracks without speaking to him.[40]

According to Hox's version, Reinl had suggested that "I should check up first to see whether there was anything to this rumor and he said that a man like that is degraded very fast. I don't know why Reinl talked to me." He claimed to have told Reinl he would report the situation to Capt. Wattenberg. He did send Guenther Bleise to gather the men on Reinl's list.[41] Bleise (a

Drechsler victim) said he told Hox: "I know more people";[42] and after the game he went twice around the barracks ordering everyone "who had had something to do with Drechsler or who knew something about him, [to] report to the orderly room of the First Company,"[43] Hox's office. None of Drechsler's crew would go.[44]

Hox's inquest began around 8:30 P.M. Bleise claimed to have arrived too late to hear much. Fourteen or fifteen may have come and gone, but nine were certainly there: Oberfunkmaat Friedrich Murza, Funkmaat Siegfried Elser, and the sailors Walter Nieswand, Heinrich Ludwig, and Rolf Wizuy and his four friends. Kuelsen had followed Wizuy there. Franke had spotted Wizuy from the canteen next door. Reyak and Fischer had come, after Bleise's call, to report their recent conversation with Drechsler. However, four victims of Drechsler's spying were not present: Friedrich Wagenfuehr had to tend the water heater in one of the shower rooms until curfew. Lothar Mandelkow had "wanted at first to tell . . . but my crew said to me: 'Keep your hands off. There will only be trouble; otherwise you will probably be taken away sometime for an interrogation and we want to remain together.'"[45]

According to Murza, Hox asked for all the details of what had happened "at the interrogation camp near Washington, D.C. and . . . what names [Drechsler] had assumed and what he had asked the men. . . . All told the same story." According to Wizuy, Hox wanted to be certain that this newcomer "actually was the traitor Drechsler." Fischer spoke of being spied on by another SP, Wosnitzka, and about his conversation with Drechsler. Kuelsen and Wizuy told of his outrageous denials.[46]

After Hox heard everyone, he said something like "it seemed to be a clear case."[47] The American officers assigned to investigate the case, determined to prove that Nazi conspirators had set up a kangaroo court, would try their best to prove that Hox's remark had a sinister meaning; but he was neither a conspirator nor a leader.[48] On the pretext that he could not exceed his authority, he gave these aggrieved men neither orders nor advice. He would even complain to the interrogators that the men at his meeting gave him no instructions! When he had said "all is clear," he had merely meant that Drechsler was clearly a traitor, not that it was clear whether he should be punished, or how. "I didn't talk about any measures to be taken because after the conversation I left."[49]

The interrogators also labored to prove that camp spokesman Wattenberg had masterminded the lynching. Only Wizuy mentioned that someone at the meeting had suggested that Hox contact the captain, and that Hox had dismissed the idea "because in this case [the captain] wouldn't be able to do anything about it."[50] Hox himself claimed he had promised to report to Wattenberg in the morning (no one else remembered this!) so that the captain "could make a report to Headquarters so that Drechsler would be removed from the Camp."[51]

So Hox declined to lead. Fischer recalled: "About the punishment of Drechsler there was no talk but we said: 'Something must happen.' We said this in Hox's office. I assume that Hox heard it."[52] Wizuy thought Hox said "It's hard to advise you. You have to know yourself what you are doing."[53] Franke heard: "I cannot do anything about this matter. You must know yourself best what to do with Drechsler"; or else, "You have to know that best; first, I don't know that man, and second, I do not have the right to punish Drechsler." Ludwig confirmed Franke's version.[54]

Only Kuelsen implied that Hox may have sent a double message. When someone asked what should be done, he had said approximately: "'I can't see much in this matter. I don't want to give any orders in this matter,'" while looking ambiguously at the ceiling.[55] Only one person, NCO Siegfried Elser, felt that Hox had approved any action at all: "After a short silence . . . Hox told us that he couldn't do anything in the matter. All we could do was beat him up or something to that effect."[56] (Elser was trying to convince his interrogators that a beating was all he had expected to happen.)

The investigators would conclude in their report that Hox had said: "You must know yourself best what to do with Drechsler," implying encouragement.[57] Richard Whittingham adds up the facts this way: Hox had presided over a "kangaroo court" in a "crude and spurious courtroom,"; which had declared the evidence of Drechsler's "gross scar of Treason" to be so overwhelming that it condemned him to death in absentia. Hox, lacking the authority to act, had encouraged "the people against whom the crime had been committed" to render whatever "inexorable judgment" they chose.[58] The facts do not fit either Whittingham's scenario or the War Department's notion of a Gestapo-led reign of terror.

Although the investigators labeled Hox an accessory, he would never be charged with any wrongdoing. He had proceeded sensibly, if reluctantly—but not far enough. By default, these aggrieved and fearful young enlisted men were left to deal as best they could with a traitor to their country. "To every one of us it was clear that something had to be done," Fischer said later.[59] But what? They gathered outside Hox's office, driven by anger at the traitor and by fear for their own safety and for that of Germany.

Later, no one could say exactly who attended this brief gathering or what had happened there. The NCOs Elser and Murza, and perhaps Bleise before he returned to his job at the canteen, stood in one group. Murza suggested a severe beating. Elser was willing to help. He told investigators that he also wanted Drechsler ejected from the compound, but as for hanging, "I personally could not do a thing like that." Murza recalled: "We only discussed that for a moment and then went over and joined the second group," which was already dispersing.[60]

In the other group of perhaps a dozen men (including six future assassins), Reyak recalled that "each one" had expressed "his opinion about what he thought the Obersteurmann [Hox] had meant."[61] Rolf Wizuy recalled that some wanted only to administer the "Holy Ghost." Others opposed that, "particularly myself." As Fischer put it, "when Drechsler leaves from the Compound he could tell all our names." Most of them (and, Wizuy believed, most prisoners) also thought that the Americans had sent Drechsler there either to continue spying or to get rid of him. Drechsler had not appeared among them by accident, Wizuy told the group. "If we give Drechsler the 'Holy Ghost,' tomorrow he will be in another compound and will continue to harm our Fatherland. In Germany he would not live very long. . . . To hang him would be best."[62]

Germany was far away. Hox was silent. It was up to them. Later, Wizuy said that if only they could have counted on remaining alive to testify against Drechsler in a German court, they would merely have given him a good beating;[63] but in that anxious moment, they felt that unless they acted immediately, he would escape to the hospital. Then he would have the inconvenient witnesses to his treason eliminated. Ludwig summed up the conclusive argument: Drechsler must not "leave the compound and continue his betrayal of other German prisoners of war."[64]

The two NCOs must have joined the second group about then. Murza thought Wizuy was saying "that a complete job should be done." Elser said he heard "that Drechsler should be questioned immediately . . . and afterwards either transferred out of camp or hung."[65] But Heinrich Ludwig remembered it this way: "One of the three [*sic*] non-commissioned officers asked who would like to participate in this matter," knowing that "we had the intentions of hanging Drechsler." He, Wizuy, Kuelsen, Reyak, Fischer, and Franke "volunteered themselves."[66] According to Wizuy, his four close friends had done so only for his sake. (The investigating board would interpret this to mean that "under the urging of . . . Wizuy" they all decided "that a 'complete job' should be done.")[67] Franke told the investigators: "Who decided to hang him I don't know."[68] They all accepted the decision. As Helmuth Fischer put it, a mere beating was "too easy for a traitor to the Vaterland. We agreed on the idea that the scoundrel should be hung one head higher and separated to make our preparations."[69]

No one had a watch. They could not agree later on the time or the order of events. According to Ludwig, they agreed to meet "later on when it was dark" at an empty lot across from Drechsler's barracks. They reassembled about 9:00, he recalled. Then someone, perhaps Murza, warned them about fingerprints and they separated again to get gloves.[70] Elser also fetched his—not to help lynch Drechsler, he said later, but merely to show solidarity with the comrades. He still intended to convince the others "to beat up on Drecchsler during a discussion and afterwards to push him out of the Compound gates." Murza changed his awkward wooden clogs for regular shoes. Then the two NCOs joined the others, who had exchanged their "Sunday clothes" for work outfits. Next they all headed for the vacant lot.[71]

According to Reyak, a "group . . . larger than the one" in Hox's room accompanied them. On the way, they made "plans . . . how best to handle the situation." But Kuelsen recalled: "We didn't make any definite plans. At first all the men wanted to participate in the action and then we all went to Drechsler's barracks and slowly the number of men in the group decreased"[72] (although the number of spectators would keep growing). Elser and Murza wandered away from the others, toward Drechsler's barrack. Wizuy noticed this. "I assume they didn't want to have anything to do with that hanging," he said, although "they didn't express any opinion."[73]

Only then did someone ask how they were to lure Drechsler outside. Would his own petty officers do this for them?[74] Franke and Wizuy headed for the NCO barracks where, according to Franke, Wizuy told Drechsler's petty officers that if they would only get him out, "we would take care of him," although "we did not mention that we wanted to hang him"; but they "didn't want to have anything to do with this matter."[75]

Drechsler's petty officers had already faced a parade of people asking about him. They were feeling more and more offended by his behavior. Some of them were beginning to think that, in Rudolf Wiemer's words, "he could be [a traitor] for the simple reason that he never came to greet us at this camp." He added: "I figured out he had a bad conscience; otherwise, he would have come to see his Comrades right away." Nevertheless, Wiemer said they told Wizuy "we had nothing against Drechsler, we couldn't prove anything."[76] According to Joseph Hoeller, after Wizuy and Franke left, someone said "we should have gone over to see [Drechsler] and see what was wrong," but Hoeller had disagreed. Duty and protocol demanded that the enlisted man should approach the officer first.[77]

Did any of Drechsler's petty officers imagine, then, that his life was at stake? None of them had asked Wizuy why he wanted them to get Drechsler out. Obermaat Reinl said, "I thought inwardly that Drechsler would probably get the Holy Ghost but I didn't hear this word."[78] Wiemer said they had understood Wizuy "surely meant to beat him," although "I believe he had a terrific hate against Drechsler and that he wanted to get even." This bothered Wiemer.[79]

Shortly after that, Drechsler's closest friend, U-118 seaman Hermann Polowzyk, came to the NCO barracks. Someone he did not know had stopped him as he was leaving his job at the canteen to tell him he should visit Drechsler. He asked Obermaat Wiemer to go with him. Weimer agreed, in spite of his opinion that Drechsler should make the first move.[80]

According to Fritz Franke, he and Wizuy returned from the petty officers' barracks to find that the others had strung a noose over a rafter in Fifth Company's bath house, and had put a bench beneath it. Even then, as they waited for the lights to go out in Drechsler's barracks, they were still "undecided how to begin." The crowd was growing. Wizuy thought that some of the "many groups" of men "walking around" there "just came to be spectators"; but he assumed that some of them also intended "to do something about Drechsler."[81]

Heinrich Ludwig, a stranger to the five friends, said that he and "one other" had stayed in the shower room "to be ready" while Kuelsen had gone inside the barracks, finding everyone asleep. (Kuelsen had not done this.)[82] Reyak recalled waiting in the shower room with "one who could be Ludwig," preparing the rope and waiting for someone "to get Obermaat Höller, who was to lead Drechsler out to the shower room, but he did not come." Reyak eventually joined the others on the vacant lot, where he saw Wizuy (or perhaps someone else) bring a "reddish-blond Obermaat of Drechsler's crew" to fetch him out.[83]

This was Rudolf Wiemer. On their way there, he and Seaman Polowzyk had encountered Wizuy and some others he did not know.[84] According to Wiemer, "this group asked me if I wouldn't go and get Drechsler out of the barracks because they wanted to give him the 'Holy Ghost.'" He had agreed, but had whispered to Polowzyk, "No, we don't want to have anything to do with it." When they arrived, Wiemer asked Polowzyk to go in alone, "because Drechsler didn't greet me directly." Polowzyk soon reported that Drechsler was asleep "and that we shouldn't wake him up." After that, Wiemer said, "I went with Polowzyk back to our Company and didn't bother myself any further with this thing." Shortly afterward, when they heard that Drechsler had been hanged, some of the U-118 crewmen would finally accept the idea that

Drechsler was a traitor, on the ground that there must have been a reason why he was lynched. Wiemer would conclude that "he had a bad conscience. Otherwise he would have come to see his comrades right away."[85]

Meanwhile the two petty officers, Murza and Elser, had been standing halfway between the Third and Fourth Company washrooms along with their fellow NCO Bleise, the Drechsler victim Mandelkow, and other spectators. "News went from mouth to mouth," Murza said, becoming garbled.[86] He heard that someone from Drechsler's boat was fetching him out. No, he was already asleep. Elser heard that when two volunteers had asked the traitor "for a hearing on the outside," Drechsler had said he was sleepy "and we have time tomorrow." At that point, Elser said, he had "suggested that the matter should be postponed until the next day" and had walked away, expecting the others to follow him. About forty men kept standing there. Elser paused to debate with some others who were saying Drechsler should be dragged out by force, when he saw five men moving through the dark toward Drechsler's barracks. He had just decided to return to his own quarters with Murza and Wiemer when they heard screaming and turned back.[87]

The keenest observer in the crowd was Otto Stengel, prowling around for gossip. He had already told his barracks buddies that men were guarding the doors of Drechsler's building while other small groups milled around; and "there is talk in the camp . . . that Drechsler wanted to leave for the hospital." His buddies had told him: "Only that little? Now you smoke a cigarette and go again."[88] He did as they asked, sealing Drechsler's fate and his own.

CHAPTER 4

Unschädlichmachung

The action began when night fell and the American guards left the compound. The following account is pieced together from the testimony of bystanders and from the (involuntary) statements of the actors. It contains the differences one expects from men acting in darkness, intent upon *Unschädlichmachung* (preventing harm, neutralizing a poison by force and violence.)[1]

A bystander later told investigators: "One comrade said to me: 'They are probably going to hang Drechsler. Come on, let's go.' Then we left down to the toilet and there was quite a bit of excitement in Camp, quite a few walking around."[2] The number of men around Drechsler's barracks kept growing. Ignoring them, the six who had "volunteered" decided to drag Drechsler from his barracks.[3]

At lights out, Wizuy, Kuelsen, Franke, and Fischer headed for Drechsler's cot, near the door by the soccer field on the camp's outer edge. Fischer: "Somebody pulled the comforter away from him and he . . . jumped up, and asked 'What is happening?' and we answered: 'You know that better than we do.'" Franke: "He asked what we wanted from him. We said that he was a traitor and he had questioned his own buddies in the interrogation camp and so betrayed his comrades and we talked to him for a long time." Kuelsen: "He said first that we should listen to him." Fischer: He said: "Comrades, I'll tell you everything tomorrow" (a mistake, since they knew he would be leaving the compound at sick call). Then somebody said "not to talk too long but to take him out right away. After that we grabbed him." Reyak: "Everybody grabbed and just how each one grabbed it was hard to tell because it was dark." Kuelsen: "Of course he defended himself and he was beat up."[4]

Reyak: "We took Drechsler out of his bunk together with his bedding." Fischer: "One kicked him in the ass and one must have hit him in the mouth.

. . . Somebody put his hand over Drechsler's mouth but [he] continued to scream." Ludwig: "After they had [dragged] Drechsler outside he defended himself and hollered like he was wild." Franke: "He screamed so much and he got loose from us and we let him go back," (Fischer:) "in order not to make this thing too conspicuous"; but "because so many men had arrived in the meantime, Drechsler got up and said: 'Buddies, somebody, come closer' and we told him nobody would come closer towards him." Then Reyak warned the others that "a guard was coming by . . . just outside the compound" fence. (Stengel, standing among the observers, also thought a sweep of searchlight from a guard tower startled them.) Then "they all let go and ran" while Drechsler dodged back inside, (Kuelsen:) taking his bedding with him.[5]

According to Obermaat Murza, watching from about a hundred meters away, Drechsler's screaming drew even more onlookers.[6] Why did those American guards fail to notice a screaming man draped in a bed sheet surrounded by a crowd? At night, Americans stayed outside the fences. The road was about 175 feet away, beyond the soccer field. Inside the wire, where only a few weak lights still burned, the prisoners knew to keep moving back and forth, or to stand in small groups around the latrines and bathhouses where men would normally be at that time of night.

Otto Stengel, out for gossip, stood on the far side of Drechsler's barracks during this first attack. The account he gave in his first involuntary confession is probably accurate—with due allowances for his compulsive dramatizing and painful situation. He had begun his new round of fact-finding, he said, with a tour of the washrooms. When he reached Third Company, he "heard a cry—somebody was distinctly calling for help." Rushing closer, he saw Drechsler on the ground. Someone "kicked him with his foot and Drechsler shouted and then he jumped up from the gravel," mounted the barracks steps, and yelled "'Come over if you have the courage?' . . . He was full of blood—around his nose and mouth." Because of his shouting, the "men told him 'Go on—get inside of the barracks.'" He did, and they "parted in a hurry in opposite directions."[7]

The investigating board asked Stengel leading questions for the record: "Did a petty officer come down" when Drechsler was lying on the ground? Yes, he remembered the "Leader of Company 5," whom the sergeants called Helmut. He had told the onlookers, "Go away and let the six men do what they want to." After the group had stepped back a few feet, and after Drechsler dodged back inside, this petty officer had walked away.[8]

Had the searchlight fallen on any of the attackers? Here Stengel overreached himself: No, only two had faced the light. They had cloths over their lower faces, "and they were dressed with heavy overcoats and gloves, mufflers, and some of them wore caps" (in mid-March in the Arizona desert). No wonder Stengel was compelled to confess again! After another thirty-hour session with interrogators at Byron Hot Springs, he would confess falsely to being the ringleader of that first attack as well as the one that followed.[9] (Stengel had to manufacture a description of the first foray. He did this by ascribing incidents from the second attack to the first one.)

Meanwhile, Drechsler returned to his cot. He could not run outside into that crowd. He could not appeal to his barracks mates, who were ignoring him for fear of the "black cow": As one neighbor who had ducked under his blankets explained, that meant "the night was dark and you can't see anyone" who comes "to take care of" a person who "does something wrong." He had minded his own business, never even discussed the event afterward. "One has to be careful to whom he talks to."[10] This man was certainly wiser than Drechsler.

Otto Engler, the only man in the barracks willing to describe what went on, slept at the other end of the barracks, fifty feet away from the action. He heard someone yell, "I want to stay here. I don't want to go away from here." When Engler and some others sat up and asked what was going on, a voice had said: "This is none of your business" and "this man is having an epileptic fit so don't bother yourself over it." Engler had done nothing because "when the black cow walks it is best to mind your own business." He added that the killers "must have been someone who knew him personally. We were all strangers."[11]

So Drechsler sat alone while his attackers reassembled to figure out what to do next. Rolf Wizuy, who had insisted on hanging him, changed his mind: "It's no use now. The beating will be enough and will do him good." Some others agreed. Bernhard Reyak thought: "It wouldn't make any sense to continue as so many men had come as spectators, and the Holy Ghost . . . would be sufficient punishment." Then "Stengel appeared suddenly, I don't know where from." (Otto Stengel acted on impulse. Later, he would say "I was the only one that didn't have any gloves on. I didn't think I would be in on it, but that I would only be the reporter.")[12] As Franke recalled, Stengel said, "What are you doing here? Can I help you?" even though "he knew what was going on. He must have been standing there and he knew all about it." Kuelsen said simply: "Otto Stengel joined us and he said: 'Can I be of assistance to you?' and we didn't say anything. He was welcome." Reyak said that Stengel, who had never had anything to do with Drechsler, "patted me on the shoulder and encouraged me to go on with it . . . and not back out at this stage of the game." Wizuy remembered: "He seemed to have a great hatred for Drechsler. He took things assuredly into his hands."[13]

In his second involuntary confession, Stengel took full credit for masterminding the second attack. His determination "amazed" his comrades, he said, "but inside of me there was hatred for the traitor and faith in my Fuehrer to whom I had sworn Faith and whom Drechsler had shamefully insulted."[14]

> The comrades suggested to let it go now. "Drechsler certainly thinks that that is all." "It was a fine Holy Ghost and let's hang him a few days later." Now I remarked: "Then he will go to the Americans tonight and will cause still more trouble for German women and children." My comrades agreed to that and now decided to enter immediately but to take a rope along with them in order to put it around his neck to prevent him from screaming. Two men went away to get a rope.[15]

Stengel suggested they attack through both doors at once. "We were all convinced and divided into two groups" (Reyak), waiting only until the crowd had thinned (Kuelsen) to try again. Ludwig did not even know if "the man who made those remarks went with us." For his part, Stengel was unaware of Ludwig's existence, since he had been waiting in the shower room during the first attack.[16]

During this second attempt, the attackers still wanted to hear Drechsler admit his treason. Fischer: "What did you do in Washington?" Ludwig: "He denied . . . that he had even been there," then claimed "that they made a pig out of him. Whereupon we answered him: 'And you have made so many other comrades pigs.'" Drechsler wept and pleaded for time to explain. He "started again to tell us to listen to him, that he was not to blame, that they had put him into the interrogation center, that he was forced to do so and that we should wait until morning," when they knew he would escape them. Then he said something that sent them over the edge: "Comrades, let me explain." Ludwig said: "That was too much, that a traitor still used the word 'comrades.'" Stengel said, "The word 'comrades' nauseated us. We told him: 'You have no more comrades, remember.'"

According to Fischer, "we grabbed him again . . . and he noticed then that we were serious and started to scream endlessly 'Help! Help!'" When Fischer tried to muffle him, Drechsler bit the middle finger of his gloved right hand until someone "slapped him in the mouth." Until now, Stengel had only been watching "as the space was very limited," but he took credit for freeing a bitten comrade by grabbing Drechsler's jaw.[17]

While Drechsler kicked and screamed, Franke took the dog leash from his pocket and throttled him. "Ludwig helped me tighten it." (Ludwig: "I don't remember for sure but I think we had a little rope which we put around his neck right in the barracks.") Stengel, of course, embroidered: The rope was intended only to stifle his screams. "He was supposed to always get a little air." Wizuy could not recall any rope except the noose in the bathhouse.[18]

When a spectator opened the barracks door, Reyak went out and "tried to disperse our friends on the outside," who began asking questions. Then "somebody suddenly cried: 'They got one.'" The others emerged carrying Drechsler. Reyak tried to follow the crowd into the washroom; "but somebody held me back and told me that it was none of my business." It took him a moment to free himself.[19]

Five of them hauled Drechsler along feet first, face down. The two at his head had one hand on the rope and one in his hair. According to Stengel, who carried a leg, whenever they loosened the rope to let him breathe, "he offered quite a bit of resistance"; but Franke, holding his head, said "he didn't move any more." Had Stengel detected death spasms? Fischer would say: "When Drechsler died I do not know as I am not a doctor. . . . It is possible that he lost consciousness on the way over because he didn't scream any more." Wizuy thought he might have been dead, although "it was dark already and I was very excited and I didn't pay attention."[20]

In the bathhouse, Stengel said he and Wizuy put Drechsler's feet on the ground "and the others pushed [him] up." Fischer climbed up on the bench and took hold of his hair, and someone helped put his head into the noose. Kuelsen arrived just as it tightened. He had paused to close the barracks door and to tell the crowd "to disappear." By the time Reyak forced his way in, with the crowd at his heels, "somebody cried: 'Everything is all set, let's beat it.'"[21]

Petty officer Elser, who had been pacing around outside, was "deeply moved" when he saw them carry Drechsler into the shower room. Distance and darkness kept him from recognizing anyone, he told interrogators, "and I was also too frightened to observe accurately." He and Murza returned to the NCO barracks together.[22]

The crowd remained and grew. Murza thought "there might have been 100 or even more." Nieswand said "almost all" of them went in to look at Drechsler. Stengel, lingering to savor the drama, said "there were about 200–300 prisoners who, to my knowledge, went inside the shower room."[23]

Heinz Taubert, one of Drechsler's ex-roommates who had searched in vain for him that afternoon, said anger had caused "most of the comrades" to watch. As soon as someone reported the hanging, he had set off from his barracks with a large group and found "about 40 or 50 men assembled outside and inside of that washroom." It was too dark to see much, and "I didn't feel well about it so I returned with my buddies to the barracks." He went back for a daylight view. "He looked very bad and I couldn't recognize him for sure."[24]

Johann Matzke, Stengel's barracks mate, was playing cards when someone brought the news, "Let's go down there and look." On the way, he met Stengel, who told him: "Go away and don't be conspicuous. . . . A man has been hung." Matzke turned back, but most of the others went on.[25]

Six of the killers kept their mouths shut afterward (even among themselves, according to Wizuy). Although the five friends had gone to their company washroom to rid themselves of bloodstains, Reyak only learned the next day that Fischer had been badly bitten. Later, Reyak said, "several people" in their barracks "asked me what had happened but I refused to answer."[26]

Otto Stengel was incapable of discretion. By his own account, he appeared in his barracks with bloodstained face and shirt, borrowed a towel, and went off to wash. "Returning to the barracks," he wrote, "I simply must tell them what has happened." His buddies "wanted to know more, saying 'How did it happen?' I told them all the details and they asked me, 'How is it that you know it so exactly?' I answered, 'I myself had participated in the crime.' After that, I went to sleep."[27]

One of Stengel's barracks mates, Alfred Friedrich, most unwisely bragged to camp officials that he knew one of the killers but would never reveal his name. At Byron Hot Springs, he would be compelled to do so. He would describe how morning roll call provided Stengel with another audience. Someone had asked who had done it. He had "laughed and said 'I don't know'" in English, "and everybody in the line who overheard him assumed" that Stengel had been there and seen "how it had been done." Then Stengel had described how "the man cried out loud and . . . tried to defend himself and made noise and had to be hit to be kept quiet," and that a traitor "deserved more than a hanging"; but most of the men in line "thought the hanging was enough." Some of them were "mad that Drechsler had been beaten as much." Stengel had mentioned five or six confederates, Friedrich would say, though no one knew who these were. "No one else spoke about it except Stengel who was always bragging." Friedrich believed the killers must have been Drechsler's victims at "Fort Meade" and this puzzled him, since Stengel was a stranger to the traitor.[28] Friedrich would also add that he heard an American officer say there were fingerprints on Drechsler's neck. When he told Stengel this, he had said: "Those are my own fingerprints because I wore no gloves." Friedrich added that if he himself had helped kill Drechsler, he would have kept his mouth shut.[29]

Stengel, however, relished a good story and he probably felt no danger. He was among comrades. Furthermore, he had no idea that the Americans could punish him. He expected to tell a German court how he had murdered a man who had

> committed countless murders. My sister-in-law has been bombed out, my cousin, a woman, was killed during an air raid, and how many more women and children, even more so, how many brave U-boat soldiers were sent to their death by Drechsler. Should we Prisoners of War wait until the war is finished to avenge the traitors of Germany? I love my Fatherland and cannot wait that long because [by] the end of this war Drechsler could have killed my wife and children also. I have committed a murder; however, I don't consider myself a murderer but a conscientious German soldier.[30]

The other prisoners agreed that this was a German affair, that traitors had to be dealt with. At Byron Hot Springs, Willi Peters would confess to hearing a rumor at roll call: the compound spokesman Hox had a confession, signed by Drechsler, "to the effect that he was a traitor and the men who participated in the crime would own up to the crime in Germany."[31]

According to the Geneva Convention, POWs were to be judged and punished by the laws of the Detaining Power—the very enemy whom these prisoners considered morally responsible for Drechsler's death. According to Fischer, "it was said among German prisoners of war, that American authorities also have to take some of the blame, because they had knowledge that Drechsler was a traitor and sent him to our camp in spite of that fact."[32]

None of the men who heard Stengel brag would ever have denounced him to the Americans. This was definitely not because they feared him, even though he liked to pretend he had ominous connections. One barracks mate said, "'So, Otto, Gestapoman, I'll keep my mouth shut.' . . . The title 'Gestapoman' was given to him by an American colonel." Another, Willi Peters, would say he paid no attention to what Stengel said during that roll call "because I know Otto Stengel."[33] Heinz Taubert, who did not then know Stengel's name, heard him saying two or three days later: "'I am from the Gestapo, I am interested in the case.' He bragged about the crime and . . . the fact that he was connected with it." Then "the buddies of my labor detail" said, "'Don't listen to the man, he is only bragging.'" In camp, "several comrades said that Stengel was stupid and had an inflated ego."[34] One way or another, Stengel escaped detection for a very long time.

CHAPTER 5

"Thorough Investigation Is Requested"

Early on March 13, a guard telephoned the camp's new provost marshal "that he believed there was a dead man in Compound 4." First Lt. Cecil S. Parshall, an ex-policeman, inspected the shower room before calling the post surgeon and the commandant. In Drechsler's barracks, he found "a large bloodstain about two and a half feet in diameter" in front of a cot. The neighboring bed held "a bloody comforter and a piece of ragged hemp rope, also bloodstained." Parshall would give these items to Capt. Leland Hebblethwaite, the post's internal security/identification/signal and summary court officer, who took charge. Hebblethwaite would lose them.[1]

Hebblethwaite began making photographs and taking fingerprints to confirm Drechsler's identity by comparing them with his personnel record—according to which Drechsler was nothing but an ordinary prisoner.[2] The two camp doctors who performed a gross autopsy (without lab work) at a local funeral home disagreed as to whether he had died from being garroted or hanged, but both decided that his injuries could not have been self-inflicted.[3] Drechsler had been murdered. Unfortunately, the commandant, Col. Means, had already informed the press that a prisoner named "Breschler" had committed suicide.

Some camp official concluded that whoever had beaten Drechsler so savagely must also have bruised himself. At the noon roll call, a medical officer examined everyone in the compound, without success. These naval prisoners always formed up "in the German way," packed together as if standing on a narrow submarine deck. Helmuth Fischer easily hid his bitten finger by slipping up into another row. (Camp rumor credited Stengel with this maneuver.)[4]

Next, Capt. Hebblethwaite tried disinformation. He announced that fingerprints had been found on the corpse's neck.[5] Guenther Kuelsen also heard rumors that camp officers only wanted the "names of the men who had participated in the crime in order to have proof for a report to Germany through Red Cross channels."[6] Of course none of the prisoners talked, but few knew anything definite. Some thought Drechsler had been dispatched by members of his own crew, others that his victims had done the killing. Not even the bystanders knew how many killers had been involved.

On the third day, Capt. Hebblethwaite decided to isolate the men he considered the most likely suspects. He shifted Drechsler's forty-seven barracks mates and ex-spokesman Hox to another compound. Drechsler's boatmates from the U-118 went into the stockade, along with all suspected Gestapo agents. Stengel's barracks mate Gerhard Richter was doubly suspicious, an alleged Gestapo man who worked in the camp personnel office with someone from Drechsler's boat.[7] For two futile weeks, these men were bullied by Hebblethwaite, other officers, and possibly an FBI agent. (When the POW Norbert Gabler described Drechsler's hanging as "German 'quick justice' [Schnellgericht]," his questioner "showed his police certificate and said: 'this was the Gestapo just as much as in Germany.'")[8]

As soon as they could, Gabler and other outraged suspects exercised their Geneva right to complain to their Protecting Power.[9] Two NCOs from the U-118, Paul Reum and Werner Reinl, reported hearing someone in the next room of the stockade "screaming pitifully as if he were being hanged" or "struggling for his life." Reinl described how his interrogators placed Drechsler's bloodstained noose around his neck, demanding "whether it was Capt. Wattenberg or Coxswain Hox [spokesmen for the camp and Compound 4] who gave me the order to commit the act"—or had he, himself ordered it, as Drechsler's senior NCO? He might as well confess, Reinl was told, since two of his mates had already "told everything." Hours later, Reinl was shut into a cold, empty cell where he "stood the whole night leaning against the wall." The next evening he was given access to a "toilet and washing facilities . . . in a condition not fit for human use." His treatment, he wrote the Swiss Legation, "was not in accord with the provisions of the Geneva Convention, and was not that of a German prisoner, but of a criminal."[10]

Wattenberg was demoted. The new camp spokesman, Fregattenkapitän Paul Keller, collected these letters to the Protecting Power and added one of his own, which listed "a series of violations against the Geneva Convention and against the principles of criminal trial law": These men had been locked in unfurnished cells with no covering but their summer work clothes, compelled to sleep on the very floors on which they had to relieve themselves. Nearly all were told they would hang for murder, "even when plainly no evidence for such was available." Two NCOs "were bodily attacked by a Captain."[11]

Capt. Keller's letter and those of the others were dated in late March, but at the camp commandant's request he held them back until the Service Command had completed a second investigation. Col. Means did not take possession of these complaints until July 22, by which time Drechsler's killers had already been forced to confess. Furthermore, the PMG's Office would not send these letters to the Swiss Legation until August 12—a mere three days before their trial.

Long before then, Drechsler's death had caused diplomatic trouble. On March 14, 1944, thanks to Col. Means's "loose lips," the *Washington Post* and the *Washington Times Herald* carried small Associated Press reports announcing that the German POW "Breschler" had hanged himself. The *Times Herald* added that the suicide had occurred "shortly after Army officials had frustrated a second escape attempt" from Papago Park "within the past month." The *Post* quoted Col. Means's assurance that the two events were unrelated.[12] From these articles, the Protecting Power learned that a German prisoner had met an unnatural death. Naturally the ambassador from Switzerland demanded to know why his government had not received formal notice. This was not the first time such a thing had happened. The Secretary of State had already promised Switzerland that it would not happen again.[13]

Communications involving the Swiss Legation, the State Department, and the War Department could be painfully slow, particularly if the War Department had not initiated the contact. On March 17, State's Special War Problems Division (SWPD) passed the legation's complaint to the War Department's Prisoner of War Division (PWD) in the Provost Marshal General's Office (PMGO), with the State Department's standard request for information on "the nature of the reply to be made." Could this "Brechsler" be the Werner Drechsler mentioned in a recent War Department note to State's SWPD announcing his "suicide by hanging on March 13, 1944"?[14] (Actually, Drechsler had died on the twelfth. And when the War Department had sent that message to the SWPD, on the sixteenth, it already knew he had been murdered.)[15]

Drechsler's lynching posed several inconvenient problems for the War Department. It aggravated fears of Nazi terrorism in the camps and caused concern that Berlin might interpret Drechsler's death as proof that the United States was too weak to protect its German prisoners from violence, as the Geneva Convention demanded. The situation seemed to call for silence and obfuscation. The Pentagon decided to give the Swiss Legation as little information as possible; but to appease the ambassador, it announced new guidelines for reporting prisoner deaths from suicide, murder, or "suspicious circumstances." Camp commanders were to notify the PMGO immediately by telephone and telegram. The PMGO would then telephone the legation immediately. After receiving word of the investigation, it would later communicate "full details of the incident . . . through the Department of State."[16] The War Department's skimpy notion of "full details" would cause great, if predictable, problems later.

The newspaper articles about "Breschler's" suicide also produced a citizen complaint. A Mrs. Herrmann from New Jersey wrote Col. Means at Papago Park: "I am greatly distressed, as a citizen of our glorious country, and a mother of a boy in the service, that our prisoners are learning nothing about democracy and that Nazis are allowed to hang those of their countrymen who disagree with their philosophy. Can we not segregate the brutal Nazis from those who do not follow their beastly teachings?" The War Department was touchy about such complaints and always responded promptly. The PWD's assistant director assured this lady that her suggestion had received "careful consideration . . . and will be filed for appropriate reference."[17] This public relations bump was also a sign of future trouble.

The Pentagon's interest in the Drechsler case increased on March 25, when another death by "Nazi terrorism" occurred. According to the intelligence officer at Camp Chafee, Arkansas, a "cooperative" prisoner, Hans Geller, had "considerably enraged" the camp by accusing two men on his work detail of being "sent there by someone for the purpose of spying on him." The next night, after those two had been disciplined, an unknown person lured Geller from his barracks, where he was beaten by "several prisoners of war in waiting." Geller was sent back to his cot with nothing but a sleeping tablet. By morning, he was comatose and he later died in the post hospital.[18]

On April 29 Camp Chaffee investigators charged a single German NCO, Sgt. Edgar Menschner, with being "the instigator of the 'gang' which committed the crime," even though Menschner had been teaching a class when the beating occurred and no member of his alleged gang could be identified. His interrogators found his evasiveness under questioning suspicious enough to warrant the charge.[19]

Because of the Drechsler case, the Pentagon had already intensified its war on terrorism. On March 24, the day before Geller died, the Adjutant General had issued a circular calling for vigilance. On April 3, the Provost Marshal General announced this new policy to his superior, the Commanding General of the Army Service Forces (ASF): "Some German prisoners of war have been beaten and killed by their fellow prisoners for reasons which remain unknown to the camp authorities until after the violence is committed." Some victims who had considered warning "the American camp authorities of their impending danger" had been "dissuaded from doing so by spokesmen and other prisoners." Therefore, the following notice should be posted "upon the bulletin board of every German prisoner of war compound":

> Any prisoner of war, regardless of faith or political belief, who fears that his life is in danger or that he may suffer physical injury at the hands of other prisoners of war will immediately report that fact personally to any American officer of this camp without consulting his spokesman. From that time on adequate protection to such prisoner will be assured by the Camp Commander by segregation, transfer, or other means. Prisoners who mistreat fellow prisoners will be severely punished.

The camp commandant was to sign each copy.[20]

On April 5, the day before these posters went up, "terror" (or more accurately a sordid squabble) struck again. A prisoner, Horst Guenther, was found hanged at Aiken side camp, South Carolina. The War Department notified State that Guenther "had been classed as a traitor" and his "extermination . . . deliberately planned." He had been strangled, then "tied to a large pole" to simulate suicide.[21] A suspicious camp commander had called "for expert investigators from the Service Command . . . to determine if foul play was involved."[22] (Later, the War Department would boast that this murder was the last link of that ominous chain of Nazi "kangaroo court" assassinations.)

The National Archives files on the Guenther and Geller murders contain communications between officials in the Eighth and Fourth Service Commands and the PMGO.[23] Files on the Drechsler case do not contain this sort of correspondence—which, given the Pentagon's lively interest, must surely have existed. Its new policies bear witness to that interest.

On March 24, twelve days after Drechsler died, the Adjutant General issued a circular to all ten Service Commands in the United States. It was inspired by the War Department's fear of camp terrorism and its contradictory need to wring maximum labor from prisoners who worked much better if supervised by their own NCOs. The AG's circular permitted this practice to continue, but warned the commanders to be vigilant against apparently cooperative prisoner spokesmen and supervisors who were secretly organizing

> discontent, acts of violence, work stoppages and slowdowns and other disorders. . . . A majority of the German officers and noncommissioned officers with years of service in the regular German army are indoctrinated completely with the Nazi theory of discipline which permits them to terrorize enlisted men by any means available. "Kangaroo courts," secret threats of violence and family reprisals cause the prisoners to fear such noncommissioned officer prisoners more than they respect the orders of the American Camp Commander.

The AG directed the Commanders to warn camp personnel to take appropriate measures.[24] In a telephone call to Seventh Service Command, Assistant PMG Bryan added that German NCOs must not wield any command or disciplinary authority at all. They must be carefully watched to prevent "unauthorized control" over other prisoners. "Experience" showed that NCOs could pretend to be cooperative while organizing "subversive activities based upon their terror tactics." Camp commanders dealing with these threats must not allow themselves to be influenced by the prisoners' complaints "to the State Department or the Protecting Power."[25] Bryan also read parts of the AG's circular to someone at Ninth Service Command headquarters, where Maj. Gen. McCoach was probably still smarting from the official reprimand he had received,[26] thanks to complaints from the Papago Park camp spokesman Wattenberg and the compound spokesman Franz Hox.

Then, on March 28, McCoach received a secret telex from the legal branch of the PWD, signed by the PMG: "Necessary segregation and surveillance of Prisoners of War are authorized in order to effect necessary investigation of murder of Werner Drechsler. Promise of necessary protection should be made to prisoners willing to reveal information . . . even though it may necessitate transfer to other camps. Thorough investigation is requested."[27] At about the same time, McCoach also read a report from the commandant of Papago Park, Col. Means. It revealed that after two weeks, his officers had uncovered "no information of value whatever" about Drechsler's death. Some prisoners were even saying that "the American authorities were responsible" because they had sent this traitor into a camp full of honest German fighting men. This notion deeply offended McCoach. If those assassins could not be brought to justice, he said, this would be "an admission that murder in the United States may not necessarily be a crime." On March 29, therefore, the general appointed his own board of investigators.

Everyone on McCoach's staff must have known his unwritten agenda: to protect his personal and professional turf by finding and punishing the killers.[28] This situation is called "command influence" and it bore directly on the military justice system. Under the American Articles of War, a commander not only controlled a criminal investigation, but was also the "convening power" who appointed the court-martial and the "reviewing power" over the sentences passed by that court. The commander's subordinates investigated crimes; organized trials; named and served as judges, prosecutors, and defenders, and conducted the first judicial review of the sentences. All these men were dependent on him for promotion. A mere remark from the commander could prejudice their work. Under today's Uniform Code of Military Justice, command influence constitutes reversible error (a mistake so grave as to nullify the sentence).[29]

Gen. McCoach himself plainly suffered from command influence. On April 26, three weeks after appointing his investigators, he received another telex: Provost Marshal General Gullion brought to his attention the fact that he had not sent a "report of details" of Drechsler's hanging. The Swiss Legation had "complained of delay in not receiving full particulars." Gullion ordered McCoach to send them at once, by airmail.[30] But McCoach had nothing at all to report. His investigators, however ruthless, would achieve nothing until mid-May and would not produce a preliminary report until July 1.[31]

Meanwhile, the Swiss Legation continued to be dissatisfied with the War Department's response to its protest against the newspaper leak about "Breschler's" suicide, yet the War Department continued its policy of silence and delay. Not until May 18, two months after his death, would the PWD inform the State's SWPD that Drechsler had not died by his own hand; a board of officers investigating "the incident" had found that five or six of his "former mates," not yet identified, had apparently condemned him as a traitor. The State Department would eventually convey this information to the Swiss Legation on June 1, two and a half months after the legation's first complaint.[32]

Meanwhile, the War Department produced another scheme for fighting the Nazi "reign of terror" by means of prisoner segregation. The planning involved personnel from the PWD in the Provost Marshal General's Office, the Chief of Staff for Service Commands, the Director of Intelligence in the Army Service Forces Office, and the Office of the Commanding General of the Army. The PWD criticized G-2's assistant chief of staff for insisting that all NCOs were "ardent Nazis and must be segregated to remove the pressure which is making the privates tow the Nazi party line." Removing all NCOs would disrupt the labor program, in which about 45 percent of the NCOs were performing volunteer supervisory work amounting to 15 percent of the total man-days. Segregation by politics, not rank, would minimize the disruption, though it would involve constant rescreening by trained (and unavailable) American personnel and the use of informers who might be secret Nazis.[33]

The newly appointed Acting PMG, Brig. Gen. Archer L. Lerch, sent a long memorandum on May 10 to the ASF's Deputy Chief of Staff for Service Commands, entitled "Segregation of Persecuted German Prisoners of War": Five deaths by beating and three forced suicides showed how some prisoners "persecuted, coerced and terrorized" others. These incidents also produced "considerable unfavorable publicity" for the War Department. Furthermore, Geneva's Article 2 mandated that "prisoners must at all times be protected, particularly against acts of violence and insults." Therefore, he asked the ASF's Director of Intelligence to coordinate "procedures and policies" for screening and segregating all unsegregated German POWs. This would be a time-consuming task, but "complete segregation of the opposing factions" would most effectively control "the gangster methods" in the camps, which "arise from political differences."

Gen. Lerch also mentioned the notice, now posted in each camp compound, "requiring" fearful prisoners to seek protection from an American officer. Then he described an elaborate scheme for allowing prisoners to get protection "without further endangering themselves." The screening process could be rigged to look like an ordinary transfer. Prisoners, arriving with all their belongings, would be scrambled to prevent them from keeping track of each other. One by one, they would enter a "control station" where each would answer questions under "conditions of absolute privacy." Each would then be given a written statement explaining that the American government was protecting him "against violence and injury in accordance with the Geneva Convention." When he left, the prisoner would see two exits. He could choose the "non-Nazi" exit, which would lead to a screened-off assembly point for immediate transfer "to appropriate camps designated by this office." The scheme was to be tested at Camp Campbell, Kentucky, "where optimum conditions exist."[34]

The plan must have been approved, for on May 30 the ASF Deputy Director of Intelligence requested the Adjutant General to send a secret letter entitled "Segregation of German Prisoners of War" to all nine Service Commands: "In order better to insure the maximum employment of German prisoners of war, to obtain a maximum of information from cooperative prisoners, to fulfill this country's obligation of providing adequately for the physical protection of all prisoners, and to permit orderly administration of the individual camps," the commanders were made responsible for the complete political segregation of German prisoners.

Navy prisoners were to be separated according to whether they were non-Nazi or "other" officers and enlisted men. Army officers and enlisted men would be labeled pro-Nazi, non-Nazi, and all other. There would also be a fourth category: NCOs who were not cooperating in the labor program.

For Army prisoners, the pro-Nazi category would include "individuals that are leaders among the ardent Nazis, members of the Gestapo, or otherwise so imbued with the Nazi ideology that they go to extreme lengths in 'punishing' the unbelievers or attempt to instill in other prisoners an attitude of non-cooperation in the orderly administration of the camp." The non-Nazi category covered all prisoners "not in sympathy with the Nazi ideology." (The term "non-Nazi" was considered less offensive to POWs than "anti-Nazi," since some could be loyal Germans but not pro-Hitler.) This category also included "non-Germans who have been impressed into the Army and others who not only hate the Nazis but are also willing to aid the Allies."

The service commanders were to segregate German Army NCOs immediately, unless camp administrators knew by experience that an individual was cooperative and had not "engaged in political activity." Such individuals could be transferred later if they behaved badly. So could segregated NCOs who ceased to "engage in political activity" and became willing workers.

Segregation and classification had to be a continuous procedure, though an extremely difficult one because the Nazis ruthlessly "correct[ed] the views" of those suspected of non-Nazi leanings, and the non-Nazis feared what the Nazis could do to them and "their families at home in Germany." American personnel must take the greatest care to ensure that the prisoners always remained unaware that they were being segregated. "Experience [had] shown" that if the Nazis suspected it, "several of them, usually trained Gestapo agents, [would] realistically pose as non-Nazis and attempt to be transferred accordingly." After identifying the real anti-Nazis and reconverting whomever they could by threats and blackmail, they would "demand a transfer to a pro-Nazi camp." Any carelessness in the screening program might also touch off "a wave of mayhem and murder against the newly-discovered 'traitors' to the Nazi cause." (The directive also mentioned the great lack of "personnel who are fluent in German" and who also had the aptitude and experience necessary "for intelligence work of this nature.")[35]

When this document was written, Werner Drechsler had been dead for over two months. His killers were still unknown.

CHAPTER 6

"Are You a Member of the Volksgemeinschaft?"

Although the Service Commands were not authorized to use their Security and Intelligence Divisions to investigate crimes, Ninth Service Command's Gen. McCoach ordered Lt. Col. Gerald L. Church, Chief of Intelligence, to find Drechsler's killers. Three weeks later the rule was changed for the sake of fighting Nazi terrorist conspiracy.[1]

Col. Church's investigating board included two German-born majors. Hermann J. Zabel was about to retire. Francis P. Walsh was also Chief of the Military Justice Branch of the command's Judge Advocate Office. They were aided by two sergeants, a German-born interpreter, and a recorder. The only record of the board's work would be a secret report (BR) assembled after the fact by Maj. Walsh. It would be an English-language document containing neat transcripts of suspiciously orderly interrogations, surely the result of protracted off-scene grilling and canny editing.

Ninth Service Command's investigating board was in for some rough work. No German POW would cooperate with it, whether from dislike of their country's enemy, loathing for a traitor, sympathy for Drechsler's victims, or fear of reprisals. Furthermore, being interrogated by a board of enemy officers was particularly intimidating.

In the Eighth Service Command the previous January (1944), Lt. Col. Leon Jaworski had explained this fact to a conference on POW affairs. Jaworski had been appointed to prosecute the Beyer Five, whose trial would shortly begin. (The general who introduced him remarked that he "understands these Germans perhaps better than some of us as he speaks the German language.") Jaworski warned his high-ranking listeners that using a board of officers to interview German POWs "is certainly not" a method "that seems to work well," since German trials were held by boards of judges. If prisoners felt they were "about to be tried and sentenced, they [would] certainly not cooperate." Evidently this message did not reach the newly appointed board in the Ninth Service Command, though it seemed to take to heart a statement by the colonel who led Eighth Service Command's POW symposium: "Spare nothing in the investigation."[2]

Col. Church's investigating board began with Papago Park's American personnel. It swore all witnesses to secrecy, including the medical orderly who had driven Drechsler into camp alive and out of it dead, and the senile post surgeon who had to be taken to the shower room to jog his memory of the crime.[3] After a search for the autopsy report, which had gone missing, two doctors cheerfully described their task. The board was particularly interested in Drechsler's severe bruises: "Just for the record, what is the scrotum?"[4] The camp's assistant engineer presented maps, upon which Lt. Parshall marked Drechsler's cot, the blood spots, and so forth. Capt. Hebblethwaite authenticated the photographs he had taken and told of matching the corpse's fingerprints with Drechsler's record.[5]

His personnel record seemed perfectly ordinary. It noted Drechsler's transfers from the naval hospital in Norfolk, Virginia, to Fort Meade, Maryland, and—after a blank space—to Fort Leonard Wood, Missouri, and Papago Park, Arizona. Most U-boatmen went through Fort Meade. Even assuming that Col. Church knew that this transit camp camouflaged a secret interrogation facility, he was ignorant of Drechsler's role there. The board assumed, when it began interrogating prisoners on March 31, that the camp spokesman Wattenberg had ordered Gestapo agents and NCOs to hold a "kangaroo court," which had condemned Drechsler to death for being a "good" (cooperative) prisoner. These assumptions reflected Wattenberg's notoriety and War Department bias. Even after the board discovered Drechsler's career as an SP, weeks later, it never quit trying to incriminate Wattenberg and the NCOs. As a result of its mind-set and the prisoners' universal unhelpfulness, the board faced a very frustrating month.

Since the Geneva Convention ordered Custodial Powers to treat war prisoners in the same way as their own accused soldiers, the Board Report scrupulously documented its obedience to the Articles of War. When it began to interrogate any prisoner (at least for the record), someone read him AW 24: No witness "shall be compelled to incriminate himself or to answer any question the answer to which may tend to incriminate him, or to answer any question not material to the issue when such answer might tend to degrade him." Then, the report shows, each prisoner was quizzed to make sure he understood.

Many were astonished to hear that they were subject to American military law. They considered Drechsler's treason a purely German matter.

The board began with Drechsler's nearest barracks mates. Otto Behrens, who had shared his ambulance ride to camp, described how Drechsler had "wanted to put his bunk up next to mine." When Behrens's friends had crowded him away, he had asked, "Where should I go now?" Behrens had suggested "the other side near the corner," by the door. No, Drechsler had not said he was "afraid of something." That night, Behrens said, he woke to hear someone near the door, whose voice he had not recognized, calling for help. He saw four or five shadows. It was dark.

The board asked, "Isn't it a fact that some men in your barracks in Indianola, Nebraska, were beaten during the night?" Yes, and when someone there had cried for help, Behrens had been threatened for rushing up to see what was going on. This time he had pulled the covers over his head and gone back to sleep because he was ill, injured, not exactly afraid, "but the younger ones sometimes look at us older fellows as not being Nazis." He had minded his own business because the "black cow" was there. If he had been nosy, "I would probably get one on top of the head myself." Besides, he only weighed 130 pounds. If he had been a six-footer, that might have made a difference. Furthermore, Behrens said, he'd had no idea that someone was about to be hanged. In the morning, when "I grabbed my towel and soap," some "fellows standing around the pool of blood" told him there was a body in the washroom. He had gone to look, but "you cannot recognize a naked man from the behind." At roll call he learned its identity. He had not discussed the crime with anyone. "One has to be careful to whom he talks to."[7]

Emil Witt, the sergeant of the barracks who slept directly across the aisle from Drechsler, swore that when he heard "some noise" that night, he thought someone was having "epileptic fits." He had gone back to sleep. In the morning, "after I saw the blood I reported it immediately to the First Sergeant" (in charge of Fifth Company), only to be told "I would immediately have to tell the American authorities." He had not done so. No one knew who had hanged someone, or why.[8]

Arthur Bender, whose cot lay eight inches away from Drechsler's, professed to have slept soundly all night. No, no one knew why this man was hanged. "I think that he wasn't a comrade." Col. Church asked: "Do you think somebody hanged him because he was a traitor?" Bender thought that one might suppose so, but when he had spoken to Drechsler on the train he had thought he was a good fellow. Why had Bender not reported the blood? It was none of his business.[9] Benno Unfried, sleeping eight inches from Drechsler's other side, swore that he heard nothing but a muffled cry, "a fellow having a fit" he thought. "I always sleep with the covers over my head and I have ear trouble."[10]

The last witness of the day was alleged Gestapo agent Gerhard Richter, from Otto Stengel's barracks. The board asked him over and over if he had known Drechsler "at Camp Stringtown, Oklahoma?" (where he had never been, as his record showed!). Who had Richter corresponded with "relative to Drechsler"? Richter was "a member of the German gestapo at this camp," wasn't he? Richter politely denied everything. He had only overheard at the ball game that a traitor had arrived.

Col. Church asked: "Do you know whether he was tried by a German Naval Court Martial?" No, only that the new compound spokesman had said that his predecessor Franz Hox "wasn't involved in this case." Richter had also heard that fellows from Drechsler's own submarine had called him a traitor, but he was not acquainted with any of them. After a tussle, Richter finally admitted that "some of the fellows" at the ball game had said that Drechsler "should be" killed, rather than "might be," and that he had agreed; but these were only opinions. None of them knew "who could or who would" actually do anything.

The board grilled Richter again on June 2, still fishing for information about a kangaroo court. "What is your belief in Germany regarding the punishment of a traitor?" In Richter's opinion, "if a German soldier endangers the German Reich or the German people," he should be executed. Yes, he admitted, "even in Germany" an accused person was given a trial; but if Drechsler had been tried, "I didn't hear of it." Church asked: "Do you believe that German prisoners of war have the authority to appoint their own courts-martial . . . and impose punishment?" Richter had never heard anything of the sort. He doubted it. Even though in Germany a traitor would be executed, even though he himself "would do away with a man if the welfare of the German people were at stake," neither he nor anyone he knew would want to take "the responsibility of killing anybody." And if he had gone to the Americans to report the rumor that a man might be hanged: "[I] would get the rope around my own neck perhaps. . . . Yes, they would have come to get me," because then he also would be a traitor.[11]

Paul Reum, who was Richter's co-worker in the camp personnel office and a crewman from Drechsler's boat, had little to tell. After the football game, he had played cards. (The board asked what game, with whom, and who had won.) After he had gone to bed, "the rumors started flying around that someone was hung in the washroom." He had gone to see. Had Reum known about Drechsler's treason? After a struggle, he admitted that in Stringtown some newcomers from "Washington" (Fort Hunt) had spoken to him about a traitor there. His crew had suspected it was Drechsler, but they knew nothing "for sure." The board asked: "Now in Stringtown the plan was made up to hang Drechsler wasn't it?" On his oath, Reum knew nothing about that. Had not Reum already admitted to camp officials that he knew who killed Drechsler? A board member quoted Hebblethwaite's inadequate minutes of the camp-level investigation: When asked "How many from the ship were among the murderers?," Reum had supposedly replied, "Can't tell—were some." Now Reum swore he never said that. "Do you think German prisoners of war hung him?"[12] Well, who else had been in the compound?

Next the board called Alfred Friedrich (another of Stengel's barracks mates), who had bragged to Hebblethwaite that he knew one of the killers. Now Friedrich refused to be sworn and demanded to see a German officer. The board interrogated him anyway, badgering him to admit that he had met Drechsler at Stringtown, Oklahoma (an impossibility). Friedrich did mention a rumor that five or six men had killed him. "I know one for sure," he said again, but he would never tell his name because then he himself would be a traitor like Drechsler. Yes, this person was in camp. In what compound? Where else but the one where Drechsler was hanged? Friedrich refused to say which company.

Did Friedrich consider Drechsler's hanging "a legal murder"? Yes, because he was a traitor. Even without "first letting him have a court hearing"? Yes, because "enlisted men arriving in Papago Park" had said "he spilled stuff at Fort Meade." Had Friedrich heard this from an officer, Church asked? "No, sir, they never congregate with us at any time." Had not "Captain Wattenberg [the camp spokesman] talked to you just before the hanging?" No, they had never spoken. Well, Church asked, if Wattenberg gave him permission to speak, would he do so? No, unless the captain ordered him to do it and assured him that he "wouldn't be a traitor."[13]

When called before the board, the feisty Capt. Wattenberg brought his own interpreter and disdained to be sworn. "As an officer of the German Navy and as a gentleman I am prepared to say the full truth." His duty, as senior officer and camp spokesman, was to represent all the prisoners to the Protecting Power and to the American officials. He looked after all the prisoners' well being and saw to it that their Geneva rights were observed. No, he did not "go about the Camp at frequent intervals" addressing speeches to the men. He had been in Compound 4 only once—on March 12 (the day Drechsler had arrived)—to give a standard welcoming pep talk to some new arrivals, whether in Company 4 or 5 he could not recall. He had introduced himself as their "representing officer, face to face" and let them know that he was "looking after their welfare." No, he had not spoken to a Gerhard Richter. He did not know him.

Wattenberg had learned the next day that someone or other had hanged himself. The news "came through the fence" as "common talk." In his opinion, Drechsler had killed himself for shame after being beaten as a traitor. "Now captain, if you had definite proof that he was murdered, would you say that the murder should be punished? Now think that question over." His thoughts were irrelevant. "Now captain, we have definite proof, both medical and physical," that Drechsler was a murder victim. "Now if you knew the names of the men who did it, would you tell this Board?" After Wattenberg evaded that question, the board informed him that a prisoner who knew one killer's name would tell it, but only if Wattenberg allowed him to do so. "According to the convention of Geneva," Wattenberg replied, "it is not my task." Furthermore, he could not issue a military command; "I am a prisoner of war myself. . . . This is your matter." No, he did not condone murder or allowing prisoners to take the law into their own hands. But in this special case [the board] must understand how POWs felt about treason. [If I authorized one to talk, the others] "would shout that . . . I am a traitor." His duties as senior officer did not involve helping American investigators. After the war, he would report what he knew to the German government, and it would investigate "to find out whether it was murder or not."[14]

The board would never cease trying to implicate this unflappable man.[15] For now, it returned to the task of questioning Drechsler's barracks mates. After a fruitless day and a half of that, it switched to its only other suspects, Drechsler's crew.[16] From them, it learned that Drechsler had not been an ordinary prisoner after all. He and another man, Wosnitzka, had been left behind in a Norfolk hospital when their boatmates had gone to an interrogation camp in "Washington" where, they strongly suspected, these former comrades had become traitors. Still, Drechsler's crew refused to condemn him without proof.

When Seaman Gustav Behlke revealed that he had seen Drechsler once in "Washington" through a window, the board scented conspiracy. Did Behlke know Alfred Friedrich? Yes, at Stringtown; but no, Friedrich had never mentioned Drechsler. After a struggle, Behlke admitted avoiding Drechsler on the ballfield the evening he arrived because "somebody told me he was a traitor." Who did? Men from other boats. "I just heard it when I walked around." Behlke kept denying that he had known beforehand that Drechsler would be killed. He had only expected someone or other to beat him. The board pressed hard: "As a matter of fact, the noncommissioned officers of your boat were going to beat him up, weren't they? They always administer the punishments on the U Boats don't they?" No, only commissioned officers did that. "What made you believe that Drechsler was to be beaten?" Behlke had read that such things were done in "the last war." As for knowing who had planned Drechsler's punishment, "there are one thousand men in the compound." His crew had nothing to do with it.[17] Try as it would, the board could not make him say otherwise.

The next day, the Board Report shows that it questioned only two of Drechsler's crew (though all of them were undoubtedly being grilled intensively to prepare them to speak "for the record"). Erhardt Lenk refused to be sworn in, even when threatened with a court-martial. After dismissing him, the board heard Herman Polowzyk describe how he had received "a greeting" from Drechsler, how he had started to visit him but had changed his mind. When had he learned of Drechsler's death? That night, when he had heard someone report a hanging in Fifth Company, he had known that it must be Drechsler. Whoever killed him, "I am sure it couldn't have been anyone from our boat. . . . No one from our crew could say he was a bad fellow because he was a good kid. No one from our crew knew for sure that he was a traitor. . . .They only heard that he was."[18]

The next day, April 7, the board questioned Seaman Klaus Preuss, who was still bitter about his experience in "Washington": "We were threatened and interrogated like common saboteurs," not war prisoners. "We were told that we would be shot as saboteurs." He thought Drechsler had been hanged for treason. In Stringtown, newly arriving men had said "that there was one in Washington that questioned German prisoners and then would turn around and betray them and give the information to the Americans." No, he could not name these informants or their boats. He had no idea what, if anything, Drechsler had supposedly betrayed. The crew "couldn't believe that he was [a traitor] because he was one of us." Did Preuss think so now? Yes, because why else would they have hanged him? Preuss did not know who "they" were. "Did they give him a trial before they hung him?" Preuss kept denying he had heard anything like that, though the board pressed him hard. "If you knew who hung Drechsler would you tell us?" No. He would never have taken the oath if he had known anything.[19]

Turning to Drechsler's NCOs, the board asked the chief radio operator Josef Hoeller: "Didn't you see [Drechsler] at the Interrogation Camp near Washington, D.C.?" Hoeller had glimpsed someone who resembled him, walking with an American officer, "but I am not sure." Rumors about him had circulated in Stringtown because he had not rejoined his crew. They kept wondering about his absence, but "you can't say a person is a traitor until you are absolutely sure." Rumors were not proof. If Hoeller knew who hanged Drechsler, would he tell? He was happy to say that he knew nothing. Neither did his comrades.[20]

Werner Reinl, the chief boatswain's mate, had also glimpsed Drechsler at "Washington," taking the air with an American officer. "He must have just come from the hospital as he was limping and had bandages on his leg." Reinl had not spoken to him then or at the ballgame. "I thought he recognized me, I wasn't sure, and I thought he would come over to my barracks to see me within the next couple of days." The board asked: "You know that he was killed because he was a traitor didn't you?" Reinl finally admitted hearing talk at Stringtown. "It was only talk." He could not recall exactly what "some new fellows" had accused Drechsler of doing, "but they said he was sent into the rooms with other comrades to listen to what they had to say and then reported it."

Reinl first learned of his death at morning roll call, when "a little fat sergeant . . . came running down from the Third Company and told the officer that there was a man hanging someplace." Had Hox, the chief quartermaster, been in the compound that night? (Where else could the compound spokesman have been?) Yes, Reinl said, but he had not spoken to him about the hanging.

Suddenly, according to the record, Col. Church asked, "Are you a member of the German People's Party"? Reinl would have heard the translator use the word *Volksgemeinschaft*. The translator gave the colonel this confusing reply: "All Germans belong to the German People's Party, but I am not a member of it." When the board demanded that he explain what this party's purpose was, he said it was not a party at all; it was "all the German people united together."[21] The word meant the entire German ethnic community.

Church was following orders from the PMG's Office, which had just sent him three letters that the G-2 censors had found suspicious. The writers had used the term *Volksgemeinschaft*, surely a sinister secret organization! Two of the letters were from prisoners in Compound 3, separated from the crime scene by double rows of barbed wire. The other was from the infamous camp spokesman, Juergen Wattenberg. The PMG's Office believed the board "could use these letters to advantage in eliciting information. . . . Every reasonable effort should be exerted to have these prisoners of war divulge any information they may have regarding Drechsler's death." Assistant PMG Bryan suggested that "maybe solitary confinement will induce them to talk."[22]

The Army censors had translated one letter this way:

> This morning a traitor to the fatherland was executed in the 4th Compound by the German People's Party (Volksgemeinschaft). This man interrogated and betrayed his own comrades for the Americans. The Americans found him swinging, beaten black and blue. Whosoever should break his oath to the flag and betray his country in hope of deriving personal benefit is a dog and has no right to live. It is a good thing the Americans sent him to a camp where there were people who immediately recognized him, otherwise he would have done more mischief.[23]

The board soon learned that the writer was only repeating rumors. When it asked: "Were the men that hung [Drechsler] from the Volksgemeinschaft?" the man was amazed. "That is no party." That is "the whole people, everybody in the nation belongs to the Volksgemeinschaft."[24] The board dropped the issue, but the censors remained vigilant.[25]

As for Wattenberg's letter, he had written in mid-November 1943 to his parents, Mr. and Mrs. Professor and Doctor of Medicine O. Wattenberg, to say he would miss them at Christmas. He had concluded:

> We must be victorious because we are tough—in contrast to the Jews and others—and we know for what we fight. We all know here what attitude to take in our fidelity to Führer and people and, not to be mentioned last, our duty and honor for the dead who gave their lives for the Reich. Weaklings and defeatists, in the event any should arrive, would find no response in our camp.[26]

If Drechsler had found "no response" at Papago Park, he would not have died!

After its *Volksgemeinschaft* detour, the board resumed its inquisition of Drechsler's crew. In spite of hard pressure, NCO Hans Siebert kept denying he knew the killers. Furthermore, he said, if he did know anything, he would not betray his comrades by telling the board. In fact, he announced, the Americans were responsible for Drechsler's death "because [they] sent him into this camp." The next day, April 8, the board asked Seaman Walter Schiller whether he had seen Drechsler at Stringtown (impossible), or knew what sort of treasonous thing he had done, or who killed him. "If I knew it, as a German soldier I would not tell." Hermann Wiedemann (the wounded NCO who had first spotted Drechsler) took refuge in vagueness. Those rumors about Drechsler spread by unknown men in Stringtown were "all talk." Did he believe them? No, "because [Drechsler] was always a good soldier but I can't make any judgment now. It is too late now."[27]

Rudolf Wiemer, another NCO, admitted that in "Washington," an American naval officer who was urging him to talk "told [him] that Drechsler talked quite a bit." When he failed to show up at Stringtown, Wiemer concluded he must have been a traitor. He must have had a bad conscience, or "he would have come to see his comrades right away" at Papago Park. If he was a traitor, then "I guess he got what was coming to him"; but aboard the boat "he was always a very good soldier" and none of the crew would have hanged anyone without "positive proof that he was a traitor."[28] The petty officer Werner Wilke also admitted that Drechsler might have been a traitor, "because he was hung." No, he did not know who did it. "If I had known I never would have swore."[29]

The board questioned Paul Reum again, the U-118 man who had worked with Gerhard Richter in the personnel office, demanding to know why had he not told them about having seen Drechsler at "the interrogation camp at Washington, D.C." Reum had forgotten. He had been nervous. He had entered the mess hall just as Drechsler had been leaving and had been reprimanded for looking out the door. The board told Reum that (according to Hebblethwaite's notes of the fruitless camp-level investigation) he had made this reply to a question about which NCOs had killed Drechsler: "I won't tell" or "I won't talk." When asked "How many from the ship were among the murderers?" his recorded answer was: "Can't tell—were some." Reum denied having said such things. "I can't tell how many men there were because I don't know who they are."[30]

By then, the board had labored for a week without obtaining any better results than Hebblethwaite's committee. Capt. Wattenberg flaunted his refusal to cooperate. Nothing tied Drechsler's boat comrades to the crime. The anonymous people who had spread rumors about Drechsler's treason in "Washington" were untraceable. There was no evidence of any Nazi organization at work. There was nothing to report, and nothing for the board to do but keep slogging down the list of Drechsler's barracks mates.

The board's frustration kept mounting. So did the Pentagon's interest in the case.

CHAPTER 7

"I Can't Control My Blood"

On April 10, 1944, the board finally found someone in Drechsler's barracks who would talk. Otto Engler, a thirty-four-year-old marine "engineer on land," said he had been awakened by shrieks from the opposite end of the building. He and his neighbors had asked questions, but had not intervened. No one knew "that they were going to hang the man." Anyway, "when the black cow walks it is best to mind your own business." Engler had no idea who had killed Drechsler or why. There "could have been 2, 3, or 4" attackers. "It must have been someone who knew him personally. We were all strangers." Had Engler heard that Drechsler's own crew had killed him? Church asked. No, only "that he was supposed to have given some information away about the U boat." If Engler knew what that information was, would he tell it? "I am not a National Socialist but I am still a German soldier." He would never betray his comrades. Neither would the next thirty-six men in the barracks, who said nothing worth recording.[1]

The first useful witness, on April 13, was Chief Warrant Officer Josef Gross, the U-118's only surviving officer. He spoke of the treasonous things Drechsler was rumored to have done in "Washington"—or Wosnitzka did; he kept confusing them. At Stringtown, new men had arrived describing Drechsler exactly, with great resentment, saying he had bragged about the forbidden things he had told the Americans: his boat's name, number, commander, and mission (mine laying), his specialty (torpedoes). In an obviously bugged room, he had spoken of "things that a German soldier has been told not [even] to tell to another German soldier," mentioning secret devices that "were not even yet installed on our own submarine." Gross and the fellows in the officers' compound "got to wondering what kind of a man

[Drechsler] was." After leaving "Washington," Gross said, "all the comrades get together and ask each other what happened." Then Drechsler's victims saw more clearly that "there was something strange going on." Gross refused to name his informants.[2]

Had the U-118 men been angry when they heard these rumors at Stringtown? He did not know. He had been transferred to another camp. He had only learned of Drechsler's death the morning after, when his crew had sent "some soldier" to shout the news through the wire. He had only heard the details when he encountered his men while on an errand to the compound to which they had been moved. They also told him that "Drechsler or Wosnitzka showed pictures of himself . . . with American girls." Captain Hebblethwaite had also met with the compound spokesmen and told them how severely Drechsler had been beaten. Gross thought his killers, whoever they were, "could have done it in a little cleaner way."

Had Drechsler been condemned by some sort of court? Gross had heard a rumor that this "might have been possible" but he had no idea who could have held it. At any rate, the Americans were more guilty for placing Drechsler among them. If Gross had been there, he "would not have lifted one finger" to save him. "This man had hundreds of comrades' lives on his conscience and every decent American soldier would have felt the same way" about him as his killers did.[3]

Gross had clarified the crime's motive, but added nothing to its solution. At an impasse, the Board traveled to the anti-Nazi camp at Fort Campbell, Kentucky, where a few intimidated prisoners had been transferred from Papago Park. Only one was from Drechsler's Compound 4, but surely anti-Nazis would testify against Nazi terrorism. At least they were all eager to talk.

The merchant mariner Oskar Meyer said he had been beaten at a camp in Texas for being a pro-American Communist. At Papago Park, he had appealed in vain for protection. He had panicked after Drechsler's death because his company leader had stared at him while saying that there were others "that we should get rid of. . . . Be sure and not forget the gloves." The rumor in Compound 3 was that one of the five who had killed Drechsler "had gloves missing."

Meyer's second appeal for protection got him transferred to the guardhouse, where he had played a bit part in Captain Hebblethwaite's inept investigation. His role was to accuse Paul Reum of murder. Now, however, he told the board that to the best of his knowledge neither Reum nor any other man from Drechsler's boat had been involved. No, he had not heard Capt. Wattenberg's speech to new arrivals the day Drechsler died; but afterward "all the fellows" had quoted the spokesman as saying: "Here among us are quite a few who do not think like we do and these people must, under the circumstances, be taken care of so that they can't talk anymore."[4]

The next three witnesses, also from Compound 3, had heard about the death of an "anti-Nazi" from someone on their work detail, an interpreter from Compound 4, who thought the traitor had been killed by his own crew. These three also told the board something it badly wanted to hear about Capt. Wattenberg. Rolf Fitzner, a teen-aged merchant mariner, told of being frightened when the senior NCO in Compound 3 had said "these anti-Nazis" should be hanged. When the board suggested that this speaker could have been Wattenberg, Fitzner obligingly recalled that he himself had heard the captain say this, on the Sunday afternoon "after the hanging."[5]

John Neumair, a coast guardsman, also described how, on "the same day this man was hung," Capt. Wattenburg had made a speech forbidding electricians, mechanics and tool makers to work for the Americans, unless they used the opportunity to do whatever sort of damage they could. Furthermore, anti-Nazis "should be weeded out and given a good beating," and "the one who is a traitor to his fatherland, it is not worth for him to live." And prisoners "should guard themselves with gloves so that whoever they beat, they wouldn't get any scratches on themselves."[6]

According to Rudolph Wilhelmy, a marine anti-aircraft gunner, Wattenberg had said that "all those that were not good Nazis should be . . . done away with." Had the captain said anything about beating traitors? Yes, he had said "that he would greet those people that would do away with a traitor." Had he said something about the men wearing gloves when they beat up the traitor? Yes, something like that; at least the spokesman for Compound 3, who had conversed with Wattenberg that day, "told us once that he hoped they have gloves on whenever they do anything like that." And had that interpreter on the work detail not remarked "that anybody else who talked would get the same treatment?" Yes, that was right. A talker would be a traitor and traitors were hanged.

No, Wilhelmy had not heard Wattenberg say that anyone working for the Americans should commit sabotage; but some Nazis had threatened to beat him for working too fast. The morning after Wattenberg's speech the compound spokesman had told him: "[You] should get out of the Camp; . . . the ones who are traitors [will] be done away with." No, he had no idea who killed Drechsler; but of course it had to be someone from Compound 4! There was someone from Compound 4 who knew the murderers' names.[7]

This hot lead fizzled when Seaman Herbert Wollenweber's "murderers" turned out to be ordinary bullies who had taunted him that his turn was coming. Wollenweber thought Drechsler's crewmates had killed him. "There must have been 10 or 12 men, like a commando unit, that took Drechsler out" on the orders of an officer.[8]

The board's last Kentucky witness, the merchant mariner Guenter Albert, was certain that Drechsler's crew had killed him for telling "military secrets on his comrades." He added: "You probably know that Captain Wattenberg gave the orders that anyone who thinks different or is a traitor should be done away with; that he should be hung." I was there when he said so, and that might even have been on the same Sunday Drechsler was killed.[9]

The trip to Kentucky was another dead end. After two and a half weeks of hard work, Church's board had learned only one solid, very sensitive fact: Drechsler had been a stool pigeon at a camp called "Washington." As a last resort, Col. Church went to Washington. It took him four days, April 16–20, to find any solid information. The Army knew little. According to Whittingham, Naval Intelligence was hostile, "saying in effect that they had no intention of helping the Army," which "had sent Drechsler to his death."[10] However, the Board Report credits ONI's Prisoner of War Branch with "greatly" facilitating its investigation.[11] At least ONI gave Col. Church a list of nineteen prisoners who had roomed with Drechsler at Fort Hunt.[12] Twelve of these had ended up in Papago Park's Compound 4.

Surely G-2 and ONI must have been alarmed when Col. Church told them how much ordinary POWs knew about their secret camp at Fort Hunt. Military intelligence had to be protected at all costs. In addition, the PMG's Office was even more concerned about squelching Nazi conspiracy. Six days after Church left Washington, the PMGO telexed Ninth Service Command's Gen. McCoach, ordering him again to report the details of Drechsler's hanging at once, by airmail.[13] Unfortunately the general still had nothing to report and would not until Church's committee solved this crime.

At least Church returned from Washington with new powers. The court-martial records contain an undated, unsigned memorandum from Ninth Service Command headquarters that states: "Colonel Church flew to Washington and received certain instructions known only to him. . . . By authority granted to Colonel Church, apparently at that time, the prisoners suspected were transferred to a questioning center in California."[14] However, that transfer would not take place for more than a month. It would take the board that long to locate a set of viable suspects and witnesses.

Church also left Washington with a new weapon. The FBI loaned him Dr. Leonardi Keeler, a lie detector expert. There is evidence of very high-level involvement. The Board Report contains a stray piece of onionskin paper, the transcript of a telephone call dated April 24. A Col. Pierce, Chicago School, told a Col. Miller that he'd had to obtain "a three priority" to get Keeler an immediate airplane flight. Such a high rating should have come from Washington, but the WAC officer with whom he dealt had said that if Col. Miller "and the Provost Marshal were interested in it, she'd go ahead and take a chance." Since Col. Church was probably watching the airport, Miller should tell him that Keeler would arrive "some time around noon today."[15]

The Board Report itself contains only one oblique reference to the use of a lie detector (in Gerhard Richter's testimony on May 8). At the court-martial of Drechsler's killers in August, Col. Church would imply that he used the lie detector on only three prisoners. (But many more had already written indignant letters to the Protecting Power!) According to Whittingham, "over 125" of Church's suspects were strapped to the device. Behind the scenes, the board re-interrogated its earlier targets: Drechsler's crew and barracks mates, the "Gestapo element," Capt. Wattenberg, and the automatically suspect NCOs.[16] The board would eventually find a few likely suspects and witnesses, thanks to three factors: Dr. Keeler's machine; ONI's list of Drechsler's roommates, which gave the board a new category of suspects; and sheer dumb luck. Curiously, the Board Report dates the interrogation of its thirteen new suspects from April 21 to 23, before Dr. Keeler arrived—although the transcripts show signs that a polygraph was already being used (more proof of Maj. Walsh's creative editing).

On April 21, Funkobermaat (radio man second-class) Friedrich Murza admitted sharing a room for about three days with machinist's mate Niemer (one of Drechsler's aliases). What sort of questions had this man asked Murza? The same unanswerable ones the interrogators at "Washington" had asked, which Murza refused to repeat to the board. At Stringtown, when some newly arrived prisoners told about a fellow in "Washington" who "didn't act right," he had described his own experience. The unmistakable conclusion was that one fellow was using different names and ranks. Everyone mentioned the wound on his right knee. Well, perhaps the left one. "He limped a little."

No doubt cornered by the lie detector, Murza became the first witness on record to implicate a fellow prisoner by name. He, NCO Elser, and Seaman Wagenfuehr, he said, had learned Drechsler's true name from the NCOs of the traitor's own boat, the U-118. Then the board called the roll of the forty or so NCOs in Murza's barracks and all the U-118 survivors, asking repeatedly if Murza had spoken to that person about Drechsler. (This was a polygraph technique. Guilty knowledge made the needle jump.) Murza protested that Drechsler's arrival "was common talk among all of us" NCOs.

The board asked: "Now what did they tell you they were going to do with Drechsler?" Nothing, except that "he would probably come to trial some day in Germany." After his death, the NCOs had merely wondered about "how they beat him." Which one of them had told Murza "that he knew who hung Drechsler"? No one! Had anyone at Stringtown told Murza that POWs "were going to try him for being a traitor? . . . that they thought he should be punished? . . . that they were going to punish him?" No, in each case. The polygraph apparently caught Murza out when he claimed he had never mentioned Drechsler to the compound spokesman Franz Hox. He finally admitted that they had talked a little, but only once, at Stringtown, "in a general way," but not about the crime—although he had overheard Hox say that it would have to be brought to the "attention of the German authorities . . . after the war."[17] Murza was now a prime suspect.

When Lothar Mandelkow was strapped to Mr. Keeler's machine, this nineteen-year-old seaman denied he had ever been to "an interrogation center near Washington," or had ever heard of this Drechsler before he died. He had no idea who had killed him (which was probably true, since Mandelkow had not attended the meeting in Hox's office—an event still unknown to the board). Mandelkow was sure that none of the enlisted men from Drechsler's crew were guilty. They slept in his barracks. No, he knew they had not sneaked out "because it was supposed to have happened about the time we went to bed." The board asked, "Didn't somebody tell you that it was the noncommissioned officers from his boat?" No. Mandelkow refused to name anyone who had called Drechsler a traitor, because then he "would be betraying all of [his] comrades in this Camp," who would then "be gotten out and questioned too." When the board read Mandelkow the names of the U-118's seven surviving enlisted men,[18] the polygraph evidently did not react.

Guenther Bleise was next, on April 22. (He had gone with two of Wizuy's friends to speak with Drechsler and had also rounded up men for Hox's meeting.) Now Bleise claimed to have known nothing about Drechsler until he died. Drechsler's "own crew didn't talk much about it because it was one of their own comrades;" and no, they had not hanged him. How did Bleise know? "Because they themselves didn't know anything about it," and neither did he. "We think you do know," the board told him. "No, I don't. If I knew I would tell you." Bleise must have been a good liar. The board would not take him to Byron Hot Springs with their other suspects and potential witnesses.[19]

Another NCO, Paul Buchholz, refused to take the oath even when threatened with a court-martial.[20] Dismissing him, the board turned to Rolf Wizuy—the first killer to be interrogated. He seemed quite cooperative. Yes, he had roomed with a dark-complected NCO named Leimi, who never asked him direct questions. "He was just another prisoner of war like myself." What had Wizuy heard about Drechsler at Stringtown? The U-118 crew had "mentioned that one man was missing. . . . I said that this 'Leimi' was from [their] Boat." They also said he was "a traitor didn't they?" the board prodded. "We couldn't say that exactly but we took it for granted because this man was missing a long time." When had Wizuy first learned of Drechsler's death? "We didn't know exactly what was wrong" until the morning, he lied. No, he didn't know who had killed him. Was Wizuy sure about that? "If you knew who hung him would you tell?" No, said Wizuy, "I don't believe I would."[21] It was a brief session, but the lie detector must have been busy. The board would take Rolf Wizuy to Byron Hot Springs.

Obermaat Siegfried Elser said he had spent only an afternoon and a morning with Drechsler at "Washington." They had only spoken of ordinary things. Before Papago Park, Elser never heard rumors of his true identity. "Now who told you at this Camp that the man was Drechsler?" Elser said he could not recall, but it happened the day after the hanging. He also told other lies: yes, he knew Hox; but no, they had not spoken about the killing.[22] Elser would be taken to Byron Hot Springs.

Friedrich Wagenfuehr and Walter Nieswand did not rouse the board's suspicion, though they had roomed with Drechsler. Wagenfuehr (whose work as a water heater attendant had kept him from Hox's meeting) said he had spent a month at "Washington," being transferred from room to room and grilled about his boat, his home, France, "military questions." Once he had been with "Limmer." He noticed at once "something peculiar about him," the way he asked questions and said things that "even two Germans shouldn't discuss . . . among themselves." At Stringtown "several" strangers, whose names he could not recall, had asked him about Drechsler. None was from the U-118. He had no idea who the killers were.[23]

Walter Nieswand told the board he had been with "Limmer" for two or three days during his month at "Washington." They had only spoken "about ordinary things, home, women." He had never heard of "a traitor in Washington, D.C." while at Stringtown, nor even the name Drechsler, until after the hanging—and he had never discussed that event with Drechsler's crew, who shared his barracks. No, he had never heard Hox "talking about Drechsler" (a lie). He did not know Hox personally. There were "over 500 men" in the compound. He couldn't know everyone.[24]

Nieswand got away with his lies. Heinz Taubert (who had not attended Hox's meeting) would be sent to Byron Hot Springs, however—possibly because he said: "I do not believe in any Church, I am a National Socialist," and because he knew far more than he should have about the camp "near Washington." Before he arrived there, he said, he had already been told he could "be interrogated by one of our own kind." The board demanded details. More than a hundred parachute troops had told him that "one should be very careful when they go in there." Taubert even named seven missing members of his crew who had been held back at the interrogation center. He thought they had probably been sent to an anti-Nazi camp, because "I found out later from other comrades, these men were also supposed to have told different secrets."

During his four weeks in "Washington," Taubert said he had roomed with two snitches, the machinist's mate Werner Globus and Werner Limmer (Drechsler); Limmer had claimed "that he was engaged to a movie star in Germany" and had asked Taubert about his boat. "I just told him the very opposite of what was true." When he had first arrived at Papago Park, about three weeks before the hanging, both Drechsler's crew and men from the U-boat *Graf* had questioned him "about these men, Globus and Limmer." Another crew also asked "if 'Limmer' was truly a traitor and I had to answer them because I knew 'Limmer' personally."

When Taubert learned that Drechsler was in camp, "I looked for him but I couldn't find him." That night someone had run into his barracks saying, "There is someone hanging down there. Come and take a look at him." It was too dark to see much, so Taubert had returned the next day. Who did it? "I think that it was some who had been interrogated by him or it might have been some of the crew or some other friends who turned against him." Yes, Taubert knew Hox. They had both been transferred to Compound 2. They had never spoken about Drechsler (a lie).

The board attacked: "As a matter of fact the men who hung Drechsler were from his ship weren't they? . . . They were the only ones who would have any grounds for it?" Taubert thought it possible, but "the whole Compound was angry at this person when he was sent in there." No, Taubert did not have anything to do with killing him. "I am sorry I didn't have."[25]

On April 23 the board interrogated Heinrich Ludwig and Peter Duer, who had been Drechsler's last roommate at Fort Hunt. Only Ludwig triggered the lie detector. (Duer had not attended Hox's meeting.)[26] Ludwig, the second murderer to be questioned, lied about everything. During his three weeks at "Washington," he vaguely recalled a roommate who may have asked a few things about his boat, amid "ordinary talk" and card playing. "What I could answer I did but what I couldn't answer I didn't." No, no one at Stringtown had mentioned a traitor. He had never seen Drechsler at Papago Park and he did not know who killed him.[27] Ludwig was definitely considered suspicious.

The board always asked about Capt. Wattenberg. On April 28 it interviewed a lieutenant whom the captain had been harassing. He described the spokesman as a duty-obsessed micromanager capable of inciting murder. "I know that Wattenberg told the officers at Crossville [Tennessee] that every officer would be annihilated who showed weakness" or anti-Nazi leanings. The lieutenant had been told "they tried to hang a man there." When word of Drechsler's hanging reached the officers' compound, the younger ones "educated in the Nazi principles . . . agreed with the whole thing." The lieutenant was afraid that they might spot his distaste for hanging people without trial; "maybe they would think I am an anti-Nazi." No, he had never heard who killed Drechsler or why, but he believed that Wattenberg knew, after the fact—although he knew the captain was "inspirational to hanging people up." So, Church prodded, "he would approve any act of that kind?" Yes, because of the story about the man killed at Crossville.[28]

That was on April 28. On May 8 Wattenberg would be deposed as camp spokesman and isolated from his fellow officers.[29] Such a notorious Nazi had to be guilty of something. That same day, the board formally re-interrogated, "for the record," Gerhard Richter, alleged Gestapo agent, and Alfred Friedrich, who had foolishly bragged of knowing one of the killers but had refused to tell.

After reminding Richter of his oath, the board asked more acute questions than before. Yes, he now admitted, he had discussed the traitor in "Washington" with other crews at Stringtown, although not with Drechsler's crew, whom he had only met in the stockade. The board pressed him extremely hard, again, to admit he had overheard men on the ballfield conspiring to kill Drechsler. He kept insisting they had only spoken of possibilities. After great resistance, he finally told the board that these men had been from First Company, though he still refused to name them.

When had Richter heard about the hanging? He was not sure. "The whole barracks was suddenly talking about it" and it "spread all over the place." No, he had never spoken to Hox about it. A friend had told him "that Hox didn't have anything to do with this case," which had surprised him. He had thought that spokesmen were "responsible for everything that was going on in the Camp." Surely "somebody must have told him." Who did he think was most interested in hanging Drechsler, his crew "or the people that he interrogated"? Richter had no idea. Did the men who had discussed hanging Drechsler on the ballfield belong to either group? No, they were just people from Richter's own company.[30]

Having failed again to establish a conspiracy, the board moved on to re-interrogate the boastful Alfred Friedrich, Richter's (and Stengel's) barracks mate. The transcript shows that Friedrich had already been forced to reveal the killer, without ever uttering his name. At the Sunday soccer game, the man standing next to him had said that "that night a traitor was supposed to be hung. . . . I didn't believe him because I didn't think it was true." Who had said that? "I remember but I . . . won't tell you." Later on, he heard "that a man was hung." He didn't believe it until he saw the body.

"You have already told us . . . that you know one of the men who helped hang him. How did you find that out?" the board asked. "He himself told me that he was among them"—not Friedrich personally, but the whole group standing at roll call the next day. "I overheard it and I took it for granted that he was there," because he told in such detail "about how they beat him." What, exactly, had he said? "He just talked about how the man tried to protect himself" when they hit him, "and how they beat him and that he was a traitor and that is all."

No, this man had not said how he had known Drechsler was a traitor. He may have said that five or six had helped him, but he had not named them. In Friedrich's opinion, "they must have been the men who overheard him at Fort Meade." But the "one whom you know" had never been interrogated by Drechsler, said a board member. Yes, Friedrich said, that fact "is bothering me too." The board made him confirm that the man recounting such gory details was the same individual "who told you the day before that there was going to be a hanging." Yes, the same man. "You told us the other day that this one man is in Barracks 3, Company 1, didn't you?" Friedrich admitted it, bitterly.

After Friedrich had remarked that he never mixed with anyone but First Company, the board had read all the names to him. When they read the roster of his own barracks, "my blood showed . . . that must have been it. I can't control my blood." With satisfaction, a board member added: "And when the name of Otto Stengel was read to you, you couldn't control your blood there either." Friedrich still refused to say his name. "The machine will have to tell you."[31]

How preposterous that the first killer to be identified was the only one without any prior connection to Drechsler, his crew, or his victims. The board still had no idea who Otto Stengel's confederates had been, but thanks to the lie detector and luck they now had a manageable list of probable suspects and likely witnesses. What the board did not have, after five weeks of frustrating work, was any evidence linking anyone to the crime. Therefore, if the guilty were to be brought to justice, Nazi terrorists confounded, camp labor disciplined, and the service commander's reputation shored up, these suspects would have to be forced to incriminate themselves. For that task, the board needed experts.

On May 14, 1944, Col. Church transferred ten prisoners from Papago Park to the secret interrogation camp at Byron Hot Springs, California.[32] It took him only five days to arrange train transport—proof of high priority.

CHAPTER 8

Ploys and Complaints

Prisoners who were released from the Papago Park stockade after the investigating board departed for California soon used their Geneva right to complain to the International Red Cross (IRC) and the Swiss Legation. Their letters went via their spokesmen to the camp's commandant and from him to the Provost Marshal General's Office. Normally POW letters were delivered to the addressees, but the War Department kept translations of these embarrassing complaints for its files. From these, we learn that the new spokesman for Compound 4, Karl-Heinz Jaeger, charged the United States with grave violations of the Geneva Convention. Papago Park's new commandant, Col. George Barber, forwarded Jaeger's collection of letters to the PMG's Office on May 12, 1944. Three days later he forwarded a joint letter from Jaeger and the Compound 2 spokesman, Karl Voelker, dated May 11, which summarized several other POW letters that the two intended to send along later. The camp's new spokesman, Fregattenkapitän Paul Keller, sent still more complaints, which were not forwarded from the camp until July 22.[1]

Capt. Keller strongly protested the American practice of swearing witnesses to tell the truth. In Germany, no suspected criminal was ever sworn. German police were not authorized to administer oaths. What were his men to think when some officers claiming to be agents of the FBI, which "corresponds to the German secret state police [Gestapo]," had used "deceptive tricks" to get military information? These interrogators had repeatedly accused "the POW soldiers" of being spies, had threatened to hand them over to the "civilian authorities for final disposition or delivered over to Russia or to Brazil; or said that other Prisoners of War already told all things worth knowing," or threatened that the agents could "cause the soldier to disappear unnoticed."

They would tell a "soldier" that since there was proof of his guilt, he "would be hanged as the first one," the very next day. They would say "that the German Government desired the use of the electrical apparatus [lie detector], the staged deception of hanging scenes, etc., etc." The POWs, seeing through these ploys, had naturally assumed that the oath was another "police trick." Therefore, those who refused to swear must not be accused of "a criminal intent to commit perjury."

Two prisoners, Drechsler's victim Lothar Mandelkow and U-118 seaman Walter Schiller, wrote letters describing their outright resistance to the "electrical apparatus." (The board's transcripts contain no trace of these incidents.)[2]

The two most troublesome complaints were written by Willi Peters and Walter Nieswand. Peters told the IRC:

> On May 2nd, 1944 . . . I was ordered to sit down and the civilian strapped a rubber covered steel-pipe around my chest, put over my right hand a clasp and fastened on my left arm above the elbow a steel-pipe with a rubber bandage, which was filled with air. I had to sit quite calm and was not permitted to move. The interpreter now read aloud to me about 50-60 names of the first company with an interval of about 30 sec., and after each name I had to reply: "No."

When Peters questioned the process, he had been assured "that the usage of that appliance be allowed according to the Convention of Geneva. I replied, that so far as I know, the application of extortion be not allowed." He threatened to complain to his spokesman, only to be "told that Kapitän Wattenberg had sat here exactly like me." When Peters ceased to cooperate,

> suddenly the major said in English that I had hanged Drechsler. I answered that I be a German soldier and I therefore demand for examination in German language, and I would not stand that accusation.
>
> Upon that the major screamed, that I be able to speak English and he struck at the back of my head. At once I jumped up but the major stood before me with clenched fists and ordered me to sit down. I said that this not be a treatment for a captured soldier, and the examination be terminated for me. Then I was told that I be belonging to the secret M.P. or to the Gestapo, but that seems only laughable to me. I then again was accused of murder, and finally I was brought back to the camp.

(The Board Report does not mention Peters's interrogation at Papago Park, but four days after writing his complaint he faced a new set of inquisitors at Byron Hot Springs!)[3]

Walter Nieswand, a Drechsler victim, complained that when forced to sit at the apparatus he "stood up again. Then I was slapped from behind upon my head, my hands were hold fast, one man, who stood behind me, took with his arm the air away from me." He could complain if he liked, they said, but he was only getting German-style treatment.

The letter cowritten by the compound spokesmen Jaeger and Voelker alleged serious Geneva violations. Their men had been isolated in tiny cells in oppressive heat for four to eight weeks, deprived of their mandatory two hours of daily outside exercise. Every time the spokesmen had asked to visit their men in the stockade, they had been refused. When some men were released, they told of being "compelled . . . to have an electric apparatus applied to them, which is used otherwise only with known criminals." Several "comrades were slapped, beaten, and otherwise mistreated." One man had a rope tightened around his neck while being "beaten upon his head, and, when he demanded to loose[n] the rope, he was told one could do with him what one wanted." These insults were "a very rough violation of the honor of every German soldier and are against all regulations of the Geneva Convention." Jaeger and Voelker promised that letters from eight "mistreated comrades will soon be forwarded."

The spokesmen asked Papago Park's new commandant, Col. Barber, to send their letter in triplicate to the IRC and the Swiss Legation and in duplicate to the Provost Marshal General but, following standard procedure, he merely sent the lot to the PMG's Office with a note of his own: The "machine referred to" was a lie detector, used by officers from Service Command headquarters to investigate the Drechsler hanging. The suspects' "treatment and food was identical to that in other compounds." They had been "segregated on orders of the Commanding General, Ninth Service Command and on his verbal orders "transferred to Angel Island, California" (the cover address for Byron Hot Springs).[4]

These letters made trouble, of course. If they were not delivered, as the Geneva Convention commanded, the Germans would likely retaliate by blocking the complaints of American boys; but what would happen when this particular set of complaints reached Berlin? It was time for damage control. Fortunately the Geneva Convention did not specify prompt delivery.

On May 18, a military police translator telephoned Col. Church in California. He summarized Peters's and Nieswand's letters and asked, "Do you know anything about that, Colonel?" Church (who obviously knew what was going on) said that both men were questioned under oath, with and without the polygraph. They had asked "if such a thing was permitted by the Geneva Convention." When he had reassured them "that their own senior German Naval officer at that camp, Captain Wattenberg, had been examined on the machine without any objections," they had then meekly submitted—as the polygraph records proved. The machine "recorded their blood pressure, their pulse and their skin electricity and the amount of perspiration that came into the hands." The apparatus would not work unless "the subject remain[ed] absolutely quiet." Furthermore, Church "was present during all of it."

Maj. S.: All right, and you saw no active violence perpetrated upon them?
Col. C.: I did not—definitely not.
Maj. S.: Well, that seems to answer the question then.

Church added: "Now there's one thing I want to make clear." Mr. Keeler had snapped—not slapped—Peters on his right ear with a finger, by surprise, to "see if the polygraph was reacting on the galvanometer." That was "the only thing that could be construed as being hit on the head." Major S. responded, "I see. Well that's very fine and I'll pass this information on. . . . And thank you, Colonel Church."[5]

Four days later, Assistant PMG Bryan telexed the Commanding General, Ninth Service Command, that Peters's and Nieswand's allegations would be forwarded to the State Department in two days (May 25) for transmission to the Protecting Power. He ordered Gen. McCoach to write an explanation to accompany their letters.[6] The task was bumped down to Col. Barber at Papago Park, who replied on May 24 that he had "no knowledge" of any mistreatment.[7] Of course he did not. Church's investigation had been secret. Barber had not been present.

The PMG's Office made creative use of this scant information. Col. Francis N. Howard, director of the Prisoner of War Division (PWD), sent two messages to Mr. Bernard Gufler, head of the State Department's Special War Problems Division (SWPD), for transfer to the Swiss Legation. The first message, dated May 26, was a note conveying only one item, the joint letter by Jaeger and Voelker, with a note explaining that it had to do with the ongoing investigation of "the incident Drechsler" (about which the War Department had informed State on May 18).[8] Some suspects had been "segregated to prevent them from influencing" one another. According to the camp commander, "exercise was not denied prisoners held in Compound 3 and . . . their treatment and food was identical with that in other compounds." (The complainers had been moved to the stockade!) The eight letters from prisoners which the spokesmen mentioned would be examined when they arrived and, if they contained pertinent information, "forwarded to your Department."[9]

The second communication from PWD to SWPD, dated June 1, 1944, contained Peters's and Nieswand's letters of May 3 and May 9 respectively, and the two notes by spokesman Jaeger (May 11) and Col. Barber (May 12). The PWD explained that the "complaints arose" from the rigorous investigation of Werner Drechsler's death, which "was quite probably the result of murder by prisoners of war." The lie detector was necessary because "as usual" German POWs did not want to identify their guilty comrades.

Then the PWD's note to the SWPD put Church's words into Barber's mouth! The camp commander, who was (*not*) present during the two interrogations, was quoted as saying that "there was no mistreatment or violence." "Although they both objected orally," these two prisoners had willingly sat down for the examination. The polygraph operator merely "snapped" Peters's "right ear with the end and back of his finger" to make the machine react.[10]

On June 17, State's SWPD finally sent the Peters, Nieswand, and Jaeger/Voelker complaints to the Swiss Legation, with a note of its own which (innocently, one assumes) amalgamated those two War Department communications into one highly misleading message: "The Department of State transmits herewith" letters from three POWs at Papago Park "relative to the treatment allegedly received by certain prisoners following the 'Drechsler incident.' The Legation is informed" that, according to the camp commander, the "prisoners held in compound 3" [*sic*] were not mistreated. "Evidence marshaled by the investigation indicates that certain prisoners" who "were *particeps criminis*" in the Drechsler murder were segregated to prevent their influencing the testimony of others. Col. Barber, who was (allegedly) present, denied that Peters and Nieswand were mistreated. The operator had merely flicked Peters's ear to get a mechanical reading. As soon as the State Department had "a further report" of this ongoing murder investigation, it would "again communicate with the Legation."[11]

By June 17, the day State delivered this note, the inquisitors at Byron Hot Springs had already compelled eighteen prisoners of war to testify against themselves and their closest friends, in clear violation of AW 24—the guarantee against self-incrimination, part of the American Articles of War which, by order of the Geneva Convention, applied to POWs in American hands.

Perhaps the War Department congratulated itself for delivering these letters in compliance with the Geneva Convention, while covering up the treaty violations they mentioned; but there was more trouble to come. On June 20, Col. Barber forwarded a new appeal from the camp spokesman Keller to the Protecting Power: Since "a number of enlisted men will have to appear before a court-martial in the near future," their "former commanding officers" desired to appoint, as their defense counsel, "Director of Supreme Court Dr. Hans-Georg von Wick at present Lieutenant P.o.W. at Crossville/Tenn., Compound 4." Would the Swiss Legation "kindly notify the Provost Marshal General to this effect?"[12] Geneva gave war prisoners the right to choose their own defenders, but of course this legitimate request had to be denied.

Meanwhile, what of those five former SPs from Byron Hot Springs, Barthel, Linke, Petratschek, Mueller, and Vogler? On April 5, 1944, the PMG's Office had ordered Seventh Service Command not to remove them from Camp Indianola, Nebraska, without its prior approval.[13] Two days later, the PMGO ordered that all anti-Nazi prisoners be sent to a special camp. The five had been sharing an entire 250-man compound with Indianola's 25 anti-Nazi prisoners. Once these had been transferred, the camp urgently needed the space and guards for crowds of newly arriving prisoners. The five could not mingle with regular prisoners, not even new ones, for even those who were "not fully informed as to their previous work" were too hostile.[14] Since the five had seemed trustworthy and cooperative, Indianola's executive officer decided they would be safe enough back on a ward in the post hospital—without guards this time.

At first the five former SPs were content with these new quarters and other "small privileges;" but as Karl Linke put it, they periodically asked the commandant if Washington had responded to the "exacting report about ourselves and our work" that they had written upon arriving at Indianola the previous December. He repeatedly told them "to be patient and that something would be coming." Their dramatic, irregular appeal to the Secretary of State through the U.S. mail had led to an interview by a major from a G-2 screening team, who had assured them "that all details of their former work and their entire case was known to Washington,"[15] but that was all.

In mid-June, the friends became "somewhat disturbed"—as the stockade commander put it[16]—to learn that Camp Indianola was closing down. They were to be transferred to Camp Atlanta, Nebraska. According to Marcel Barthel, the news caused Herbert Vogler so much stress that "he went slightly out of his mind" and began planning with Anton Petratschek to escape. "Before he could get us into trouble," Barthel said, and do something foolish that would get them placed under guard again, he and Linke decided to stage another breakout, still believing that they could resolve everything by explaining their case in person to some government official. Washington knew "that our work and the results were excellent"; therefore, "there must be some facts that are not yet clear enough to reach a decision."[17] Albert Mueller, the sailor, mentioned another motive: "We were all still anxious to do something to fight the Nazis."

Linke and Barthel had intended to go alone, on the assumption that as deserters from the German Army they might have a better chance than men captured in battle. At the last minute, they decided to take Mueller with them. Barthel said: "We did not include Petratschek in our plans because he is married, and also because he doesn't exactly know what he wants. We did not include Vogler because, since he is so young, we thought he might make trouble for us."[18]

The three planned to contact the IRC first, for help in contacting Barthel's government in exile (Luxembourg) and the War Department. Then they would try to find a lieutenant with whom they had worked in California to learn if he knew "whether anything was being done about us."[19] "We had no intention of causing any disturbance or any sabotage," Linke said, "but merely wanted to reach Washington, take care of our case and then return to camp"[20] (as he and Barthel had done in California, with potentially fatal results).

On June 15, one of them managed to purloin a claw hammer in the officers' mess. They spent their evening as usual, singing, talking, squabbling, until Vogler and Petratschek had gone to bed and the guard had made his regular check of the stockade's double fences. Then the trio put on every article of clothing that might pass for civilian, latched Barthel's door, and crawled out his window. Neatly replacing the fencing they dislodged with the claw hammer, they took off east down the railroad tracks, avoiding the towns, lying low during daylight. When they hopped a train the next day, Linke lost hold of the laundry bag containing all their assets: cigarettes, several candy bars, and six pennies. By the morning of June 19 they were in St. Joseph, Missouri, hungry and tired.

Along the way, the three decided that if they were caught, they would ask to see an FBI agent and a reporter. "We wanted to give our whole story to the newspapers," said Linke; Mueller added, to "catch the attention of Washington and help our case to be cleared." They soon had their chance. When they could not produce their draft cards for a Missouri highway patrolman who spotted them walking along the highway, he took them in handcuffs to the Buchanan County jail. The sheriff had already received a wanted notice about them in his mail. First he notified the authorities back at Indianola. Then, being an amiable man, he fed his prisoners and fetched them a reporter and an FBI agent![21]

The reporter arrived first. Harold M. Slater's article in that afternoon's edition of the St. Joseph *News-Press* trumpeted: "NAZI FUGITIVES ARRESTED HERE. Escaped War Prisoners, Bitter Against German Militarism, Say They Want to Enlist in U.S. Army." The unarmed fugitives had been without food for four days when "State Highway Patrolman Jack Inman made the arrests single-handed. . . . Sheriff S. J. Shepherd ordered a large meal for them." Slater repeated their life stories. Barthel, Linke's fellow deserter from Rommel's Afrika Korps, who "spoke clearly although with an accent," told Slater how, aboard ship, they had to be segregated because they "gave valuable information to the English." They were there in St. Joseph, Missouri, because they all wanted to become American soldiers and fight Germany. That was why they had escaped a second time. On their first attempt, they had gone "to the F.B.I. in California in an effort to get into the army," Slater wrote. Now they were spending the afternoon with FBI agents at the jail. (The FBI's Washington office denies receiving any report of this, in spite of a Freedom of Information request.)

The prisoners were anxious to enlist because Germany was so near defeat, Slater continued. That was why they "wanted to get to Washington and straighten up" their cases. People at the Pentagon surely turned pale when they read in this small town reporter's article that Barthel had mentioned "a secret prisoner of war camp in California," where these fugitives had "rendered service to the United States by questioning other German prisoners. 'We had a lot of freedom. We wore United States army sergeant uniforms.'" Barthel had added: "We know that if we ever are sent back to Germany after the war we will be killed" because too many prisoners knew how they had helped "the enemies of Germany."

Slater also mentioned the arrival of "a United Press dispatch from Denver," which said that two other German escapees from Camp Indianola (Petratshek and Vogler) "had been captured by army officers at Cambridge, Neb."[22] Speaking of the wire services, not one of them picked up Slater's sensational article. None of the papers in Denver, or Omaha, or St. Louis, or even Kansas City, fifty miles to the south, repeated it. Only the War Department could have smothered such a human interest story.

Petratshek and Vogler had panicked when they realized their friends were gone. The night of June 15 had seemed normal, Petratschek said. Vogler had gone crying to his room after "a little argument with Mueller," complaining of being picked on. Petratshek had tried to console him. Later, when they missed the others, they "thought it might be a joke" until they realized that Mueller's clothing and cigarettes were gone and Barthel's window screen removed. Petratshek had wanted "to notify the American authorities"; but Vogler, afraid that this "would incriminate[them]," said that the only thing to do "was to leave also." Petratschek agreed because he could not allow Vogler to go alone. They wondered how to get out. Vogler said they would simply climb over the fence, "and if the guards shot it would be all right since everything was ruined anyway. Vogler was in a high emotional state at this time."

They headed east, planless, with seven candy bars and no money. At dawn, they hid in a ditch. By evening, they felt so hopeless that they no longer hid from passing cars.[23] Soon two officers from Camp Indianola drove by, recognized them, and turned around to approach them from the rear in case they panicked and scattered into the fields. One officer "got the idea" that the prospect of a little food would make them "feel better." It did. "The fugitives climbed on the running board—one on each side." The officers decided: "if we kept them away from crowds we could reason with them better." They drove to the home of a civilian secretary whose mother "very kindly took everything in stride, fixed up some food." After the prisoners had a drink of water, they protested that they were too dirty to go inside. "They were, but they scraped their shoes, knocked the dust out of their clothes, and went in" and ate, until the captain said, "it's about time to go, isn't it, boys?"[24]

An investigating officer would describe Petratschek as "not too intelligent, but probably the most sincere one of the five," and Vogler as "very immature in his emotions, highly excitable, and with a definite persecution complex." Since these five prisoners were so unusual, and because "additional information" might clarify their cases, he gave each of the five "the privilege of making a voluntary additional statement" to the authorities.[25]

Once again the five explained themselves and their escapes.[26] This time, hard feelings surfaced. Petratschek said: "The fact that Barthel and Linke, while working at Angel Island, fled to report to the FBI could not be helped by us since both of them have exerted strong influence on all three of us." Therefore, "it is my and Vogler's express desire never to be together again with either" of them. Petratschek asked permission to join a Czech military unit or the American army. Vogler begged for work "similar to that which I performed at Angel Island" or at least for any sort of military assignment, even in the Pacific. "My life would be in danger were I sent to another Prisoner of War Camp." At Angel Island, "we were assured on several occasions that for the future everything would be done to protect us against all physical violence and mental persecution of whatever source." Now he asked that this promise be honored.[27]

Was this what the investigating officer called Vogler's persecution complex? When the commandant of the Atlanta, Nebraska, camp forwarded what they wrote, he informed the Commanding General, Seventh Service Command, that their former work was "common knowledge" among his 120 other prisoners, who had "openly expressed their intentions to do away" with them, even threatening "to poison these men if food was furnished them from their Mess." He urgently requested that "some disposition be made." When Indianola closed on June 30 there would be "no facilities available for subsisting" these five.

In the Security and Intelligence Division at command headquarters, the chief of the Prisoner of War Branch promptly forwarded the escapees' reports to the Prisoner of War Division of the PMG's Office, commenting only that Petratschek and Vogler wanted nothing to do "with the other three."[28] Eventually, according to John Hammond Moore, all five were moved to a prison camp in Canada for their safety.[29]

Was Barthel ever permitted to speak to the Luxembourg government in exile, or to join the American army to "fight for common ideas—for Allied Victory and Freedom all over the world"?[30] Was Vogler ever allowed to return to intelligence work? There was an urgent need for personnel trained in the German language and culture. But even if these five merely languished for the duration behind barbed wire, they were protected. This fact made their lot better than Werner Drechsler's—and also spared other German war prisoners the ordeal suffered by Drechsler's killers.

CHAPTER 9

"Dachou" Treatment

The island that Conquistadors named for Mary, Queen of Angels, is a state park now, "a naturalist's delight" six miles from San Francisco.[1] From 1910 until 1940 Angel Island's Fort McDowell held Asian immigrants. During World War II, this grim installation became a transit camp for POWs and also camouflaged and fed the illegal interrogation camp at Byron Hot Springs, on the mainland. No historical marker informs picnickers of this fact.

During the war, one clueless inspector from the PMG's Office reported that the Angel Island Camp had a "very close connection with the Ninth Service Command Headquarters," bypassing Fort McDowell. Another found it "peculiar" for a camp on a military post to enjoy "the status of an exempted station." The camp commander claimed he had "written authority not to establish a canteen for the prisoners"—and the camp used nonstandard forms![2] Inspectors from the State Department, the IRC, the Swiss Legation, and the Spanish Embassy (which protected Japanese nationals) failed to detect such bureaucratic nuances.

Byron Hot Springs, a bankrupt spa fifty-four miles from San Francisco near Tracy and Stockton, was never inspected.[3] Even the FBI had to beg information, though it was responsible for tracking down escapees. J. Edgar Hoover had ordered all Special Agents in Charge (SACs) to "locate . . . and to maintain close liaison" with POW camps. The FBI's San Francisco office reported that while G-2's Western Defense Command said that Angel Island was "the only camp in the area," it had heard from "other sources" about a Camp Byron, "allegedly . . . maintained jointly by the Army and Navy" for interrogating Japanese prisoners. Local G-2 and ONI officials told the SAC "they were not permitted to discuss any such installation."[4]

Hoover did not like to be kept in the dark and he knew how to pull strings. A few weeks later, Byron Hot Springs' commandant himself, Col. D. W. Kent, visited the FBI's San Francisco office.[5] Later, he gave the SAC a personal tour. Agent Pieper's report described Camp Byron as invisible, because the old hotel and other buildings lay "in a shallow hollow." Prisoners were driven there under armed escort from Angel Island or the Oakland train depot in converted ambulances with sheet metal bodies and indirect ventilation, fixed so the passengers "have no idea where they are going." The former hotel rarely held more than twenty POWs, though it could hold forty. The POWs were quartered on the fourth floor behind double locked doors. Guards patroled the corridor day and night. Outside the building were double fences with guard towers. Escape seemed "impossible," but in case it ever happened, Col. Kent would direct the nearest FBI office to "to get in touch with PO Box 651, Tracy." Escapees must be said to have fled from Angel Island. Though Col. Kent was "very pleasant," the SAC said, he constantly asked for secrecy.[6]

Not even Col. Church's investigating board was allowed to see what went on at Byron Hot Springs. Two interrogators calling themselves Capt. Oscar S. Schmidt and Sgt. Paul Held took over the suspects from Papago Park and proceeded to do whatever got results. (One of them would ask Otto Stengel if he wanted "some more of Dachou [*sic*] treatment." Dachau had not yet become a public byword for infamous cruelty.) In addition to Stengel, the board had brought Alfred Friedrich and Gerhard Richter, who had fingered him; five of the eleven men in Compound 4 who had roomed with Drechsler at Fort Hunt (Heinz Taubert, Rolf Wizuy, Heinrich Ludwig, and the NCOs Friedrich Murza and Siegfried Elser); and three others (Willi Peters the complaint writer and Rudi Stoessel were both innocent bystanders; the third, Johann Matzke, evidently served as Church's stool pigeon). After the interrogators did their job, the board would learn that only three of their ten were murderers.

The board's minutes say that it convened on May 30 at "Place—Secret." Church swore in the interrogator Schmidt to replace its own interpreter. Major Zabel took over the duties of the board's reporter. The board's third member, Major Walsh, returned to Ninth Service Command headquarters on "official business."[7] These maneuvers greatly reduced the number of outsiders involved in the project. The truncated board had only to wait out of sight and hearing until Byron Hot Springs' expert interrogators presented them with a set of docile, extremely well-rehearsed witnesses. This arrangement also gave the board deniability. At the court-martial, Church and Zabel could testify under oath that they knew nothing about interrogations conducted by anyone other than the board itself.[8]

On May 30, after reminding him of his rights under Article of War 24 (the alleged guarantee against self-incrimination),the board listened while a very subdued Gerhard Richter finally named the men who had stood near him on the ballfield the Sunday Drechsler had arrived. He described how "Stengel remarked that the traitor should be hung." Then he told something new: that night Stengel had also announced to their whole barracks: "Do you know that the traitor is already hung?" He had said that men who "had been at Fort Meade with Drechsler" had done it, but Stengel didn't know their names. Who had been listening, the board demanded? "According to my opinion anybody that wasn't asleep." Richter said he had lied to the board earlier, because he had not wanted to involve Stengel, who "was married and had two kids."[9]

The next morning, it was Alfred Friedrich's turn. The board had to pick answers out of him, but he finally confirmed that it had been Stengel who had said, at the ballgame, "that a traitor should be punished." The board kept trying to make him say that Stengel had predicted that he would be hanged, but Friedrich kept insisting he only "heard that somebody was going to get the Holy Ghost." No, Stengel had not said how many men had killed Drechsler. Rumor said five or six.

The board's next question shows that it had a script of the prisoner's revelations to the interrogators Schmidt and Held: "What did Stengel say about having his fingerprints taken?" This was a new detail. When Friedrich had repeated Capt. Hebblethwaite's announcement "that fingerprints had been taken from the dead man's neck," Stengel had remarked "that he didn't have any gloves on." (The board considered gloves to be evidence of premeditation.) Friedrich said he and everyone in the compound assumed that the killers were men whom Drechsler had gravely wronged at "Sing-Sing" camp. No, he had not heard any names. "No one else spoke about it except Stengel who was always bragging."[10]

By the next day, June 1, Otto Stengel begged his tormentors' permission to give his statement to "the small board." He had resisted Schmidt and Held as long as humanly possible, in spite of suffering from chronic appendicitis. (At his trial, Stengel would say that as a precaution, they had kept a doctor with him "at all times.")[11] The board would reject Stengel's first confession. After another working over by Schmidt and Held, he would confess again on June 2, both orally and in writing. On June 5 he would be allowed an appendectomy.

On June 1, with Sgt. Held as interpreter, the board treated Stengel as a first-time witness (at least "for the record"), putting him on oath, reading him AW 24—the prohibition of compulsory self-incrimination. Stengel's last-ditch resistance took the form of piling up irrelevant details and names, putting his own words into other people's mouths, and posing as a mere observer. At Stringtown, he had heard of a traitor, not Drechsler of the U-118 but a man from the boat *Heidman*. What had he heard that Sunday at Papago Park? That a traitor named Drechsler had just arrived. No, he could not say who told him this, just someone on the ballfield. When he had told Heinz Richter that a fellow townsman named Drechsler had arrived, "somebody from a different group altogether called out . . . 'That man is a traitor, that man will receive the Holy Ghost tonight.'" How had Stengel known that Drechsler was Heinz Richter's friend? "Drechsler himself told me" the name of his hometown. He had spoken to the newcomer, not realizing that he was the traitor, "because I was interested to hear news from other Camps." Had Stengel himself said that Drechsler would be hanged or beaten that night? No, no one had mentioned hanging; but that other group had "called over" the information that "he wouldn't see the next day or would get the Holy Ghost." Had Stengel then said that "the traitor should be hanged?" Well, he had asked Richter's group, "What is wrong with Drechsler?" They said they didn't know. But later, Stengel admitted, he began telling people he met on his way back to thebarracks that he had heard "that he won't survive until the next day or that he will receive the Holy Ghost."

Then his barracks buddies ordered him to get them more news because "somebody will be hung!'" Who had said that? Just somebody on the other end of the room, not one of Stengel's crew. "The other men in the barracks joined in: 'Aren't you on your way yet? We want to hear something new.'" Why had they said that? "Because I am, so to speak, the source of information." Did Stengel mean he was a gossip? "Yes, all the men come to me with the news because I took care of their laundry."

Commissioned by his buddies, he went to Fifth Company, where he "noticed a guard on each door" of the fourth barracks. One guard shushed him and said: "'Something is happening here' and I continued my walk because I knew then what was going on." The guard's name was Otto Heldt, a newcomer. Back at his own barracks, Stengel had described the door guards, the people walking around, and "talk in the Camp, I don't know where the talk is coming from, that Drechsler wanted to leave for the hospital the same day." His buddies had told him: "Only that little? Now you go ahead and smoke a cigarette and go again." He had gone.

Stengel described seeing Drechsler lying on the ground being kicked, then jumping onto the steps, shouting until "the six men" attacking him had ordered him back inside, then scattered. Yes, there had been enough light to see that much, but not enough to identify anyone because "they had something—I don't know—it was a piece of cloth in front of their mouth—on their lower part of their face." Yes, they wore gloves, too.

The board (consulting its script) asked: "Did an under-officer come down at that time?" Yes, the Fifth Company leader had ordered the spectators to "go away and let the six men do what they want," then had walked away. The onlookers had only backed off a bit. "Wasn't it at that time that the guard from one of the towers threw the searchlight on the group?" Yes, but it had only lit up two faces. Then Stengel the yarn spinner overdid himself. Those two were not only masked but "they were dressed with heavy overcoats and gloves, mufflers and some of them wore caps" (in Arizona in March!) Had he recognized either of these men in the spotlight? No, but they resembled Sgt. Ernst Hilderbrandt and Lance Corporal Viktor Drobek.

Then, Stengel said, he saw some men go into one end of the barracks and exit the other carrying Drechsler head first, face down. "The first two men had a rope in their hands and Drechsler's neck was in that rope." The procession had passed within twelve feet of him, double timing to the shower room. After they left, he and two or three hundred others had gone inside. Some "lit matches to see better." Some said, "There he is hanging, the traitor." Was Drechsler dead? "I do not know but he was hanging like he was dead . . . . There was a peculiar odor in the washroom so we did not stay very long."

Had Stengel recognized anyone at the crime scene? He named several nonentities. He had been in a hurry to report to his buddies. Then "all of the men but three of my boat's crew went there to look." Which three? Stengel named three petty officers (hardly barracks mates) who had been afraid they might throw up. No, he did not tell everyone in his barracks about it, only a few on his end, and some others from the middle who came over to ask him questions.[12] The board sent Stengel back for another session with the inquisitors.

The next witness poked more holes in Stengel's testimony. From *Funkobermaat* Freidrich Murza, who had broken down after twenty-four hours in Capt. Schmidt's hands, the board learned two new things. There had been two separate attacks on Drechsler, and the compound spokesman Hox had held a meeting in his office beforehand—evidence of premeditation. Murza described how the U-118's wounded machinist's mate, Wiedemann, had been the first to spot Drechsler. Murza had discussed the newcomer with the U-118's sergeants before supper that Sunday. After a spate of name-listing,[13] the board finally asked what, exactly, the NCOs had said to each other? They had decided that Drechsler was in their camp because the Americans "didn't need him any more at the interrogation center." They had also thought that it took "a lot of nerve" for them to send him to Papago Park. No, they had not "discussed right then" what should be done with him.

After the ballgame, during which he had spotted Drechsler and pointed him out to others, Murza had attended a class. Then Guenther Bleise had ordered him to report to Chief Quartermaster Hox. "There were altogether about 15 men at the office." The board made Murza name everyone he knew. He listed Ludwig, Wizuy, and Elser (who were also there at Byron Hot Springs), Mandelkow and Nieswand (Drechsler victims), and (erroneously) Polowzyk and Reinl from Drechsler's boat. After more name-listing, the board had him describe the meeting. "Hox asked each man whether he had been with Drechsler at the interrogation center near Washington, D.C." and what had happened there. Murza had described how "Werner Nimmer" had questioned him about his submarine. The others had told their stories. (Again Murza had to recite names.) The board said: "There was some discussion about what should be done with Drechsler. What was said?" Nothing, in Hox's office. The spokesman had simply said "everything is clear," and everyone had left.

Where had they gone? Murza told how two groups had gathered outside. In the first, "I said the man should be beaten up." Then "in the second group we said that a complete job should be done." What did that mean? "Probably that he should be hanged." Who had said that? Murza could not recall. The men were already scattering. "I believe they wanted to change . . . they all were in their Sunday clothes." He had waited with Elser until he saw the men gathering again. Several newcomers joined them. He thought he saw Rudolf Wiemer, an NCO from Drechsler's boat. When the "entire group" arrived at Fifth Company, "about half the men went inside the barracks and got Drechsler," including Wizuy, Ludwig, Nieswand (an error), and five or six more from First Company. Murza had been watching from about a hundred meters away, close enough to see how Drechsler fought and yelled and got away. No, he did not see him fall on the ground or hear anyone ordering the crowd back. How had the attackers been dressed? Like everyone else, all in blue pants and shirts. He noticed that they had gloves "because their pockets were bulging."

Then, Murza continued, after a short conference four men had reentered the barracks. Perhaps two minutes later they ran to the washroom with Drechsler, one man on each arm or leg. Who were they? Murza named Wizuy, Ludwig, Fischer, and (mistakenly) Nieswand. Then he and Elser had returned to barracks, but "due to the screaming many men came—there might have been 100 or even more." That was all he knew. The next day he had taken ill and been hospitalized.

Ordered to retell the story in his own words, Murza named Wizuy as the one who had said "a complete job will be done." The board asked if there had been enough light for him to recognize those who had carried Drechsler? Yes, Wizuy and Fischer; but now he was not sure of the other two, nor of the five or six he thought had made the first attack. Had they worn caps? Hardly anyone in camp did that. It was too hot.

Consulting its script, the board asked: "What happened to Fischer?" The next afternoon, a doctor had examined everyone's hands. When Fischer had slipped from one row to another to avoid him, Murza had noticed "that somebody had bitten him on the thumb."[14]

On June 2, Schmidt and Held re-delivered Otto Stengel to the board. In the thirty hours since his last appearance, they had brainwashed him into believing that he had been the leader of both attacks on Drechsler. He would still be saying so weeks later and casting himself as the mastermind.

After reminding him of his oath and the farcical AW 24, the board said sternly: "Prisoner of War Otto Stengel, do you have a statement to make?" This time, they let him recite without interruption. When he heard that a traitor named Drechsler had been recognized by the "men who were interrogated by him," he had gone searching for him because "I was inquisitive" and wondered "what he looked like." He described their meeting again. (He never repeated a conversation the same way twice). When Heinz Richter had asked him who this hometown boy was, Stengel had replied, "Yes, it is Drechsler," and had pointed him out. "He was dressed in an Africa uniform." Stengel still insisted that somebody from another group had shouted that Drechsler was "a traitor." "It is possible that he will get the Holy Ghost tonight or that he won't live until morning." After the game, Stengel had gone around repeating those words.

Now Stengel described his second conversation with "the traitor, comrade Drechsler," who had dared to cast doubt on German victory and to criticize Hitler and Göring. Stengel had warned him that this sort of talk would "get him into trouble. . . . He got mad again and said 'I will take it up with you at any time!' and I answered 'That is all right with me.'"

After describing again how his buddies had commissioned him to gather more news, Stengel truly bore false witness against himself, manufacturing a tale about the first attack by borrowing incidents from the second one. He had obviously taken cues from his tormentors. He now said that he had asked one of the groups standing around Drechsler's barracks the following:

> "What do you intend to do with Drechsler?" and somebody made a movement of strangling with his hands. I said: "Is it really clear and understood that he is a traitor?" and the other men said "Yes!" In this group there was only one man whose name I know—it was Wizuy. They answered: "We only don't know yet how we will be doing it," and I said: "You already have a rope handy?" and they answered: "Everything is clear and ready." I told my buddies: "Do you need another man for it?" and they answered: "Yes!" and I said: "I will go with you!"[15]

Inside the barracks, Drechsler had started a mighty fight. He was even winning until he rolled into the aisle where they could all grab him. Stengel saved one buddy's finger by forcing Drechsler's mouth open. They dragged him out the door. Stengel stuck to his account of how Drechsler had fallen to the gravel, of how the searchlight had swept over them. "The four men who were in front of us kicked Drechsler on the behind" and ordered him back in. At that point a guard driving by outside the compound fence shined a flashlight in their direction. "Drechsler noticed it too and he shouted to us: "Come closer if you have the courage!" The board asked: "Were they Americans in the car?" They must have been, said Stengel, because they were outside the fence.

Next, he continued, his confederates "discussed whether [they] should be satisfied . . . because it was really a [good] Holy Ghost." They decided that he would only keep serving the Americans, doing more damage than before. (In later versions, Stengel would give himself credit for inspiring the group to try again.) His account of the second onslaught was even more dramatic: "Please, buddies, let me go." . . . "You coward. Now you can prove that you are a man. Through your fault many wives and mothers have lost their lives and how many submarines has Germany lost through your fault." They battled again. This time, Drechsler tackled Stengel, who had to dig his fingers into the traitor's neck to stop his screaming. (In his written confession, he said he did this to force Drechsler to release the buddy's finger.)

Then, when they had Drechsler under control, the comrades had told Stengel: "Go away. We will get him now"; but he had helped carry one of Drechsler's feet. "He offered quite a bit of resistance" whenever the rope around his neck slackened. That was a throttling rope, Stengel explained, which two buddies had fetched after the first attack. They had used it just enough to keep Drechsler from screaming. "He was supposed to always get a little air" as they carried him away.

In the bathhouse, Stengel said he had merely watched the hanging. Then, after washing off the bloodstains, "I went back to my barracks and my buddies said 'What is happening' . . . and I told them." Aside from telling Friedrich "that it is possible that fingerprints found on the neck were mine—that is all."

Actually, Stengel had more to say: "I have made this statement because during the entire time in my room" [I had pictured] "how Drechsler was hanging there." He had not told the whole story the first time because "I had believed that the matter could be delayed until I could present myself to the authorities in Germany." He had also been "a bit afraid"; but in his room he had told himself that a soldier had to tell the truth. "If I am put before a courts-martial, then I wish that I can say something in my defense because in every German heart it feels bad that one sees such a man to turn traitor." Drechsler had many things on his conscience, including Stengel's own relatives, who "have lost their homes and my woman cousin has lost her life in a bombing attack and if I am put before a court-martial I will be standing before soldiers who will have an understanding of this matter."[16] Stengel was better at storytelling than prophecy.

When the board finished with him at 9:00 that night, it allowed him no rest. At the trial, Col. Church would describe how, after each prisoner had made his oral statement, he

> was told he would be furnished with pen, ink and paper and that the Board desired that he go to his room and write out all the facts and circumstances including names, dates, times and places concerning the murder of Prisoner of War Werner Drechsler. That he should date the first page and that he should start it substantially: this is a statement of Otto Stengel, German serial number, Prisoner of War serial number, that this is concerning the murder of Werner Drechsler. That the pages be numbered consecutively and that his signature be appended to the end of the statement.[17]

In some cases, these written statements were nearly identical to the oral testimony. Furthermore, the statement Stengel produced on June 2 is copybook neat and perfectly chronological.[18] So are all the others, with very few scratch-outs or additions above the line. Nearly all have a narrative flow surprising in men with only seven or eight years of schooling. Were the prisoners that well rehearsed, or were they also working from scripts provided by the inquisitors?

Though Stengel said his conscience had made him confess, the real cause was torture. The court-martial transcript contains his description of it (in the English of the official court translator, Capt. Oscar S. Schmidt of Byron Hot Springs!). Stengel told of being driven at great speed across rough open fields in a closed vehicle containing an iron bar, suspended so that it swung viciously at him with every bump. After seven hours of this without food or water, "the guard dragged me to the questioning. I could not walk any more because the trip was too hard." When he still refused to confess, he was left inside that vehicle, which stood for two hours in the California sun while the drivers enjoyed a meal. When that did not break him,

> three heavy coats were put on my shoulders and one [guard] opened the steam heat. My shirt and underwear were torn and my sex organs were hanging out, at which time I was pushed toward the steam heat and burned myself. That was not enough. The American Lieutenant went out to get a gas mask, which was put upon my head. At that time the American Captain [Schmidt] said, or yelled at me, "Will you confess now or will we give you some more of Dachou [*sic*] treatment?"

(They were indeed using Nazi methods. The National Archives hold a G-2 document dated eight months earlier, entitled "Violations of the Geneva Convention and Treatment of American Prisoners of War by the Germans." It describes how "at least one American airman in Dulag Luft, Oberursel, has been subjected to the 'hot box,'" a room "specially constructed to retain the heat," equipped with "over-sized" radiators. "Windows were closed and the room unbearably over-heated. This, along with solitary confinement for extended periods, is a form of torture designed to elicit information.")[19]

The "hot box" and genital torture did not break Stengel, but another treatment did. (Reminder: this is Capt. Schmidt's translation of what Stengel said at his court-martial.)

> Somebody got an onion and garlic which was smashed and put into the gas mask. The Lieutenant stood next to me and pushed me and stubbed me every time I closed my eyes.
>
> Suddenly the interpreter, the Sergeant [Held], stood behind me and yelled at me "Stand straight. Behind you stands a German Feldwebel [sergeant]." I was not able to stand straight any more. My legs were too weak because the three American coats were too heavy for me. This was not enough yet. The American Lieutenant . . . closed the inlet holes of the gas mask. At that time he was looking at his watch to find out how long I could stand without air. The American Captain [Schmidt] said "Now you see how it is if slowly the air gets out." "That is the way you have done it with Drechsler." When he had done this with me about 8 times . . . until

> I collapsed unconscious. An American guard told me later that I have, while unconscious, called for my wife and children until the time one has poured water on my face. I was not altogether conscious yet and they lifted me up and already reached for the gas mask again. "Do you want any more of that stuff"? yelled the Captain. I said no, it is enough for me. I wanted to talk to the Major [Zabel]. I want to give an oath. The Sergeant said, "You can't do it" but another Lieutenant said, "If you want to give an oath, I will call for the Major." Thereupon the Major . . . came to my room with the Sergeant. I was afraid to tell all of it at this time and I only told part of it. . . . I said to the Major, "I would like to see the small board" and they went out to get Colonel Church. After about 15 minutes Colonel Church arrived and I confessed about half [on June 1]. Finally, one let me back to my room. It was by that time about 4:30 A.M. Only after two days I confessed all of it, the true matter.

He had confessed, Stengel said, "because I heard continually how innocent comrades were punished. I continually believed to be shot because I had shortly before seen of a shooting."[20] Had a shooting been staged for him, too?

Later that night, Schmidt delivered *Obermaat* Siegfried Elser to the board so well rehearsed he needed little prompting. He described how he had searched the compound for Drechsler without finding him. About 8:00, someone had ordered Elser to Hox's office, where he had explained how Drechsler had betrayed him. He had heard Ludwig and Buchholz do the same. Hox had only responded that he "couldn't do anything in this matter. All [the men] could do is beat him up or something to that effect." In the group outside the compound spokesman's office (Elser could only recall Murza, perhaps Ludwig and Wizuy) they had discussed grilling Drechsler "concerning his conduct," then expelling him from camp or hanging him. Elser claimed he had tried to guide the others away from killing. After *Oberfunkmaat* Wiemer and another U-118 man found Drechsler asleep, "I suggested that the matter should be postponed until the next day and I retired from the group," thinking the others would follow. Instead the group, now grown to about forty men, discussed taking Drechsler "with force." Then he saw five of them enter the barracks.

Elser telescoped the two attacks into one. As he, Murza, and Wiemer paced around Fourth Company's washroom among "several" small groups, they heard screaming and saw "four men carrying a comforter running in the direction of the shower room." He had been too far away to identify them. This was the truth as he could recall it. After so many weeks, and "due to many stories I heard from all sides . . . I don't remember any more whether it is my own experiences" or someone else's.

Now the board fixated on gloves. Who had Elser seen wearing them? Why had he worn them, if he was trying to prevent a lynching? Well, someone had said to get them. He had not wanted to exclude himself from the group. And why had the group gotten gloves? "In order to hang Drechsler"—but Elser still claimed he had not meant to help them. At that moment "they were all too excited" to listen to him.

Col. Church asked: "Who in Hox's office said that Drechsler should be hung?" No one. But had that not been the very purpose of the meeting? No, only to tell Hox about him. No one had spoken of punishment until afterward. Who had done so? Murza, Wizuy, probably Ludwig; but he, Elser, had only agreed to help beat Drechsler and expel him. The board replied that this still made him an accessory before the fact. He was an NCO. "The privates are willing to follow your lead isn't that right?" No, said Elser, "it is different while being prisoners."[21] The board sent Elser off to write his statement.

After resisting the interrogators for over twenty-four hours, Rolf Wizuy was ready to talk by mid-morning, June 3. He described his ordeal at the court-martial (through the court translator Oscar Schmidt): He had been awakened in the small hours of June 1 and moved to a dark, unfurnished cell. After breakfast, he had been taken on a wild four-hour ride, falling "all about in the car." He, too, had been left sweltering inside the van while the drivers lunched. Back at camp, "an American Lieutenant, Captain Schmidt, the interpreter [at the court-martial], and two guards" forced him to stand at attention while Schmidt pulled, prodded, and braced him. "The Captain . . . smelled of alcohol. His eyes were bloodshot. He kicked me in the back of the knee to find out if I really stood at attention." When Wizuy told him he had eaten nothing for twelve hours, Schmidt had said that a superman like him could take that. "It would continue until I would talk." At around 11:00 that night, Wizuy was finally allowed to sit down but not to sleep. A guard kept him awake all night.[22]

Tadeusz Wittlin, a veteran of the Soviet gulag, has described how Stalin's NKVD chief, Lavrenty Beria, routinely forced a victim to talk by simply making him stand in a corner with arms extended out or above his head, forbidden to move them. Soon exhausted by intolerable pain, he would be "ready to admit to any crime of which he was accused." (For variety, or to save time, he might make someone stand "half straddle, neither upright nor sitting on his heels.") Today this technique is called "using pressure points."[23] Another Stalinist technique, the "conveyor belt," involved sleep deprivation combined with "continual interrogation . . . for hours and days on end."[24]

These two methods also got results at Byron Hot Springs. When Schmidt started in on Wizuy after his second sleepless night, he finally betrayed his four best friends, whom he had fiercely tried to protect.[25]

At Byron Hot Springs, Wizuy told the board that after becoming so angry at Drechsler for lying about his identity, he and Guenther Kuelsen had gone to see whether the traitor's NCOs would "participate in any action against this man." They had refused. Later, at the meeting, Hox had listened to everyone without giving "any positive advice." Then Bleise had returned to his job in the canteen. About ten others had gathered outside. Wizuy named Helmut Fischer, Fritz Franke, Bernhard Reyak, Guenter Kuelsen, Friedrich Murza, Siegfried Elser; "and I assume that Heinrich Ludwig was there. It is even possible that he was with us at the office of Chief Quartermaster Hox." Some thought Drechsler should be beaten; but Wizuy had reminded them that "tomorrow he will be in a different Camp and will continue to do espionage work for the Americans," who had sent him there to Papago Park. Wizuy told the board about the questions Drechsler had asked Kuelsen concerning missing men "who were suspected of being traitors" and illegal shortwave radios. Under the circumstances, Wizuy had told the others, this spy "must be eliminated some how."

When the five friends "and I believe Ludwig" had arrived at the Fifth Company's washroom, there were already "several other groups" there, presumably also intent upon doing something to Drechsler. By then Elser and Murza had walked away from the project. Someone attached a rope to a washroom rafter. Then they waited until the barracks lights went out. Church asked: "Stengel had not come yet?" No, said Wizuy. "That came later." Only "the six of us" had seized Drechsler, beaten him, and let him go when he screamed and pulled loose. After that, "I myself was of the opinion that Drechsler had his beating and we should let that be all. Then Otto Stengel joined us. I really didn't feel like continuing in this matter and he, so to speak, took over the command."

The seven of them entered the barracks and began accusing Drechsler, who freely admitted his treason. "He said . . . we should let him go until tomorrow when he promised to give some kind of explanation." They "threw him out of the bunk" and beat him again—that was when he bit Fischer's thumb—then dragged him outside, unconscious. As for details of the hanging, "it was dark already and I was very excited and I didn't pay any attention." None of them had discussed the matter afterward.

Then Wizuy realized he had gotten off script: "I believe I forgot to mention that Chief Quartermaster Hox had stated that a report to Captain Wattenberg wouldn't lead to anything because the officers as such wouldn't have anything to do with the case and they couldn't do anything in this matter." Finally, the board asked Wizuy why he had made his statement. "I came to the conclusion and conviction that it would be the best for myself, my comrades and everybody who is involved in the crime to tell the truth and nothing but the truth." Yes, he had lied earlier, but he had "stated the truth today," as he recalled it.[26]

Several hours later, it was Heinrich Ludwig's turn to face the board. Before Hox's meeting, he said, "all the men" betrayed by Drechsler had discussed "what to do with him."[27] Obermaat Reinl from Drechsler's boat had said: "We should think this over. We should not act in too much of a haste." Then, since Hox merely told them "he couldn't do anything in that matter as he didn't know the man personally," they had continued their discussion outside his office. Some NCO—Elser, Murza, or Reinl (not present)— had asked, "Who wants to participate in it?" Then he, Kuelsen, Franke, Fischer, Wizuy, and Reyak had volunteered. To do what, exactly? "We didn't have any orders whatsoever." Murza and Elser only wanted to beat him, but the others said that he would only "continue to play tricks on other comrades." They had separated without making plans.

When they reassembled, they realized they should get gloves. After that, they wondered how to get Drechsler out of his barracks. When Kuelsen slipped in and found everyone asleep, four had gone inside to fetch him. Ludwig had waited in the washroom with someone he didn't know, then rejoined the group after their attempt had failed. Another stranger had come up and said, "Go ahead—go ahead!" Ludwig did not know if that man had remained with them when they returned to their task.

Inside the barracks, they ordered Drechsler to admit his treason. He had whined that the "Americans had made a guinea pig out of him" in "Washington." Then he had enraged them by saying "Buddies, let me explain!" They beat him and, "I don't remember for sure but I think we had a little rope which we put around his neck." Ludwig had carried his right leg out to the washroom, where it was too dark to recognize who climbed on the bench and who handed the traitor up. Church interrupted: "No, wait a minute, you pulled the bench out first didn't you?" Ludwig had wandered from his script.[28]

On that same day, June 3, the board ordered a second contingent of prisoners extracted from Papago Park: Rolf Wizuy's four loyal friends Fischer, Franke, Reyak, and Kuelsen, as well as Obermaat Reinl and Chief Quartermaster Hox. While awaiting their arrival, Church and Zabel began to make cosmetic changes to those coerced confessions. Their colleague Maj. Walsh, who was in Salt Lake City planning the court-martial, had no doubt warned them that these statements must be made to seem voluntary. Since they would be the only proof of guilt, the whole case would depend on doing so. Starting with Otto Stengel on June 7, Church and Zabel began to require that the POWs add this "certificate" to their handwritten confessions:

> I, a German Prisoner of War . . . [name, POW and German service numbers], do hereby certify that the statement above and concerning the hanging of Prisoner of War Werner Drechsler, on [the total number of] pages numbered one (1) to __ inclusive, was voluntarily written by me in my own handwriting on [date], without any offer of reward, threats, promises or duress of any kind whatsoever.[29]

They all signed before witnesses, in the presence of their tormentors.

(At the court-martial, the incompetent defense would ask Maj. Zabel whether, while signing his certificate, Stengel had mentioned "any coercive action taken against him personally by anyone?" Zabel replied: "He did not," and seized the chance to add that, when Wizuy had signed, he had turned and asked: "How does the Major feel about being waited upon [in the officers' mess] by a murderer at Papago Park?")[30]

On June 7, Maj. Zabel, as "acting recorder," formally presented Ludwig's and Stengel's original handwritten confessions, and their English translations, to the board (himself and Church).[31] On that day also, Col. Church's superior, the Director of Ninth Service Command's Security and Intelligence Division, informed the commanding general that "certain German prisoners of war have been interrogated and the guilty ones are to be tried by a General Court Martial."[32]

Next, Church and Zabel interviewed the small fry. Heinz Taubert and Rudi Stoessel produced a few inaccurate rumors, including the notion that the killers had promised Hox in writing to confess to the crime back home. Willi Peters appeared with his statement already written out.[33] So did Johann Matzke (probably the board's stool pigeon), with a lame tale about Ludwig's asking him "What should I do? How should I conduct myself?" at the interrogation.[34]

The next day, June 8, the interrogators brought Fritz Franke to the board. He told how Wizuy had searched out and confronted the traitor. Later, at the canteen, Franke had spotted his friends next door and had stepped into Hox's meeting as it was breaking up. He thought Hox had said: "You must know yourself best what to do with Drechsler." After his friends had conferred, Franke had returned to his barracks for a piece of rope, "a dog leash," then had accompanied Wizuy to see the Obermaats from Drechsler's boat. "We did not mention that we wanted to hang him." No, Stengel was not present during the first attack. He had stepped up afterward and asked, "Can I help you?" Had they told Stengel what they intended to do, Church asked? "He must have been standing there." He "knew all about it."

During the second attack, Franke said, he and Ludwig had used the dog leash to stop Drechsler's "biting and screaming. Then we carried him out. . . . I always carried Drechsler's head on the rope." Church wanted details for the record: "You had the rope in one hand and Drechsler's hair in the other?" Yes, but aside from Ludwig he did not notice what the others did. In the washroom, "I helped pull him up from his feet." Was he already dead? Franke thought so. "He didn't move any more when we carried him."[35]

Next it was Guenther Kuelsen's turn to hear the board inform him of his right not to incriminate himself, then order him to tell "everything . . . including times, names and places." Kuelsen described his encounters with Drechsler on the ballfield and then with Wizuy, when the traitor had refused to recognize the man for whom he had fetched an ice bag after his appendectomy in "Washington." At Hox's meeting, when "somebody, I don't remember his name, asked what should happen to Drechsler," Hox had "looked at the ceiling, it was a kind of an ambiguous movement," and had said something like "I don't want to give any orders in this matter." Outside afterward, Kuelsen had told the others that Drechsler intended to go to the hospital the next morning; "and then we came to the opinion that it was best to hang him." At first, "all the men who had been in the meeting" wanted to help, but many of them dropped out on the way to Drechsler's barracks.

When they had regrouped after the first attack had failed, "Otto Stengel joined us and he said 'Can I be of assistance to you?' and we didn't say anything. He was welcome." Kuelsen did not know who put the rope around Drechsler's neck. While the others carried him out, Kuelsen had picked up the bedding and closed the door. By the time he got to the bathhouse, Drechsler's head was in the noose. Finally, the board asked Kuelsen, "Why did you make this statement?" He realized that resistance was senseless; "and I like to stick to the old proverb 'Honesty is the best policy.'"[36]

After Bernhard Reyak was AW 24'd, sworn, and ordered to tell everything, he recalled Hox saying something like "Everything is clear." Then they had assembled outside to discuss what he had meant and what they should do. After fetching his gloves, Reyak had found an even larger group near Drechsler's barracks. Then they considered "how to best handle the situation," whether to get one of Drechsler's crew to lure him out or simply grab him themselves. While "Wizuy or Nieswand" was asking Drechsler's NCOs to help, he had gone to the shower room "with one who could be Ludwig and one or two others whose names I don't recall" and prepared the noose. After giving a vague description of the first attack, Reyak became the third witness to make nonsense of Stengel's second confession. Reyak was in the process of telling his discouraged partners, "He got a good beating. Let's forget about it," when Stengel "appeared suddenly, I don't know where from," and warned them: "If you stop now, he will be gone in the morning." Other bystanders agreed. "Stengel insisted that the man must be killed even though Stengel had nothing to do with" him. "We were all convinced" and took his advice to enter through both doors at once.[37]

By the time the inquisitors began working on the last killer, Helmuth Fischer, they already knew everything. They tortured him anyway. Perhaps he was unusually resistant, for the board had to pick his story out of him. He had gone to Hox's meeting to tell about the conversation he and Bleise or Kuelsen had with Drechsler, the time he had asked about illegal radios. No one at the meeting had spoken about punishment, but "we said: 'Something must happen.' We said this in Hox's office. I assume that Hox heard it. He shrugged his shoulders and said: 'Everything is clear.'" Church asked if that was German Navy slang, meaning "to go ahead." No, merely that "there is nothing left to think over." Afterward, he and his friends had decided to hang Drechsler because if he got away, "he could tell all our names."

Fischer had been tortured into reciting his interrogators' script. Why else would he say that Stengel joined the group before the first attack after helping them decide what to do? Only Stengel had uttered this falsehood. After the barracks lights went out, Fischer said, the "four" attackers split up, entering by both doors "in order to prevent Drechsler from running out the back while we came through the front" (Stengel's suggestion before the second attack). At the barracks door, "because so many men had arrived in the meantime, Drechsler got up and said (as only Stengel had reported): "Buddies, somebody come closer," before retreating inside.

When the attackers regrouped, Fischer said, "somebody" warned that it would be useless to stop there, because "Drechsler would leave the Camp the next day" and have them arrested. So they returned, berated him for being a traitor, and beat him again while he "started to scream endlessly 'Help! Help!'" Fischer had "terrific pains" when Drechsler bit down hard on his right middle finger, glove and all. One of the buddies freed him. Fischer recalled vaguely that someone had "tried to limit [Drechsler's] breathing facilities" before they carried him out. The only rope he remembered was the noose in the shower room. "When Drechsler died I do not know as I am not a doctor," but "he did not scream any more" as they carried him off.

After describing how he had escaped notice at roll call, when hands were inspected, Fischer ran out of steam: "I have nothing else to add." Why had he decided to tell the board the whole truth? "The reasons are first, I know that in this thing there are many men involved who had nothing to do with it and these men should not be implicated in this matter. Second, because I want to own up for what I did. That is all."[38]

At the court-martial, Fischer would describe how he had been made to "own up." He had stood at attention for nearly four hours, until 7:00 in the morning. Schmidt had forced him to keep his hands "cross to" his body while pressing his chin on his chest. Then he had to stoop and clasp his no doubt exhausted arms under the seat of his pants while Schmidt stepped on them, forcing his body backward. This treatment had lasted for about an hour and a half "under continuous yelling." Schmidt had asked him not only about the crime but also about the "pig dog" Hox and about the "super Nazi," Capt. Wattenberg.

> Further, I was asked if I knew Dachou. I said no to the question and Captain Schmidt asked me if he should show me some things about Dachou. I said, "No." I was asked if I would like to see Hox who was very little. I also said no to this question. Thereupon the interpreter [Schmidt, the official trial interpreter] asked me if my undershirt and my shorts were bothering me. If they did bother me, I should denude myself.

By then Fischer "was shaking all over" (unsurprising, after being explicitly threatened with genital torture! The allusion to Hox's being "very little" could not have referred to his height). Pain, fear, exhaustion, and finally hopelessness broke Fischer down. The interrogators told him that "all the others had confessed and there would be no further use" in resisting.[39] They showed him the statements that his friends Franke and Kuelsen had already made. (Using one person's confession to break down another's resistance is extremely improper. At the trial, Col. Church would deny strongly, on oath, that this ever happened.)[40]

After dismissing Fischer, the board resumed its task of conferring the appearance of free will upon such forced confessions. It asked Friedrich Murza and Siegfried Elser, under oath: Is this statement written by you? Is it true? When both answered yes, their confessions became exhibits for the prosecution. The next day, June 9, the board asked the same questions of Franke,

Kuelsen, Reyak, and Fischer, adding: "Was anyone present when this statement was written?" These confessions were also marked as exhibits pending the court-martial.[41]

The board still had two more men to hear, Franz Hox and Werner Reinl, the U-118's senior petty officer. Reinl described how he had assembled a list of Drechsler's victims, ten or twelve names. He had given it to Hox, who had said, "What should I do with it?" Church asked: "Why are you telling the full truth now?" When questioned at Papago Park, he said: "I was afraid . . . because I figured if I told you about the piece of paper . . . you would confront [Hox] with the men mentioned on it and I would be considered a traitor." Since they already knew the names, he felt free to speak.[42]

The board had never yet questioned Hox, the former compound spokesman, even though he was an NCO from Capt. Wattenberg's boat. Odder still, the board seems not to have challenged his story. It pressed him very hard to identify the men at his meeting; but of the twelve or fifteen, he could name only six, including two who were never there (Reinl and Polowzyk from the U-118). Why had he called that meeting? "Because there was a big excitement in the Camp. I tried to find out whether Drechsler was a traitor." He had listened to the men, but no one had discussed punishment. "I didn't talk about any measure to be taken because after the conversation I left."

Thus far Hox's story agreed with the others, but then he added: "I said: 'Drechsler seems to be a traitor. Let's wait and I want to report the case the next day to Captain Wattenberg.'" Sensing a plot, the board prompted: "During the time that you were at Papago Park you had various talks with Captain Wattenberg did you not?" Yes, he had. "And you discussed with Captain Wattenberg the fact that some of the men from the submarines were traitors?" No. But, as a spokesman, didn't Hox have an identification card that permitted him to visit other compounds? Yes, but he could not enter the officers' compound at will. And that Sunday, Wattenberg had come to Compound 4 only to introduce himself and to welcome the new men. Well then, had the captain said anything "to the effect that if any traitors were to be punished the men should wear gloves so that they could not be detected?" No, Hox was positive he had not.

Had Hox spoken to Reinl that day? "No, he passed me only and he told me: 'Here seems to be a traitor. Everybody is excited and you should report that to Captain Wattenberg.'" Yes, Reinl had given him "a little piece of paper," which he had pocketed without reading. Reinl had said: "These are the names of men that Drechsler had been together with at the interrogation center near Washington and that I should check up first to see whether there was anything to this rumor and he said a man like that is degraded very fast. I don't know why Reinl talked to me." He had told Reinl: "That is all. It is settled," and refocused on the ball game. What had he meant when he said "the case was clear"? Just what he said. And why was he going to report to the captain? So he could tell camp headquarters and have Drechsler removed from there. Aside from that "I didn't talk about this case whatsoever." He stuck to that story.[43]

After recalling Hox and Reinl on June 9 to identify their statements, handwriting, and signatures under oath, the truncated board adjourned. On June 13 the full board, including Maj. Walsh, reconvened at Papago Park to interrogate a few more prisoners. It learned nothing new. By June 20 its work was done. Maj.Walsh undertook to prepare the official Board Report. At the trial, which Walsh was already planning, the prosecution would base its case upon this report, though the document itself would remain secret, unknown to the defense. Maj. Walsh himself would be the prosecutor.

CHAPTER 10

Thorough and Impartial Investigation

Although the prisoners from Byron Hot Springs remained, on paper, "permanently interned" at the Angel Island processing station, special guards scattered them about and remained to watch them. Two NCOs connected with the "fatal disturbance" at Papago Park were sent all the way to Ninth Service Command headquarters at Fort Douglas, Utah. Siegfried Elser was confined in the guardhouse and Friedrich Murza in the psychiatric ward of the fort hospital, possibly for treatment. The officers in charge of these facilities were told that in the interests of "military security and secrecy," only someone with "express authority" from command headquarters could speak to these two—who must not be allowed to send letters or notes.[1] According to a second order, they could not even possess paper or writing instruments; but as an afterthought they were allowed to exercise daily under guard, smoke, purchase reading material "from personal funds," receive medical attention, and "be afforded sanitary facilities including washing of their personal clothing."[2] Presumably they had been denied these amenities.

The seven confessed killers remained in California. Ludwig, Wizuy, and Stengel were conducted to separate base hospitals. Stengel needed postoperative care; perhaps the other two also needed medical attention. Fischer, Franke, Kuelsen, and Reyak were held at Turlock, a military prison.[3]

"A special chosen armed guard" moved seven material witnesses from Papago Park to remote Camp Florence in southern Arizona, near Coolidge, where the trial was to be held. The command's Director of Security and Intelligence warned the commandant there that the very presence of these men must be kept secret. They were not to converse or to correspond with anyone without "express permission from this headquarters." When the commandant asked questions, he was told to mind his own business.[4]

On June 20 at Papago Park, Col. Church's investigating board finished its findings and recommendations: Werner Drechsler had been hanged on March 12, 1944, by Otto Stengel, Rolf Wizuy, Heinrich Ludwig, Helmut Fischer, Fritz Franke, Bernhard Reyak, and Guenther Kuelsen, who should be charged with murder. Two NCOs, Elser and Murza, should be charged as accessories before the fact.[5]

Neither Murza (mentally unstable?) nor Elser would be charged or even listed as witnesses. However, a first lieutenant in the command's Judge Advocate office formally accused the others of violating AW 92 by "acting jointly and in pursuance of a common intent, . . . with malice aforethought," to feloniously "kill one Prisoner of War Werner Drechsler, a human being, by strangulation."[6] This underling also swore that he had "investigated the matter" and found it "true in fact, to the best of his knowledge and belief."[7] When the Ninth Service Command's Judge Advocate advised Maj. Gen. McCoach to appoint a court-martial, he also affirmed that his own "searching inquiry as to whether the confessions were obtained in a lawful manner" had shown that they were all "free and voluntary."[8]

This "searching inquiry" never happened, although the American Laws of War required that a pretrial investigator review all the evidence, interview the accused and the witnesses against them, and then decide if there were sufficient grounds for prosecution. Another underling, First Lt. Harry A. Baldwin,[9] left Utah for California on June 30, carrying with him the formal charges, a copy of the secret Board Report (to be returned "when it has served its purpose"), and an order directing the commandant of Angel Island to "immediately appoint an investigating officer to make a thorough and impartial pre-trial investigation." This order added: "The Commanding General, Ninth Service Command, concurs in your appointment of First Lieutenant Harry A. Baldwin."[10]

Baldwin's own orders were "to carry out the verbal instructions of the Commanding General."[11] One may deduce what these were from Baldwin's actions. He interviewed no witnesses. He ignored every circumstance that might have mitigated guilt. Instead, he neatly trapped the seven defendants into testifying against themselves again.

Having turned over the secret Board Report to Angel Island's commandant, Baldwin evidently worked from copies of fifteen confessions. Seven belonged to the accused. Two belonged to the former Compound 4 spokesman Franz Hox and to the highest-ranking NCO survivor of Drechsler's boat, Werner Reinl. At least these two were named on the official list of witnesses. The other confessions belonged to Murza, Elser, and four utterly insignificant figures, Heinz Taubert, Willi Peters, Johann Matzke, and Rudi Stoessel.[12] When he interviewed the accused, he would not refer to any of these statements unless one of the defendants asked him a direct question.

On July 3, 4, and 5, Baldwin spent three hours with Stengel, nearly three with Fischer, two with Wizuy, an hour and a quarter with Kuelsen, and less with the others. Reyak got five minutes of his time. Speaking through an interpreter, the lieutenant introduced himself to each of them as an impartial investigator. "I am not the prosecutor, nor do I represent the prosecution. I am not your counsel. I am here merely to inquire into the truth of the charges, and to recommend what disposition should be made in the interest of justice and discipline."[13]

Next, Baldwin read the murder charges and the list of witnesses. Stengel said he could not "understand how all these people" could have witnessed against him. Kuelsen said that he could not imagine how "the men who did not participate in the crime itself" could possibly "have said anything against me . . . personally."[14] Baldwin did not explain.

Next he read AW 70, "Charges, Action Upon": no trial could take place until there had been a "thorough and impartial investigation" into "the truth of the matter," during which the accused must be given "full opportunity" to "present anything he may desire in his own behalf, either in defense or mitigation." Uncounseled, isolated, six of the seven took him at his word: they believed that this was their chance to explain and defend themselves. When Baldwin asked each man to restate AW 70 in his own words, Kuelsen said: "It is possible for me to make statements in my defense and for leniency. . . . I will tell the truth, so I am not afraid that anything I might tell might be used against me in a bad sense," for he had "participated in that crime" to help his buddies, whom Drechsler had harmed, and to prevent the traitor from doing further service to the Americans. Kuelsen also said he could not "imagine how I can be under the American laws." Acting as a German soldier, he had killed another German.[15]

Wizuy's understanding of AW 70 was that, since he could "make statements which would be helpful to me before the Court Martial," he wanted "to describe the mood and the spirit and the eventual reasons which led up to this crime"—although he did not wish to speak under oath. Baldwin responded that it was immaterial whether he spoke under oath or not. Ludwig responded: "I can make statements in my own defense, or which may serve as reasons for leniency." Reyak was puzzled. He wanted to know which of the witnesses had identified him at the "noosing." None of them had, said Baldwin. Still puzzled, Reyak said that everything was in his confession. Did the lieutenant wish him to repeat it?[16]

Baldwin never told these men that those confessions they had made at Byron Hot Springs would not be admissible in court because they had been coerced. He did not say that those confessions were the only evidence against them. Instead, he re-read AW 24 (against self-incrimination), put some of them under oath, and had all of them formally identify, as their own, the statements they had written there (including those "certificates" alleging that they had acted voluntarily). Each had to verify the date, his signature, and his handwriting, and say whether he had been alone when he wrote. When Baldwin asked, "Are all the facts stated therein true?," each innocently said yes—including Stengel, whose second confession contained patent fictions.

Then this "investigator" told each man that if he had anything to say in explanation or extenuation of his deed, this was his chance. Only Helmuth Fischer failed to take the bait. After declining twice, Otto Stengel could not resist retelling his saga—this time presenting himself as the ringleader of both attacks on Drechsler. Not even the board had believed that![17]

Even though these men (or the translator) used the term "crime," they wanted it understood that they had acted justifiably. Had not the Americans sent Drechsler among them? Like soldiers in every army, they were obliged to deal with a traitor! If they had not acted when they did, Drechsler would have escaped. Then he would not only have kept on spying for the enemy, he would have made sure they themselves did not live to testify against him in a proper German court.[18] In justifying themselves, these seven men inescapably expanded upon the statements wrung from them at Byron Hot Springs. At the court-martial, the resulting transcripts would become exhibits for the prosecution.[19]

How could these prisoners have known that the prosecution would now be able to claim that they had not only validated their first confessions, removing all taint of improper pressure, but had also confessed a second time, allegedly without threat or compulsion? Baldwin's sham investigation also provided a double fail-safe insurance policy for the prosecution: if those POWs had freely "validated" their "first" confessions under oath, their statements from Byron Hot Springs were now untainted, acceptable evidence. In case that ploy failed to hang them, their "uncoerced second confessions" would do the job. (In fact, both tricks would work! The "first" confessions would be accepted by the court-martial judges and by Ninth Service Command's review board. Reviewers in the Judge Advocate General's Office would look slightly askance at the "first" but accept the "second" ones.)

But were these "second confessions" uncoerced? Neither the hand-picked Lt. Baldwin nor his stenographer spoke German. They understood nothing but the words of the translator assigned to them by Angel Island's commandant —and he was none other than Staff Sgt. Paul Held, whom the prisoners had last seen at Byron Hot Springs translating for Col. Church's board. He had also been present during some of the harshest interrogations. According to the (English-only) transcripts, none of the seven defendants mentioned Byron Hot Springs at all, nor did anyone allege that he had been mistreated. Was this remarkable lapse due more to Held's translations, to Held's intimidating presence, or to their own inability to understand their peril?

Amazingly, in spite of the fact that the defense would call Sgt. Held to the stand, fruitlessly, to ask about "third degree" methods at some unnamed facility, no one ever noticed Held's role in obtaining the "uncoerced" second confessions. Nor did anyone notice that Baldwin's report revealed slipshod work. He forgot to place any of the defendants except Kuelsen and Ludwig under oath. He had asked Stengel, at the end of their interview: "and all the statements you have made to me this afternoon you have made under oath?" (Stengel imprudently replied, "Yes.") No one noticed that Franke had said nothing to Baldwin that could possibly be called a "second" confession.

Baldwin also affirmed in his report that he had examined "all available witnesses and documentary evidence in the presence of the accused," then had added that "to conserve time and expense, the witnesses listed on the Charge Sheets were not personally examined by me for the reason that their testimony was exhaustively developed" in the Board Report. "The attached confessions of each of the accused indicate their guilt. . . . Trial by General Court Martial is accordingly recommended."[20] Of course.

Later, Ninth Service Command's staff Judge Advocate would praise Baldwin's skill, "sense of justice," and "liberal views." As his trial testimony showed, "confidence in this officer was not misplaced."[21] (Baldwin's testimony was sprung without warning upon the befuddled defense after which he was hustled out of town during a recess.)

The principal planner of this court-martial was the third member of the investigating board, Chief of the Military Justice Branch of Ninth Service Command's Judge Advocate staff, Maj. Francis P. Walsh, who was assisted by the staff adjutant and the Director of Security and Intelligence. Walsh had been planning this trial since early June, when he had conveniently absented himself from Byron Hot Springs. Later, he had written the official Board

Report, including an introductory "Summary of Evidence" upon which the prosecution would base its case. Furthermore, Walsh would soon become the trial judge advocate (TJA), or prosecutor.

This would be no ordinary trial. Ninth Service Command's JA staff may have sanitized the confessions, but it also had to satisfy the letter of international law. The Geneva Convention required that POWs be tried in exactly the same way as the Custodial Power's own soldiers, with additional safeguards: a defender and a translator of their own choosing. Obviously, if true choice were allowed, dangerously inconvenient remarks could end up in the trial record. That record would become the basis for two judicial reviews required by the Articles of War. The first review was at the service command level; the second review was conducted by the Judge Advocate General's Office in Washington and by the Secretary of War. If the record were not kept clean, the sentences might be overturned, besmirching the careers of Ninth Service Command personnel.

Furthermore, since Geneva gave the Protecting Power the right to certain information about prisoner trials, and this information would certainly end up in Berlin, the trial record must not reveal the existence of Fort Hunt, which had provided the motive for Drechsler's killing, nor that of Byron Hot Springs, where the killers had been forced to confess.

The Protecting Power could also send an observer to the trial of a war prisoner. Fortunately for the planners, the Geneva Convention allowed secret trials under certain circumstances. On July 11, the command's Judge Advocate office sent a request to the War Department. Would the Provost Marshal General advise the Protecting Power that this trial would involve "testimony of a secret nature, the disclosure of which would compromise methods and operations employed by the United States Military Establishment?" The Swiss Legation should also be informed that seven prisoners would be tried for murder at the POW camp in Florence, Arizona, on August 15 and that their defender would be Maj. William H. Taylor, field artillery, stationed at the Presidio of San Francisco. "Arrangements will be made prior to trial for the service of a competent interpreter for the accused."[22]

Ignoring both Geneva Article 64, which gave POWs the right to choose their own defender, and repeated requests by the Papago Park spokesman Keller that a specific German lawyer be appointed, Walsh followed the routine American practice of choosing the defender himself.[23] The trial planners also routinely drew up a list of officers (six colonels, two majors, and five captains), which Maj. Gen. McCoach, as the "Convening Power," would automatically appoint as judges.[24] (According to the 1928 Code of Military Justice only one judge, known as the Law Member, need have any legal knowledge.) When the staff Judge Advocate, Col. Thomas J. White, informed Gen. McCoach of these arrangements, he added that the trial judge advocate would obtain "a competent interpreter for the accused, if requested, . . . locally."[25] Then the TJA—Maj. Walsh—appointed a German-Jewish immigrant who worked as a translator in a California POW camp.[26] Walsh probably did not expect this man to sympathize with the defendants.

Cpl. Erwin Gruenebaum set out for remote southern Arizona in ignorance of his new assignment. He would not set eyes on the defendants until the trial opened. As their translator, his job would be to make sure they understood the court proceedings. Another man, the official court translator, would turn each prisoner's words into English for the judges—not one of whom, according to Gruenebaum, understood German—and for the court record; and this record would be the only account of the trial and the sole basis for judicial review. For the key job of court translator, Walsh chose Capt. Oscar S. Schmidt of Byron Hot Springs. He could invisibly intimidate the prisoners while skewing any inconvenient phrases.

Meanwhile, the trial planners ordered a psychological assessment for Otto Stengel. An Army psychiatrist reported on July 17 that Stengel was "apparently getting along well" with his wife and two children! He was cooperative and spoke "quite freely, . . . which does not suggest paranoid or projection mechanisms." Assuming that Stengel's saga was "based on fact, there is no evidence of Psychosis elicited from this examination."[27] Walsh was well aware that many of Stengel's "facts" were falsehoods. All he wanted was some expert's opinion, in case the defense argued that Stengel's confessions were the products of an unsound mind. (It would never occur to the defender, chosen by Walsh, to make such a plea.)

For the trial's diplomatic aspects Walsh had to rely on the Pentagon to deal with the State Department. Oddly, the information about the trial that State passed on to the Protecting Power on July 15 did not mention that it would be secret. The Swiss Legation signed a statement that it had received "good and sufficient notice of at least three weeks before the opening of the trial as provided by Article 60 of the Geneva Convention,"[28] which the Judge Advocate General's Military Justice Division forwarded to the Ninth Service Command on July 21, along with a reminder that Geneva's Article 62, Paragraph 1, "should be complied with prior to the trial."[29] Accordingly, at Camp Florence, Arizona, on July 27, just nineteen days before the trial, the defendants finally received written copies of the charges against them. After collecting their signed receipts for these, Maj. Walsh also required them to sign this statement in English and German: "In compliance with Paragraph 1, Article 62, Geneva Convention, I have been advised of my rights to have qualified counsel of my choice and the services of a qualified interpreter." They signed in the presence of their "chosen" defender, Maj. Taylor.[30] This is the earliest recorded contact between him and his seven clients.

Maj. Taylor spoke no German. If he had interviewed his clients in California, who had translated for him? If he did not meet them until they arrived in Arizona, who translated? Someone provided by the prosecution? The defendants' "freely chosen" translator Cpl. Gruenebaum would not appear until the trial opened. One assumes Walsh planned it that way.

On July 19, the PMG's Office informed Fort Douglas that "the Legation of Switzerland does not contemplate having a representative attend the trial."[31] The Protecting Power probably had no choice, since Geneva allowed the Detaining Power to keep sensitive military issues secret.

Since secrecy was vital, then the War Department must have been keeping a nervous eye on those Papago Park POWs who were still exercising their Geneva right to complain to their Protecting Power. The PMG's Office had already resorted to delay and misrepresentation to blunt their bitter protests against being threatened, manhandled, and forcibly hitched to an "electrical device" (see chapter 8). On July 1, the PMGO's Prisoner of War Division (PWD) had finally given State's Special War Problems Division (SWPD) the letter that the camp spokesman Keller had sent on June 17, asking the Swiss Legation to help him get a learned POW lawyer appointed counsel for the defense. PWD instructed the SWPD to tell the Swiss Legation that the investigation into Drechsler's death "was still proceeding," and no one had been accused yet.[32]

On July 11, the Protecting Power asked the State Department to refer Keller's request for a German lawyer "to the appropriate American authorities." On August 8, a week before the trial and just over a week after the legation had consented to a secret trial, War's PWD told State's SWPD that the PMG had declined to appoint Director of Supreme Court Lt. Dr. Hans-Georg von Wick of Camp Crossville, Tennessee, to defend the men about to be tried for murder.[33] War prisoners could serve as defenders only if interned in the camp where the trial was held or "within a reasonable distance." (Maj. Taylor, Cpl. Gruenebaum, and the seven defendants had traveled over seven hundred miles from California to southern Arizona.)

This note of August 8 added that the PMG's Office was complying with Geneva Article 62 "by placing at the disposal of the accused prisoners an adequate number of competent defense counsel from whom they may choose."

The Swiss Legation had no reason to question this fiction. Four months earlier, when some Italian prisoners (also under Swiss protection) were to be tried, the State Department had given the legation a list of persons near their POW camps who were "qualified to present the defense of prisoners of war before a court-martial." After a Swiss diplomat had observed the trial, the legation had called the arrangement entirely satisfactory.[34] So when the legation received Taylor's name—along with those of two alternates—as proposed defenders in the Papago Park case, it saw nothing amiss. (Taylor had already been appointed three weeks earlier.)

Meanwhile, the PMG's Office was fielding another letter from Keller enclosing several more complaints from prisoners at Papago Park, accusing the United States even more bitterly of violating the Geneva Convention.[35] The officer who translated Keller's scorching denunciation wrote: "This is a MURDER case" involving prisoners' claims "that they were given '*the works*' and '*3rd degree*' by U.S. Army officers and F.B.I. officials. . . . This being a matter of real seriousness a complete translation of *all* the contents was required." A Maj. Sullivan commented on the prisoners' "delusion that *German law* and *German law court procedure*," not American law, applied to them.[36] Keller's letter, which Sullivan found "particularly difficult to translate," contained yet another request that POW Lt. Dr. von Wick defend his men in case they were "summoned (to court) for having hanged Machinist 1st Cl. Drechsler because of his activity for the American Intelligence Service, or for their having committed perjury in the investigation of this matter." Keller enclosed nine letters from POWs complaining of "a series of violations against the Geneva Convention and against the principles of criminal trial law."[37] These complaints made it clear, he said, that "the chance must be given to the arrested soldiers, to talk with a legal counselor whom they can trust."

After summarizing complaints about the first, camp-level investigation, Keller reviewed those concerning the board's lie detector and the oaths administered by police officials. He cited physical abuse and threats, particularly "the ever-recurring" accusation that since the prisoner was really a spy, he would be "handed over to the civilian authorities for final disposition or delivered over to Russia or to Brazil; that other Ps.o.W. already told all things worth knowing; that one was to cause the P.o.W. soldier to disappear unnoticed, and much more of that sort of ideas." As for the twenty-two men who had been arrested and "transported away," Keller did not know "where they were brought to and what they were charged with." Their unexplained disappearance "had caused great unrest and anxiety in the camp." Keller asked that copies of his letter be sent both to the German government and to Dr. von Wick.

The PWD had already sent copies of the prisoners' accusations to Ninth Service Command headquarters on July 22, demanding an explanation.[38] On July 31, the deputy director of the command's Security and Intelligence Division would reply that the foul "conditions concerning special confinement" at Papago Park had been corrected. If camp officials had used "improper methods" of interrogation, these had been "corrected" by the appointment of a new investigating board (Church's board!), which had proceeded "without incident." The "electrical device" was a lie detector, which was not harmful "in any way." Since the only prisoners still being confined were "those accused of murder, material witnesses in the case and those in protective custody as a result of giving information," there was no longer any cause for complaint.[39] The PWD repeated this message to State's SWPD but would not forward Keller's July 3 letter for delivery to the Protecting Power until August 12—three days before the trial began.

On the day the trial opened, the director of War's PWD forwarded a third letter from spokesman Keller, in which he said: "To my knowledge at least a few, if not all of those soldiers accused, will of their own accord choose the Lt. Dr. Hans-Goerg von Wick, as their counsel for the defence." He begged the Protecting Power in its "conferences with the proper American authorities, to point out this fact as well as the 62nd Article, paragraph I of the Geneva Convention, which assures POW defendants the right to choose their own counsel." The PWD merely instructed the State Department to remind the Protecting Power that Lt. Dr. von Wick's appointment had already been denied.[40]

Capt. Keller kept on trying to obtain justice for the men in his care, but that was out of the question. In Utah, Maj. Walsh could not allow them a competent defense, much less a German one. In Washington, high military bureaucrats were well aware that any hint of America's violation of Geneva by extorting confessions would compromise military intelligence, embarrass the government, and endanger GIs in German camps.

Six days before the trial, on August 9, the Swiss Legation would receive another sensitive complaint accusing the United States of violating eight provisions of the Geneva Convention. According to Capt.Wattenberg, the (former) commandant of Papago Park had refused to let him defend his "ever correct behavior as Camp Spokesman." After "unheard of insults," he had been placed in solitary confinement where he lacked "mental stimulus and distraction" and, worse, "the comradeship and society of my fellow officers." Germany would never treat an American officer of his rank in such a way, he said.[41]

Any such accusation was serious. Papago Park's new commandant, Col. William A. Holden, explained that Wattenberg's segregation was necessary "for the comfort and well-being of the rest of the prisoners" in camp, and that Geneva allowed such "special considerations." Capt. Keller also asked the legation to get Wattenberg transferred to some camp where an officer would be treated properly.[42] American authorities would regret leaving him at Papago Park. In December, he would mastermind one of the war's greatest mass POW escapes.[43]

Meanwhile, Werner Drechsler's death caused someone in Washington to at least consider ways of protecting discarded stool pigeons. On July 16, Col. Martin Tollefson, the PWD's assistant director, received a secret memorandum: Seven war prisoners had been charged with murdering an informer who had helped interrogate prisoners "at Meade or some other installation in this vicinity." "After his usefulness had been exhausted" this informer had been shipped to a camp containing "numerous Navy prisoners," who had recognized and murdered him. "This result could or should have been foreseen, to put it mildly." The author of the memo also mentioned those five former stool pigeons from Byron Hot Springs. They were "comparatively safe" in Nebraska. He recommended that "some arrangement" be made for the intelligence services to alert the PMG's Office whenever "prisoners who have assisted the American authorities" were sent to internment camps. "Under the present system, the responsible officers who are transferring such prisoners without taking any steps to provide for their safety are bringing about their deaths more rapidly and efficiently than our courts-martial are trying the murderers."[44]

When this memorandum reached the desk of Assistant PMG Bryan, he routed it back to the PWD's legal branch with a testy comment: "We cannot set up a camp especially for this type of person. If he is an anti-Nazi, send him to an anti-Nazi camp." Bryan added that he had "no objection to attempting" to keep such a POW safe, if G-2 would only "notify us as to who is an informant and who is not."[45]

The outcome, in early August, was a mild request from the PWD to G-2's Captured Personnel and Material Branch: In "a few instances," prisoners had taken reprisals against fellow POWs who had "assisted" the intelligence agencies. Would G-2 please notify the PMGO "when prisoners who have acted for American Intelligence are ready for release to normal imprisonment, in order that steps may be taken to safeguard them?"[46] A few days later, someone replied that G-2 considered such special notice unnecessary because "a high percentage of prisoners is giving information at this time"; but in case G-2 believed that an individual might be in danger, "your office will be advised."[47] The barn door was now closed.

CHAPTER 11

Judgment

The first POW murder trial, that of the Beyer Five, had been held at Camp Gruber, Oklahoma, in January 1944. This was where the crime had occurred. The seven-day-long court-martial had been attended by a prominent diplomat from the Swiss Legation, a "high-ranking officer of the Provost Marshal General's office," and several other Washington functionaries.[1] The seven sailors from Papago Park, however, were tried in an isolated corner of southern Arizona, in secret. They would be condemned in less than two days.

It took Cpl. Erwin Gruenebaum a week to travel by rail from central California to southern Arizona. He dragged all his possessions in two duffel bags because he thought "it was a permanent transfer." An NCO who descended from another car of the train with only "a shaving kit dangling off his little finger," asked him if he was "in the prisoner of war trial," too. It would only last a couple of days, said Sgt. Held. That was Gruenebaum's first inkling of his new assignment. He spent the next four days wilting in the heat, drinking sodas, and changing his clothes every two hours.[2] He finally met the defense counsel, Maj. Taylor, at "the same time I met the prisoners, when the trial opened" on August 15. He was immediately suspicious. "Even the stupid person could tell that it was nothing but a fake," he said fifty years later. "It looked fishy, it felt fishy. It smelled fishy. It bothered me all these years and I repressed it. I pushed it back like the concentration camps out of my mind." He soon found himself feeling "sorry for these kids," the defendants. He was surprised by their intelligence and their youth. "They were all give or take 20, 21, or 19. . . . They were Germans, they were enemies, they were—heck, . . . they were all kids. . . . I had no reason to love them, really. After all, my grandmother died, then my uncle died, then my aunts died." Still, he knew "those kids" were not Nazis. He also thought his own job was unnecessary because they "could speak English as well as you and I."[3]

These "kids" did not face a jury of their peers, but a board of judges. The president, infantry Col. Cassius Poust from the Presidio in San Francisco, was also Law Member, the only judge required to have any legal knowledge. His colleagues on the bench were five more colonels, two majors, and five captains.[4] "I never saw that many high-ranking officers," Gruenebaum said. He insisted that Poust was not a colonel but "definitely a general," and that Maj. William Taylor, the defense, was only a "stupid lieutenant" who was "panic stricken when he saw the court. . . . He was scared spitless. . . . All the brass arrayed against him! A whole United States Army . . . you know he was awed." Furthermore, Taylor "was the most inept person I say they could possibly have. . . . I don't even think he was a lawyer." His clients were not "overly impressed" by their defender, either.

Gruenebaum sat at the defense table with Taylor, translating whatever was said in court to the prisoners immediately behind him. He was sure that none of the judges knew German. They relied entirely on the official court translator, Capt. Oscar S. Schmidt. "He was a bastard, that one. . . . I was under the impression that he was an enforcer. . . . The way he spoke was all muscle. . . . I don't know, I just didn't like him."[5] He and Schmidt were sworn in together.

Next, Trial Judge Advocate Walsh asked each of the accused "whom he desired to introduce as counsel." Having no alternative, each named Taylor. The man they might have challenged with great cause, Capt. Schmidt, had already been installed.

After the court was sworn and Walsh had taken his oath as Trial Judge Advocate (TJA), he asked Col. Poust to warn everyone that the trial was secret. Then he set about establishing the corpus delicti: the fact that Drechsler had indeed been murdered. He entered into evidence a map of the camp, the noose, and photographs of the corpse and his bunk. On cross-examination, Taylor quibbled about the measurements of the shower room and the height of the bench beneath the noose.

Walsh called Capt. Hebbelthwaite, who described how he had taken custody of Drechsler at train side on March 12, fingerprinted his corpse, made the crime scene photographs, and preserved the noose. Taylor questioned the rope's authenticity and whether the puddles in the photographs were really blood. Then he asked: "Do you know whether or not [Drechsler] had ever aided the United States in giving information?" Yes, Hebblethwaite had heard about that, after Drechsler's death. Had he ever described Drechsler as doing the country "a lot of good"? Walsh objected: the question was incompetent, irrelevant, and immaterial. Although Taylor protested that this conversation "might have some bearing on the status of Drechsler as a traitor," President Poust sustained the prosecution. Taylor then complained that two of Drechsler's fingerprints were smudged.

Next, Capt. Claude Stafford enthusiastically described his autopsy of "a white, young male adult, blood all over the face, dead, of course," from strangulation. Taylor quibbled about the body's identity. Stafford replied that identification was not the point of the autopsy. When the other doctor, Capt. Max Marks, gave an even gorier account of Drechsler's wounds, Taylor merely asked about time of death.[6]

Next on the stand, Col. Gerald L. Church admitted that he, Zabel, and Walsh had investigated Drechsler's death. "Where was that investigation conducted?" asked Walsh. "You mean the place the board went?" Oh no, Walsh meant where it had begun investigating. After looking slowly around the courtroom at Walsh's invitation, "the witness walk[ed] over to the accused, pointing each one out as he stated their names." Had Church told these men—"for instance, Fischer"—anything when they appeared as witnesses? Yes, Church said. Through an interpreter each had heard AW 24, the guarantee against self-incrimination, and had been quizzed to make sure he understood. Only then had he been put under oath.

"After the accused Fischer testified before the board, what developed?" asked Walsh. Fischer had been given paper, pen, and ink and sent alone to his "room" to write out his statement. The next day, the board had reminded him again of his oath and his AW 24 rights, and asked whether that statement was in his own handwriting, with his own signature. "Then [*sic*] he was asked if he minded appending a statement to it, the gist of which was that it was a free and voluntary statement, and to sign it." Fischer had done so, after being assured that he might refer to "traitor" Drechsler rather than "Prisoner of War" Drechsler if he wished.[7]

Walsh then set about verifying the English translation of Fischer's confession so that it could be entered into evidence. "Colonel, who was the interpreter to the board at that time?" Church, misunderstanding, told the truth: Staff Sgt. Held, then quickly added that the board's interpreter, Sgt. Blank, had translated the document. Bringing Held's name into the record was potentially a bad error. The rules of cross-examination limited the defense to whatever was raised in direct testimony; but when his turn came Taylor would not be bright enough (or well enough informed) to seize the chance to clarify who this man Held might be.

Church gave the same testimony about the other six defendants. Otto Stengel, he noted, had testified more than once but had been reminded of his AW 24 rights each time. The colonel also made much of the fact that Stengel had signed the "certificate" affirming that he had confessed "freely and voluntarily, without duress."[8] After getting Church to repeat that each defendant had thoroughly understood his rights, Walsh asked: "Colonel, where were these Exhibits . . . received by the board?" Church replied: "At a secret military installation in the State of California."[9] This was the court's first inkling that all this willing statement writing and declaration signing had not occurred at Papago Park.

How was Taylor to inquire about a "secret military installation"? In wartime, one respected military secrecy. When he asked Church whether any of the defendants had been "interrogated by any other officer or person outside of your own board?" Walsh hotly objected. This was not proper cross-examination because Col. Church had only testified as to "the identification of certain exhibits." If the defense wanted to call Church later as its own witness, well and good. President Poust sustained Walsh again, over Taylor's protest.[10]

Taylor then asked Church:

> How did the board arrive at a point where statements were asked of the seven accused whom you have testified statements were made by?
> [Walsh:] Objection.
> [Court:] Sustained.
> [Taylor:] In what manner did the board eliminate some 100 other witnesses from the proceedings at the time these—
> [Walsh:] Objection.
> [Court:] Objection sustained.[11]

At least Taylor kept trying. "When the accused appeared before the board on the 2nd of June, what questions were asked them leading toward their making a statement?" Walsh objected again, "on the ground that the questions should be confined to each particular accused"! Taylor made another stab, and finally hit something:

> Q. Colonel, what witnesses appeared before your board on the 2nd of June?
> A. Otto Stengel. [He did not mention Siegfried Elser.]
> Q. What questions were propounded to him by you or other members of the board to establish or lead to his statement?

Church sidestepped: "The last time?" Walsh, who had no intention of presenting Stengel's first confession into evidence, intervened again: "Just a minute. May it please the court, the record of the board proceedings is the best evidence as to what questions were propounded by the board." This time Col. Poust ruled that Taylor's question was proper, but suggested that he should recall Church later, after Walsh had offered the board's proceedings as evidence. Of course, Walsh had no intention of doing that: "We don't feel it is necessary."

Then Poust told Church he "had better answer" to the best of his own knowledge. "Obviously I can't remember exactly," he said, but "substantially" Stengel had appeared before the board, been reminded of his oath and his AW 24 rights, and "told to tell all of the facts and circumstances within his knowledge concerning the hanging of Werner Drechsler." The board's only questions had been designed to clarify details. "Prior to the time the board convened, Prisoner of War Stengel had notified me through a guard that he wished to see me. He was brought to an interrogation room and said substantially 'I am guilty and want to confess. Will you convene the board?'"

Now even Maj. Taylor could force Church a step further:

Q. To your knowledge, had accused Prisoner of War Stengel been questioned prior to the time he make the statement that he wished to confess?

A. Yes, sir.

Q. To your knowledge, had coercion or violence ever been used?

A. Not within my presence.

Q. Do you have any information as to the use of coercion outside of your presence?

A. I have some information.

Taylor obliged Church to admit that Stengel "had been interrogated at considerable length by other persons than the board." When Taylor asked: "Was this interrogation done by proper authority or not?" Walsh objected. Now Poust was interested: "If [Church] knows he may answer it." Church waffled: "I am not sure I understand who is proper authority." Taylor meant anyone "who is authorized to issue orders or assigned the duty of interrogation." Walsh objected, to be overruled again. Church sidestepped. Was Taylor asking whether Stengel had been interrogated by "anyone with authority over the prisoner?" Taylor said yes, although that was not precisely what he had meant. Church was able to say that Stengel had been questioned by an authority.

Taylor moved a step closer: "Do you know what individual did the interrogating you have spoken of?" Again Walsh objected, but Poust was becoming annoyed as well as intrigued: "Colonel Church, pay strict attention to the questions. Don't presume to hearsay or anything of the sort. If you can't answer it of your own knowledge, say so." This gave Church an out: "I cannot answer of my own knowledge."

When Taylor asked, "Do you know of the methods used in the interrogation?" Church gave the same answer, then added: "But there is something that occurred to me. May I tell it now?" After Judge Poust warned him once more against hearsay, Church trailed a red herring: "Three of the defendants were, I guess you would call it interrogated," when "Leonardi Keeler, the lie detector expert," had applied his machine to "three of the defendants at various times," in Church's presence, at Papago Park in April or early May.[12]

The trick worked. Taylor dropped that promising line to ask, rather incoherently, if any defendant had been brought to confess by being shown Stengel's statement. (That would be highly improper, since a confession could not legally be used against anyone but the confessor himself.) Walsh objected: Taylor's question was too broad. He could not ask about all six as a group (though they were being tried as a group). Poust sustained him, so Taylor said: "I refer to the board which met on the eighth of June" (the date on which Kuelsen, Fischer, Reyak, and Franke had all confessed). "Objection sustained. Ask another question." Taylor seemed unable to single out one defendant. The prosecution called his attempts "incompetent, irrelevant and immaterial."[13]

Finally, after some kindly coaching from Poust, Taylor focused on Fischer. (This should have been a good choice, for the next day Fischer would say that his interrogators had shown him his two friends' confessions and told him it was no use to hold out. Taylor was too inept to make any use of that statement, or this response to another question: "Were you advised of your rights before the interrogation you just described?" "No." Taylor would drop the matter there, not even commenting on the fact that Fischer had obviously been threatened with genital torture.[14] The most charitable explanation is to assume that Taylor expected the court to take unsworn statements by enemy prisoners at face value.) But on that first day of the trial, Col. Church resolutely denied that *Stengel's* confession had been used to put pressure on Fischer. Painfully, question by question, Taylor got Church to say that he could not recall that anyone's confession had been used that way.

At last Church stepped down, permanently. Taylor never called him as his own witness, although Walsh had suggested it and Col. Poust had told him that this would allow him to grill Church on issues that Walsh had not brought forward.

The prosecution's next witness was Maj. Hermann Zabel, a former board member. He had made sure, he said, that each of the accused had understood his right, under AW 24, not to incriminate himself. He described the "certificates" each man had added to his statement. Walsh asked specifically about Stengel's and Wizuy's, establishing that neither of them (the worst-treated defendants) had complained to Zabel about ill treatment while signing statements to the effect that there had been none of it. Zabel volunteered that after signing his certificate, Wizuy had said: "How does the Major feel about being waited [in the officers' mess] upon by a murderer at Papago Park?"[15]

After a supper recess, Walsh gilded the lily. He asked Zabel to scrutinize Stengel's "certificate" and affirm that he had dictated the wording which the defendant had "signed of his own accord." Walsh had him read it aloud for good measure: "voluntarily written by me . . . without any offer of reward, threats, promises or duress of any kind whatsoever." Taylor asked Zabel, after some thrashing about, if he knew "of any coercive methods used upon [Stengel] or any of the other prisoners?" Zabel denied it before Walsh could object, so the president let the answer stand.[16]

Walsh called the board's interpreter, Sgt. Blank, to authenticate the translations.[17] By then, it was growing late. President Poust asked if the prosecution ever intended to introduce these confessions into evidence. He did, Walsh said, with the understanding that a late-arriving witness would provide "supporting proof in evidence" the next day. Then he proceeded to read every confession aloud, offering each in evidence "against the accused only . . . in the absence of any objection." Taylor made none at all.[18] Finally, at 9:00, the court adjourned.

The next day, August 15, Walsh's "supporting proof" turned out to be First Lt. Harry A. Baldwin, pretrial "investigator." He described each of his interviews with the defendants, always emphasizing how Sgt. Held (by name!) had informed each defendant, in German, of his rights. Again, Taylor sat dumbly while Walsh introduced Baldwin's transcripts as prosecution exhibits. The only question he could think to ask was whether Kuelsen had said: "Anyone would have to be on a sinking submarine to know the attitude of such a person toward a traitor who divulged Military information to the enemy." Baldwin replied that he had recorded the prisoner's every word. (He also repeatedly praised the work of his translator, Sgt. Held.)[19]

Since Walsh had failed to share Baldwin's transcripts with the defense beforehand, how was Taylor to know what they contained? Furthermore, Walsh did not immediately place them in evidence. What he did next was to take the stand himself while his assistant asked him whether he had advised the defendants of their right, under Geneva Article 62, to have a qualified counselor and interpreter of their own choosing! While Walsh made a production of presenting into evidence the prisoners' signed acknowledgments that he had formally so advised them,[20] Baldwin left town.

Only then did Walsh read each of Baldwin's transcripts aloud. This took most of that hot morning. Finally he presented them in evidence, while Taylor once more sat mute. Even if the defense had comprehended the trick Walsh was playing, Baldwin was unavailable for cross-examination.

After a break for lunch (and the president's stern reminder that "this is a secret proceedings"), Taylor began his defense by calling Staff Sgt. Paul Held, a most unfriendly witness. Held refused to identify himself except by name and rank. "I cannot reveal my organization by order of the War Department. I am sworn to secrecy." Taylor did get him to admit that he worked as an interpreter "at a Prisoner of War processing station and besides that at a secret installation which I cannot reveal." Yes, "sometimes" he had interpreted for the board. Had he been present at Otto Stengel's interrogation? "I was for a very short while but I interpreted all the board procedure, sir."[21]

The board's "procedure" was not the "interrogation" Taylor was trying to get at, but he failed to make this vital point clear to the court. Held did his best to keep the issue confused. When Taylor asked what officer had conducted Stengel's interrogation "on or about June first, 1944," he replied: "One of the officers of the board, sir. I could not remember his name." Taylor then asked him directly: "Were you present when Captain Schmidt conducted the interrogation?" Walsh immediately objected that Taylor had asked a leading question. President Poust sustained the point but offered Taylor a friendly hint: "Assuming that Captain Schmidt did some investigation and some questioning, first ask if he did any and then inquire into it." Walsh objected again when Taylor asked: "Did Captain Schmidt conduct any investigation at which you were present?" Poust overruled him. Held had to answer: "Yes, sir."

"Aside from interrogation, what other means were used in questioning Prisoner of War Stengel?" Held was vague. "Nothing as far as I can remember, sir. I was only there for a very short time . . . at the end. Very late in the evening. . . . Around 9:30." He could not say when Schmidt had begun interrogating Stengel.

When Taylor asked if Held noticed "anything about the manner of Prisoner of War Stengel's being dressed," Held was cornered. "I remember, sir, that he had an overcoat, sir"—but the weather had been "very cool" and the room unheated. No, he did not remember if the prisoner was sweating. Had Held seen or heard of "any third degree methods" being used there? "No, sir."[22]

Walsh objected again: Taylor was making a "highly improper" attack on "confessions already introduced in evidence." Poust overruled him, so Taylor kept fishing. Had Held questioned Stengel? No, he did not think so. Had he acted as an interpreter for Stengel at any other time than the June 1 incident? Yes, "before the board several times, sir, and before individual members of the board." (Since it would never be introduced into evidence, Taylor could not have known that the secret Board Report recorded only two sessions with Stengel.)

Taylor assumed that Held had been present during those "approximately 15 minutes" of Stengel's interrogation because Schmidt had called him to translate (though Schmidt, the court interpreter, obviously knew German). Taylor tried several times to make Held describe how and when he had been summoned. When Walsh objected, Poust was lenient: "Try not to ask leading questions. He is your witness."[23]

Taylor finally got Held to admit that he had been present during Schmidt's interrogation of Franke, Fischer, and also Wizuy for "maybe 15 minutes." Had he observed "any methods other than mere interrogation" used against Fischer? "No, sir." How had Fischer been dressed? "In his undershirt and shorts." Where had this occurred? "I cannot reveal the identity of the place."[24] In spite of this reminder that he was dealing with military secrets, Taylor kept laboring. Had Held noticed anything unusual when Schmidt had questioned Franke, Fischer, Wizuy, or Stengel? Held denied it (perhaps not considering third-degree methods unusual).

Had those four men been "warned of their rights under the Articles of War before being questioned or not?" Yes (though after some waffling Held admitted that he had not been present "in the beginning" with Stengel or Wizuy). He added that the board had drawn attention to Article 24, "at length in English and German, explanation and everything." But had Schmidt advised Franke and Fischer "of their rights under the Articles of War" when he had begun interrogating them? "Not in the beginning, sir." Had Held observed Stengel's physical condition while Schmidt was questioning him? "His physical condition was good, sir."[25]

Although Taylor surely knew that was a lie, he could think of nothing else to ask. Since Walsh had no desire to cross-examine, Held stepped down from the stand into oblivion. The court would never realize that this surly witness was the same man whom Lt. Baldwin had recently praised as his competent translator.

At least the court discovered, when Taylor called his next witness, that this "Schmidt" which Held had mentioned was its own official interpreter. He identified himself as "Oscar S. Schmidt, Captain, Air Corps, unit is secret." He admitted having seen all the defendants except Ludwig; but when Taylor asked if he recalled interrogating Stengel on or about June 1, and Walsh's objection was overruled, he took refuge in a poor memory. In his year on the job, he had dealt with too many men. He could not recall the date. Well, did Schmidt see Stengel dressed in an army overcoat? "I cannot answer that question, sir." When President Poust ordered him to answer, he said: "I am not allowed to divulge interrogation methods." When Poust ordered him again, his memory abandoned him. When Taylor asked if he had used "any forceful means or third degree methods in any way or in any form," Schmidt retorted: "What constitutes third degree methods?" When Poust ordered: "Answer. Yes or no," he claimed he had only "used ordinary interrogation methods," which he was "not allowed to divulge."

By that time, Poust was annoyed. He advised Taylor: "Ask him leading questions about what he did in this case."

Q. Is it not a fact that you did use a method upon Prisoner of War Otto Stengel which involved the use of a gas mask upon Prisoner of War Stengel?
A. Yes.
Q. Did you use a method which involved the use of an overcoat?
A. I think I did see an overcoat.
Q. In what manner was the gas mask used on Prisoner of War Otto Stengel?
A. I do not quite understand, sir.
Q. How was the use made of the gas mask?
A. It was put on his head and face and used in the ordinary manner.
Q. Was an onion used in the gas mask?
A. There was.[26]

And then Taylor quit. He did not attempt to show that this abuse had compelled Stengel to confess. He did not ask about Stengel's bad appendix or any other detail of his long ordeal. He asked nothing at all about Fischer or Wizuy. He simply quit. Since Walsh declined to cross-examine, Schmidt stepped down and simply resumed his official job.

Overestimating the impact which these snippets of fact had made upon the court, Taylor moved that Stengel's confession be stricken from the record. Motion denied. Then Taylor announced he would call Stengel to testify. President Poust ordered the defendants to stand and told them they had three options.

They could remain silent, and the court was not allowed to "indulge in any speculation whatsoever" about the guilt of a person who chose silence. They could swear to tell the truth, and then be cross-examined "with great latitude" by both prosecution and court. Finally, they could "make an unsworn statement in denial, extenuation or defense." In that case they could not be cross-examined, although the prosecution could present evidence or testimony in rebuttal. The court would give "such consideration . . . to your [unsworn] statement" as it deemed warranted.[27]

President Poust ordered Schmidt to translate this information to the prisoners. Then he asked each one: "Do you understand your rights under the warning just read to you?" Each answered "Yes." Poust did not inform these minimally educated young foreigners (or their defender) that giving unsworn statements "such consideration . . . as the court deems warranted" meant that the court might choose to ignore all or any part of them, because under American law they were not evidence. Perhaps the president's instruction gave Taylor the notion of having his clients make unsworn statements. Or perhaps he was honoring their own preference. German prisoners were strongly opposed to taking an oath. They were used to a legal system which forbade defendants to testify on oath, but which allowed them to make unsworn statements at the end of the trial.[28]

Whatever his motive, Taylor allowed only three of his seven clients to speak. Furthermore, he made no protest against the fact that their words would be translated by the very man whom they would accuse of torture. One can only imagine how Schmidt's presence made the defendants censor themselves, and how he muddied the waters. Mr. Gruenebaum believes that his translations were accurate. ("Every bit of what those kids said went to the court," but "it didn't make any difference. They weren't listening.")[29] However, the official transcript (recording Schmidt's words) reveals two interesting incidents. It has Stengel saying he was interrogated by "*a* captain who *was* acting as interpreter." He must have meant *the* captain who *is* acting as interpreter! And something about Schmidt's demeanor displeased President Poust: "Stand up and talk out loud so that everyone here can here you, interpreter. We don't want any whispered interpretation."[30]

How could the judges have failed to realize what was going on? Though they must have found those scant references to overcoat, gas mask, and onion very obscure, they knew that this man Schmidt had used them somehow while interrogating Stengel. Taylor had used the term "third degree" several times.

Stengel made his unsworn statement first. His ordeal "commenced with a ride of four hours at a speed I have never experienced," jolting over fields with a steel bar swinging around his head. His captors stopped only once, to ask if he were ready to confess. Walsh vigorously objected: This defendant was not making a statement in denial, explanation, or extenuation of the facts, as the *Manual for Courts-Martial* specified. This was "absolutely incompetent and should not be allowed." The president overruled him.[31]

Stengel continued: He was next made to "stand up in a corner quietly" (in a painful posture?) in the presence of two officers and "the captain who is here." A major came in to ask him to confess. When he would not, he was "closed in the car again and a much worse trip started." By then it was late afternoon. Having had nothing to eat, he "collapsed on the stairs coming back" so that a lieutenant and a guard "dragged me to the questioning." Stengel added: "At this time I always had appendectomy pains and I had a doctor with me in my room at all times."

When Stengel still resisted, he was taken on a third trip, and this time "left standing in the car while the mosquitos bit me and a Captain who was the interpreter" (or "*the* Captain who *is* the interpreter"?) sat in a restaurant for over two hours. Back at "the questioning camp" they loaded him down with "three heavy coats" in a steam-heated room. They tore his underwear open and burned his genitals against the radiator. "The American Captain" taunted him: "Will you confess now, or will we give you some more of Dachou treatment?" Then he had endured a gas mask filled with crushed garlic and onion, "about eight times until I collapsed unconscious."[32] The captain had yelled, "Do you want any more of that stuff?" but he had reached his limit. "I said no, it is enough for me. I wanted to talk to the Major. I want to give an oath." Then Zabel had come to his room with "the Sergeant" (Held?). By that time it was 4:30 in the morning.[33] Surely this statement drew a clear connection between torture and confession.

Had Stengel been advised of his rights before this interrogation had begun? Taylor asked. "Yes, I believe in Papago Park."[34] That "yes" obscured the fact that Schmidt had not done so at Byron Hot Springs, giving the lie to Walsh's careful claims.

When Taylor asked Stengel who had been present during his interrogation, Stengel said "Captain Schmidt and Sgt., what is his name?" Schmidt must have made some threatening movement, for President Poust felt called upon to warn the translator: "Don't carry on any conversations in German." Helmut Fischer, next on the stand, began speaking in English, whereupon Poust ruled—for who knows what reason—that it would be better to "continue the interrogation through the interpreter, instead of in English."[35] Perhaps because of what Schmidt had muttered in German, Fischer seemed reluctant to speak.

Taylor had to pick his statement out of him question by question.[36] Taylor asked Fischer: "Were you advised of anything pertaining to anyone who had confessed?" Yes, his interrogators had shown him the statements that Franke and Kuelsen had written.[37]

Then Fischer described how, beginning at 3:15 in the morning and lasting for nearly four hours, Schmidt had forced him to stand in various intolerable positions. On two occasions, Fischer had to cross his hands under the seat of his pants while "the present interpreter" stepped on them, forcing his body backward. "[In] this position I stood under continuous yelling of Captain Schmidt from about 5:00 o'clock until 6:30 in the morning." Schmidt had asked him if he knew "Dachou," and if he would like to be shown some things about it. Would he "like to see Hox, who was very little?" (not a reference to the chief quartermaster's height). He had also added that if Fischer's shorts bothered him, he should "denude" himself (a threat of genital torture). After Fischer had finally been left alone for a while, "shaking all over my body," the interpreter told him "that all the others had confessed and there would be no further use" to resist.

Taylor only asked:

> Were you advised of your rights before the interrogation you just described?
>
> A. No.
>
> Q. That's all.[38]

After a mid-afternoon break, Taylor called Rolf Wizuy, who described how he had been taken in the middle of the night to a small, dark, unfurnished cell. The next morning, when he refused to confess, he had a car ride like Stengel's, "in curves through ditches" with sudden stops. He, too, had been left baking in the sun while his tormentors relaxed over lunch. Then Schmidt and four others forced him to stand in painful positions without food or drink until 8:00 that night, while they kicked and prodded him. Schmidt "smelled after alcohol. His eyes were bloodshot." When they finally let Wizuy sit on the floor, a guard kept him awake all night. After this second sleepless night, he could take no more. "After that I was brought into another room and made statements. That's all."

Taylor asked a good question: How had this treatment affected Wizuy? He replied: "Captain Schmidt let me know that this condition would not change until I would talk. I did not have any help to make my rights as a Prisoner of War of value." Had Wizuy been told these rights before being questioned? Wizuy was precise: On the twentieth of April, at Papago Park, they had been mentioned. Schmidt had not done so.[39] (Later, two sets of reviewers, ignoring Wizuy's statement, would argue that there was no connection between the mistreatment and the confessions!)

Then, without comment, Taylor dismissed Wizuy from the stand and abruptly rested his case. Walsh slyly allowed him to make the first closing argument, revealing his cards. After a plea for fair treatment, Taylor read from the *Manual of Courts-Martial*: "An accused can not be convicted upon his unsupported confession. A court may not consider the confession of an accused as evidence against him unless there be in the record other evidence, either direct or circumstantial, that the offense charged has probably been committed; in other words, there must be evidence of the Corpus Delicti other than the confession itself."[40]

Incredibly, Taylor proceeded to challenge the corpus delicti! Two of Drechsler's three fingerprints had been smudged. The rope had not been "absolutely proved beyond a reasonable doubt" to have been "connected with the body of the deceased which is alleged to have died by the acts of the accused." Taylor wanted these items "stricken out and disregarded" as evidence. Only then did he get to the heart of the case, quoting again from the *Manual*:

> It must appear that the confession was voluntary on the part of the accused. . . . Facts indicating that a confession was induced by hope of benefit or fear of punishment or injury inspired by a person competent (or believed by the party confessing to be competent) to effectuate the hope or fear is . . . evidence that the confession was involuntary.

(So that was why Taylor had asked Col. Church whether the interrogation was "done by proper authority or not?")

The accused were prisoners, Taylor continued, "constantly under fear of punishment at any time." Therefore, "a threat made to a Prisoner of War might well have a stronger effect" on him than upon "an intelligent soldier of our own Army who knew his legal rights." True, the defendants had been read their rights, "at least in most cases"; but was that enough to give a war prisoner "full confidence" that he would "receive justice and . . . not be punished at the will of the threatening officer"?[41]

Taylor did not mention Lt. Baldwin, who had trapped his clients into incriminating themselves twice over. Nor did Taylor draw the court's attention to the extreme disparity between Stengel's, Fischer's, and Wizuy's accounts of how they were brought to confess and Church's pretty picture of amenable prisoners writing in their "rooms." He did emphasize that Schmidt had "definitely admitted" under oath to questioning Stengel while using an overcoat, a gas mask, and an onion. "Such methods are not countenanced." Stengel could not have confessed voluntarily because his "thoughts must have been influenced" by fear of having "to go through it again." Even though his motion to strike Stengel's confession had been rejected, "I plead with the court that if these methods were used in some cases, they could have been in all cases. In all probability, and beyond a reasonable doubt, perhaps [*sic*] they were used on all the accused."[42]

His seven clients were accused of first-degree murder with "malice aforethought" and of "unlawful" murder, that is, "without legal justification or excuse,"[43] Taylor continued. "Malice aforethought" meant "unlawful killing without mitigating circumstances." Certainly there were extenuating circumstances for the court to consider. In very convoluted language, Taylor suggested that the defendants' confessions proved that each had acted in the knowledge that Drechsler was a traitor serving their enemy.

Taylor presented an analogy: American prisoners of war in Germany were interrogated by a turncoat "acting on behalf of the German government." They refuse to give him military information "because they are loyal Americans." Later, this same soldier appears in their prison camp. Those misused Americans "become suddenly so bitter that that very night, knowing he had so divulged information which perhaps contributed directly to the death of other American soldiers and sailors, killed him." His German clients were just as bitter as "our soldiers" would be, Taylor said, and they had done what they believed to be their duty by executing a traitor who was still spying for their enemy. Unfortunately, Taylor had utterly failed to place any evidence into the record that Drechsler had, indeed, been a traitor in American pay.

Taylor ended by praising American justice, which the court had a "solemn responsibility" to uphold. "In this country, we do not inflict harsh punishment upon people, be they our people or Prisoners of War."[44] The summation was the best part of Taylor's case. Erwin Gruenebaum took credit for this sudden improvement: "I was the defense. . . . I kept saying to the lieutenant . . . our soldiers' oath requires us to do this. . . . I kept poking him. . . . I told my lieutenant, I said you tell the court that every American soldier would have done the very same thing because a soldier owes his life and he got up and . . . he did everything I told him. . . . The man had no idea . . . I don't think he was a lawyer."[45]

With or without help, Taylor was no match for Walsh, who thundered that although no one condoned treason, "neither you nor anyone can condone the treatment which was received by this poor boy before he was hung"—dragged screaming from his bed, beaten "unmercifully and cruelly," then tormented again before being carried "to a wash room where, gentlemen, there was a noose already prepared for his neck." His assassins had then gone home to sleep. "How can anyone argue that this was not cold blooded and premeditated?" And: "Gentlemen, you have seven confessions of those (pointing to the accused) seven Prisoners of War before you."

Then, despite Poust's remark that the court could not "indulge in any speculation whatsoever" about a witness who chose to remain silent, Walsh asked if there was "any evidence in this record" that "four of them—Franke, Kuelsen, Ludwig, and Reyak"—had confessed involuntarily? "No."

As for Otto Stengel, "he should have been a novelist. He is one of the greatest story tellers I have ever heard. . . . But, gentlemen," his "beautiful story" incriminated him. He had confessed under solemn oath and then, unsworn, had claimed he had been compelled to confess. The pretrial investigator had not used any force on Stengel! Furthermore, he had warned him

> fully of his rights and he couldn't tell his story fast enough. He bragged about it. . . . He came along this night and said "Boys, do you need any more help?" As a matter of fact, his story shows, and the stories of the other boys show beyond any contradiction that he was the motivating force behind some of the boys. Then he tries to say that the story was forced out of him by brutal treatment. I will tell you who received the brutal treatment in this case—the poor victim who didn't have a chance. He didn't have a prayer. Was it his fault he was brought into this Prisoner of War camp?

All war prisoners in the United States were subject to its laws, which his killers broke when they beat Drechsler, carried him off "partly by the hair of his head," and hanged him. Defense said they acted as German soldiers. Would real soldiers have "cruelly tortured" Werner Drechsler like that?

The Law Member would advise the court, Walsh said, that "any question about the invalidity of these three confessions" from Stengel, Fischer, and Wizuy "is absolutely cured by the confessions and statements" they later made to Lt. Baldwin.[46] As for their three unsworn statements, Walsh quoted Winthrop's classic *Military Law and Precedents:*[47] While "all due consideration" should be given to such a statement "properly presented, the statement is *not evidence* but a personal declaration of the defense, and cannot legally be acted upon as evidence by the court or the reviewing authority." (This was a misstatement. The court could consider such statements if it pleased.) Therefore, Walsh said, the fact that Held and Schmidt had mentioned an overcoat and a gas mask did not matter, because "anything done in that interrogation center was wiped out and cured when these men went before an Investigating Officer and reaffirmed their stories again." Since unsworn statements "can not be used as evidence, I say there is not one scintilla of evidence in this record to show that Wizuy, Reyak, Ludwig, Kuelsen, Franke and Fischer [he omitted Stengel] were compelled to tell their stories." Could anyone under coercion "really tell those beautiful but gruesome stories"?[48]

Then the thirteen judges retired to consider the case. By secret ballot, they promptly and unanimously decided that all seven defendants should be hanged by the neck until dead; but in the name of secrecy, President Poust "directed that the findings and sentence not be announced."

The fact that no sentence was pronounced "flabbergasted" Cpl. Gruenebaum. He had no doubt that the seven were guilty. "You didn't have to torture them. They were tickled pink to let you know. . . . They were proud of doing it, as I would have been proud under the same circumstances." Still, the secrecy of the sentence confirmed his belief that the trial was "a fake," which bothered him for fifty years.[49]

Walsh did not even disclose the verdict to the Commanding General of the Ninth Service Command, the reviewing authority, merely informing him that the trial was over.[50] The defendants themselves were not told. When they received carbon copies of the trial record on September 2, the verdict was left blank. Walsh did not even want the typists to know. He wrote the sentences by hand on each of two original copies. He sent one of these to the PMG and flew with the other to San Francisco to obtain the signatures of Poust and Taylor as president and defense counsel.[51]

One assumes that Taylor must have been dismayed to learn the verdict; however, at no time did he enter a plea for mercy. Such a plea might have touched the Secretary of War or the President, who had to approve all executions.

The case still had to face two judicial reviews, which would be based upon the court record alone. The first review, at the Service Command level, was no doubt conducted by reviewers who were as carefully chosen as the pretrial "investigator" and the defense had been. But at the Pentagon level, trained reviewers scrutinizing the documents might have noticed details that Taylor never had a chance to spot: for example, Franke had never made a "second" confession to Baldwin, and Baldwin had omitted to place Wizuy, Stengel,

Fischer, and Reyak under oath before they made theirs. At the Pentagon level, they might have spotted irregularities that Taylor lacked the wit to see, such as Sgt. Held's part in Baldwin's "investigation." They might have objected to Schmidt's double role. Such details might have made a difference.

CHAPTER 12

Fair and Intelligent Review

In 1946 Congress had to revise the Laws of War. According to the Vanderbilt Committee report, "the command frequently dominated the courts." Defenders "were often ineffective" for lack of knowledge and "a vigorous defense attitude." Sentences were often "excessively severe and sometimes fantastically so." Pretrial investigations "were frequently inefficient or inadequate." After the trial, the prosecution still exerted such control that "a fair and intelligent review" was impossible.[1] Nor were there any provisions for judicial appeal.

To be sure, Maj. Walsh had not found Lt. Baldwin's pretrial investigation "inadequate" for his purposes, nor Maj. Taylor too inexperienced, although the latter's "defense attitude" had been just vigorous enough to place inconvenient material in the trial record. The Ninth Service Command's JA staff benefited from the fact that the first reviewing power was the very commander for whom they had investigated the crime, convened the court, and prosecuted the case; nonetheless, the review that the staff would now compose and present to Gen. McCoach for his signature would not be an easy task.

The command's staff Judge Advocate, Col. Thomas J. White, not only had to justify the seven death sentences well enough to win approval with the Judge Advocate General's Office in Washington, which automatically reconsidered all General Court-Martial sentences. He also had to deal with a new judicial ruling that made nonsense of the Papago Park case. Furthermore, before the review was complete, Ninth Service Command would have a new reviewing power which favored mercy.

In June 1944 the *Bulletin of the Judge Advocate General of the Army* had digested a case in the European Theater in which a soldier named McDonald had been bullied into confessing a theft. A week later, he had confessed again to a pretrial investigator. The reviewers had rejected both confessions and overturned his sentence on the ground that McDonald had never been told that involuntary confessions were inadmissible in court. In confessing anew, he "may well have thought that he could not make his case worse than he already had made it." In effect, "the influence of the prior improper inducement" had tainted both confessions.[2]

The McDonald case decision was very unpopular. Field commanders had no use for legal niceties that interfered with a court-martial's primary purpose, discipline; and military lawyers always resisted constitutional limits.[3] Therefore, when Col. White read the McDonald trial transcript, he recognized a fine political opportunity. The reviewers in Utah calculated that the reviewers in Washington could be led to confirm the Papago Park sentences as a means of preventing McDonald from becoming a legal precedent.[4]

Col. White gave three assistants six days to write the review.[5] They began with a vivid description of Drechsler's corpse. They explained that his killers called him a traitor because he had "interviewed" them "at a previous station under an assumed name for the purpose of obtaining information for the detaining power."

The reviewers fairly paraphrased, without comment, the three unsworn statements, including Fischer's charge that he had not been advised of his rights before his ordeal and Wizuy's charge that Capt. Schmidt had told him "his condition would not change until he talked."[6] They also noted that Sgt. Held had mentioned seeing Stengel in an overcoat and Capt. Schmidt had referred to a gas mask with onion in it. Then the reviewers emphasized how carefully the investigating board had explained to each defendant his AW 24 right not to incriminate himself. Furthermore, each one had signed, without protest, "certificates" stating that they had not been coerced. Each one had "in effect confessed anew" to the pretrial investigator. Major Zabel had testified that he knew nothing of any coercion, and Col. Church that "he had no personal knowledge of any coercion being used on any of the accused, but that he had been informed as to its use outside of his presence in the case of accused Otto Stengel."

The reviewers then said they found "no errors, omissions or irregularities" in the trial procedure "injuriously affecting the substantial rights of the accused."[7] Though there had been "instances of the interpreter being improperly requested to make explanations to, or ask questions of, the accused," this was apparently a result of the court's "abundance of caution to assure that each accused understood his rights"; and since the defendants had "an interpreter of their own choice . . . no harm befell" them.[8] (The review did not mention that the court twice admonished this [un-named] interpreter for speaking to Stengel and Fischer before they made their unsworn statements.)

The command's reviewers also took care to explain three improper comments Walsh had made in his closing argument. First, he had said that Stengel's story showed "beyond contradiction that he was the motivating force behind some of these boys," improperly using one defendant's confession against another; but this must not have misled the court, which "had been carefully instructed" about the laws of confession. (The reviewers, like the court, ignored Fischer's description of how his interrogators had shown him his friends' confessions.) Walsh's second impropriety was to say that unsworn statements could not be considered as evidence. However, the court presumably "understood its prerogative" to consider them if it wished. (The reviewers had to presume. American judges leave no record of how they reach their verdicts, a practice so different from German procedure that it would cause much trouble later.)

Finally, Walsh improperly maintained that if there had really been any coercion, all seven prisoners would have spoken up. Defendants clearly had the right to remain silent. However, since Walsh had merely been commenting on the voluntary character of their confessions, not on their guilt or innocence, his error had not "injuriously affected the substantial rights of the accused."[9]

These reviewers also found the trial "refreshingly free of procedural errors." Using the official interpreter, Capt. Schmidt, as a witness for the defense was not an ideal situation; but since neither the prosecution nor the defense made any objection, there was "no impropriety" and the "substantial" rights of the accused were not "prejudicially affected." The reviewers ignored Schmidt's original role as inquisitor at some secret camp. They did not mention that Sgt. Held, who had testified to witnessing extremely odd methods of interrogation, had also translated the defendants' statements to the "impartial investigator" Baldwin. They did not challenge the claim that these statements were second confessions reinforcing those certified "first" confessions in the defendants' own handwriting. Therefore this evidence conclusively established the defendants' guilt.

The defense had neither objected to the confessions' being admitted into evidence nor asserted that the four silent prisoners (Reyak, Franke, Kuelsen, and Ludwig) had been coerced. As for Stengel, Fischer, and Wizuy, who had spoken, the reviewers admitted that "a somewhat different situation" existed in their cases. Each had attempted to imply, but had not expressly stated, that his confession was "improperly influenced."

The *Manual for Courts-Martial* gave "no hard and fast rules" for determining whether a confession was voluntary.[10] It could be presumed voluntary if nothing suggested that there should be "further inquiry as to the circumstances"; or if the accused stated that he had confessed "freely without hope of reward or fear of punishment"; or if "just before he made the confession" he had been told of his right to remain silent and informed that his words "might be used against him" (AW 24). Ignoring the fact that Oscar Schmidt had not read anyone his rights, the reviewers found it "apparent" that both the "first" and the "second" confessions were valid and "properly admitted in evidence."

Therefore, those three unsworn statements (which were not legal evidence) raised "only" two questions: Had the court been required, "as a matter of law," to investigate "the circumstances" under which Fischer, Stengel, and Wizuy had confessed? And had those three confessed voluntarily? Wharton's classic text on criminal evidence said there were no fixed rules.[11] If a first confession was coerced, the presumption in law was that a subsequent confession was also involuntary, unless there was "positive proof" that it was "free of the original improper inducement." It was generally assumed that improper influence was removed "where the accused is properly cautioned" before he confessed anew.[12]

Therefore, Fischer's alleged mistreatment was irrelevant. Sgt. Held had testified that "nothing unusual" had occurred at any time during his interrogation. The defense had not questioned Capt. Schmidt on this matter, nor objected when Fischer's confession had been introduced, nor moved to strike it from the record. In his unsworn statement, Fischer never even implied (via Schmidt) that the treatment he described had "influenced" his confession. In fact, if his unsworn statement "be assumed as factual," what had actually induced him to confess was having been told—"after all interrogations had ceased"—that holding out was useless because "all the others had confessed."[13] Since Fischer's first (written) and second confessions had obviously been voluntary, made in full knowledge of his rights, the court had not been obliged to inquire how they had been induced.

The reviewers applied the same reasoning to Wizuy. When Wizuy had described how Capt. Schmidt "drew his arms down and pressed his shoulder blades together," he had not (via Schmidt) complained "of being either frightened or hurt." Furthermore, Wizuy had confessed under oath but had complained unsworn. This fact had prevented the court "from asking clarifying questions" that might have shown "whether further inquiry is indicated." The court was "justified in attaching no weight" to Wizuy's words.

Stengel could not be dismissed so easily. He had said plainly that his tormentors frequently asked him to confess. There was some corroborating testimony. Schmidt had admitted to "seeing" an onion, a gas mask, and an overcoat. Nevertheless, "Stengel had at no time expressly stated" that he had confessed "under fear of further coercive action."[14] This could only be inferred from his unsworn statement![15] Furthermore, the defense had already allowed Stengel's even more detailed "second" confession to be placed in evidence, without protest. Lt. Baldwin gave "clear and convincing" evidence of using "extreme care and caution," during the pretrial investigation, to explain Stengel's rights. All this and "the absence of any person connected with obtaining the prior confession" [*sic*] demonstrated Stengel's "complete mental freedom." Even if one assumed that he had originally been coerced, any possible effects "had entirely ceased to exist" by the time of Baldwin's interview.

Now, turning to the McDonald case, the reviewers argued that it had no bearing at all. The Supreme Court had ruled that a second confession was valid when the accused had "mental freedom" at the time he made it.[16] If Stengel had not possessed such mental freedom, then "certainly he or his defense counsel" would have said so!

In conclusion, the reviewers said, the trial record proved "beyond all doubt" that all seven defendants had acted together with malice aforethought. Since "there is no plea of, or recommendation for, clemency appearing in the record," and since Drechsler had been killed in such a cold-blooded way, death by hanging was "eminently proper."[17]

White, the staff JA, now had to present this review to Ninth Service Command's newly appointed reviewing authority, Maj. Gen. William E. Shedd. His predecessor, Maj. Gen. McCoach, had taken Drechsler's murder as a personal insult; but Shedd favored mercy on the ground that no one would condemn GIs under similar circumstances for doing away with an American traitor! To placate him—and to dodge criticism for having brought seven patriotic German soldiers to trial on inadmissible evidence—White wrote a concurring opinion to the review which pretended sympathy for the defendants while justifying their execution.[18]

Drechsler, he began, "had given much information to the Armed Forces of the United States of apparent military value," which caused certain "devoutly loyal" German prisoners to judge him a traitor. Drechsler was "unfortunately" sent to Papago Park, a fact that his killers knew before he arrived. (The board had never found evidence of this, nor had the prosecution claimed it.) Drechsler's body "showed marks of a horrible beating before death brought him relief from his tortures." Maj. Gen. McCoach had remarked at the time that unless the perpetrators were identified, "murder in the United States may not necessarily be a crime"; and he had appointed an investigating board composed "of the most competent, skilled, and trained officers within the command." After two and a half months of "pitfalls, failures and disappointments," this board's labors were "crowned with success" when seven killers confessed.

Then, White claimed, his own office had made "searching inquiry as to whether the confessions were obtained in a lawful manner." Only after finding them "free and voluntary" had he recommended trial. Although some of his "thoroughly qualified and experienced officers" had disagreed about "several complex legal questions" in the trial record, the three senior staff members who reviewed the trial had unanimously supported the death sentences.

Four of the seven defendants posed no problem at all, for their "certificates" showed that they had freely confessed. Defense had not hinted otherwise "until almost at the close of the trial," nor had he called them to the stand. Although Trial Judge Advocate Walsh's efforts to prove that the other three had also confessed voluntarily were "somewhat short of that desired," these men had also signed and certified that they had acted freely, without threat. Therefore all seven confessions "met the minimum legal requirements." White implied that Taylor must have agreed, since he had not objected to their admission into evidence.

White did admit that Wizuy's, Stengel's, and Fischer's unsworn statements contained allegations "casting the gravest doubt" upon their admissibility. In fact, White was inclined "to say that there had been an utter disregard of that fundamental fairness essential to the very concept of justice"— but cold facts had forced him to stifle this "fleeting thought." The court had been free to take whatever notice of these unsworn statements it saw fit, and it had taken none at all. White was "most reluctant" to cast doubt on the decision of such richly experienced and distinguished American officers.

In order "to do substantial justice," White continued, POWs had to be treated exactly like American soldiers. "Here lies an opportunity to prove by deed and act" the superiority of the American system. "We have no right to question" the patriotism of any man imprisoned for his military service. "These men are strangers in a strange land. They have been separated from their armies, and . . . from the system of justice to which they are accustomed." Therefore, one should not simply assume that because Stengel, Fischer, and Wizuy had failed "to insist upon the right" to speak under oath, they were rejecting the right to testify. Nor was it enough to say the accused had all been "fully advised of their rights." A "realm of doubt" remained, even though their defense counsel, "who was skilled in the law, undoubtedly advised them to make unsworn statements." Therefore, Col. White continued, "legal support for these confessions must be found by some other process of reasoning."

Neither Fischer, nor Stengel, nor Wizuy had claimed that his confession was untrue, nor had anyone denied his guilt. This was "persuasive but not conclusive," since guilt and admissibility were different matters. Then—with great hypocrisy, since he had undoubtedly helped Walsh, the chief of his own office's Military Justice Branch, to devise his courtroom tactics—White resorted to the cozy scenario that Church and Zabel had painted under oath: Each defendant, after hearing his rights thoroughly explained (via Held or Schmidt), had obligingly confessed and, when the board had politely asked him to do so, had retired to his private "room" to write down his misdeeds. When asked "if he minded" certifying that he had written "freely and voluntarily," without promises, threats, or duress, each had willingly complied. The record thus showed that Fischer, Stengel, and Wizuy had confessed in exactly the same way as the other four.

Therefore, White concluded, "whatever the means of inducing a desire to confess, those restraints and compulsions were terminated" when Fischer, Stengel, and Wizuy were each sent to his room. There was no indication, White said (ignoring Stengel and Wizuy again), that they had been "told to confess a part of this crime." In fact, all seven defendants (captives in a strange land, under unknown laws) had been "as welcome" to proclaim their innocence as to confess to the execution of "the deceased traitor." Since each had written whatever he chose "in absolute privacy," then "the effect of prior coercion was dissipated through the lapse of time and circumstances." Therefore every one of the "first" confessions had been "free and voluntary."

Furthermore, White continued, all the defendants (except the unnoticed Fritz Franke) had confessed again one month later to First Lt. Baldwin, a man "whose legal views and commendable sense of justice are well recognized," who had been named investigator "because of his experience, skills, training and liberal views," and whose testimony showed how scrupulously, with what "exemplary care," he had read them their rights. In fact, "I know of no instance where an American soldier has been so carefully and so fully informed" of them.

In spite of Baldwin's warnings, Stengel, Wizuy, and Fischer had not only reaffirmed their previous confessions but had given "additional details and explanations." White shed some crocodile tears: "It would be a most happy conclusion" if one were able to say that these second confessions were as inadmissible as McDonald's, whose pretrial investigator had not informed him that his first confession was not admissible in court, leading him to assume that he might as well talk because the harm was already done. Too bad, White argued, that the two cases could not be compared!

The Judge Advocate General, White said, had never meant to "lay down . . . an iron clad rule" that a prisoner should be warned that the only proof against him was invalid, that he then be asked for a fresh confession so that one could "legally request the stretching of the neck until life departed." White declared that he longed to follow "the dictates of [his] conscience" and mercifully set aside all the confessions, but the Law would not allow him.

The facts spoke for themselves, said White. If Fischer's, Stengel's, and Wizuy's first confessions were good, the second ones were "only superfluous . . . evidence," a mere procedural error. If the first were questionable, then the second ones, made freely and voluntarily, were nevertheless "adequate for all purposes. We either have too much in the record or just enough, whichever view may be taken." Therefore, White continued, certain other troublesome aspects of the case were now nearly irrelevant. The fact that Taylor sat "idly by without objection" when the confessions were introduced "only served to mislead the Trial Judge Advocate and complicate the record"! If Walsh had only known that Taylor would later question the confessions, he "no doubt would have made a more presentable and readable record." He could have "introduced rebuttal testimony to counteract the effect" of these three unsworn statements. On the other hand, Walsh had wished to avoid unnecessary controversy, which would only lengthen a trial record that was so impressively sufficient.

White meant no criticism of Maj. Taylor, he said. Taylor had "made the best defense possible," within the limits of his conscience, his sense of justice, and the law. "He even sought to influence the court by pointing out that it may well be the duty of every soldier to treat a traitor as such." Indeed, White claimed, he himself entertained "an almost conscientious objection to the imposition of the death penalty upon a soldier who murders a fellow soldier known to be a traitor." Even though "legalized murder in these United States cannot be countenanced," White still wondered if, in such circumstances, his "own natural self-restraint" would give way to "hatred and contempt for a fellow soldier who betrayed [him]and [his] comrades in arms."

White would, if only he could, recommend that his new commanding general commute the sentences to life imprisonment; but, alas, the general was "powerless" to take that advice. "He can only recommend" mercy to those who had the power to grant it[19]—someone further up the chain of command.

Gen. Shedd took his staff JA's legal advice. He accepted the review and White's brief, both of which ignored, denied, or explained away any ground for clemency, with this terse comment: "The sentence of each accused is approved and the record of trial is forwarded for action . . . with the recommendation that the sentence of each of the accused be commuted to life imprisonment."[20] These three documents were laid atop the trial record and forwarded to the Pentagon.[21]

Less than a week later, Maj. Walsh found himself in hot water. Former president Poust informed Gen. Shedd that Maj. Taylor believed that Walsh might have altered the trial record after he and Poust had signed it. Walsh had asked two staff JA officers in California whether they thought he had "committed reversible error in his closing argument by commenting upon the fact that some of the accused had failed to take the stand." (Reversible error would nullify the trial.) When these officers had said it was "a close question," Walsh had said that "if there were any doubt . . . he would have the pages showing his closing argument rewritten."[22]

Walsh frantically telephoned Poust, the two staffers, and a fourth official who called Gen. Shedd's chief of staff to say that although Walsh denied changing anything, "these people were still unsatisfied." Poust felt "a little bit shaky about it," the officer said, but thought "he would have to make some report of it because the Defense Counsel knows" about the matter. Poust was "afraid he will be kind of criticized."[23] Then someone at headquarters recalled that the newly written review had called Walsh's remark improper, but not an error. Walsh took an oath that he had not tampered with the record and that ended the matter.[24] White never informed the Judge Advocate General's Office about it.

In Washington, the Judge Advocate General's reviewers might well have honored Gen. Shedd's plea for mercy. It was common practice "in World War II for court-martial panels to administer stupefyingly heavy sentences and then leave it up to 'the old man' to cut them down to whatever dimensions and shape he envisioned justice to be."[25] But this was not an ordinary case.

In 1944 JAG review boards examined eighteen thousand courts-martial involving dismissal, discharge, jail time, and death. Normally, they could review a case for legal sufficiency and clemency recommendations within twenty-four hours.[26] Review Board No. 2 (Col. Terry A. Lyon, chairman, Col. Earle Hepburn, and Maj. Hermann Moyse) spent a month and a half on the Papago Park case.[27] According to Whittingham, these three even traveled to Utah to confer with Ninth Service Command personnel.[28] Their review was even longer than the Ninth Service Command's, although they repeated only one of its paragraphs.[29] They used different arguments. The Pentagon had its own agendas.

Drechsler, the JAG reviewers said, had come to Papago Park from "another prisoner of war camp in America, referred to as an interrogation center."[30] His killers' trial appeared "to have been held in closed session, without objection on the part of the defense"! After consulting Col. Archibald King, Chief of the JAG War Plans Division, an expert on international law,[31] the reviewers certified that this trial complied with Geneva Articles 60 and 64: the Protecting Power had been advised of the trial and the defendants of their right to choose their own defender and interpreter.

The JAG reviewers never questioned the myth propagated by the prosecution, that after the board's gentlemanly interrogation, the defendants had willingly confessed, orally and in writing, and had voluntarily certified that there had been no "threats, promises or duress of any kind whatsoever."[32] The reviewers praised Church's use of several interpreters as proof of his scrupulous care to be exact in two languages. They praised Baldwin's pretrial investigation "with the assistance of a competent (and nameless) interpreter." After the lieutenant had fully informed the defendants of their rights, they had neither denied their guilt nor mentioned coercion. Each had "acknowledged" to Baldwin his first confession "unequivocally." Most had "made additions" to it.

Since none of the accused had repudiated his confession, the case for the defense had no merit. However, because Gen. Shedd had recommended mercy, the JAG reviewers quoted what each defendant had said to Baldwin in his own defense—which caused them to note that Franke had never made a "second" statement.[33]

As for the first confessions, since "the voluntary nature of some" of them had been "at least inferentially" questioned at the trial, and since this was "the only feature of the case" upon which defense had presented any testimony, "the insinuation of improper pressure . . . may not merit but does require consideration." The JAG board "considered" the matter by reviewing the American officers' testimony: Col. Church swore that no coercion had been used against Stengel in his presence, though he admitted knowing that someone else had questioned the prisoners "at considerable length." Sgt. Held had never heard of any third-degree methods, though he had recalled seeing Stengel in "good" condition, wearing an overcoat in a "very cool" room, and seeing Fischer clad only in his underwear. Capt. Schmidt had denied, then recalled seeing Stengel with "an overcoat in connection with" an interrogation method. The captain had worked on too many cases to remember details of "one individual" instance. A gas mask had been used "in the ordinary manner." Schmidt had stated on oath that he never used anything but "ordinary interrogation methods," of which he was forbidden to speak.[34]

Next, the JAG reviewers scrutinized Stengel's, Fischer's, and Wizuy's unsworn statements in detail, even noting how Stengel had described calling for a board member when, after recovering his senses, "the captain" had threatened him with "more of that stuff." They did not identify this captain. They also repeated, without comment, Fischer's statement that he had not been "advised or warned of his rights" before interrogation, and noted that both Fischer and Wizuy named Schmidt as their interrogator. (The reviewers ignored Held.)[35]

Then the JAG reviewers proceeded to reject every statement made by these three German enlisted men. The record conclusively showed, they said, that all seven defendants had confessed to "a heartless, cold-blooded, premeditated murder, without legal justification or excuse," the worst example of individuals taking the law into their own hands. They had planned every detail. Acting on "rumor and inference," without giving their victim "even the semblance of a hearing or the right of explanation," these "self-appointed judges, court and executioners," pausing only for fear of detection, had mercilessly manhandled their begging, bloodied prey to the noose. The defense claim that they acted from "high motives of patriotism" was a "striking lack of excuse," based upon the assumption that "traitorous conduct justifies the summary execution of the offender by a self-appointed tribunal." Only a legally constituted court could impose a death penalty. Certainly no one would "grant this extraordinary and dangerous authority to prisoners of war." These men had hanged Drechsler for merely rumored treason, "such a flagrant violation" of the laws of the Detaining Power that it "cannot be condoned."[36]

Then, incredibly, the JAG board transformed Drechsler, the failed snitch, into a suffering saint! "Instead of being a traitor to his country, deceased may have been an outstanding patriot, whose very actions may have been governed by secret instructions given him by his government."

It seems impossible that these JAG reviewers could believe this taradiddle, but (aside from its probable appeal to Secretary of War Stimson's personal notions of justice) the image of Drechsler as "outstanding patriot" also served two fine casuistical purposes. First, if he were not a traitor, then he was the pitiful victim of depraved, cold-blooded killers who deserved to die. Second, the JAG reviewers had to defend the United States from any hint of violating international law. They found it "worthy to note" that the Geneva Convention bound the Detaining Power to protect its prisoners against "violence, insults and public curiosity." Therefore, war prisoners must be punished for harming each other "because of some real or fancied wrong." In other words Drechsler had to be defended, postmortem.

The JAG reviewers took scant notice of Ninth Service Command's labored arguments that the first confessions were admissible evidence. "Nothing in the record" overcame "the convincing proof" that they had been voluntary—this "proof" being the certificates, the "subsequent confessions," and defense counsel's failure to object to their admission into evidence. Therefore, there was "not the slightest suggestion in the record" that either *Church* or *Baldwin* had used improper methods. "On the contrary, insofar as the record is concerned," those two American officers had used "the highest degree of care and consideration, probably unparalleled in any record of trial of an American soldier," to make sure the accused understood their rights.

Without even breaking a paragraph, the JAG reviewers noted that Church had said he knew the seven had been interrogated by others "prior to their confessions to the board;" that Held had seen Stengel wearing an overcoat "in cold weather in an unheated room" (in June in California!); that Schmidt had "acknowledged" the use of an overcoat and a gas mask with an onion in it. However, "there was no testimony to show that any of these methods" had induced Stengel to confess! The *inference* that one defendant, Stengel, was on one occasion "subjected to treatment which, had it produced a confession, would have rendered that confession inadmissible, was more than offset by the declarations subsequently made by this accused."[37]

The JAG reviewers dismissed the unsworn statements out of hand. They were not legal evidence. Furthermore, proper unsworn statements were offered in "denial, explanation or extenuation of the offenses charged." Stengel, Wizuy, and Fischer had spoken "solely to the *alleged events* preceding, at a time not definitely fixed, their first confessions."[38] For good measure, the reviewers added three pages of legal opinions about the unsworn statements. Then they found a third reason for ignoring these examples: The court, had it believed these POWs, was "empowered to call additional witnesses." It did not do so. Ergo, their statements were not believable. The record established "beyond any reasonable doubt that even though some of the accused may have been subjected to severe interrogation at some time prior to their appearance before the board of officers," their confessions "were unaffected by any prior grilling they may have received. To hold otherwise would be to consider as unworthy of belief Colonel Church and Major Zabel and to disregard the solemn certificates voluntarily signed by the accused." In conclusion, the defendants deserved to hang.[39]

As a matter of fact, the review board had not reached this conclusion easily. The two senior members, Cols. Lyon and Hepburn, had favored commuting the sentences to life in prison. Only Maj. Moyse, who wrote the review, had wanted to hang them. How had he prevailed over his superiors?

The officer who stood between the review board and Judge Advocate General Cramer was Col. William A. Rounds, Assistant JAG for Military Justice. He also favored hanging.[40] So did Col. Archibald King, Chief of the JAG Office's War Plans Division and resident expert on the Geneva Convention. Even so, Col. King sent Col. Rounds a long brief criticizing the review board's work so sharply that Maj. Moyse had to write a rebuttal.[41] Both of these documents became part of the trial records.[42]

Col. King's brief stripped away pretenses. The record, he said, contained "clear indication" that Geneva articles had been violated. Capt. Oscar S. Schmidt, who had inflicted "various tortures and indignities upon Stengel, had been "used improperly as court interpreter," translating "those statements of his own misconduct for the record." Wizuy and Fischer described how Schmidt had used "nearly as severe methods" on them "in seeking to obtain their confessions." Therefore it was, indeed, "possible that the original confessions of the other four accused were similarly extorted." Schmidt admitted having interrogated them all, "except perhaps Ludwig," on behalf of Col. Church's investigating board. He had taken them to the board when they had "signified their willingness to 'talk.'" Because of this "close connection," Stengel "certainly . . . and perhaps some or all of the other accused, might reasonably be considered to have been 'obliged to admit themselves guilty' in violation of Article 61 of the Convention." They might also reasonably be presumed to have "certified that they signed 'voluntarily' while actually still under [the influence of] improper persuasions."[43]

King's honesty was unique, yet even he considered the "second confessions" extracted by Lt. Baldwin to be valid. He pointed out that the defendants had made them "nearly a full month" later, after Lt. Baldwin "very fully" informed them of their right to remain silent. Since each man had nevertheless declared that his former confession was true, it was therefore "abundantly clear" that "any prior unlawful inducement to confess had . . . been wholly dispersed by the passage of time" and by Baldwin's "very full warnings." Not even Col. King noticed Sgt. Held's intimidating presence.

Although King supported the death sentences, he also pointed out that a fundamental right, such as being judged upon valid evidence, "is not abandoned by mere silence," as Walsh had maintained when referring to Taylor's silence as the confessions were introduced.[44] Furthermore, King proposed that Geneva Article 61 might "require that the Investigating Officer, in addition to his other warnings, inform the accused that it was doubtful whether their previous confessions could be used against them," just as Wharton's *Criminal Evidence* required. King also pointed out that since Geneva required

POWs to be treated "like our own soldiers," American case law applied. Under American domestic law, a conviction based only upon a coerced confession could not stand. Nevertheless, a conviction based on other evidence was valid in spite of any coercion. Ignoring the possibility that the defendants would not have confessed anew if the investigator had warned them, King found that "other evidence" in their "later, voluntary confessions" to Baldwin. Therefore, King opined that each defendant had been convicted upon statements which he had not been, "in any legal sense, 'obliged to utter.'"[45]

King's next arguments reveal that his primary aim was to prevent the McDonald ruling from becoming a legal precedent. Since McDonald had gone free under Wharton's rule, King argued that this revered expert was wrong. The cases cited by this authority in his classic *Criminal Evidence* did not support his "unfortunate statement" that the accused must be told that his involuntary confession was useless in court. American case law had rightly ignored his dictum,[46] for it had judged every case but one (McDonald's) by its individual circumstances. Therefore there was no general rule requiring that the accused be told his prior confession might be worthless, provided that the effects of "improper inducement" had dissipated when he gave a second statement.[47] This was true in the Papago Park case but possibly not in McDonald's, who had made his second confession very soon after his "earlier, involuntary" one and who was "described as being 'pretty easily led.'" The JAG Bulletin should make it clear that the McDonald opinion had not set a legal precedent.[48]

However, King added, interrogating officers should not feel invited to force offenders to bear witness against themselves and then proceed to convict them by deliberately inducing a second confession. Physical torture was "a vicious throwback to medieval cruelty," particularly reprehensible when applied to POWs. It violated Geneva Articles 2 and 3, which granted them "protection and respect of their persons." It also employed "in the name of the United States practices which we condemn in our enemies."[49] It was morally repulsive.

King also attacked Capt. Schmidt's "contumacious" (perversely rebellious) attitude when called to the stand, where he had finally admitted, under oath, to torturing Stengel by what he called "ordinary" methods. King therefore demanded that "the interrogations of all the accused" be investigated "with a view to possible disciplinary action," because there were also "indications in the record of trial that personnel of Ninth Service Command Headquarters may possibly share [Schmidt's] responsibility." He strongly recommended that when the Judge Advocate General drafted recommendations that would accompany the trial documents to the Secretary of War, he should point out exactly where the record showed that U.S. Army personnel had tortured confessions from one or more of the defendants, in violation of Geneva and of Articles of War 2, 3, and 61. Moreover, these recommendations should add that he, Col. King, recommended investigation and punishment.[50]

But first, King said, Gen. Shedd should receive a letter criticizing Capt. Schmidt's role at the trial. An interpreter should be wholly disinterested, not a witness or "a person whose actions were a subject of dispute." The letter might also comment on Schmidt's "presumption in refusing to answer questions," and ask whether anyone at Ninth Service Command had authorized that refusal. (He seemed unaware that Schmidt answered to G-2).

In addition, King recommended that the Judge Advocate General, through his superior the Commanding General of the Army Service Forces, investigate the "interrogations of these accused, with a view to possible disciplinary action against Captain Schmidt and others" at Ninth Service Command headquarters. Furthermore, "the Inspector General, U.S. Army rather than the Inspector General, Ninth Service Command" should carry out this inquiry "as soon as possible in order to obtain the testimony of the accused" before they were hanged. If necessary, the executions should be postponed.

Postponement was all King would consider. In spite of everything, he rejected the notion of mercy. Though the defendants probably believed Drechsler was a traitor, they had cold-bloodedly conspired to take the law into their own hands "without the semblance of a trial," thereby committing the "very sort of fanatical terrorism that must be suppressed in prisoner of war camps." Unless such murderers were severely punished, the United States would stand in violation of Article 2 of the Geneva Convention, which bound the Custodial Power to protect prisoners against violence.[51]

When Maj. Moyse, the only reviewer who favored execution, wrote a response to Col. King's brief, addressed to Col. Rounds, he said that he and his colleagues had three reasons for deciding not to use the Papago Park case to modify the McDonald ruling. They feared that "interested persons" might get the "unwarranted" idea that POWs were being held to a harsher standard than American soldiers. They judged the issue to be outside their jurisdiction. Finally, the matter seemed irrelevant since, as King agreed, there was "no indication in the record" of any coercive measures against the Papago Park seven, and since their confessions to Baldwin were definitely admissible.[52]

Notably, Moyse's response to King ignored the nearly ten pages he had devoted to Schmidt's use of torture. As for King's criticism of Schmidt's role as court interpreter, Moyse remarked that the captain could not have known, when appointed translator for the trial, that he would be called to testify. No harm was done because he was a defense witness and the defendants had their own translator. Furthermore, Schmidt had only hinted that "at some stage during the long drawn out investigation, which covered a period of approximately two and a half months, [the] accused Stengel was subjected to physical discomfort while being interrogated on one occasion."[53] Since (ignoring the unsworn statements) there was "no evidence of record" that "improper methods" were used, there was therefore nothing for the Inspector General to investigate.

King's brief and Moyse's rebuttal, totaling over fifty single-spaced legal pages, now occupied the top layer of the stack of trial records. They provided two different reasons for upholding the guilty verdict and the death sentences. Review Board No. 2 had warned that if the killers were not punished, the United States might be criticized for condoning lynch law. King, on the other hand, prophesied that it "might prove embarrassing to the United States Government in the event that the accused were executed."[54]

It remained to be seen what Judge Advocate General Myron C. Cramer would do with this mountain of documents that Col. Rounds handed him. Cramer's task was to study the case and to send his recommendation, death or mercy, to Secretary of War Henry Stimson. In turn, Stimson would advise President Roosevelt whether or not to sign the death warrants. Mercy was still possible, if unlikely.

CHAPTER 13

Coddling and Confirmation

A number of things made mercy for "Nazi terrorists" unlikely. A third of the prisoners taken in the six months since D-Day had been brought over at the request of labor-hungry government agencies. By December 1944 there were 305,648 Germans in American camps, up from 150,000 in June.[1] The Pentagon therefore feared Nazi influence more than ever.

Red Cross reports of the serious mistreatment of GIs in German POW camps also made mercy increasingly dubious. In September, Secretary of War Stimson had ordered JAG Cramer to set up an interagency committee to consider how to prosecute Axis "cruelties, atrocities, and acts of aggression" against American armed forces,[2] an effort that led eventually to the Nuremberg War Crimes Trials. Although most reports about mistreated GIs would be kept out of the press until the spring of 1945,[3] in December 1944 everyone knew that American prisoners had been machine-gunned at Malmedy during the Battle of the Bulge, a brief but frightening renaissance of Nazi power.

In addition, public outrage refueled the protracted "coddling crisis." The War Department considered food to be "the most vexatious prisoner of war problem in the United States."[4] Americans, increasingly pinched by rationing, complained that enemy prisoners were gorging on meat, smoking free cigarettes, and partying over here while GIs died for freedom over there. Some critics also accused the Army of ignoring a fine chance to reeducate Nazis into good freedom-loving democrats. Others railed against the notion that these Nazis were allowed to terrorize their "coddled" fellow prisoners.

The War Department thoroughly investigated every citizen complaint. Every letter received a personal reply. Both the War and State Departments issued public explanations and denials of such charges.[5] They did little good. Repeatedly, some newspaper or radio commentator or veterans' organization[6] would make accusations that would be echoed in the French and Russian press.[7] Two such attacks particularly displeased the War Department.

Walter Winchell, the Rush Limbaugh of his day, was a constant problem. In early 1944 an officer conducting a seminar for POW personnel in the Eighth Service Command ordered them to straighten up, because Winchell had flooded the commanding general "with complaints from Washington and from prominent citizens [all] over the Service Command." He added, "the wires from Washington were hot" the day after Winchell's broadcast skewered incompetent guards. "We have to find a solution and get off the spot."[8]

Walter Winchell outdid himself on March 5, 1944, when he revealed a pathetic scandal at Camp Breckinridge, Kentucky. "Attention Mr. and Mrs. United States and General George Marshall" (the Army Chief of Staff): "The following exposé is without qualification one of the most serious and dangerous conditions ever to exist within the United States." In American camps, the Gestapo was training prisoners "as Nazi battalions . . . to take over Germany when they are returned. General Marshall, I respectfully submit to you, sir, that some of our American officers in charge of these prisoners do not even understand the German language." At one Kentucky camp, "an American colonel had led a parade of 300 German soldiers," completely unaware that they were singing out "insults to this country and our allies." These singers were "the nucleus of the next world war, an underground Nazi army [which] is here in full force . . . under the protective custody of American officers who do not realize what is going on right under their noses."[9]

The facts, which emerged when the PMG's Office ordered the Fifth Service Command's Inspector General to investigate, were nearly as bizarre as those in Winchell's broadcast: At Camp Breckenridge, Kentucky, both Nazis and anti-Nazis had been quartered in the same compound, though in separate barracks. Col. Winlock, the well-meaning, non–German-speaking World War I veteran in charge, decided that a dose of religion would improve their morale and behavior, particularly if he set a good example by attending church with them. He arranged a church parade for Sunday, January 12, 1944, from the camp to an unused post chapel more than a mile away.

That sabbath, about three hundred Nazis turned out for church. The anti-Nazis, being disinclined to pray with Hitlerites, did not show up. Col. Winlock, however, saw nothing but a smartly uniformed column of threes. He had intended to see his prisoners off, then ride ahead to the chapel. His car was late, so he decided to march along in front of his fine prisoners, enjoying their band music and their enthusiastic singing. In spite of what some critics said later, the colonel did not goose step to Lutheran services.

Winlock was so well pleased with his project that he planned a Mass for the next Sunday. That day, however, the anti-Nazis also showed up for church parade—in fatigues, since most of them had thrown their German uniforms away. This improper dress so offended the Nazis that they refused to march. Mass had to be canceled. Later, the anti-Nazi company's spokesman told the astounded colonel that those smart-marching Nazis had not been singing hymns the week before, but "hate songs." Until then, Winlock told the Inspector General, "I always considered that when a song had 'hi-le hi-lo' in it, it was jovial."[10]

The sequel was equally bizarre. The anti-Nazi prisoners at Breckinridge wrote fifty to seventy-five letters giving their version of events, addressing them to the most prominent Americans they knew, including New York's Mayor LaGuardia, Treasury Secretary Henry Morgenthau Jr., and radio journalists like Walter Winchell and Dorothy Parker.

Under normal circumstances, not one of these letters would have been delivered. The Geneva Convention permitted war prisoners to send as many complaining letters as they wished, but only to their captors, their Protecting Power, the Red Cross, and the YMCA. Delivery of these was required. Otherwise, prisoners were limited to one unsealed letter and one postcard a week, but only to close family members, in which they were forbidden to make complaints and derogatory remarks. These communications went to a censorship office in New York—after a camp official had made a list of any American addressees, to aid the FBI in case of escapes.

At Camp Breckenridge, there was only one official who knew German, the intelligence and postal officer. By chance, he was in the hospital that week. When his mail clerk noticed the flood of prisoner mail with forbidden addresses, he asked the camp adjutant's advice. The adjutant said that the censors would catch anything amiss. On his own, the clerk decided to skip the chore of recording all those American addresses. He crammed everything into one manila envelope, addressed it to the censorship office, and tossed it into the U.S. mail sack. Perhaps the thing came unsealed. Perhaps some of these letters were mailed by Col. Winlock's young son, who had the run of the camp. Some of those letters got through, enough to cause a scandal.

After the investigation, poor Col. Winlock was not even disciplined. The hapless mail clerk was. The command's Inspector General also recommended that each camp have at least three competent interpreters. Both the

War and the State Departments made public statements about the fiasco, but these left Walter Winchell unabashed and provided fodder for other critics.

The second incident that most displeased the War Department occurred in April 1944. In another radio broadcast, the gadfly Dorothy Thompson scoffed at an Army-sponsored tour of POW camps for journalists, from which she had been excluded.[11] The tour was worthless, she said, because the invitees were only allowed to speak to camp officials. They were forbidden to speak to prisoners, even though they all had one vital question: how many prisoners were Nazis? An informed source had assured her that while no more than 10 percent were "real Nazis," these were so highly organized that they ruled the camps by terror. She had heard that there had already been fourteen camp suicides and two murders.[12]

It was "perfectly clear" to her why "our good natured" but non–German-speaking camp officials were helpless. Nazi prisoners could "make absolute fools" of them, like the "chaplain" at Breckinridge who had innocently sung the Nazi Party anthem, thinking it was a church hymn. No wonder those prisoners believed that America was weak and ignorant. No wonder they allowed the Nazi minority to keep them cowed and silent.

According to one camp commander, she said, the Geneva Convention forbade teaching this splendid cross-section of German manhood anything about democracy. What nonsense! Geneva encouraged "intellectual and sporting pursuits." Surely courses in American history and values would nourish intellects warped by Nazi propaganda. So would "carefully selected libraries of brilliant anti-Nazi and humanistic writers"—if the camp Gestapo could be prevented from beating up the readers.

Then she sneered at army authorities who thought they could assure good treatment for GIs in Nazi hands by giving German prisoners more than the Geneva Convention required, while flabby American military censors were approving prisoners' letters that falsely described miserable treatment. German newspapers were full of these accounts, which could only incite retaliation against American prisoners in Nazi hands. It would be "a terrible irony" if, while defeat and disillusion were killing Nazism in Germany, it was kept alive in America's comfy POW camps.

Dorothy Thompson's broadcast resonated in the Pentagon. Two weeks later, Assistant Provost Marshal General Bryan sent a long, defensive memo to the Under Secretary of War.[13] In the first place, he said, no female journalists were ever allowed into POW camps, where they might be insulted. No journalist of either sex could interview any prisoner, because the Geneva Convention protected them all from "insults and public curiosity."

Then, passing the buck, Bryan assured the under secretary that Secretary of War Stimson himself had delegated the "difficult and perplexing problem" of sorting out Nazis and anti-Nazis to the Assistant Chief of Staff, G-2. However, military intelligence had so far screened only 5 percent of the prisoners. Bryan next claimed that the PMG's Office had gone ahead and segregated enough Nazis to prevent them from terrorizing other prisoners—at least "to a great extent." On G-2's advice, Secretary Stimson had authorized the Service Commands to transfer Nazi troublemakers to Alva, Oklahoma, to segregate "non-cooperative noncommissioned officers," and to relocate a quota of anti-Nazis to Camp Campbell, Kentucky. To date there had been only three [*sic*] murders and only three (out of thirteen) suicides clearly caused by "Nazi brutality occasioned by political differences."

If prisoners who read pro-American books were sometimes beaten, the remedy, said Bryan, was more productive labor and more political segregation. Unfortunately, German-speaking American personnel were not being assigned to American camps, but sent overseas as intelligence officers as soon as they were trained. Nevertheless, the PMG's Office had a secret committee at work devising subtle means of giving German prisoners "a greater opportunity to observe and study the American way of life."

As a result of the Breckinridge church parade episode, the PMG's Office had issued orders forbidding prisoners to sing outside of their compounds![14]

Judging by the paperwork in the National Archives, these two broadcasts by Winchell and Thompson were the worst journalistic contributions to the coddling crisis. Another journalistic attack producing strong reaction in both the War and State Departments came in the November 1944 issue of the *Atlantic Monthly*: "What to Do with German Prisoners: The Russian Solution," by Henry C. Cassidy, and "What to Do with German Prisoners: The American Muddle," by James H. Powers. The State Department's SWPD, fearing that the *Readers Digest* would condense Power's article in its foreign language editions, rallied to support Gen. Bryan, who took this attack personally.[15]

The War Department also had to defend itself against Congress. The House Committee on Military Affairs began to investigate coddling because, as one congressman put it: "It is one thing to treat [German prisoners] decently, but it is something else to give them a lot of privileges just because they happened to be captured while trying to kill a lot of our boys."[16] Although committee members junketed to camps in ten states, with much publicity, the report to the House of Representatives on Nov. 30, 1944, admitted that the committee had found no examples of dances, festivals, picnics, and sight-seeing tours.[17] Nevertheless, recognizing a good public relations issue, the committee immediately began a second investigation.[18]

The "coddling crisis" also required the War Department to address public opinion. It did this by censoring newspapers and magazines. It also fed facts and arguments to cooperative writers. Far from being coddled, POWs were being treated "fairly and firmly" according to the Geneva Convention. One could not disobey the Geneva Convention because a treaty ratified by Congress was as much the law of the land as the Constitution itself. Furthermore, ill treatment could cause prisoners to sabotage the labor program. (The War Department could not yet brag in detail about this valuable program, for fear that prisoners might sabotage it.) Department mouthpieces also warned that noncompliance with Geneva would incite Hitler to take bloody reprisals against American boys, whereas compliance would shame him into treating them well.[19] (Until the early months of 1945, the War Department credited Hitler with treating American prisoners according to the convention.) Both the War and State Departments also announced that enemy soldiers were surrendering in large numbers because America treated her war prisoners well.[20]

As an example of War Department information management, in December 1944, Assistant PMG Bryan asked Bernard Gufler in the State Department's Special War Problems Division to critique an article by John Brown Mason, an official in the SWPD's internees section, because it contained much information "available only to an individual officially connected with prisoner of war administration." The War Department's Bureau of Public Relations would not allow publication without Gufler's okay.[21] The finished product, which the War Department warmly approved, appeared in the *American Journal of International Law*.[22]

The Pentagon also fed information to Russell Porter, a *New York Times* reporter, for a series of articles in January 1945. Unfortunately, Porter was excessively optimistic. His first front-page article bore the headlines "Prison Camps Rid of Nazi Terrorism. War Department Lifts Secrecy Now that Gestapo Activities Have Been Stamped Out."[23] To make War Department countermeasures seem more potent, he overdramatized unpleasant details of "Gestapo" power, such as the extremely embarrassing death of a prisoner with New York kin ("Ex-Yorkville Man Slain as Prisoner").[24] After the third offering ("Violence Is Ended in Prisoner Camps"),[25] the War Department had Porter's series suppressed. The Pentagon would not feel secure enough to brag about its victory over Nazi camp terrorism until the war was over.

The War Department planted similar articles through AP correspondents and through the National Education Association.[26] In March, 1945, even the august Harvard historian Dr. Sidney B. Fay would contribute an essay to a semi-scholarly publication,[27] praising the War Department in terms strongly resembling Porter's.

The War Department's Bureau of Public Relations was very displeased when another reporter, Chester G. Hanson of the *Los Angeles Times*, submitted four articles for clearance. Hanson cited interviews he claimed to have had with prisoners at Papago Park and Florence, Arizona. He said too much about their political tendencies and he overemphasized the Gestapo's power (like Porter's columns, "which were killed," a public relations analyst remarked). Hanson quoted Papago Park's camp spokesman as saying that officers had been punished with hard labor in violation of the Geneva Convention. The public relations analyst also objected that he had revealed a "classified secret": German naval personnel were segregated at Papago Park.[28]

The Provost Marshal General himself ordered Ninth Service Command's Gen. Shedd to investigate Hanson's sources.[29] Shedd learned that Papago Park's commandant, Col. Holden, had taken Hanson's word that he "was authorized" to write about POW camps. Hanson was his personal friend. The colonel had asked his stockade officer to show Hanson around, after telling him not to interview prisoners or take pictures. The stockade officer claimed that when the journalist asked questions "regarding the hanging which occurred in March, 1944, . . . I told him that we *never* discussed that matter with the PW, nor permitted anyone else to do so." Furthermore, Hanson had never interviewed the camp spokesman. The former compound spokesman Karl-Heinz Jaeger had stepped up to ask the stockade officer a question. Hanson had seized the chance to ask him about "food, clothing and recreation supplies" and, in his articles, had promoted Jaeger to camp spokesman.[30] Of course, the War Department squelched Hanson's articles.

In spite of the Pentagon's news-managing efforts, the coddling crisis erupted again after Anglo-American troops liberated Buchenwald and Bergen-Belsen concentration camps in mid-April 1945 and Dachau at the end of that month. American newspapers amplified public horror by failing to make a distinction among death camps, ordinary concentration camps (run by the SS), and POW camps (run by the German armed forces).[31] British and American prisoners, at least, had usually been treated according to the German interpretation of the Geneva Convention, until the Third Reich began to disintegrate.

This confusion, and rising battle casualties,[32] posed another public relations challenge for the War Department. Hatred of Germany was useful for selling war bonds, but what of the grieving relatives of American war prisoners? They needed reassurance. As early as February 1945, the War Department sent a delegation of ex-prisoners on a two-month tour of "thirty key cities" to address Red Cross meetings for POW relatives and friends. They gave "thousands . . . a comprehensive picture of conditions in enemy camps."[33] Still, in the wake of the newspapers' awful revelations, even more people demanded to know how the American government could coddle those Germans in American camps. In other words, the last winter of the war, when the Papago Park sentences were moving slowly toward presidential confirmation, was no time for any official to seem soft on Nazis.

On Dec. 7, 1944, Assistant Judge Advocate Gen. Rounds gave his boss the formidable stack of documents connected with the Papago Park trial. Rounds's own recommendations now lay on top.[34] Judge Advocate General Myron C. Cramer's task was to review all this information and report his decision, death or mercy, to Secretary of War Stimson. If Stimson agreed, he would do the same for President Roosevelt.

According to the Laws of War, only the chief executive could sign a death warrant for an offense not committed on a battlefield. He might also "reject or mitigate" a sentence "at pleasure," or order a retrial.[35] But was President Roosevelt likely to exercise any of these powers unless advised to do so by the Secretary of War—who would rely on the advice of his Judge Advocate General?

And how far down such a mountain of paper could any busy executive go? Bosses have staff people to summarize such accumulations and to draft their responses. For example, the Judge Advocate's review board had already composed a letter for General Cramer to sign, recommending that Secretary of War Stimson approve the death penalties.

As for JAG Cramer, he clearly relied on Col. Rounds's advice about the matter. Colonel Rounds told him that he had only two decisions to make. First, was the trial record legally sufficient? The board of review, Col. King, and Rounds all agreed that it was. Calling attention to King's brief and Moyse's response, Rounds said the only(!) legal point "relates to the voluntary nature and admissibility of the second confession." As for "the advisability of using this case to over-rule or clarify" the McDonald decision, this was "too involved" a question to address in his memorandum. Major Moyse of the review board could provide more information.

The Judge Advocate's other decision, Rounds said, was between death or life in prison. Maj. Gen. Shedd of Ninth Service Command and Moyse's two associates on Review Board No. 2 had recommended mercy, said Rounds.

He and Moyse opposed mercy because this was the third case "in which Nazi German Prisoners of War have taken the law into their own hands" to murder an alleged traitor. President Roosevelt had already approved "execution by hanging" in the first two cases. To give the seven killers from Papago Park life sentences "would simply condone the offense of murder" and encourage POWs in "their fanatical, misguided ideas of patriotism."

The second document in the stack delivered to the JA's desk contained Col. King's argument that seven death sentences would fulfill the United States' duty, under Geneva Article 2, to protect prisoners against violence.[36] The topmost document was Col. Round's memo.

Of course Gen. Cramer approved the sentences. He signed the "carrying papers" (documents prewritten by the review board, giving "his" opinion of the case and providing forms for Stimson and Roosevelt to sign if they agreed with it). Actually, Cramer also had to sign a new set of carrying papers on January 1, 1945, in order to change the place of execution. The Provost Marshal General's POW Division had informed Rounds that it "particularly" desired to hang all fifteen German murderers at the U.S. Disciplinary Barracks at Fort Leavenworth, Kansas, as a matter of administrative convenience. Even though transporting Drechsler's seven killers from Arizona "half way across the continent" would involve some "risk of escape and publicity," the fact that Arizona and Kansas were in the same Service Command would prevent jurisdictional disputes.[37]

The prewritten memorandum which Cramer sent Secretary of War Stimson on January 2, 1945, described Drechsler's cruel murder and summarized the evidence which proved the defendants guilty "beyond a shadow of a doubt." Their defense, that they were justified in executing a traitor who had harmed their fatherland, was based "upon mere rumors and inferences." They had usurped authority to judge and condemn. Maj. Gen. Shedd's recommendation of mercy should be rejected. The document assured Stimson that all the defendants' Geneva rights had been "scrupulously protected during the trial," and it drew the secretary's attention to the draft of a letter, ready for his signature, advising the president that these seven men should be hanged by the neck until dead.[38] (The review board had also written this document.)

Secretary of War Henry L. Stimson was a very conscientious man in matters of life and death. He "took a great interest in all aspects of military justice" and carefully reviewed cases "to prevent malfunctioning of the system."[39] His diary for May 10, 1944, records that his "most solid job" that day was reviewing three trials with Judge Advocate Cramer. The "first and most important" of these was the Beyer case, the five German POWs condemned to death for organizing an

> attack upon one of their own number who was trying to affiliate with the Americans. They treated him as a traitor, called a meeting of 200 prisoners (Germans), read a letter which showed he was in correspondence with . . . the Americans, and then deliberately pounded him to death. I am told that it is typical of what the German prisoners are doing in their different camps. They are keeping their discipline and their Nazi hatred. This was a long case and I had to take a good deal of time in reading the record with General Cramer. . . . I approved the sentences of all.[40]

Five months later, he received the records of the second POW murder trial, which had condemned Erich Gauss and Rudolf Straub to death for a murder in South Carolina. According to his diary for October 5, he spent a "strenuous morning" with Cramer reviewing so many capital cases that he could not complete the task in the time allowed. One case "involved another murder by German prisoners of war of one of their number who showed some evidence of friendship for the Americans. I feel very strongly that we should be very severe on these cases. It is the old snake of Nazism beginning to raise its head in our present camps."

This second case reminded Stimson that the earlier one "has not yet gotten to the White House." He was so "troubled by the delay" that he telephoned Roosevelt's gatekeeper, Gen. "Pa" Watson, telling him:

> I thought that was a most serious case and ought to be decided on promptly and I gave him my reason why I thought the death sentence ought surely to be approved. The President had gotten some wrinkle in his head of the question of law involved and had referred it to Konenman who was too busy with political matters to touch it. I emphasized my views strongly as to the part it played in the treatment of Germany and Nazism, and General Watson agreed to put it at once up to the President and present my views to him as strongly as possible.[41]

When Stimson received the Papago Park case records, this righteously conscientious man read more than the top documents. When he found Col. King's opinion that Geneva Articles 2, 3, and 61 had clearly been violated, and his demand that the Inspector General of the U.S. Army investigate with a view to reprimanding those responsible for "third degree" methods,[42] Stimson refused to approve the sentences. He demanded that a full report be ready when he returned from his weekend.[43]

Somehow, it was not the Inspector General but G-2 who conducted the "investigation." The court-martial records contain a list of eight questions, without date, sender, or addressee: "What authority was there for the use of third degree methods?" Who gave the orders and why were they necessary? Who, within and outside of Ninth Service Command, had used these methods? "What offices or agencies did they represent?" Who were Capt. Oscar S. Schmidt and Sgt. Held? "Full identification is desired," with a "full report of the facts" of "the incident."[44]

The next document, also unsigned, undated, unaddressed, is undoubtedly Ninth Service Command's response: Maj. Zabel was unavailable and Maj. Walsh knew nothing. Col. Church, whose instructions were known only to himself, was "absent from this headquarters" just then, and "it is not known" whether Col. Church had "witnessed the procedure by which the confessions were obtained from these prisoners." "Insofar as we know," the prisoners had merely "appeared before the board and submitted their written confessions." It was believed "that all military personnel entering the questioning center are sworn to secrecy and are permitted to reveal nothing they may see or hear within. Since Col. Church received his instructions in Washington, I think the information the Secretary of War desires may be available there." The writer also understood that the official positions and true names of Schmidt and Held "are known in Washington." Would it "be proper, under any circumstances," for Ninth Service Command "to seek the information requested and to convey it in writing; and especially so since the entire details are probably known to some of your people"?[45]

This reply was marvelously diplomatic. Who meddled with military intelligence secrets? When Maj. Gen. Lerch, the Provost Marshal General himself, spoke to the Ninth Command's chief of staff on January 27, he delicately asked whether the issue involved "the installation near Tracy" (Byron Hot Springs). Gen. Wilson replied: "We have nothing whatever to do with that operation" except for housekeeping. Its commander "operated directly under G-2 as I take it."[46] Col. White, Ninth Service Command's staff judge advocate, was listening and recommended that since most of the information about third-degree methods was too secret to put into writing, Col. Church should "report verbally to the Secretary of War." The PMG wanted Church to "report personally to him," but on second thought, he would be out of town. However, "Vine [*sic*, Asst. PMG Bryan] will be here and have him report to him." Church should also "go up and talk with [JAG] Cramer and to G-2."[47]

White immediately arranged for Church to leave the conference he was attending and fly to Washington. "Colonel Church stated that he was in a position to answer all questions pertaining to the method of questioning the prisoners concerned," without any documentation from Service Command headquarters.[48]

On February 1, 1945, the day Church arrived in Washington, G-2 informed JAG Cramer that Byron Hot Springs' officials denied everything. The bus used for transporting prisoners "is not and never has been equipped with a moving steel bar of any sort," and the complainers (Stengel and Wizuy) only rode it "between points of interrogation." No prisoner could possibly have been subjected to heat or pushed against steam pipes because "the heating plant was not in operation at the time and, furthermore, there were no steam pipes in the room where interrogation took place." Prisoners were never "forced to bend over with hands crossed behind their legs or forced to assume any similar position, nor were their hands stepped on at any time while being interrogated by G-2 personnel." The "only instance" of a prisoner's being denied food was while an interrogation "lasted through the regular mealtime, in which case the interrogating officer also went without food."

However, "one interrogator," on his own initiative and "without authorization from the Post Commander, who was absent from the Post in hospital at the time," had used a gas mask rubbed with onion "for a period estimated at less than five minutes." This "distinctly forbidden" method "would not have been tolerated by the Commanding Officer," had he known of it. "Certain PWS," who were "extremely arrogant and considered themselves heroes because of the part they had played in this murder," had been "caused to stand at attention for a prolonged period but not as much as three hours." The commanding officer would not have tolerated that practice either, but the interrogating officer felt justified "as a matter of discipline for the manner in which the PW had conducted himself."[49]

According to Stimson's diary, JAG Cramer and G-2's Deputy Assistant Chief of Staff, Brig. Gen. John Weckerling, reported to him on February 10, 1945, about "the treatment of German prisoners in one of the cases" where he had been "a little worried lest improper methods had been used to extort confessions." After hearing of Weckerling's "thorough investigation," he "decided that no failure of justice had been occasioned." He approved the seven death sentences.[50]

That same day, Gen. Cramer sent a lengthy but routine letter, which had been waiting in his files for two months, to the president's gatekeeper, "Pa" Watson. It summarized the Papago Park case so that "Pa" could summarize it for the president.[51] Four days later, Stimson sent Roosevelt the case records, with a short letter reviewing the facts and assuring him that the Geneva Convention had been scrupulously observed. The accused "were ably defended by experienced counsel, with whom they expressed themselves as being satisfied. . . . All their legal rights were scrupulously protected during the trial." Stimson had investigated the testimony of three defendants who alleged improper treatment. "I find these complaints are either unfounded or are grossly exaggerated. Whatever improper treatment there may have been had no effect on their later confessions." He recommended that Roosevelt sign "a form of Executive action" ordering their executions.

Stimson also told Roosevelt that he had "taken steps to see that no further instances of this kind [of mistreatment] will occur."[52] Files from the PMG's Office contain a draft rebuke, dated February 2, 1945, warning recipients that "so-called third-degree methods cannot be tolerated in investigations involving prisoners of war." Even though there were "numerous difficulties involved" in investigating their crimes and misbehavior, it was "necessary to refrain from such methods." They violated Geneva Articles 2 and 3, mandating humane treatment, protection from violence, and respect for the prisoners' persons. They were "contrary to American concepts" and, "if flagrant enough, might result in nonapproval or nonconfirmation of a merited sentence." Furthermore, "under American court-martial procedure, a copy of the record in general court-martial cases is given to each of the accused prisoners on request." One of these copies "containing evidence of a third-degree investigation might find its way to an enemy country."

Worse still,the document said, in capital cases the Geneva Convention obliged the United States to "furnish to the Protecting Power a copy of the record or substantial summary thereof. If evidence of third-degree methods is found in the record, it cannot be forwarded." Finally, the Geneva Convention gave war prisoners the right to complain to their Protecting Power, which would report to their governments. "Third-degree methods will very likely result in retaliation upon American prisoners held by the enemies."[53]

Whoever wrote this document was a prophet. However, it was not the third-degree methods used in the Papago Park case against which Hitler would begin to retaliate—those were still secret. His government reacted mightily against the prospect that any German war prisoner whatsoever would be hanged.

CHAPTER 14

Obnoxious Material

Presidential confirmation of the "Beyer Five" death sentences caused a diplomatic crisis that lasted until V-E Day. According to Geneva Article 66, the Detaining Power had to give the Protecting Power, as soon as possible, "details of the prisoner's offense and the decisive reasons for the verdict against him." The War Department issued tardy, extremely brief notices.[1]

In January 1944, five weeks after Johannes Kunze died in a riot at Camp Tonkawa, Oklahoma, the War Department told the Swiss Legation that his company leader had called a meeting to compare his handwriting with that on an "alleged traitorous note" (omitting all details, such as Kunze's description of the camouflage protecting the main railroad station in Hamburg, and his suggestion that military hospitals might be likely bomb targets). "Belabored with blows," Kunze had been chased down and killed. "Certain of the POW company will be court-martialed for riot and murder."[2] In late January, another terse note informed the legation of the five death sentences against Kunze's killers.

The German government inevitably protested, citing its own scrupulous observance of Geneva Article 66. When Germany tried American war prisoners, it furnished the Protecting Power "with copies of the opinion of the court, giving the facts upon which the verdict was based and the evidence produced, as well as details concerning the laws under which the prisoner was sentenced." The American notices contained none of this information. Berlin wanted the "particulars as to the manner in which testimony was taken," and as to how the judges had considered both the testimony and "the statements of the accused." Exactly what facts had caused the judges to pronounce death sentences? Unless Washington sent the "written opinion of the court," Berlin might begin withholding information about the trials of American prisoners.[3] When the Swiss Legation handed this message to the State Department on September 13, the POW murder trials ceased to be the Pentagon's private domain.

The State Department expected no difficulty, for the German requests seemed reasonable. When its Special War Problems Division asked the War Department to provide "an appropriate reply," it pointed out that the Geneva Convention allowed any POW to request "a full transcript" of his trial.[4] Why not his government?

On October 3, Asst. Provost Marshall General Bryan sent the State Department a reply for the legation: American trial records contained transcripts of all testimony and copies of all exhibits, but did not include information about how the court reached either verdict or sentence. However, the Protecting Power could observe any trial and make whatever report it wished. If a secret trial should occur, as Geneva Article 62 allowed, "the Protecting Power will be informed" beforehand. As of that date, no Swiss representative had been excluded from any trial [*sic*]. Therefore, "the request of the German Government for a written opinion of the court, including a resume of the evidence and applicable law, cannot be granted."[5] This reply did not even satisfy the State Department, which asked for more information.[6]

By the time it sent this reply, the War Department had already given notice of the death sentences handed down in the other POW murder trials, against Erich Gauss and Rudolf Straub on July 13, against Edgar Menschner on August 12, and against Drechsler's seven killers on September 29. Now there were fifteen Germans liable to hang,[7] if the president confirmed their sentences. On October 9, the War Department gave notice that Roosevelt had confirmed the five sentences in the Beyer case. According to the Geneva Convention, they would be eligible for hanging on January 9, 1945.[8] (No prisoner could be executed until three months after the Protecting Power had been informed that his death sentence had been confirmed.)

On October 24, the legation delivered the predictable second German demand for a "detailed written opinion" of the court's reasoning in the Beyer case, and "the consideration given to the testimony in determining a judgment," so that "German authorities could . . . form an opinion of the process." Since apparently "the recording of sentences is not customary in the United States," Berlin would "appreciate" seeing the entire verbatim court records of every serious case and, furthermore, "a report of the plea of the defense counsel"! Otherwise, the note warned, "the German Government very soon will have to adopt the procedure of the American Authorities" when it reported trials of American POWs.[9] If anyone in the War Department wondered about Berlin's reaction to discovering that those five sergeants were to die for doing away with a traitor to their fatherland, there is no record of it; but someone there certainly did worry about setting a precedent for handing over entire trial transcripts. The real problem was the Papago Park case, which contained allegations of torture at illegal "questioning centers." Even a simple "report of the plea of the defense counsel" in the Papago Park case would include Maj. Taylor's suggestion that all seven confessions had been coerced. The Pentagon ordered the State Department to tell the legation that the reply to its note awaited "consideration by the military authorities."

Meanwhile, the Swiss minister proposed that the Beyer Five hangings be postponed to allow time for the German government to receive and study the documents it had requested. The minister pointed out that since he could not send these until time for his next diplomatic pouch, and since communications were rapidly deteriorating, Berlin would not receive them until "the end of November at the earliest."[10] The War Department refused to consider this reasonable request.

On October 28, the legation presented a third German note: Since "the lives of five human beings in their prime" were at stake, the Reich government particularly needed details of how they had allegedly killed Johannes Kunze. Geneva's Article 66 obligated the Detaining Power to send, as soon as possible after sentencing, "a communication setting forth in detail the nature and circumstances of the offenses." Nine months after the Beyer verdict, the note continued, American authorities still had not described the "circumstances and reasons leading to" the crime. Therefore, the five executions should be postponed until three months after the trial transcript "or an objective report by the counsel for defense" had reached Berlin. When the Swiss minister delivered this message, he drew the State Department's "particular attention" to this last request.[11]

On November 1, the legation sent a fourth German note containing the same request in regard to the offense committed by Erich Gauss and Rudolf Straub, criticizing American noncompliance with Geneva Article 66 more sharply.[12] Berlin also demanded "specific data" about Edgar Menschner's crime, motives, defense, and sentencing "as soon as possible."[13] In the State Department file containing this German note, one finds a secret report on German atrocities against English war prisoners. Someone at State was considering the possibility of reprisals. After all, the Geneva Convention imposed reciprocal duties. If one party failed to observe its terms, the other could legally do likewise.

Perhaps someone at the Pentagon also thought about reprisals. At least there was an uncomfortable awareness that delicate details might leak out when these POWs exercised their Geneva right to complain to their Protecting Power. At any rate, on November 8 the War Department decided to allow the Swiss Legation in Washington—but emphatically not the German government—to examine the Beyer trial transcript and to make excerpts from this secret document.[14] (Bern would decline this responsibility.)

Also on that day, Asst. PMG Bryan finally informed State's SWPD of the War Department's position on the first two German notes. The Geneva Convention made war prisoners liable to the Custodial Power's military laws. Before the Beyer trial, Bryan himself, with representatives from the Judge Advocate General's Office and from the State Department, had thoroughly explained court-martial procedure to the legation's Department of German Affairs, including the fact that in America "the record of trial, rather than a written court opinion, is the basis of review." In *future* cases involving a death sentence, the War Department was now willing to show trial transcripts to the legation *provided* that Berlin would reciprocate by furnishing "a verbatim transcript of each German court-martial" which had sentenced an American prisoner to death. (This was a safe offer. Germans did not make such transcriptions.) As for Berlin's request for "the testimony of witnesses" and so forth, Bryan continued, the legation's own observer should be able to provide that information. No record existed of "the consideration given to such testimony" by the judges. American judges always deliberated in private.

The Geneva Convention's basic intent, Bryan continued, was to make sure of five things: that the Protecting Power knew the time and place of a trial and the charges against the accused; that the accused had competent translators and defenders; that they were treated in exactly the same manner as the Detaining Power's soldiers; that the Protecting Power was notified when the sentence was confirmed; and that there be a three-month delay of execution to allow the Enemy Power to receive this information. The United States had fully complied with Article 66 on October 9, when it had notified the legation that the president had confirmed the five death sentences in the Beyer case. Any prior notices had been a matter of courtesy, not of obligation. Since the legation itself had said that documents would reach Berlin by the end of November, there was "no useful purpose" in delaying the executions (scheduled for January 9).[15]

On November 13, the War Department sent notice that President Roosevelt had confirmed the death sentences of Gauss and Straub, four days earlier. This made them eligible for hanging on February 13, 1945. On December 1, the legation delivered another German note demanding details as soon as possible about Gauss, Straub, and the last POW to be tried, Menschner. Pending instructions from the War Department, State could only tell the Swiss Legation that the subject of all fifteen condemned German prisoners was "receiving the urgent consideration of American Authorities."[16]

With the War Department so mysteriously unforthcoming and the Beyer Five execution date approaching, the State Department's SWPD took the initiative in early December and began drafting a reply to all those German notes. Assistant PMG Bryan reacted to this project by making a show of cooperation, then preempting the task.[17]

Meanwhile, the Swiss minister sent a note, attached to yet another German demand for information, which reveals that the War Department had yielded a few more inches. After the minister had refused to make excerpts from the Beyer trial records, Gen. Bryan had finally permitted him to forward the entire trial record to Bern—provided that the Swiss government would "in no circumstances" make this document "available to the German authorities." Now the minister said that his government found it impossible to "determine which details should and which should not be transmitted" to Berlin. "Appropriate American authorities" should do the selecting. The minister asked that this be done "with the utmost expediency" and that the executions be postponed until three months after this material reached Berlin.[18]

On December 26 the Swiss Legation finally received a thirteen-page reply to all the German notes (the result of Gen. Bryan's having commandeered SWPD's project).[19] It made only two small concessions. First, the Beyer Five could have sixteen more days of life! Their new date with the gallows would be three months from the day the Swiss Legation in Washington had received their trial records. This would allow the German government ample time to study them, since the legation could send its trial observer's notes to Berlin by cable or radio. Second, in all other death penalty cases, the three-month interim would begin when the legation received "copies of records of trial *or substantial summaries thereof, whichever appears appropriate to the American authorities*"—provided that Germany reciprocated, if it should ever charge any American POW with a capital crime.[20] No doubt the War Department felt that these concessions were safe. "Substantial summaries" could omit inconvenient material. Demands for "reciprocity" would ensure maximum delay.

On the day the Swiss Legation received this long document, December 26, it handed State another urgent cable: The German government rejected the American note of October 9, 1944, announcing presidential confirmation of the Beyer death sentences. The note did not "analyze the full circumstances surrounding the offence." It lacked "all details" about each defendant's motives, what each man had actually done, and what each had said in his own defense. German authorities were therefore unable to analyze "the seriousness of the offense" or the "possible basis for mitigation." Therefore, the United States had not yet conformed to Geneva Article 66 and the three-month waiting period had not yet begun. The German note ended with a delicate but definite threat: If the United States hanged these five men on January 9, Berlin would "draw such conclusions as deemed appropriate in the light of such a violation."[21] The State Department immediately sent this to the PMG's Prisoner of War Division and also to Secretary of War Stimson himself, requesting his comments.[22]

Two days later, the Swiss minister responded to the long, lawyerly State/Bryan memorandum of December 26. He wished to confine his remarks to the five men who were so shortly due to hang. The Swiss government wanted permission to send the entire Beyer trial record to Berlin. It could do this without delay since the Foreign Office in Bern already had a copy but, even so, the German government would need time to examine it. The sixteen-day extension of the death date was therefore "inadequate."[23]

The Asst. Director of the PWD, Col. A. M. Tollefson, responded on New Years' Day, yielding nothing.[24] However, something changed. On January 2, 1945, his superior, Asst. PMG Bryan, wrote this: Because "the German authorities have by now been supplied with *a complete copy of the record*," and because a presidential confirmation could not be altered, "the request for an additional extension of time [for the five executions] beyond 25 January cannot be granted."[25]

The War Department soon paid the penalty for yielding up the trial record of five patriotic Germans who were to hang for killing a traitor to Germany, while insisting that they be hanged on schedule. On January 5, the legation delivered this message:

> The following members of the American armed forces have been condemned to death by sentences imposed by the Reich Court Martial and other courts-martial:
>
> (a) Sentenced November 22, 1944, for treason:
>
> Leutnant James Meloyne Greyfield, born January 31, 1915, in Shawsheen Village, Massachusetts.
>
> (b) Captured as francs-tireurs; sentenced December 30, 1944:
>
> Oberleutnant Franklin Dent Coslett, identification number 0/801353/T/42/03;
>
> Leutnant Johann Josef Walsh, born June 12, 1922 in Waltham, Massachusetts;

> Sergeant Marvin Palver Martin, born November 24, 1921, in Palmira, Indiana;
>
> Sergeant Edward Adolf Walsh, born March 19, 1922 (presumably in Jersey City)
>
> The German Government has deferred execution of the sentences pending receipt of information from the United States Government as to whether it is prepared to exchange them against German prisoners of War Beyer, Seidel, Demme, Schomer and Scholz, of Prisoner of War Camp Tonkawa, who were condemned in the United States.[26]

After hastily acknowledging receipt,[27] State forwarded this shocker to the Provost Marshal General and the Secretary of War on January 6, the following day. Stimson took five days to respond. The PMG had no sense of urgency either, although he surely knew that the traditional laws of war permitted *francs tireurs* (partisans, irregulars found out of uniform and presumably spies) to be executed out of hand, and that the protections granted by the Geneva Convention did not apply to them. He sent this communication to the legal branch of his POW Operations Division, which sent it along to the Assistant Chief of Staff, G-1 (personnel), attention Lt. Col. M. C. Bernays of the Special Branch,[28] whose job was to keep track of Americans in enemy hands. This took six days.

In contrast, Asst. PMG Bryan immediately sent Judge Advocate General Cramer this message: Germany and the Swiss Legation had protested that the official notifications of the Beyer and Gauss and Straub death sentences "were insufficient in detail." The PMG's Office had now conceded that the three-month waiting period would begin only when the legation received either the court record "or a substantial summary thereof." This policy would also apply to the Menschner and the Papago Park or "Fischer" cases, after presidential confirmation.

> It is believed that the record of the Fischer case contains material which should not be submitted to the Legation and through it to the German Government. The obnoxious material will be apparent upon review of the record.

Bryan asked Cramer to prepare "a substantial summary" for both cases[29]—assuming, perhaps, that excisions from the Papago Park records alone would seem suspicious.

Meanwhile, on January 6, Secretary of State Stettinius had sent an urgent cable to Ambassador Huddle in Bern, ordering him to find out whatever he could about the five condemned Americans. In particular, had the Germans violated Geneva by failing to notify Switzerland of the charges, trial dates, and sentences? How could Lt. Walsh, Sgt. Walsh, and Sgt. Martin be deprived of their status as war prisoners, which they had enjoyed ever since the German government had reported their presence at Stalag Luft 3 eight months earlier? And how could Lt. Greyfield commit treason against an enemy country?[30]

On January 9, the Swiss Legation informed the State Department that the Beyer trial records had reached Berlin only three days earlier. Even if the United States rejected the exchange proposal, it should postpone the five executions—now only sixteen days away! In spite of that, the State Department for some reason took four days to acknowledge receipt of this note and to send a copy to the War Department.[31]

Secretary of War Stimson finally responded to the German exchange offer after five days, on January 10. Because "the German authorities have trumped up charges" against five Americans in order to delay justice or "to compel the release of the German murderers," he wrote, the State Department should send "an urgent message" to Berlin "in the sense of" a ten-page secret memorandum he enclosed. This scolding, schoolmasterish document conceded nothing at all. First it bragged that the United States had fully respected every Geneva right pertaining to those five German murderers. They not only had "qualified and adequate" American defenders but even "German counsel selected by them from among their fellow prisoners of war." Not only had the American government kept the Protecting Power informed in detail of every step. It had also sent the complete trial record and had reset the execution date to three months after its delivery to the legation. By contrast, all the "purported" German trials violated the Geneva Convention. If the German government executed those Americans, it would also be violating the traditional laws of war, which forbade "an unlawful killing of prisoners." The American government therefore expected Berlin "to insure that this does not occur" and to inform Washington immediately of the steps it had taken to prevent it.[32]

Stimson also enclosed some supporting documents. One was a letter he had written Secretary of State Stettinius on August 8, 1944, which referred to several German enlisted men found guilty of "heinous murders." Stimson had rejected some unnamed course of action on the ground that it would provide Germany with an incentive "to try and condemn Allied prisoners on trumped-up charges," as bargaining chips "for procuring the release of German prisoners whose continued detention is an imperative military necessity."[33] This "supporting" document shows that the War Department had walked open-eyed into this crisis!

Stimson was an old man, and often so ill that Under Secretary Robert Patterson had to stand in for him. Furthermore, Stimson became sidetracked. On January 8, two days before his note to Stettinius, the Secretary of War had a long conversation with Col. Thomas D. Drake, a General Staff Corps officer recently repatriated from a German POW camp for ill health. Drake assured Stimson that his experience at Oflag 64 had taught him that Germans only understand "threats and rough talk." They "violate[d] the Geneva Convention all the time" by humiliating prisoners and denying them decent food and shelter. They got away with it because the Swiss and the International Red Cross were very partial to the Third Reich.[34]

Stimson was far less concerned with those five endangered GIs than with the thousands of other American boys in German hands. Blaming Swiss camp inspectors for all their sufferings, he resolved to force the Protecting Power to do its duty. When he met with Admiral Forrestal and Secretary of State Stettinius the next day, January 9, he repeated Col. Drake's revelations and urged Stettinius to appoint "someone who would represent us vigorously in Switzerland." A week later, Under Secretary of War Patterson repeated Col. Drake's bitter complaints to this "Committee of Three," accusing the State Department of "letting up on Switzerland" because it was also the Protecting Power for GI prisoners in Germany.[35]

Stimson had already acted on his new anti-Swiss obsession by ordering his close advisor, Under Secretary John J. McCloy, to investigate Bern's shortcomings. Col. Drake sent McCloy a long memorandum entitled "Improper Attitude of Swiss Government," which he labeled "pro Nazi." American and British POWs commonly called it the "Neglecting Power." One camp inspector had told Drake that "of course it was necessary to 'tone down' reports to prevent retaliation upon German Prisoners of War in America." Drake found that odd, for "it is a genuine well known fact that we lean over backwards in our treatment" of them.

Drake described two cases in which Bern had fired its camp inspectors for trying to make improvements. On the other hand, since the Germans were "more afraid of unfavorable opinion of the neutral world" than anything else, even "the mere report of an impending visit by the Swiss Legation" made the Germans improve conditions—but only temporarily, said Drake, because the Swiss inspectors neither investigated violations nor reported them to Bern. The Swiss government often ignored prisoners' reports of German violations of their Geneva rights. Even the Swiss-controlled Mixed Medical Commissions, which selected sick prisoners for repatriation, left many deserving Americans suffering in German camps without proper food or medicine. Furthermore, Drake concluded, he had letters to prove the "definite fact . . . that the International Red Cross, also a purely Swiss organization, has failed to properly carry out the intent and wishes of the American Red Cross in caring for American Prisoners of War." Under Secretary McCloy would pass this memorandum along to the deputy chief of staff, who would refer it to the Inspector General.[36]

The State Department hardly welcomed Stimson's anti-Swiss crusade. The Protecting Power was not only the main source of information about captured Americans but the only direct means of pressuring Berlin to treat them decently. For example, Ambassador Huddle had sent State an urgent telegram from Bern on December 16, reporting the possibility that "a colonel close to SS circles" had become the director of the German army command's POW information bureau, and that some SS in Wehrmacht uniforms had taken over the hiring of camp personnel, intending to replace them with SS officers. Secretary Stettinius had immediately told Huddle to keep alert, to ask the Swiss to inspect the camps more often, and to thank them for their helpfulness. Secretary of War Stimson saw Huddle's telegram as ominous proof of Switzerland's failure to protect. McCloy added it to the growing arsenal of documents he was sending to the Inspector General.[37]

On January 12, State began receiving hourly telegrams from Ambassador Huddle. The first, at 6:40 P.M., reported that Thomas Jefferson Snowden, an NCO from Rutland, Ohio, had been sentenced to death on December 29, 1944, for assaulting a superior officer. He had slugged a guard who had slapped his breakfast bread out of his hand when he refused to stop eating and get to work. The Swiss Legation in Berlin had already protested that "other similar cases receive much less severe sentences" and had asked that Snowden's be canceled. Furthermore, the Germans had violated Geneva Article 60 by holding his trial sooner than the announced date.[38]

At 6:57 P.M. another telegram gave more information about the first five American hostages: Franklin Dent Coslett had been sentenced on December 30 by the "Court of Second Parachutist Detection Corps for illegal possession of arms." He had been captured in civilian clothes behind German lines in a pillbox containing arms, ammunition, and maps. Lt. Johan Josef Walsh, Sgt. Marvin Palver Martin, and Sgt. Edward Adolf Walsh had been condemned on the same day by the Court of Commandant of POWS in army sector 8 for "helping the enemy." They had been captured in Italy in civilian clothes, carrying propaganda leaflets. Lt. James Melvin Greyfield's treason consisted in his learning German state secrets—by means of German News Service articles—and sharing this information with "American organizations." The Germans had not notified the Swiss of Greyfield's trial date before holding it on November 22.[39]

At 7:34 P.M. another telegram announced that on December 30 the Court of District No. 402 had pronounced a death sentence against a seventh American, Sgt. Angelo Nicosia, for assaulting a superior. Again, the Swiss Legation in Berlin had asked for cancellation of this unprecedentedly harsh sentence. Nicosia's trial date had also been advanced by two weeks without notice.[40]

At 8:27 P.M. came the news that on September 23 Lt. Col. William Schaefer and Lt. James Schmitz had been sentenced to hang. Schmitz's offense was to have stood in front of a bulletin board on which a German guard was trying to post a notice, thereby hindering a superior by force and threats from carrying out an order and obliging him to neglect his duty. Col. Schaefer had "wilfully supported a subordinate's punishable action."[41] Their trial date had been advanced without notice. So had that of Pvt. Willard Davis, sentenced on December 30 for assaulting a superior. The Swiss had asked that all three sentences be canceled for undue harshness.[42] Now ten Americans were liable to hang, if Hitler confirmed their sentences.

Five days after this series of telegrams, the head of the State Department's SWPD, Edwin Plitt, sent a document entitled "American Prisoners of War in Germany Under Sentence of Death" to Asst. Secretary of State James Dunn "for possible use in your meeting this morning," in case Dunn had not seen the draft of the "strong protest" being prepared in cooperation with the War Department. This "strong protest" demanded that the Germans cancel all ten "reprisal" sentences while virtually ignoring the German exchange proposal. "Although this is primarily a War Department matter and the attached note has been drafted in accordance with the War Department's wishes," Plitt pointed out, the SWPD felt compelled to warn that if the American public ever learned that the government had failed to accept a German exchange proposal, "wide spread repercussions may result."[43]

The State Department acquiesced uneasily to that "strong protest," which had been crafted by Col. Tollefson according to his, or Gen. Bryan's, specifications. An official in State's Division of European Affairs informed Asst. Secretary Dunn on January 19 that he had "initialed the note . . . with reluctance," since it would do nothing to prevent the Germans from killing the ten Americans "against whom they have quite obviously trumped up charges." Since the PMG's Office refused to exchange the condemned Germans, he suggested that Dunn "might want to take up the matter with some of the high officials in the War Department in an effort to get them to accept the German proposal."[44]

This must have seemed unlikely. Only two days before, on January 17, SWPD had received a letter from Col. Tollefson, giving the PWD's reply to Switzerland's repeated requests to hold off hanging the Beyer Five. Neither the PMG's Office nor Secretary Stimson, he said, saw any valid reason for delay. Therefore, these executions "will take place on or shortly after 25 January, 1945"—in only eight days.[45]

On January 19, Secretary of State Stettinius ordered Ambassador Huddle "urgently to investigate" a report, "believed reliable," that the Germans had condemned an eleventh American prisoner, Col. Henry R. Spicer of Stalag Luft I.[46] The Third Reich was on its way to matching those fifteen Germans whom the War Department was so eager to hang.

Germany's actions moved the Joint Chiefs of Staff to propose that the United States, Britain, and Russia issue a strong warning. A draft addressed to the Secretaries of War and Navy, JCS/164/4 of January 23, 1945, states that the JCS was "impelled" to reconsider "measures to deter Nazi atrocities against allied POWs, given recent indications that . . . the German government has already adopted and . . . will carry out a policy of murder and mistreatment against them." Appendix B, "Facts Bearing on the Problem," referred to the ten Americans under sentence of death on trumped-up charges and to the Malmedy massacre, as well as other incidents. The Joint Chiefs decided that this warning should state that "for each Allied prisoner of war murdered by the Germans, 1,000 German prisoners or other German males would be detained subsequent to the imposition of peace terms" for however long the Allied governments thought proper.[47]

Meanwhile, the War Department had been dealing with another problem. In his long memo to State, Gen. Bryan had bragged that the United States was fulfilling Geneva Article 67: No POW under sentence for a crime could be deprived of the right to complain about his condition to the American authorities or to his Protecting Power.[48] How awkward, then, when some of those condemned Germans began to complain! When Walter Beyer wrote about being denied exercise and hot meals at Fort Leavenworth, War held on to his note for a while before delivering it to State on October 28, with an explanation that the delay was being investigated.[49]

Far worse, two letters reached the Protecting Power directly, through ordinary mail. One, dated October 5, was from Oberfunkmaat Fritz Murza, who had once been denied writing materials while incarcerated in the Fort Douglas hospital psychiatric ward. The Swiss Legation presented State with a partial translation of his letter: "In connection with" Werner Drechsler's death, he had been taken from Papago Park to "a hearing camp near San Francisco," arriving on May 13. "On June 9 I was transferred to Utah and held there for 41 days in a prison unworthy of human beings." Since July 20 he had been held in solitary confinement at Florence, Arizona, where lack of exercise and companionship were causing "symptoms of illness, such as stomach trouble." Although he had been listed as a witness in the trial of Drechsler's murderers, he had not been called to testify. "The verdict was rendered on August 16 and I do not know why the authorities continue to hold me here." He was not permitted to exercise, although "several other comrades" in solitary confinement enjoyed this Geneva right. Murza's Protecting Power asked for an investigation into his condition. (He seems not to have mentioned his mistreatment at the "hearing camp." Perhaps he was ashamed to admit he had ratted on comrades who had executed a traitor.) State's SWPD waited nearly a month before acknowledging receipt of Murza's complaints or asking War for its views "in order to phrase a proper reply."[50] State had no reason to believe that this matter was sensitive.

When the Swiss Legation received a second irregularly delivered letter, from the condemned killer Guenther Kuelsen, it asked the State Department to determine "the status of all those German prisoners of War still being confined in connection with the Drechsler case." Kuelsen had complained that solitary confinement denied him "the freedom to which he is entitled under the provisions of the Geneva Convention." The Swiss note arrived on October 14; the SWPD forwarded it to War on December 13.[51]

Fortunately for the War Department, Otto Stengel's complaints arrived through regular bureaucratic channels. Since all such POW letters had to be delivered to the Protecting Power (eventually), and since War did not usually make copies, their contents must be inferred from the State Department's accompanying notes, which were based on information provided by War Department's PWD. On December 12, Col. Tollefson informed State's SWPD that, according to the commandant at Camp Florence, Stengel's claim to have been denied "medical attendance, tobacco and toilet articles" during and since his trial was false. Stengel was one of seven convicted murderers held in solitary confinement. Their condition had been investigated by "the Surgeon and the Director of the Security and Intelligence Division of the Headquarters of the Ninth Service Command," which was also investigating why Stengel's complaint had been so long delayed. However, Tollefson failed to send Stengel's letter with this note. The SWPD had to ask for it. Stengel's letter of November 10 finally reached the legation on December 20. State's accompanying note seems to deny the lack of medical attention and toilet articles.[52]

Had this greatly abused man merely griped about toilet articles? Perhaps he accepted his guilt, having been brainwashed into believing the false confession wrung from him at Byron Hot Springs. Perhaps he had been ordered to limit his complaints to current prison conditions.[53] Or perhaps he was suffering a certain disintegration of personality caused by solitary confinement.

According to a British soldier who spent years in German hands, prolonged solitude could make a prisoner accept the aggressor's moral rightness. As he put it, "should powerful captors wish to make certain arguments accepted, an averagely weak character could be made to believe anything and indeed would seek, without compulsion, to adopt the views of the dominant influence. Only strong men and saints and possibly old lags can be sure of themselves. I was glad not to be put to the test."[54] Otto Stengel had certainly adopted his captors' views.

As for the irregularly delivered letter from Murza, Col. Tollefson did not respond to the Swiss Legation until December 22, when he blandly denied everything. Murza had always been "permitted to exercise in his quarters," which were so far from being "unworthy of human beings" that his "private hospital room with adjoining bath facilities" was now occupied by American personnel. The commandant at Florence had already been told to allow regular outdoor exercise "in future instances of this nature" and Murza had already been released from solitary. His treatment had been "similar in all respects" to that of an American soldier being held as a material witness in a murder case. The State Department repeated all this to the Swiss on January 9, 1945.[55]

Also on January 9, more than a month after the legation inquired about the letter it had received from Guenther Kuelsen, Tollefson informed the SWPD that his complaint and Otto Stengel's were so similar to Murza's that his own note of December 22 should suffice for both of those cases. He assumed, he said, that when the legation had asked about "the status of all those German prisoners of war still being confined in connection with the Drechsler case," it had not been referring to the seven condemned killers. If any other prisoners were still in solitary, he would inform the legation.[56]

As long as the War Department had to allow POWs to correspond with their Protecting Power, as the Geneva Convention demanded, its only defenses against embarrassing revelations were delay, prevarication, and denial.

CHAPTER 15

War versus State

Secretary of War Stimson continued his campaign to force Switzerland to force Germany to obey the Geneva Convention. He wrote Secretary of State Stettinius on January 19, 1945, that his informant Col. Drake, a "thoroughly reliable" American officer with "first-hand experience," could prove that Switzerland was "more interested in retaining German goodwill than in properly protecting American prisoners"; but that whenever the slipshod Swiss camp inspectors did do their job, "conditions in the camps have improved temporarily." Stimson wanted Stettinius to tell Bern to adopt "a firm and vigilant attitude."[1]

The next day, the War Department sent State a version of Col. Tollefson's "strong protest," beginning and ending with passages from Stimson's letter to Stettinius.[2] It contrasted America's honorable protection of the rights of German murderers with Germany's scofflaw railroading of innocent GIs. Furthermore, it accused Berlin of providing "only scanty and inadequate information . . . regarding alleged grounds for trial and sentencing of American personnel!" How could Lt. Greyfield have obtained state secrets from a German news service? How could Lt. Walsh and Sgts. Martin and Walsh cease to have Geneva rights, eight months after being reported as war prisoners?

Furthermore, Germany was violating its own code of military law, which provided that an act producing only insignificant consequences might be punished by "hard labor for not under two years." If Walsh, Martin, and Walsh had significantly harmed the Reich, why was their case "allowed to remain dormant" until the politically useful moment? The death sentences clearly violated "the spirit and letter" of Geneva Articles 2, 60, and 67, which prohibited reprisals and required that the Protecting Power have prior notice of all trials. The traditional laws of war also forbade unlawful killing of prisoners.

Germany's "purported trials" and harsh sentences against the second set of five GIs (Davis, Snowden, Nicosia, Schaefer, and Schmitz) also revealed "the wide discrepancy between German and American concepts of justice." The United States had tried four Germans for assaulting or willfully disobeying a superior, potentially a capital offense under Articles of War 64; yet one of these was serving a mere ten-year sentence. One had been sentenced to eighteen months and another to only one, having mercifully been charged with lesser crimes. The fourth was serving a life sentence, but he had also incited others to riot.

This "strong protest" completely ignored the German exchange proposal, demanding instead that the Reich Government cancel its ten death sentences. At least the unenthusiastic Secretary of State was permitted to inform the Swiss Legation that "the American Government will not (repeat not) take any step of reprisal as a result of the German action."[3]

No doubt irked by this lack of enthusiasm, Secretary of War Stimson developed a scheme for bypassing the State Department by hitchhiking on the mission of Lauchlin Currie of the Foreign Economic Administration. Currie, one of Roosevelt's "six all-purpose administrative assistants," would soon travel to Switzerland for some delicate trade talks. Roosevelt was "rankled" that Switzerland continued to trade with Germany even though no longer surrounded by Axis powers. In mid-January, addressing the Swiss president as though he were "eager to deprive the Nazis of any further assistance," Roosevelt announced that Currie would lead a delegation "to renegotiate" any prior American trade agreements. Currie's unstated goal was to cut off Switzerland's strategic exports to the Reich and to prevent the Nazis from hiding their pelf in Swiss banks.[4]

Before Currie left Washington on January 27, Asst. Secretary of War McCloy sent him a long, poorly written memo summarizing Col. Drake's accusations, which, McCloy said, had been "checked informally" with State. McCloy also told Currie how to give the Swiss "opportunities for improvements." In case Swiss trade negotiators referred "to the importance of their services as a protecting power," Currie was to "comment on their shortcomings in this regard." If the Swiss did not mention it, he should still "needle" them, hinting that there could be "a very substantial deterioration" in trade if they did not begin at least monthly inspections of POW camps containing "substantial numbers" of Americans. Whether or not the Swiss agreed to this, Currie was to remind them that they had not adequately investigated serious complaints from American prisoners.

The Swiss, McCloy told Currie, must teach their camp inspectors to be firmly assertive, to reject German excuses for violating Geneva, and to look at matters from the prisoners' viewpoint. Currie should also pressure Bern to challenge the German ban on stockpiling Red Cross food parcels. He was to find out "how far the Nazification of camp administration and control have gone." What were the Swiss doing about this and about "American prisoners who probably have been or will be moved westward" away from invading Soviet armies?[5]

When McCloy showed these instructions to the State Department, Acting Secretary of State Joseph Grew urged caution: "I consider it of the utmost importance," he said, to make "an objective evaluation" to verify "whether the facts fully support" these grave charges, based upon "information supplied by an American officer formerly detained in a POW camp in Germany."[6] McCloy interpreted this reply to mean that the State Department approved War's campaign against Swiss malfeasance. He placed Grew's letter in the documentary arsenal bound for the Inspector General's desk.[7]

The Swiss government was already displeased with American newspaper accounts of maltreated GI prisoners (based on War Department releases), which reflected badly upon the Protecting Power. The Swiss ambassador complained through an unlikely medium: Archibald MacLeish. The noted poet and State Department employee reported that, after apologizing for "broaching a subject outside of MacLeish's jurisdiction," the Swiss minister had expressed "unhappiness over the stories about his country." He had also remarked "that Nazi prisoners who murder fellow prisoners on the ground that they have given information to [the United States] Army might perhaps be considered as less culpable than those" who did violence for reasons other than "loyalty or discipline."[8]

The Swiss minister sent the State Department another cable, marked urgent, on January 23, about forty-eight hours before the Beyer Five were due to hang: The Germans now agreed to send trial records, though these contained "merely a general description of the proceedings." Because American records did not show how or why judges reached their decisions, the only way the United States could comply with Geneva Article 66 was to make entire court records available to the German government. Those for the Beyer trial had arrived in Berlin on December 30, 1944, after seven days in transit. Hanging the Beyer Five sooner than three months after that date would violate the Geneva Convention.[9]

Immediately after this cable arrived, E. Tomlin Bailey, head of State's SWPD, telephoned both Asst. PMG Bryan and Col. Bernays of G-1's Special Branch;[10] Col. Bernays kept track of captured American personnel and was close to Secretary of War Stimson. The next day, January 24, Stimson grudgingly reversed his policy: "Solely in order to remove all grounds" for

Germany's claim that the Beyer Five had been denied any Geneva right or protection—Stimson told Stettinius to make that motive clear—the War Department had given orders to "defer the execution of these sentences until March 31."[11] Grew so notified the legation on January 25 (the old execution date). He also telegraphed the American Legation in Bern: "Please request Swiss urgently to inform their Legation [in] Berlin."[12]

Why had Stimson unbent? His diary for January 25 records a meeting "in respect to German atrocities on American prisoners," at which he told John McCloy that he had yielded not so much because the Nazis threatened to kill a few "perfectly guiltless" Americans to prevent the just execution of Germans who murdered their own comrades for undue friendship with America, but because of the Nazi failure to treat "American prisoners in general" according to the Geneva Convention. "And we are now afraid that there will be mass murders as the Russian troops and our troops converge on the present camps in Germany where our prisoners are being held. It is a very ticklish and trying situation." The Joint Chiefs of Staff were urging him to announce that for every American the Germans killed, "we shall set aside a thousand of their prisoners . . . and hold them subject to being disposed of after the war . . . either by turning them over to the Russians for forced labor or otherwise." Stimson was still considering this suggestion (though Geneva forbade reprisals against war prisoners).[13]

Two days later, on January 27, the legation handed State another "very urgent" and very angry cable from Berlin. The Beyer trial records revealed that the deceased Kunze

> had been in traitorous association with the American information service. The American authorities are to be blamed to a considerable extent for his death, because after having used him for their purposes they left him to remain among honor-loving German prisoners of war, although the authorities undoubtedly had been aware that he would be in danger there.
>
> The German prisoners of war upon learning of his acts of treason had no opportunity to have him brought to court and thereby prevent him from continuing the traitorous activities.[14]

Furthermore, the American trial records contained no proof that any of these five loyal soldiers had inflicted any sort of injury upon Kunze. "The only thing against them was participation in a fight in the course of which Kunze was killed," either by accident or by an unknown person. The just penalty according to German law would be "at the most . . . a few years' imprisonment."

The extraordinary severity of American law, evidently "based on special circumstances of American civil life" (Jim Crow?) was not suitable for German war prisoners. Since the United States refused to abide by the Geneva Convention, the German government had to conclude that such unjustified severity was a pretext for terrorizing all German war prisoners. "Therefore, the German Government expects that this execution will not be carried out." State immediately sent this note to Gen. Bryan and Col. Bernays.

American authorities were also learning more about the GIs that Germany had condemned. On January 26, two men from the Judge Advocate General's Office and two from the State Department interviewed two repatriated ex-prisoners at Walter Reed Army Hospital.[15] One of them, Lt. Archie W. Sornberger, had been briefed at Stalag Luft 1 to report on the trial of Col. J. S. Spicer, senior officer in a compound of fifteen hundred Americans. One night, after the commandant had threatened to cut off the prisoners' coal supply unless they returned an iron bar stolen from a latrine window, the guards had demanded that Spicer assemble his men for a midnight head count. Spicer not only refused but, rumor had it, "threw the Germans out of his room."

When the guards made a bed check anyway, Spicer "got 'sore.'" Next morning at roll call, instead of asking his men to return the iron bar, "he said among other things (a) The Germans are the same bastards as in 1940 when they were winning the war. (b) The Germans shot prisoners of war at Arnheim so that they could not be recaptured. (c) He would be willing to stay in a prisoner of war camp ten more years if it would kill more Germans." He was not trying to foment mutiny, he announced, but "only expressing his personal opinion. There was a loud cheer from the Americans."

Lt. Sornberger did not know if Col. Spicer had a defender at his trial, around December 27. He did have a cot to sleep on in solitary confinement. No one spoke of any "beatings or other mistreatment." There was a rumor, started by "a German G-2 man" at Stalag Luft I, that Spicer "had been condemned to death in order to exchange him."[16]

Another repatriated soldier, Col. Hasket (Hoskot), described how Lt. Col. W. H. Schaefer and Lt. James Schmitz had been condemned to death.[17] While Schaefer, always "a thorn in the side of the Germans,"[18] was serving as acting camp spokesman at Oflag 64, a friendly interpreter named Diest [*sic*] asked his secretary, Lt. Schmitz, for permission to place a poster on a bulletin board reserved for American notices. (There was another for German orders on the opposite wall.) The poster contained a provocative warning from the commandant that escapees would be shot. Schmitz checked with Col. Schaefer, who refused permission and told him to "offer token resistance if

Diest insisted." Schmitz then stood in front of the notice board until Diest nudged him aside. Col.l Schaefer then complained to the commandant.

Several weeks later, an Abwehr (military intelligence) officer began asking questions. In early December, Col. Schaefer was taken away to become, the GIs were told, senior officer at a new camp. Later, a guard revealed that he had been sent to the infamous maximum security camp at Colditz.

On December 26 the camp spokesman, Col. Goode, was told that he and one interpreter might attend the trial of Schaefer and Schmitz the next day. He was permitted to telegraph the Swiss Legation in Berlin but forbidden to bring a fellow officer who was a lawyer.[19] The next morning he was allowed to speak to Col. Schaefer in the presence of a German interpreter. A civilian lawyer from the Swiss Legation, arriving five minutes before the trial, was forbidden to speak to either defendant.

After a three-hour trial, the court took twenty-five minutes to levy the death penalty "for using force against the Reich." Back at camp, the Germans "were horrified," Hoskot said, and some of them said the two had been condemned "for their value in exchanging hostages."[20] Even "Colonel Schneider, the German Camp Commandant, came into the compound to call on the Senior American Officer, something which he particularly never does, and expressed his regret." Lt. Schmitz remained at Oflag 64 in solitary confinement, but the commandant allowed the prisoners to send him comfort articles such as books, food, and fuel, "and the Germans seem to be doing all they can for him."

Col. Goode had been told he might petition either the military district headquarters or Hitler himself for leniency. Diest, the German translator who had hung the poster, told Col. Hoskot that he had worked all night for two nights translating Goode's petition.[21]

Col. Schaefer was returned to Colditz Prison, a place where the High Command sequestered its prime hostages and most escape-prone prisoners. According to the German security officer there, "We put Schaefer in solitary confinement when he came back. Hitler himself had been advised of the affair, as head of the Holding State."[22]

In his memoir of Oflag 64, published in 1983, Clarence Ferguson vividly describes the Schaefer-Schmitz trial and the tensions leading to it. (Ferguson was a lawyer who defended fellow POWs in a dozen trials.) Although German POW camps were under military control, after the failed attempt to kill Hitler in July 1944 the Nazi Party expanded its influence. One instance of this was a ban on war prisoners using sidewalks. In October 1944 three officers from Oflag 64 were court-martialed for refusing to walk in the gutter. Ferguson, sent to the town of Greniesen to defend them, describes how the camp guards were replaced by party troops, "an ominous detachment in full field uniform" led by Hauptmann Zimmerman, "the hated Nazi commander of the area." He and the defendants were forced to walk in the streets, emptied of traffic but lined with gawking civilians and armed party officials. "We must have been publicized as very dangerous men," Ferguson thought.

Fortunately, the judges were regular army men and there was a Swiss observer at the trial. Ferguson's case for the defense was that gutter walking was an affront to military honor. He quoted famous German jurists on the subject of human dignity. The men were declared not guilty (for the time being; see discussion in chapter 16).[23]

In Ferguson's opinion, this verdict wounded Hauptmann Zimmerman's pride. His need for vengeance led to the provocative notice posted by "one of Zimmerman's underlings." (Diest was evidently serving as his interpreter.) Schaefer objected because the poster personally slandered every man in camp, violating the Geneva convention. The "young Nazi" replied that Germany was not bound by that. Schaefer then ordered Schmitz to stand in the doorway, but to move at once if he were touched. He believed that any physical contact would allow him to accuse the Germans of assault in the performance of an illegal act. About two weeks later, the two were charged with interfering with an officer and Schaefer was removed from camp.

Ferguson was not alarmed. He had experience with such vague charges.

> Charges filed against POWs were drawn in such a way as to be extremely confusing. I could never determine whether this was widespread or not, but at least in this area they were ambiguous. Equally difficult was the determination as to whether or not a charge was serious or trivial. This charge failed to say whether it was in violation of the military or civilian code. We were denied a copy of the criminal code or military regulations regarding this offense. Even when we inquired about these charges, we were told they were prepared by higher echelon, and no information was available. This was not unusual.

"The underground" said that Schaefer had been sent to a camp for troublemakers. Ferguson thought that would be the end of it. Then, when he was taken to Greniesen on December 28 to defend the two, he was forbidden to speak with Schaefer in private, in spite of his protest that the Swiss government had designated him as the defense. He saw his client for only fifteen minutes in the presence of a German officer. He entered the courtroom cold, without knowledge of the German penal code, the range of punishments prescribed, or the case to be presented by the prosecution.

The prosecution called the German sergeant who had pegged up the poster. He did admit that he had been kept from carrying out his orders for perhaps two or three minutes, and that Schmitz had moved as soon as he was touched. But he could not provide a copy of the poster in question, nor a copy of the orders under which he had acted. Next, a Capt. Pieper, a Nazi party official who had served at Oflag 64 for two weeks on special assignment, testified that Schaefer was a troublemaker. Ferguson challenged this as hearsay evidence. He was overruled. Nor was he permitted to see the report of the incident submitted by the sergeant. When Ferguson implied that Pieper knew nothing about the situation, the chief judge rebuked him: "The witness is an officer in the German Army and as such I instruct you that he cannot tell a lie. You will therefore not question this witness further." Ferguson stated, "If I am not permitted to test this witness as to the source from which he draws his conclusions, we cannot even know the weight to be given his testimony," but to no avail. German law did not permit cross-examination.

Neither Schaefer nor Schmitz was permitted to speak. Although the prosecution made the mildest speech Ferguson had heard in any of the dozen trials he had witnessed, he knew by then the trial was a farce. None of the six judges would make eye contact with him. He used all the arguments that had served him well so far: the honor of soldiers, German legal precedents back to the famous Puffendorf, the contempt to be expected from world opinion if Geneva were breached. Then, after a short wait, they were summoned back to court by "an attendant with tears streaming down his cheeks." Whatever Ferguson had expected, it was not the sentence of "death for an innocuous triviality that at most should have been punished [with] no more than a reprimand."

That night, Hauptmann Zimmerman himself stood guard at the door of Ferguson's cell. Ferguson concluded that "each of us could also be executed at any time." He felt lucky to make it back to camp with Schmitz, who was placed in solitary confinement. Ferguson was pleased that German camp personnel went out of their way to be "good to him when he needed it most."[24]

The next month, the able-bodied prisoners were marched away from camp to prevent their liberation by the Red Army. Ferguson describes their ordeal, and mentions that Lt. Schmitz made several attempts to escape. On one occasion, the commandant barely saved him from being shot out of hand. He finally succeeded in slipping away.

In Washington meanwhile, on January 30, the American Legation in Bern notified State that the Swiss government had formally protested German violations of Geneva Article 60 and their use of the death penalty for petty offenses. The German Foreign Office had denied these charges, but had assured the Swiss ambassador "that competent authorities had received [the] order [to] suspend for [the] time being execution" of all death sentences, including that of Louis Biagioni—a new name!—who had been condemned on September 30. The Swiss had not been notified of his trial.[25] Biagioni made the twelfth American at risk of hanging. The State Department replied through Ambassador Huddle on February 2 that Germany was, indeed, violating Geneva's Article 60. Any trial conducted sooner than three weeks after the Protecting Power was notified of it, was illegal.[26]

Meanwhile, the War Department continued its anti-Swiss crusade. On January 31 Asst. Secretary McCloy (then Acting Secretary) gave a long memo to Maj. Gen. Thomas Handy, Deputy Chief of Staff to George Marshall, Army Chief of Staff.[27] Handy supervised, among other vital things, the General Staff and the three major army commands.[28] Now McCloy gave him an errand, informing him that the Secretary of War, inspired by Col. Drake, was interested in preparing Mr. Lauchlin Currie for his trade mission to Switzerland. Currie would "appreciate" being provided with every specific example Handy could find of Swiss failure "to press the interests of our prisoners of war to the fullest extent possible." These examples should be sent by courier, as soon as possible, to Switzerland.

The Deputy Chief of Staff should also make "a complete investigation" of Germany's improper treatment of POWs "and the possibility of remedial action," McCloy said. As his starting point, he was to use a short report just composed by representatives of G-1 (personnel), G-2 (intelligence), OPD (the Operations Division),[29] and the State Department. Handy should also "make full use not only of Colonel Drake's material but of any other available source." For example, repatriated prisoners should be routinely asked whether the Swiss had adequately represented their interests, how this representation could be improved, and how the Germans had "failed to live up to the obligations of the Geneva Convention." Handy should also conduct his investigation "with a view to obtaining the 'objective evaluation' requested" (allegedly) by Acting Secretary of State Grew on January 27.

The Deputy Chief of Staff handed the task, and McCloy's stack of documents, to an assistant, who, on the advice of G-2, assigned the investigation to the Inspector General (IG) of the Army, with a two-week deadline. The Assistant Chief of Staff of G-2 sent interrogators to interview thirty repatriated GIs at Walter Reed Hospital.[30]

The IG's preliminary report, dated February 8-21, included a long memorandum in which Col. Drake (known to have the secretary's ear) recited instances of Swiss and German perfidy and offered his notion of remedial action: the Swiss, who needed the United States and who, "like their German counterpart will respect a forceful, strong stand," must be made to see that they were too conciliatory. Drake also thought that "publicizing the inhumanity of the Germans will bring speedy relief. The German will go to any extent to prove he is a misunderstood person. He admires force and assumes that conciliatory treatment is weakness."[31]

The IG's investigators knew that the best source of information was in Bern, Switzerland, which was beyond their reach. They consulted the Red Cross instead. Then, looking at the situation in Washington, they found bureaucratic anarchy. The State Department's SWPD was supposed to evaluate "all information regarding violations of the Geneva Convention" and to ask the Swiss to investigate them. The IG's inspectors found twenty file cabinets of correspondence which, for lack of manpower, had never been cross-indexed or classified. In addition, G-2 in the Adjutant General's Office, the War Crimes Commission in the Judge Advocate General's Office, and the Prisoner of War Information Bureau in the Provost Marshal General's Office all had massive files on camp conditions, atrocities, and Geneva violations. G-1, at the General Staff level, was supposed to be "the coordinating and liaison agency," giving State all the War Department's information on prisoners and receiving copies of State's.

The IG's Preliminary Report was limited to what McCloy considered most urgent: specific instances of Swiss deficiencies and German violations. It found that Swiss agents did not visit German camps frequently enough, nor inspect them well enough, to produce any permanent benefit. Camp inspectors minimized certain complaints and failed to report others. The Mixed Medical Commissions were improperly preventing full enforcement of disabled prisoners' Geneva right to be repatriated. On the other hand, the IG also blamed the American POWs themselves. Those repatriated GIs at Walter Reed knew almost nothing about the Geneva Convention. Since Article 27 made each country responsible for informing its soldiers about their rights, the War Department was not doing its job.

The Preliminary Report also found that the Germans disregarded sections of the convention, or interpreted these "at a level far lower" than the United States did. The Germans always used disproportionately harsh discipline against POWs who violated camp regulations. They improperly interrogated prisoners by "duress and violence." Their atrocities included killing prisoners who surrendered after attempting to escape; beating and shooting prisoners for not working hard enough; transporting them under cruel conditions; wounding, killing, or sentencing them to death for minor infractions; and making unreasonable use of solitary confinement.

Although the Protecting Power had reacted to individual atrocities, the report continued, no American agency had made a comprehensive protest. None had considered establishing a policy for treating German prisoners, "if not on a comparable basis," at least according "to the minimum requirements" of the convention. The IG expected that things would inevitably get worse, for Gestapo or SS troops were taking command of POW camps. Half of all American prisoners had been marched away from their camps in subfreezing weather without adequate shelter or supplies.

The Preliminary Report had several recommendations for Lauchlin Currie: He should ask for more frequent camp inspections and more information about the Mixed Medical Commissions. He should ask the Swiss to obtain, from the German government, its written interpretation of Geneva's rules about such things as food, clothing, sanitation, and working conditions, for comparison with the American interpretation; and also "a list of minor and major offenses . . . and the corresponding average penalty appropriate for such violations." Currie should also ask the Swiss to protest "against the practice of preferring the capital charge of 'opposing the Reich' for minor acts." However, Currie should coordinate his demands with the American Legation in Bern.[32]

In his Final Report, dated March 1, the Inspector General skewered the War Department.[33] Too many of its agencies handled only those bits of information pertinent to their special spheres. Since there were now "upwards of 100,000 [U.S.] military personnel" in enemy hands, someone should be responsible for compiling and evaluating information about them.[34]

The Final Report warned that, since Bern was where "most of the action" took place, only the American Legation there had "detailed current information." It took six to eight weeks for the State Department and the American Legation in Switzerland to communicate with each other. Therefore, "this report, and the preliminary report, and the information upon which they are based, are . . . necessarily inconclusive" for justifying criticism of the Swiss government.[35]

Much as Secretary Stimson despised the Swiss, the fact remained that they were the only protectors of captured Americans and also the chief source of information about them. Therefore, like it or not, he sent a report on the IG's work to Secretary of State Stettinius, who, he hoped, would make "an early approach to the Swiss Government" in accordance with it and with the memorandum for Mr. Currie. These documents, with "material . . . undoubtedly available to the American Legation," should provide a "solid foundation" for improving the lives of captured American personnel. Germany's deterioration made it urgent to ensure that Switzerland become, and remain, as effective a champion of American interests as possible. "It is from this point of view, and with this objective, that the War Department would wish to have the matter approached." In spite of the fact that the report was stamped SECRET, the State Department should feel free to use it to that end.[36]

A few days later, State received the Swiss government's very stiff response to Lauchlin Currie's efforts:[37] Switzerland would inform its representatives of the American complaints, even though they were already taking "all measures in their power." The IRC, which was the responsible party in some cases, agreed absolutely with the Swiss government. More camp visitations called for more inspectors, which depended upon German permission, which had been several times denied. Should that be obtained, then of course Switzerland would send more inspectors, which would require more automobiles and gasoline, which Switzerland did not have. The camp inspectors' reports should provide conclusive proof of their intimate knowledge of the Geneva Convention and their concern for the prisoners' well being. There followed a lecture on the practical problems of examining sick prisoners and of delivering food parcels in a country whose transportation system had been destroyed by Allied bombs.

Germany was disintegrating. Not only did bombs deprive prisoners of food and fuel,[38] but their captors brutally removed them from the path of advancing armies—not due to bloody-minded fanaticism, as in the case of the pitiful holocaust victims, but in obedience to Geneva's rule that prisoners be removed from combat areas for their own safety. Rather than leaving them to be liberated, their guards were marching them to overcrowded, ill-provisioned camps in central Germany.

Secretary Stimson's diary shows his deep concern. He told Col. Luther Hill, acting director of public relations, how important it was to get the message out that the American government and the Red Cross were making "very substantial efforts . . . to get food through the German lines to these men." Newspapers had been printing "a lot of atrocity stories which are very true," but hard on the prisoners' relatives.[39] He and his public relations man discussed "the best way to handle" the fact that "several people with an ulterior motive" were saying that German prisoners were pampered—the coddling crisis, again.[40]

Stimson and the Joint Chiefs of Staff feared that the Nazis might begin slaughtering war prisoners. To his credit, on February 8 he and Admiral Forrestal decided to stifle the Joint Chiefs' plan for a public proclamation that for each murdered American, "we shall set aside a thousand of their prisoners" for postwar forced labor "or otherwise."[41] The United States should not be the first to speak of renouncing the Geneva Convention—the very treaty which forbade reprisals against war prisoners. The Joint Chiefs' warning would probably "lead to a reprisal race" in which the Germans would have all the advantages, being desperate and unrestrained by "normal humane considerations." Threats of widespread punishment would discourage surrender and play into the hands of the propaganda minister, Goebbels.[42]

Stimson was goaded into immediate action by a cable from Gen. Eisenhower on February 19, describing German death marches. The general wanted to tell the Germans that if they left their prisoners behind "with adequate supplies of food," none of them would be returned to combat. In only one day, Stimson had a proposal ready to send to London, Moscow, and Bern. The effort left him feeling "very much relieved at having" galvanized his mammoth bureaucracy so promptly.[43] The British agreed, but Foreign Commissar Molotov refused to allow American personnel to come behind Red Army lines to aid to GIs left wandering around Poland and the Ukraine. This perfidy partially deflected Stimson's anger away from the Swiss government and the IRC.

Meanwhile, the coddling crisis continued. The Provost Marshal General's Office still believed that a minority of Nazi fanatics were controlling the prisoners in nearly every American camp.[44] The public relations goal, of course, was to keep this knowledge from the public and, in particular, from Congress.

In mid-February 1945, PMG Lerch addressed a joint meeting of the House and Senate Military Affairs Committees,[45] to reassure them that Nazis were being controlled, not coddled. He told the congressmen that he was going to discuss "three principal secret matters which cannot be made public": indoctrination, the release of POWs willing to fight against Germany, and the execution of POW murderers.

In regard to indoctrination, "the War Department early became aware that Nazi elements would try to dominate the camps," and "early" began coping with this very difficult problem by "painstaking intelligence work, screening and more screening to separate the good from the bad." It was not easy, screening "over 300,000 Germans—enough to completely populate a city the size of Jersey City, Denver or Omaha." Some were Gestapo agents, "but they all looked alike, talked alike, and to an untrained eye, thought alike." Mistakes were made; but today "the known trouble-makers have been segregated" from "cooperative prisoners." In addition, "every camp" had a notice on its bulletin board announcing that any prisoner seeking safety "need only report . . . to the nearest American officer or enlisted man and he will be given protection."

These measures worked so well that the Nazis had managed "only five murders and two forced suicides," and none at all since April 1944. In fact, "the murder and suicide rate among German prisoners of war is lower than the rate shown by insurance statistics for the general German public in time of peace." The perpetrators had been caught, tried, and condemned.

As for efforts at indoctrination, these were premature "so long as Nazis were mixed with non-Nazis and anti-Nazis," with "as many as 35,000" new prisoners arriving each month. However, the War Department already had, at a secret location, seventy-six anti-Hitler prisoners, "outstanding doctors, lawyers and businessmen," busily "assisting and advising the Special Projects Division of my office."[46] Their goal was to "impress upon the German mind the benefits, the greatness, the firmness, the justice, and the power of American institutions." Lerch warned the congressmen that this noble program would fail if the prisoners ever got wind of its existence.

This was true also of the second secret topic, allowing captured German military personnel of Dutch, Belgian, Polish, Russian, or other origin to fight against Germany. If the Nazis learned that four thousand prisoners who were Soviet citizens had been "returned to the Soviet Government," they might revenge themselves by "turning our people over to the Japanese."

The final "highly secret" item was death sentences for German murderers. The president had already confirmed eight of them, in three murder cases. The first five assassins should have been hanged already, but due to a problem with paper work [*sic*], their "earliest execution date" would be March 31—and whether it would take place then "has not yet been determined." The president had not yet confirmed seven other death sentences for a fourth murder. A fifth murder had never been solved.[47]

The fact that these murders had ceased was proof that the "segregation has been fairly successful. However, we could never be sure." Lerch warned the congressmen again about loose lips. A "premature disclosure" of the proposed executions might result in reprisals against American boys. As soon as the Germans learned "through some source unknown to us" that the first five killers had been condemned, they had sentenced five Americans to death and demanded a trade.

To this audience, in secret, Lerch could brag about the labor program. The War Department had obtained $102,000,000 from 29,750,992 man-days of work from the 359,624 war prisoners on American soil, all performed in ways permitted by the Geneva Convention. Geneva, Lerch emphasized, was no "scrap of paper," but a treaty ratified by Congress and therefore, according to Article 6 of the Constitution, ranked as "*the supreme law of the land*."[48] It was the War Department's solemn duty to enforce it. That meant treating war prisoners humanely, protecting them "particularly against acts of violence, insults, and public curiosity," lodging and feeding them equally with American troops at base camp, and providing intellectual diversions and sports. "*Any deviation*" from its terms "*probably would result in instant retaliation*" against thousands of American boys in German hands.

On the other hand, the War Department had "an abundance of evidence" that good treatment of German prisoners made Hitler treat Americans better. The *New York Times* had recently revealed that British and French prisoners were eating rats, but Americans were eating as well as German civilians and base camp troops, and a weekly eleven-pound Red Cross parcel brought their diet up to American standards. Lerch quoted a Red Cross official:

> The greatest single factor which gives us strength in getting relief and maintaining regular communication with our prisoner kin is the scrupulous attitude of the American Army in fulfilling the Treaty of Geneva toward enemy prisoners. Some have lightly called this policy of our Army "mollycoddling." The truth is that the Army has maintained the highest discipline in handling enemy prisoners. It treats these men strictly but fairly and has obtained from them millions of valuable man-work hours.[49]

Furthermore, Lerch told the congressmen, America's pro-Geneva policy was lowering the enemy's fighting morale. He quoted a story about "a diehard rear guard" which, though ordered "to fight to the last bullet," had surrendered a well-fortified position because letters from captured comrades told them they could expect excellent treatment, not death or torture as their officers claimed. So, the correspondent had said, letting German war prisoners have cigarettes when ordinary citizens went without was a small price to pay for taking Nazi fortresses without resistance. "From that point of view, our policy of living up to the Geneva Convention is smart tactics."

Lerch assured his audience that every individual who dealt with war prisoners had only "one dominating thought," namely, "to do everything humanly possible to insure that our own people" would return home in the best possible physical and mental condition. "To accomplish this we are ever on the alert to avoid anything which will give the enemy an excuse for failing to give our men everything to which they are entitled." He praised the House Military Affairs Committee, whose recent investigation had "failed to substantiate any of the numerous coddling rumors," and which had understood that "the slightest deviation" from the convention "would instantly result in more than retaliatory measures" against Americans.

"Now," Lerch invited the congressmen, "let's talk a little about so-called Nazi domination of the camps." The public was misinformed by articles like the one recently published in "a magazine of wide circulation and splendid reputation," which was "replete with errors and untrue statements," by a man who had "never been in a prisoner of war camp," nor troubled to consult Lerch's office or the Army's Bureau of Public Relations,[50] which gladly checked facts, permitted camp visits, and gave off-the-record briefings to serious writers.

Those who failed to take advantage of these opportunities generated "thousands of letters from persons all over the country," some well-meant and some amounting to "deliberate harassment." The War Department gladly answered every one, though it cost "thousands of much needed man-hours." For example, after someone accused the Army of making 200,000 pairs of pajamas for German war prisoners, 125 angry citizens had to be assured that these garments were for American boys in German camps.

Lerch sympathized with the congressmen for the hundreds of similar letters they received. He urged them to consider the fact that 350,000 prisoners were being handled by only 20,000 to 30,000 Americans. Mistakes happened. All he asked was that they would not discredit the whole program on the basis of a few stunts pulled by prisoners out to embarrass their captors, egged on by "a few writers and commentators" who failed to check their facts. Lerch ended by saying that the tremendous job of controlling more than a third of a million war prisoners, while making maximum use of their labor, was a task for the whole American nation, not just the War Department. He knew that the congressmen would help get the job done right.[51]

The Provost Marshal General's speech was well timed and effective. Although the House Committee on Military Affairs would begin a new coddling investigation only two months later, its second report to the House, submitted on June 12, 1945, would tamely follow Lerch's line.[52]

Had the congressmen but known, the real story in the PMG's peroration was that the German government was threatening to execute Americans to save its own soldiers from being hanged. Of course, he did not reveal that the War Department was refusing to save American lives by trading off a few condemned Germans.

CHAPTER 16

Playing Chicken

In early 1945, the War Department made it harder for the Swiss Legation to obtain answers to its inquiries about the American interpretation of the Geneva Convention, including trials and "sentences imposed by courts-martial."[1] It refused the legation's request for a copy of its POW regulations, forcing the Swiss to ask the State Department to ask the Pentagon to answer even minor questions.[2] In addition, the PMG's Office was slow to deliver the complaints of condemned Germans—although, in the General Staff office, Col. Drake was outraged when he learned that the Germans had delayed a letter he had written as senior officer at Oflag 64. He placed this crime on his master list of Swiss, Red Cross, and German perfidy that he assembled for the Inspector General.[3]

Meanwhile, at the Fort Leavenworth Disciplinary Barracks (USDB), where most of the condemned Germans were held, Edgar Menschner, Erich Gauss, and Rudolf Straub complained to their Protecting Power that their right to correspond was being violated.

The jailers at the USDB were offended by the war prisoners' special status.[4] The fort's adjutant complained to the Correction Division of the Adjutant General's Office in early December, 1944 that they believed themselves still entitled to "the protection of all of the rules contained in the Geneva Convention." He forwarded a copy of the DB's "Instructions to Prisoners of War" designed to "correct their misunderstanding": They were to be informed that they were now only ordinary prisoners with "certain privileges." They could receive visits from the IRC and the Protecting Power "as a matter of policy" because Germany also allowed these. They were "not entitled as a matter of right" to the provisions of Geneva Articles 60 through 67—even though Article 67 declared that "no prisoner of war may be deprived of provisions of Article 42 . . . as a result of" being sentenced for a crime. Article 42 granted POWs the right to complain to their Protecting Power and to American military authorities.[5] Prisoners could still write their complaints without fear of punishment, even if these were unfounded, said the "Instructions." However, the Fort Leavenworth authorities narrowly interpreted this "privilege" to mean that POWs could complain only about conditions at the prison. POWs still might send one personal letter and postcard per week; but like ordinary convicts they were allowed only four pre-approved correspondents, excluding all females except wives and close relatives.[6] The POWs particularly resented the limits on their personal correspondence.

Menschner, Gauss, and Straub forwarded a copy of these rules to the Swiss Legation on December 29, 1944. Menschner and Beyer asked to be visited by a Swiss inspector. State delivered these letters to the legation on January 5, 1945, with the comment that steps were being taken to reconcile Geneva's rules with those at the USDB.[7]

Other complaints were not delivered so promptly. Erich Gauss wrote the legation on January 23 inquiring about a missing letter he had written the previous July, which contained a petition for clemency. Maj. Stephen Farrand, chief of the PWD legal branch, finally gave Gauss's inquiry to State's SWPD on February 3, with an explanation of sorts: Gauss's letter must have gone astray before his arrival at the DB. Farrand's office had been "unaware of the existence of the clemency appeal" and was making inquiries.[8] Gauss and Straub were scheduled to hang on March 29.[9]

Erich Gauss appealed his death sentence on the ground that neither he nor the other condemned Germans had any idea "that they would be held answerable for their crime before an American court-martial, since the affair in their eyes, was exclusively a matter of discipline among German troops." They had known nothing about the American Articles of War. The chief of SWPD at State warned Assistant PMG Bryan that "in view of the fact that this same argument had been raised in the Beyer Case, it might be advisable" to make very sure that every POW realized he was "subject to the jurisdiction of American courts."[10]

On January 29, Edgar Menschner complained that he had not received the copy of his trial record to which Geneva entitled him.[11] On March 2, Maj. Farrand, head of the PWD's legal branch, telephoned the War Department's international law expert, Col. Archibald King, for advice. The commandant of Menschner's former camp believed that he should not have it, because he had uttered a threat that the Nazis might persecute the families of the prisoners who had testified against him. King replied that Menschner knew the witnesses' names anyway. One had only to censor his mail and to black out the names in the copy or "full abstract," which had to be sent to Germany after his sentence was confirmed.[12]

Farrand had another problem to deal with. On November 6 the Swiss Legation had asked about "the status of all German prisoners of war still being confined in connection with the Drechsler case."[13] On February 8, he had State reply that only the seven condemned killers remained in solitary confinement, where they enjoyed every privilege to which they were entitled, including exercise. In the near future, they would be transferred to Fort Leavenworth.[14]

Two days later, the Protecting Power politely asked State to bring "to the attention of the appropriate American authorities" the fact that when its inspector had visited Camp Florence, Arizona, he had discovered that Helmuth Fischer, Fritz Franke, Guenther Kuelsen, Heinrich Ludwig, Bernhard Reyak, Otto Stengel, and Rolf Wizuy were "not permitted to talk with each other, to sing, or to whistle," on orders from the Ninth Service Command. Would State please obtain "a statement regarding the permissibility of such orders."[15] (Secretary Stimson should have approved such a thorough Swiss inspection.) Maj. Farrand responded eleven days later. Steps had already been taken to "modify certain of the restrictive regulations." Those prisoners were now at Fort Leavenworth, where they would "receive the same treatment as is accorded to other prisoners of war" held there.[16] He did not say what sort of treatment this would be.

The seven would have been transferred to Kansas sooner or later for the anticipated mass execution. However, they were suddenly hustled out of Arizona to prevent further contact with their Protecting Power. In spite of what the new DB "Instructions" said, Swiss camp inspectors were not permitted at Fort Leavenworth.[17] (But the Germans had allowed Col. Schaefer to see one at Colditz.)

Meanwhile, the State Department was gathering morsels of information about those condemned Americans. On February 7, the Bern Legation airmailed a copy of the German court's evidence against Sgt. Angelo Nicosia.[18] On October 24, 1944, a GI in his work party became ill "so that he had to vomit." When the guard, not observing this, ordered him to "work more industriously," Nicosia swore at him. Insulted, the guard had shoved him in the back with his gun butt. Nicosia slugged him in the eye and grabbed his gun, holding the barrel down between his legs until the foreman intervened. At the trial, which had been set forward from January 19 to December 30 without informing the Protecting Power, the president of the court had told Nicosia that his "chosen" defender would be the lawyer Zobel of Neustettin.[19]

On January 2, Zobel informed the Swiss Legation in Grosswudicke (it had been bombed out of Berlin) that he had defended the accused "upon request of the counsel of the American prisoners of war of camp Hammerstein," who had "participated in the trial" along with the camp's "man of confidence" (spokesman). In court, Nicosia had "admitted the statement of facts in principle," only insisting that he had grabbed the gun first and then slugged the guard. "The Court-Martial has considered the conduct of the accused to be an assault against a superior and regards it, therefore, according to paragraph 97, section 2 of the Military Code, as an especially serious case."

Zobel said he had defended Nicosia by pleading the "subjective" facts of his character: He had volunteered to work, though as a sergeant he was exempt. His interference, though unjustified, was an act of comradeship. The accused "believed that his life was in danger when the guard went for him with the firearm." He let go of it as soon as the foreman asked. Finally, the incident had no consequences. All the prisoners had resumed work immediately. Zobel added that he planned to protest the death penalty and, in case the sentence was confirmed, to move for its commutation to "definitely limited imprisonment."[20]

Ambassador Huddle also sent a summary of Thomas Jefferson Snowden's defense, and his petition for pardon.[21] Snowden was a mere NCO, a blacksmith from Rutland, Ohio; but his German lawyer Lommatzsch reported that "Supreme Court Martial Judge Dr. Gerhard Voigt attended his trial on behalf of the High Command of the German Army." In the petition for pardon,[22] Lommatzch did not dispute that Snowden had socked the work supervisor who had knocked his breakfast bread out of his hand, thereby violating paragraph 97 of the German military code. However, this paragraph said that in an "especially serious case" the penalty could be—not must be—either death or life imprisonment or imprisonment for as little as one year. The court had chosen death because Snowden had disobeyed before witnesses and "in the field." Lommatzch argued that the supreme penalty should logically be reserved for "a conceivably most serious case," one causing death or serious injury to a much higher superior. Snowden had only clipped a private's chin, without premeditation, and had received a blow in return—two automatic reflexes, perhaps.

There was another mitigating point, Lommatzsch argued—lack of communication. Snowdon testified that the guard never told him to stop eating. The guard had told several stories. First, that he had ordered him to quit twice, through an interpreter; then, that a British prisoner had told Snowdon he should quit; then, when the judge had asked how the guard knew what had been said, since he did not speak English, he claimed "he had made a sign to the accused with his hand" which he believed that the accused understood. Lommatzsch admitted that slugging a guard was a punishable act even if Snowden had not understood; but the possibility of noncomprehension argued for a minimal sentence. Finally, Lommatzsch suggested that since Supreme Field Judge Voigt had been present at the trial, one should ask his opinion on these points of law.[23]

Lommatzsch also filed a supplement citing a parallel case. A British prisoner was serving a mere thirty months for hitting a guard who had given him a sign-language order to resume work. Lommatzsch had asked the judge in that case, Supreme Field Judge Dr. Haebler, "whether it would be appropriate or advisable" to cite it as a precedent. The judge had replied that "based on completely objective evaluation . . . he considered it as advisable, in any event not dangerous."[24]

The State Department also learned more about Col. Schaefer and Lt. Schmitz when, three months after their trial, the Swiss Legation delivered a letter from the spokesman of Oflag 67, Col. G. V. Millett Jr. Millett explained that the poster which had caused the trouble had violated various articles of the Geneva Convention by making "unsubstantiated and derogatory statements against our allies," by "attacking the honor of the American Prisoner of War," and "by severely increasing the penalty for escape." (Since the Geneva Convention recognized the right to escape, penalties were usually light, though prisoners did risk being shot in the process.) The German Foreign Office merely commented that Lt. Col. Schaefer had "tried to hinder" two German NCOs "by openly ordering an American officer to stand in front of" the bulletin board on which they were attempting to affix this poster. "Apparently, Schaefer wanted to create an incident by this provoking attitude (for example the use of arms)." The "circumspect, cautious and extremely correct attitude of interpreter Heise" prevented this outcome. Colonel Millett's "complaint is totally unjustified."[25]

At the War Department's request, Under Secretary of State Grew had tried to learn more about German military law 97, which governed "punishable acts perpetrated in the field." The American Legation in Bern replied promptly:[26] Paragraph 97 applied to "troops who . . . have been informed officially by the commanding officer that the laws of war are applicable to them for the duration of" mobilization, and also to "prisoners of war who have been informed officially by the highest commanding officer at their place of detention that the [German] laws of war are applicable to them."[27]

The War Department received this information from State the same week in which it rejected Gauss's petition for clemency, on the ground that he had never been informed of his liability under the American Laws of War.

On February 22, Maj. Farrand of the PWD's legal branch sent the SWPD a note from Erich Gauss, thanking his Protecting Power for helping him prepare his petition for clemency. Farrand instructed the SWPD to say that the missing copy of Gauss's petition had been found attached to the trial records, which after judicial review would be forwarded by the JAG "for submission to The President."[28] Farrand omitted to say that the president had been advised to reject the plea. The War Department might contrast its own fine observance of Geneva to the Nazis' scofflaw behavior, but it never altered its intention to hang German murderers.

On February 22 Secretary Stimson wrote to Secretary of State Stettinius rejecting as "bogus" the German government's protest against hanging the Beyer Five before a proper three-month interval had elapsed. (This had been delivered on January 26.) In the War Department's opinion—with which, he understood, State agreed—the provisions of Geneva Article 66 had been more than satisfied. The German second point, that the United States was at fault for allowing Kunze, the deceased, "to be exposed to the danger of association with 'honor-loving' Nazis who considered him a 'traitor,'" was also without merit. Geneva did not oblige a Detaining Power to "ascertain" its prisoners' political beliefs or to segregate them accordingly!

Under American law, Stimson continued, mere suspicion that someone was a traitor did not justify his murder. Geneva Article 45 subjected war prisoners to the "laws, regulations, and orders" of their captor's armies. Therefore, the German contention that the Beyer case "would have merited only a light punishment" under German law, and that the true aim of the five death penalties was to terrorize war prisoners, was "wholly irrelevant" and "wholly unfounded." Those five murderers had been fairly condemned by the facts of the case.[29] Stimson ignored the German accusation that none of the five defendants had been proven to cause Kunze any specific injury. The State Department would convey Stimson's message to the Swiss Legation, with a reminder that American authorities had postponed the five executions "solely in order to remove all grounds for a claim that these prisoners of war have been denied any right or protection" to which Geneva entitled them.[30] Stimson had insisted upon that wording.

On March 1, thirty days before the Beyer Five's second date with the gallows and twenty-eight days before Gauss and Straub were due to swing, the Swiss minister delivered another German note: Berlin rejected the American note of January 20, which demanded that Lt. Franklin Coslett and Lt. James M. Greyfield should be treated as Geneva-protected war prisoners. "Coslett was active as a *franc tireur* in civilian clothing, in a combat area." Greyfield had never been given a German POW serial number because, "giving false data," he had taken "employment with a German political news agency in a foreign country." Furthermore, he was a West Point graduate whose "matriculation number" appeared on "a small metal plate worn on the wrist." He claimed to be an agent of an American information service, number FA 190. (In other words, these two Americans were still liable to be shot out of hand.) The next day, State forwarded this message to Col. M. C. Bernays of G-1, who kept track of Americans in German hands. The War Department would not respond until March 9.[31]

Also on March 2, Ambassador Harrison in Bern telegraphed the State Department that the chief of the Swiss Federal Political Department had told him of "uncontrollable rumors" in Berlin "that Germans intended to liquidate Allied POWS rather than let them fall into Allied hands." Swiss officials had suggested that the American and British governments might wish to promise that "those who well-treated our POWS" would receive special consideration "in the final reckoning." Acting Secretary of State Grew sent a Miss Willis to hand-deliver this message to Bernard Gufler of the SWPD, asking "particularly that this be given careful attention." Gufler later phoned to "give her the background of the case" and to tell her that the White House had been informed.[32] He also told Edwin Plitt, the SWPD director, that she would take the matter up with Mr. Chip Bohlen and that he had sent the White House "a draft warning to the Germans against mistreating our people" (which ironically threatened to publicize the complaints made by prisoners in Hitler's hands.)[33]

On February 28, the American Legation in Bern reported that a Swiss inspector visiting Oflag IV C (Colditz) had heard that "higher German judicial authorities" had confirmed Schaefer's and Schmitz's death sentences.[34]

The fact that Germany was threatening American lives in order to save those of German boys was supposed to be secret, but secrets leak. Coincidentally, in civilian life, Lt. Schmitz had been the secretary of the governor of Illinois, so Illinois's Senator Wayland Brooks wrote the Secretary of State (on Senate Appropriations Committee letterhead) that he was "very much interested" in the case. He had heard that Schmitz and Col. Schaefer were due to die at "Kolitz" prison "on or about March 27, 1945, for impeding the progress of the Reich." Brooks also knew that Swiss authorities had been asked to "arrange for exchange or reduction in sentence if possible." He had been "informed by various divisions" that State's SWPD was handling the matter and that "the War Department can do nothing" until German authorities confirmed the sentences. The senator from Illinois would appreciate being informed at once of any new developments.[35]

Acting Secretary of State Grew replied on March 10, correcting the senator's spelling of Colditz. Their trial was illegal, he said, because the Germans had not given correct notice of its date to the Protecting Power. The two officers were in no immediate danger of execution. "We shall bring all the pressure we can upon the German Government not to proceed." Grew warned the senator that the War Department considered this matter "highly confidential. Since their personnel are involved, I feel that we should accept their decision and request that you do not communicate any information" to anyone else.[36]

The senator's letter must have made State Department employees even more worried about how the public would react if news got out that the government had spurned a chance to save American lives by exchanging a few Nazis. On March 2, Ambassador Harrison cabled an informal suggestion from someone in the Swiss Foreign Office: Schaefer and Schmitz might be exchanged for Hitler's adjutant, Wursche. "Highest German officials" had already proposed this "via Swiss Legation Washington."[37] On March 7, Harrison sent an urgent telegram: his next airmail pouch would contain the report of a Swiss inspector who had seen Schaefer at Colditz and obtained a copy of his appeal.[38]

Before these documents could arrive, someone in the War Department decided to respond at last to the German government's two-month-old proposal to trade the Beyer Five for five condemned Americans. The PMG's Office, G-1, and State's SWPD drafted a note which Acting Secretary Grew delivered to the Swiss Legation on March 9. It was an astounding document in light of War's fierce history of foot dragging. The government of the United States was "prepared to give consideration to exchanging" Americans for "a like number" of Germans. It listed the eleven condemned Americans (a twelfth, Henry R. Spicer, would be added later) and all fifteen Germans, including the Papago Park seven, inviting the German government to choose any eleven of these. In addition, if Berlin gave Washington the full facts about any other Americans at risk of a possible death sentence,[39] the United States would consider adding them to the list and allowing Germany to choose an "equivalent number" of its men. Furthermore, no German would be hanged until the Protecting Power had received a new three months' notice, or at least until April 5, provided that the Germans did likewise. Berlin had until April 5 to consider the proposal. On that same day, March 9, Acting Secretary Grew cabled the text to Bern, with a note asking the Swiss Foreign Office to convey it to its legation in Berlin "for its information and for use in negotiating with the German Government." In case the Germans agreed, the exchange could occur at the Swiss border.[40]

So the Germans had won a diplomatic victory in the face of military defeat. The very nearness of that defeat certainly helped the War Department alter its tactics, though not its strategy. Dangling the promise of exchange would avoid possible bad publicity while preventing the immediate hanging of American boys. When Germany surrendered, those boys could probably be rescued. Then those German murderers could be hanged anyway.

The Swiss camp inspector Rudolf Denzler's report on Col. Schaefer at Colditz prison had arrived on March 7. (Bernays and Bryan received copies on March 26.) Denzler had been allowed to interview him on February 6, though not privately. He found him adequately housed and "in a fair physical condition," although "the strains of past events were evident."

Denzler reported that Col. Schaefer had appealed his death sentence on several grounds. The American senior officer at Oflag 64 had ordered him to protest the hanging of an insulting poster, "but under no circumstances to resort to force." Schaefer had told Lt. Schmitz to stand in the way, but "to move aside as soon as he was touched by a German." The gesture had only been intended to demonstrate objection, not to offer resistance or to provoke force. Schaefer had not been aware that the poster was being displayed on orders of the German High Command.

At the trial, furthermore, the court "permitted itself to be misled by Counsel for the Prosecution on matters of law." Paragraph 96 of the German military code allowed light sentences in "the absence of force, threat or any guilty intent." Schmitz had only delayed the officer by "a matter of seconds," intending no harm. The court also "permitted itself to err in matters of fact" because the witnesses for the prosecution suppressed "defence evidence vital in the interests of a fair and proper trial." Finally, the court "permitted itself to err on a matter of procedure," in denying Schaefer a chance to prepare or present his defense.

Schaefer also implied that the court ignored what little evidence it had allowed. Unteroffizier Heise had testified that Schaefer had neither threatened him nor prevented him from hanging the poster. Unteroffizier Loeffler had said that the Lageroffizier later scolded him for using a notice board reserved for American messages and ordered him to move the poster across the way to the one for displaying German announcements. The camp security officer had testified that Schaefer "had a clear, exemplary conduct sheet." Other witnesses would have testified in Schaefer's defense, had they been allowed to speak: Col. Millett, the camp spokesman, would have confirmed that he had ordered Schaefer to protest strongly, but without using force. The Lageroffizier and a "German captain on the parcels staff" would both have testified that "this mode of protest had been used" twice before without objection.

Schaefer had received only a few hours' notice before his trial began. He had repeatedly been denied permission to see the text of the law under which he was charged. Furthermore, his counsel, arriving at the last moment, had repeatedly been denied permission to consult with him, leaving Schaefer "in no fit condition to defend himself in a trial in which his life was at stake." Therefore the court had rushed to judgment, a procedural error. In sum, Schaefer had "not been treated in full accord with the standard which natural justice dictates."[41]

A week after these documents arrived, State received a cable from Ambassador Harrison: the German Foreign Office saw no reason to cancel the death sentences of Coslett, Greyfield, Biagioni, Martin, Walsh, and Walsh. However, it believed that these five "might be exchanged" for six condemned Germans.[42]

Another proposal offered to exchange either "news reporter Biagioni," or Lt. Col. Schaefer, or Lt. Schmitz for both Erich Gauss and Rudolf Straub. If the Beyer Five were kept alive during discussions for their exchange, none of these five Americans would be hanged in the interim. In addition, the Swiss government delivered the German excuse for not announcing the advanced date for the Schaefer and Schmitz trial: the court had accepted the defendants' choice of Col. Goode and Capt. Ferguson of their camp to defend them.[43] On March 20, the Department of State told the Swiss Legation that the United States rejected this excuse. Moreover, the American government would not respond to any German exchange offer until Berlin responded to its proposal of March 9[44]—which had obviously not yet reached Berlin, although the Swiss Minister assured Stettinius that he had cabled it to Bern immediately.

Communications were so bad by now that the German army commands were losing contact with their courts and with the government. Furthermore, the Swiss themselves were confused about American policy. On March 22, Ambassador Harrison telegraphed State that he was airmailing the text of a German note which expressed confidence that the United States would discuss prisoner exchange as soon as it received copies of the "grounds for sentence in the legal procedure" against the American soldiers. "Unfortunately transmission of these statements . . . could not (repeat not) be accomplished to date as [the] German courts concerned were moved. However, they will be transmitted as soon as technically possible." In view of this fact, the German government was assuming that the United States would postpone those five hangings until the "exchange question is elucidated." Berlin would likewise not execute its five Americans. The German Foreign Office asked Switzerland to confirm this assumption as soon as possible, as well as its expectation that Gauss and Straub would not be hanged while the proposal to exchange them for Biagioni or Schaefer or Schmitz was under consideration. Meanwhile, Biagioni would not be executed. The note concluded ominously: "It may be stated with regard to above mentioned exchange proposal [that the] three months period as applied to death sentences against American POWS Schaefer and Schmitz has not (repeat not) been enforced," so far.[45]

Acting Secretary Grew telegraphed Ambassador Harrison on March 24 to keep on cabling all the information it could gather about anyone on the March 9 exchange list.[46] That same day, the Swiss minister in Washington delivered a German note, dated March 1, which revealed a thirteenth and fourteenth American eligible to hang. It offered to exchange Erich Gimpel and William Colpaugh for the two German prisoners sentenced to death on February 15, 1945;[47] but no German had been sentenced on that date.

A few days later, Grew asked the Swiss government to cable another note to Berlin on the "most urgent basis." First, it pointed out that the latest German communications had crossed an American offer of March 9 to postpone all the executions, as Berlin desired. That note contained "inclusive proposals for exchanges" which, if accepted, would resolve all questions. The American government would wait until April 5 for a direct German reply. As to Schaefer and Schmitz: Since the German government had never provided a statement about the "nature and circumstances surrounding the offense as provided in Article 66" of Geneva, "they should not in any case be executed for at least three months after the delivery of such document to the Protecting Power."[48] (Did Grew realize he was speaking German lines?)

With the April 5 deadline fast approaching, Stettinius sent the following message on March 30 both to the Swiss Legation in Washington and, by urgent telegram, to the American Legation in Bern: Although Germany had not yet replied to the March 9 proposal, "the American Government . . . appreciates that the delay may be due to difficulties of communication. In view of the humanitarian considerations involved," the United States extended the moratorium on executing German prisoners to May 1. It expected the Germans to follow suit. The Swiss were requested "to make every effort" to see that the message was delivered to as many responsible German authorities as possible, including the Army High Command, before April 3, and to report when it was delivered and to whom.[49]

On April 7, Ambassador Harrison cabled another note from the German Foreign Office: Germany agreed to postpone its executions "as long as negotiations for their exchange are in course." If an execution were contemplated, Germany would notify the Protecting Power "in due time,"[50] not a reassuring idea in view of the chaotic communications. Someone at the State Department was also considering the rumor that Germany would slaughter all war prisoners. One finds the word "Malmedy" penciled in the margin of another urgent telegram from Bern, dated April 10: the Swiss had "twice intervened" with the German government, at State's request, to ask whether any American war prisoners had been executed. The German Foreign Office had replied that its inquiries had not revealed any.[51]

Meanwhile, the American public was still reacting to atrocity stories about German camps. The War Department's Bureau of Public Relations prepared a statement which Secretaries Stimson and Stettinius released to the press on April 11: Since the beginning of the year, the German government had increasingly failed to provide for its prisoners "according to the standards established by the Geneva Convention." Allied armies had already liberated around 15,000 Americans from 27 of the 78 camps where they were held. "However, the German Government hastily evacuated 36,000 American prisoners into the interior," in vile weather, without food or medicines, to join about 34,000 others. That made 70,000 GIs living in misery because of "Germany's fanatical determination to continue a hopeless war." Sweden, Switzerland, and the American and International Red Cross were doing everything in their power to get supplies to them. Since the railroad net was in ruins, everything had to be sent from Sweden and Switzerland by trucks using donated gasoline, sometimes driven by paroled war prisoners. The two secretaries promised that the perpetrators of deliberate neglect and cruelty "shall be brought to justice."[52]

Secretary Stimson's department continued to sabotage prisoner exchange. On April 12 the Swiss Legation finally delivered Berlin's response to the March 9 offer: "The German Government is prepared to exchange the fifteen American prisoners of war under sentence of death for an equal number of Germans under sentence of death," meanwhile postponing all executions. After receiving this message, the Pentagon remained silent for fifteen days, half a month.[53] This must have seemed incomprehensible at the State Department.

In the interim, the Pentagon reversed one of its policies by proposing to hand over to Russia all prisoners of Soviet origin captured in German uniforms. (That was Stalin's quid pro quo for allowing Americans into eastern Europe to aid GIs liberated by the Red Army.)[54] At the State Department's SWPD, Gufler and Plitt began drafting a response to this proposal, warning that it was very dangerous. Five-sixths of Germany's American prisoners had not yet been liberated. It would be "most inadvisable" for State to endorse a policy "which might jeopardize the welfare" of American boys. The Germans had warned that "if we make distinctions among [captured] wearers of German uniforms . . . on a basis of nationality they will have to do likewise."[55] Nazi reprisals might be anything from hanging those condemned men, to killing Jewish GIs, to bloody mass murder.

Finally, on April 27, the PMG's Office gave the State Department a reply to the German note of April 12: "The Government of the United States has noted that the German Government is prepared to exchange fifteen American prisoners of war under sentence of death for an equal number of German prisoners" so sentenced. However, Germany had mentioned only eleven condemned Americans! Two of these had now been liberated. Therefore, the United States would appreciate prompt information as to which nine condemned Germans were to be exchanged, so that these could be transported as soon as possible to the Swiss border.[56] Whatever the State Department may have thought of War's response, it dutifully delivered it to the Swiss Legation that same day.

The next day, April 28, the American General Staff adopted this new policy: "No death sentence imposed on German prisoners of war in this country will be carried out, and . . . *no steps will be taken to obtain confirmation by the President of any death sentence not yet confirmed*, until further orders from the Personnel Division," G-1. The pretext was the German threat to execute Americans.[57] The real reason was the War Department's reluctant agreement to hand over trial records as soon as a death sentence had been confirmed. The solution to keeping "obnoxious material" top secret was to freeze presidential confirmation of the remaining eight sentences!

The General Staff soon learned that a dying bee can still sting. The German army must have been scouring the camps for new hostages. At Oflag 64, for example, before Schmitz's and Schaefer's railroading, four lieutenants had been tried in October 1944 for disobeying a guard who was marching them to a nearby town for medical care. The guard had demanded that they walk in the gutter. They had refused to leave the sidewalk and had been court-martialed for their defiance. They had been acquitted conditionally, upon approval of higher authority. Suddenly they were scheduled to be retried on a capital charge. One of them, John Rathbone, now knows that he was a pawn. At the time, he said, "I just thought they were being snotty."[58] Their entire camp was marched away from the advancing front lines before their trial could take place.

On April 26, the American Legation in Bern sent the State Department the gist of a communication from the German High Command to the German Foreign Office. The High Command would not hang any American condemned so far. However, six new trials were pending, involving seventeen Americans who might be sentenced to hang. Three had taken advantage of air raids to commit the crime of plundering: Walter Barrett had stolen thirty-six soup spoons, eight coffee spoons and five knives. David Hazard and George Ball had entered a partially destroyed building and stolen some food which had been intended for the wounded. Their trials had been set for March 21, but the High Command did not know what the verdicts had been. In a third case, Maj. John Tozzi, Lt. Georges Peck, NCOs Mario Mussi and David Colin, and Pvt. Viktor Berruti had all been "accused of having endeavored to engage in espionage." Their trial had been scheduled for April 13. On April 17, Loyd Mathis, Leo Senechal, William Sargent, and Gus Hinson were to be court-martialed for assaulting a home guard, threatening him with his own pistol. Pvts. Orian Manning, Carl Ramberg, Ernst Puntorno, and Ralph Cruse had assaulted two home guards, knocking them down with their own rifles. Finally, the trial of Sgt. Fenton Bean, accused of tearing planks out of a barrack floor and of assaulting a German sergeant with a piece of iron, had been fixed for April 3. All seventeen Americans would be "eligible for exchange." The High Command asked the Foreign Office to inform the Protecting Power of these new trials and to "kindly" see to it that the Americans hanged no Germans "for the present."[59]

This document was dated March 28. It had taken a month to travel from the German High Command to the Swiss Foreign Office, to the American Legation, and thence to Washington, where it arrived on April 26. Worse, on April 28 Ambassador Harrison sent another urgent telegram: the Swiss Foreign Office told him that the German Legation in Bern was no longer able to communicate with the "responsible authorities in Germany," but that it nevertheless believed it might assume that neither country would execute any of its condemned prisoners until the exchanges were organized.[60]

On April 30 Harrison telegraphed that a representative of the "competent section" of the German High Command had told someone at the Swiss Legation in Germany that his section was "completely unaware" of the current location of the American war prisoners "considered eligible for exchange." The Swiss diplomat believed it "highly probable" that these men had been marched away to southern Germany, along with thousands of others. The Berlin legation was "making every effort to ascertain [their] present whereabouts," but did not expect to "meet with early success," considering "present circumstances."[61]

A week later, on May 8, what was left of the Third Reich surrendered unconditionally. The War Department had won the battle to suppress the Papago Park trial record.

CHAPTER 17

Honor and Execution

Drechsler's killers were suddenly removed from Camp Florence on January 27, 1945, and taken to a location where Swiss camp inspectors could no longer have access to them. After a two-day train ride to Kansas City in handcuffs (a common violation of the Geneva Convention), and twenty-five miles in a closed truck,[1] they joined the other eight condemned POWs at the Fort Leavenworth Disciplinary Barracks. In the basement of wing 4 of a building known as the "Castle," they were locked into 5 foot by 10 foot cells with heavy steel bars in front and foot-thick brick walls between them.[2] Soon enough, there would no longer be an intrusive Protecting Power.

On May 9, the State Department announced that "in view of the conclusion of the war in Europe, there no longer exists any need" for a Protecting Power.[3] Switzerland's summary dismissal had nothing to do with a handful of war prisoners in Kansas and everything to do with postwar Europe. The convention required prompt repatriation of war prisoners; but the Soviet Union, which had never signed it, plainly intended to keep their captives for forced labor. "By early 1945 the Americans, too, were planning to use German soldiers in ways not accepted by the Geneva Convention, such as mine clearing."[4]

The Combined (Anglo-American) Chiefs of Staff also realized that they could not easily feed approximately four million new war prisoners by Geneva standards. There was little enough on that ruined continent for the liberated peoples and the refugees who began fleeing Soviet control in unexpected millions. The occupying armies also had to be supplied, and the war in Asia needed all available transportation. The two democracies found a semantic solution to their Geneva obligations. German soldiers surrendering to the Americans after V-E Day were not POWs but DEFs, Disarmed Enemy Forces. British captives became SEPs, Surrendered Enemy Prisoners. Without a government, the Germans were "unable to protect or even to ask others to protect" their imprisoned sons.[5] Americans, once liberated, needed no protection. Now the War Department was free to get on with its hangings.

Richard Whittingham bases his account of the prisoners' last days at the Disciplinary Barracks upon his interviews with the Catholic chaplain, Capt. George Towle. They were cell-bound except for brief, solitary exercise. Father Towle obtained permission for them to mingle in the corridor for most of the day and to have a table there for playing cards. He described Drechsler's killers as "very likeable young chaps, all of them," but very bitter.[6]

Months passed without any sign that the president had confirmed their still unknown sentences. They remarked several times to Father Towle that if they could survive until the war ended, they would probably get to go home. After V-E Day, they told him that "they were not sorry for what they had done. They had acted as they were supposed to do as sailors in the German navy." Since the United States was no longer an enemy country "perhaps the authorities would view their act with more understanding eyes." Father Towle had to reply that he could not make a prediction about that. "He felt there was something terribly inhuman about the long wait for a decision as to whether these young men would live or die."

Whittingham referred to the "humanitarian considerations" which had moved the War Department to delay their executions, adding that "it was certainly not anyone's fault," just "tragic bad luck" that the exchange negotiations "were slower than the Allied war effort."[7] More realistically, he recognized that once the imperiled Americans were safe, fifteen German lives became valueless.

Until the president confirmed their death sentences, the Papago Park seven and Edgar Menschner could still theoretically be reprieved. The president had the power to "consider the provocation, if any, which led to the offense," and all mitigating circumstances. He could reject a guilty verdict or lighten any sentence "at pleasure," or order a new trial.[8] In fact, the overwhelmed Truman was not likely to exercise any of these powers unless advised to do so. He reprieved Menschner because Secretary of War Stimson recommended it upon the advice of the Judge Advocate General, whose trusted aide had found a defect in the trial.

Edgar Menschner was a petty officer—a suspect category—whose alleged crime fit the War Department's model of Nazi terrorist kangaroo court conspiracy far more closely than did Drechsler's murder. He had been sentenced to death in July 1944 for "acting jointly and in pursuance of a common intent with persons unknown . . . wrongfully and unlawfully organizing" a *Soldatenrat* (soldiers' council),[9] which his prosecutors defined as "a clandestine organization composed of ardent Nazis whose function it was to act as political police in POW camps." Having decided that Hans Geller was too friendly with the Americans, this cabal supposedly organized a *Rollkommando*, "a special secret and select group whose function it was to carry out the sentences . . . and to administer beatings to the victims."[10] While unknown men lured Geller from his barracks in Camp Chaffee, Arkansas, and beat him to death, Edgar Menschner had been teaching a class.

There were other striking differences between the investigation of his case and that of Drechsler's murder. The major who served as Eighth Service Command's pretrial investigator seems to have made an honest inquiry.[11] Furthermore, Menschner spoke little and signed nothing at all, not even an acknowledgment that he had been informed of his trial date and of his Article 62 right to a qualified counselor of his own choice named Maj. Jones;[12] and he never testified against any fellow prisoner. One may conclude that he was not tortured.

Unfortunately for him, Menschner's prosecutor was the ambitious Lt. Col. Leon Jaworski, who had already obtained five death sentences in the Beyer case. Fortunately, his case was assigned to a different JAG review board than the one which had considered the Papago Park verdicts. Although two reviewers approved his death sentence, the third wrote a dissenting opinion strong enough to convince Col. William A. Rounds, Asst. JAG for Military Affairs.[13] Rounds told Judge Advocate General Cramer that the available evidence did not prove Menschner's leadership beyond a reasonable doubt.[14] Cramer told Secretary of War Stimson that the accused had indeed "unlawfully organized a beating detail . . . a very serious species of disorder and one that cannot be tolerated." Although the maximum sentence for that offense was hard labor for life, Cramer recommended twenty years. That is what Under Secretary of War Patterson would have advised the White House if the General Staff had not frozen the process for confirming death sentences until after the war.[15]

On June 12, 1945, Maj. Farrand, chief of the legal branch of the POW Operations Division in the Provost Marshall General's Office, unfroze the War Department's bureaucracies with a long memorandum to the Asst. Chief of Staff of G-1: The prisoner exchange negotiations had "failed by reason of Allied military victory over Germany," he said. According to the Adjutant General's Office, ten of the fifteen condemned GIs had been liberated. Since there was no reason to fear that the other five were still being used as hostages to free the condemned Germans, G-1 should restart the process of confirming death sentences. Provost Marshal General Lerch signed Farrand's memo on behalf of the Commanding General of the Army Service Forces.[16] A week later, G-1 notified the PMG's Office that "the prohibitions . . . are removed. Necessary action will be taken."[17] On June 23, the Asst. Secretary of War's office gave its approval to the Deputy Chief of Staff's office.[18]

On June 28, Asst. PMG Bryan directed JAG Cramer to prepare the hangings. The next day, he directed the AG's Military Justice Division to report to him when the president had confirmed the last two cases.[19] On July 8, the Commandant of the Fort Leavenworth DB, Col. Eley, received an inelegantly worded order: he should execute the Beyer Five as soon as he "received official notice that there had been full compliance with Article 66, Geneva Convention." Since such compliance had already occurred, Eley could therefore proceed at once.[20]

While Col. Eley was building his gallows and composing orders for the execution and burial details, the JAG's Office extracted the remaining confirmation paperwork from its files. Four months earlier, Review Board No. 2 had drafted two letters for Secretary Stimson to sign, recommending death for the Papago Park seven; one was addressed to Roosevelt's gatekeeper, Gen. "Pa" Watson.[21] Now one of the reviewers re-addressed it to Truman's military aide, Brig. Gen. Harry H. Vaughan.[22] Truman signed the enclosed death warrants on July 3, as soon as he received them. In the same way, he would approve the recommended twenty-year sentence for Edgar Menschner.

Over in Kansas, on July 6, a lieutenant and two guards told Menschner: "Get your things; you're moving upstairs. . . . You're a very lucky bastard." As the guards hustled him out, one of the others called, "What about us? What are they going to do with us?" The lieutenant did not answer.[23]

Three days later Col. Eley abruptly entered the basement flanked by the Catholic and Protestant chaplains. He coldly informed Walter Beyer, Hans Demme, Willi Scholz, Hans Schomer, and Berthold Seidel that they would be hanged, beginning at midnight the next day, July 9. When that hour arrived, the others watched as they were removed, one by one. Two days later, Col. Eley and his party gave the same message to Erich Gauss and Rudolf Straub.

The Papago Park seven would remain alone in that basement for another forty-eight days. Otto Stengel tried to make a joke of it, often asking Chaplain Towle: "You don't think they've forgotten us, do you?"[24] Perhaps they took heart from the fact that the death sentences of their seven dead comrades had already been confirmed by the American president. Theirs had not been, as far as they knew. Perhaps they would join Menschner upstairs. They had no idea that they owed their extra days of life to red tape.

The "executive action" President Truman had signed was identical to those in the Beyer and the Gauss and Straub cases: "The sentence of each of the accused is confirmed and will be carried into execution" at the time and place chosen by the Commandant of the Fort Leavenworth DB, "after he has received official notice that there has been full compliance with Article 66" of the Geneva Convention.[25] Article 66 said that no war prisoner could be executed until three months after his government had been notified, through his Protecting Power, that his sentence had been confirmed. Someone in the JAG's Corrections Division belatedly pointed out that there was no German government to receive the report and no Protecting Power to deliver it.[26] On July 11 the Acting Chief of the International Law Division told the Chief of the Military Justice Division that, since "Article 66 has not been and can not now be complied with," the Corrections Division should be told not to hang the seven just yet.[27]

On July 18 JAG Cramer sent new memoranda, new death warrants which did not mention the Geneva Convention, and a summary of the case to Acting Sec. of War Robert R. Patterson, with a draft letter explaining to Truman why he had to do the same job twice. Patterson signed them immediately,[28] but Truman was too busy. When he got to it, the new warrants were dated "The White House, July 28, 1945," though he was in the mid-Atlantic in route to the Potsdam Conference on that date.[29]

With obstacles cleared, there was no need for haste. Not until August 21 did the Acting AG telegraph a copy of General Court Martial Orders No. 406 to Col. Eley at Fort Leavenworth, directing him to hang seven Germans, "all of Prisoner of War Processing Station Angel Island, California."[30]

Two days later, at 9:25 that night, Col. Eley marched into the basement again. The prisoners were ordered to stand at attention (probably handcuffed) while Eley read them their fate: "The orders signed by the President of the United States and issued by the Secretary of War will be carried out here August 25, 1945, commencing at zero zero zero one hours." He allowed the chaplains to stay until 10:00, lights out. Father Towle gave them all Holy Communion. He would spend the next day with them also, until he had to join the execution party.[31]

Col. Eley merely adjusted the special orders he had written for the execution of the Beyer Five,[32] who had been hanged between 0001 and 0600, Central War Time, on July 10. Eley had ordered those proceedings to be carried out privately by himself, a surgeon, a chaplain, four official witnesses with the rank of Lt. Col., thirteen enlisted men, and "other necessary personnel." There would be "no advance announcement as to the time and place of executions" and, except for official purposes, "no photographs or motion pictures." There was to be no publicity, "except as directed by headquarters."

On July 6, Eley's adjutant had ordered the Supervisor of Prisoners to select a party of guards. These were to assemble the five prisoners in the corridor outside their cells twenty-four hours before execution, hands cuffed behind their backs, while the commandant read them the execution order in English and a junior officer translated. Then, after clearing the cells of "all articles which could be readily used by a man to injure himself," the guards were to lock them up again in tidy alphabetical order, with Walter Beyer nearest the exit. Two guards would remain with them. The prisoners' last meal would be normal prison fare, eaten with a spoon. Meanwhile, the Supervisor of Prisoners was to make sure their German uniforms were clean and neat.

At midnight, the gallows party was to gather in Building No. 467, a warehouse. The prisoner guard, notified by telephone, was to escort Walter Beyer "with his arms bound behind his back, accompanied by the Chaplain or clergyman of his choice," to vehicles waiting at the main entrance to carry him the next three hundred yards. At the warehouse, two sergeants were to conduct him "to the position designated, the Commandant and the Chaplain or clergyman leading the way." A diagram directed everyone to his place.[33]

Building No. 467, 1st floor

X X X X X X X X X X
Witnesses
X
Flag
X X
Comdt Med Off
X X
Gd X X X X Gd
X Chap Pris X
X X

Off to X
spring trap

After the adjutant had handed "pictures of the condemned man with his name appearing thereon" to him and the witnesses, Eley was to read the charges, the finding, and the sentence. After this was translated, he was to say:

> "Prisoner of War Walter Beyer, you have heard the orders read directing your execution. Have you any last statement to make? (pause) Then may God have mercy on your soul —Chaplain." At the word "Chaplain" the Chaplain begins his prayer. The Sergeant of the execution party then adjusts the hood over the prisoner's head and after moving on to the trap the ankles will be bound and the noose adjusted around the prisoner's neck. The designated officer will then place himself in position at the trigger and upon a signal from the Commandant—downward movement of hand—will spring the trap.

Then the guards were to fetch the next man, by order of rank.

The translator and another officer were to "make note of any unusual incidents or last statements," and the adjutant was to record the time of each man's arrival, the springing of the trap, and the medical officer's pronouncement of death. The Supervisor of Prisoners was to ensure that no unrest occurred among the other inmates. Afterward, Col. Eley was to report to the Pentagon while the surgeon signed the death certificates and had the bodies removed, the summary court officer disposed of their effects, and the acting quartermaster buried them.[34]

Three days before the Beyer Five were hanged, the War Department authorized Eley to invite the press. Seventh Service Command's public relations officer chose several reporters and fed them the "facts." The Leavenworth *Times*' front page announced: "FIVE PRISONERS OF WAR EXECUTED EARLY TODAY AT THE DB, Germans Found Guilty by Army Court-Martial at Oklahoma Camp of Murdering Fellow Prisoners—Trap Springs First at 12:17—A Two-Hour Session, FOR HISTORY BOOKS, First Such Incident in Annals of U.S. Army." The article continued: "Described as 'fanatical Nazis,' the five resorted to murder" of an anti-Nazi "in their attempt to maintain control over their fellow prisoners." The Catholic and Protestant chaplains and a local Lutheran minister gave them spiritual comfort. Their cleaned, pressed Afrika Korps uniforms became their burial garments. Only one of them, Beyer, had made a final statement: "I can't see why this is being done to me."

After a dramatic recounting of the crime with subheadlines such as "Traitor in Group" and "Stumbles out Door . . . Dies," the Leavenworth *Times* assured its readers that the War Department had strictly adhered to "the pertinent provisions of the Geneva Convention" by notifying the German government before the trial, furnishing it with a copy of the charges, inviting a representative of the "protesting [*sic*] power" to attend, and notifying it of the verdicts and sentences.[35]

Other newspapers printed the same information.[36] William Radford of the Kansas City *Star* produced a front-page article describing how a praying chaplain followed each man right up to the "unusual" gallows, "a removable device which can be set up in a few hours" inside an elevator shaft on the first-floor level.

> The trap itself is a three foot square opening and is operated by a four foot metal lever out of sight of those attending the condemned. . . .
>
> On the trap five soldiers busied themselves fastening the condemneds' feet with light rope and another 1/4 inch rope was tied around his waist. The hangman's rope was seven-eighths of an inch.
>
> At the second floor level a 4 by 20 inch timber was swung across the shaft opening to anchor the rope. Each time a Nazi went to his death the hangman's knot was cut off and more rope lowered from the top to compensate for the shortage. The drop was 7 feet into the shaft to the basement of the building.

The average time between pulling the lever and declaring a prisoner dead was sixteen minutes.[37]

Eley's adjutant prepared identical orders for the executions of Helmut Fischer, Fritz Franke, Guenther Kuelsen, Heinrich Ludwig, Bernhard Reyak, Otto Stengel, and Rolf Wizuy.[38] Each of the young U-boatmen submitted to death with self-possessed resignation—"stolidly and without murmur of hatred for his executioners," according to the Kansas City *Star*. For last words, Fischer, Kuelsen, Ludwig, Stengel, and Wizuy thanked Father Towle. This chaplain had accompanied the officer and guards who fetched each prisoner in alphabetical order (being enlisted men with no rank distinctions). As soon as one fell through the gallows trap, Towle had to run down a ramp and around the building, enter the elevator shaft, mount a stepladder as soon as each convulsing body permitted him to do so, slit the black hood with his pocket knife, and anoint the dying man on the forehead with oil from a flask in his hip pocket. Then he gave place to the doctor, who eventually announced when death occurred. On the first occasion, when the chaplain saw Fischer's convulsions, someone told him, "Don't worry, father; he's unconscious."[39]

When the guards came for Otto Stengel, he asked to be buried with a photograph of his wife and two sons, one a toddler he had never seen. When the officer hesitated, Chaplain Towle got the picture and stuck it in Stengel's pocket. He had to explain what it was when Col. Eley noticed it.[40]

This time, the fort's own public relations officer handled the publicity. According to Whittingham, both press and radio reporters were present; but this execution produced much less comment than the first one.[41] The fort's own newspaper had only a brief notice, though its viewpoints were unique. It proudly announced that a new system used at "the greatest mass hanging yet held at the Ft. Leavenworth institution" had saved more than an hour "in the procedure."[42]

Mass burial followed. After Father Towle left the graveyard, a member of the burial party contemptuously removed Stengel's family photo.[43] The fourteen executed Germans lie in a row, at right angles to the graves of American dead who, in additional dishonor, lie on a north-south axis. Traditionally, corpses lie with their feet toward the east, ready to greet Christ on Judgment Day.

The Pentagon bureaucrats gave themselves full credit for dealing honorably and well with a dangerous wave of Nazi terror. Once it was safe to do so, they bragged that their policy of observing every provision of the Geneva Convention had forced the Germans to do likewise, to the comfort and salvation of countless GIs. For example, Provost Marshal General Lerch's speech to the House and Senate Military Affairs Committees became an article published under his name in the *American Mercury* of May 1945.

The article began by describing an irate letter Gen. Lerch had received. The writer had sent a photograph of happy German war prisoners somewhere in New England and had asked: "When our sons, brothers and husbands are dying, why are these beasts petted and pampered here? Ye gods! What ails our Army anyway?" Lerch's answer was that the Army had done what the Geneva Convention required, because it was the fundamental law of the land like every treaty ratified by Congress. Treating it like Kaiser Wilhelm's "scrap of paper" would have meant "that this government had sacrificed the place of honor and moral leadership that it has earned in the eyes of the world and had sunk to the level of Japan, whose emissaries talked peace while its army went to war." The Geneva Convention, Lerch said, "was one of the few international laws that has withstood, with a considerable measure of success, the hatred and lawlessness that war breeds." It was "a seed of international comity which we hope will grow strong and serve as an inspiration and guidepost to those who would make other international laws."[44]

By the time this article appeared, the War Department had jettisoned the Geneva Convention, "honor and moral leadership" notwithstanding. Just over a year later, it would drop all pretense of bringing terroristic Nazi prisoners to justice.

CHAPTER 18

Afterwards

Before the War Department abandoned its project of bringing Nazi terrorists to justice, it reopened a cold case. A German prisoner unexpectedly confessed to helping beat Hugo Krauss to death in December 1943 at Camp Hearne, Texas. Krauss was the prisoner whose unhappy American relatives had embarrassed the War Department. The confessor, Guenther Miesel, had not even been a suspect when Krauss's death had been investigated. In fact, Miesel had been trusted enough to drive newly repaired trucks from one army base to another.

On one trip he had stopped to help a young woman with car trouble. It was love at first sight, sustained by letters and a few clandestine meetings. "She was a Christian and she hoped that I, dearest Guenther, loved Jesus too," he told a chaplain. Her influence caused this former member of Hitler Youth "agony and conflict in [his] soul," particularly when she told him that unless he repented and accepted Jesus, his sins could not be forgiven. "She did not have the faintest clue of how grave and serious my sins were." He expected her to abandon him when he told her that he had helped kill a man, but she only urged him to confess the crime. And so this new convert did, to an astonished American officer.

Miesel and six others were court-martialed at Camp Swift in Bastrop, Texas, in January 1946 and condemned to life in prison at hard labor. However, only three months later, the Judge Advocate General's review board canceled two convictions and reduced the remaining sentences to ten or fifteen years. Meisel was to serve fifteen at Fort Leavenworth.[1]

Another POW murder case was reopened when someone at the Pentagon asked why Erich Menschner should be serving twenty years at Fort Leavenworth for inciting the group which had killed Hans Geller, while his hands-on murderers had gone free. By then, these individuals were lost among the thousands of prisoners being sent home or to forced labor. A few of these suspects were finally located at Fort Eustis, Virginia, where, having been labeled "white" (good, anti-Nazi) Germans, they were enrolled in a crash course on "historical and ethical truth as conceived by Western Civilization," which would supposedly make them reliable democrats in postwar Germany.[2]

In late September 1946 the Adjutant General ordered the Commander of the First Army in New York to investigate Geller's murder more thoroughly.[3] On February 5, 1947, he reported that three of the ten available suspects deserved prosecution. However, he added, the evidence against them was "conflicting, fragmentary, secondary and inconclusive." A guilty verdict would depend, greatly or wholly, on their willingness to incriminate themselves. The trial would be "expensive in time and money," unpredictable in outcome, and furthermore pointless: "The current policy of the Under Secretary of War, acting through his Clemency Boards, is *to repatriate immediately prisoners of war convicted by general court-martial of offenses solely against their fellow prisoners, not involving United States personnel or property, and to remit all sentences effective upon repatriation*"! Because no sentence would ever be enforced, it would save time and money to repatriate these suspects immediately.[4]

The Secretary of War's office agreed. It was a new, cold war world. John McCloy, former Secretary Stimson's man, who was now High Commissioner for Germany, was engaged in releasing major war criminals and restoring fortunes swollen by slave labor. It seems that Drechsler's seven killers had not been unrealistic to hope for mercy, merely unfortunate in their timing.

So the available members of the "Rollkommando" allegedly ordered by the Nazi "Soldatenrat" to lynch Hans Geller escaped all punishment. A clemency board reconsidered the case of Edgar Menschner, the alleged Führer of this Soldatenrat, on November 27, 1946. Though all of the board commissioners rated Menschner's conduct in confinement as "excellent," two of them opposed any reduction of his twenty-year sentence. The other two suggested ten years. The Judge Advocate General's Office decided that five years sufficed.[5] One assumes that Menschner was eventually reunited with his family.

The clemency boards also repeatedly reviewed the sentences of Hugo Krauss's killers, each time with less hostility toward them. In 1948 President Truman reduced Miesel's sentence to ten years. In 1949, after serving only three years, all five men returned home, freed on parole.[6]

And what of the families of those POWs executed too soon to take advantage of this kinder American attitude? Walter Beyer's widow began to suspect that something had happened to her husband when his letters stopped coming. Her son Edgar, who was three, remembers "the moment Mother found out my father was dead. . . . She was cooking beans in the back yard when it came, a simple, open postcard. She read it and started to shake. She let out a wail that I will never forget. . . . I thought she was going to die." The card contained only the date of his death, more than a year earlier. Later, Beyer's widow received "a death certificate and a note from the Red Cross stating no further information was available." She learned more, years later, but kept the shameful secret until Edgar was about to marry. Then she "sat him down and told him his father had been executed and was buried in a criminal's grave." In 1981 an aunt gave him some money to visit his father's resting place. He had to climb the cemetery fence, since the gate was padlocked.[7]

At least Frau Beyer had obtained a death certificate. Without this document, neither a soldier's own will, nor any will in which he was named as a beneficiary, could be probated. His widow could not remarry. His orphans could not receive a pension. Mere knowledge that someone had died was not enough.[8]

Otto Stengel's widow, left with two small sons, struggled for years to obtain the documents she needed to obtain a pension. In 1957 an official of the Social Welfare Court of the State of Schleswig sent a letter of thanks to the Chief of the Correspondence Branch of the U.S. Army's Military Justice Division, who had sent copies of Stengel's sentence and Truman's confirmation of it; but the German official pointed out that "the sentence does not include the proof on which it was based." As before, the only proof was in the trial record. Weeks later, the JAG informed the Commander in Chief, U.S. Army Europe, that his office was having this document declassified. Meanwhile, the commander was to "ascertain the purpose for this request" and confirm that it would be used for "an appropriate judicial or administrative inquiry."

The next month, the President of the Sixth Senate of the Schleswig Social Court replied to the Office of the Judge Advocate for American Forces in Europe: "The widow and the children of former prisoner of war Otto Stengel claim a widow's and orphan's allowance on the ground that her husband was a victim of the war, since he was unjustly sentenced to death and executed. The court has already heard several comrades of Stengel as witnesses. However, it is urgently desirable to consider the grounds which were decisive for the Military Court to pass the death sentence." He needed to know what the witnesses had said and what laws and facts had led the judges to pass sentence.[9] Defeat and denazification had not altered the differences between German and American judicial styles.

In 1998 a *Justizoberamtsrat* for the Social Court of the State of Schleswig-Holstein informed me that since all records were confidential, he could not even reveal whether Frau Stengel got her pension. He did say that "a few companions of prisoner of war Otto Stengel were arrested. But records about these arrests are also not available."[10]

Meanwhile, the fourteen executed Germans were not completely forgotten. Flowers mysteriously appeared by their headstones from time to time, placed by a German-American lady saddened by their neglect. As noted in the introduction, Richard Whittingham and John Hammond Moore chanced upon their stories, writing books published in 1971 and 1978, respectively. Arnold Krammer mentioned the trials in his survey of Nazi war prisoners in 1979, as did the German historians Paul Carell and Günter Böddeker the next year. In Carell's and Böddeker's opinion, the hangings at Fort Leavenworth were important because they set the "gallows protocol" for executing the marshals, ministers, generals, SS-Führers, and Gauleiters of the Third Reich at the Nuremberg Trials and after.[11]

In 1980 Sgt. Ken Knox, the corrections officer, found the graves and allowed his curiosity free rein. From his office window, he could visualize each condemned German walking by, handcuffed in the midst of an eight-man guard. He "could almost hear the Episcopal chaplain, John Sagar, reciting Psalm 130, the litany for the dying: 'Out of the deep I have called unto thee, O Lord. Lord, hear my voice.'"[12] And Ken Knox involved me.

While I worked at my slow pace, Knox kept "thinking of the families in Germany who've been told their father or grandfather died as a criminal."[13] He located Walter Beyer's son and some other relatives, found an association of former U-boat sailors now living in Florida, and discussed movie rights. He also employed a man to write the story of the Beyer Five, loaning him all his documents, only to see this person dash off a mass-market paperback without a word of thanks.[14]

Knox still campaigns to have these fourteen prisoners reburied in Germany, or in a place of respect, since their only crime was to silence "a traitor in their own ranks," as any soldier would have done. The possibility of reburial has been mooted from time to time by German or American military authorities; but during the cold war, while Communist East Germany was accusing the western half of being pro-Nazi, "the West German Embassy in Washington preferred that the matter not be raised at all." Now that the wall is history, perhaps something will happen. At least a German honor guard came to the cemetery in 1990 to lay a wreath there on November 18, Volkstrauertag, the German Memorial Day.[15]

Richard Whittingham, too, has remained fascinated. Thanks to his efforts, the History Channel broadcast a program in 1998 entitled "The Last Mass Execution." He; Ken Knox; Mr. Gruenebaum, who translated for the defendants at the Drechsler trial; Tim Mulligan, the National Archives historian and U-boat expert; and I appeared on this show, which is still occasionally broadcast.

And here is my book, at last. I hope that it will inspire more interest in issues that urgently need to be addressed, unless one is willing to dismiss the Geneva Convention, kaiserlike, as a mere scrap of paper. After years of research, I was appalled to find that my subject had become timely. Today, terrorists of another sort complicate the problems of controlling the barbarity of warfare, of bringing war criminals to justice, and of insuring the humane treatment of war prisoners. Unfortunately the Bush administration also complicated these efforts.

First, President Bush denied that the Geneva Convention applied to prisoners taken in the Afghan and Iraq wars because they were not fighting in uniform under the control of a licit government. They were, in effect, all francs tireurs. Then he cut the Army and the FBI out of prisoner interrogation, handing it over to the more politically amenable CIA. Military lawyers had standards, which did not involve the use of torture. After World War II, which had revealed certain insufficiencies in the Laws of War, Congress conducted a thorough revision, the Uniform Code of Military Justice, which included for the first time the right of the accused to have legal counsel during interrogation and the right of judicial appeal. Under Bush's administration, none of this would apply to the new prisoners, any more than did other principles of law such as habeas corpus or the right of the accused to confront his accuser.

The Bush administration also ignored a large collection of international law that had come into being since World War II: a thoroughly revised Geneva Convention; the Universal Declaration of Human Rights of 1946, which made torture an international crime; the Convention against Torture and Other Cruel, Inhuman, and Degrading Treatment or Punishment, which came into force in 1987, and the protocol added to it in 2003. The United Nations has also produced a considerable list of declarations on the protection of people being tortured and subjected to cruel and degrading treatment. In 2000, the UN General Assembly adopted a declaration on the effective investigation and documentation of such practices.

Since World War II, agencies such as the International Court of Justice and the UN High Commission for Human Rights have come into being.

There are special international courts to try war crimes in Rwanda and the former Yugoslavia. There is a UN Committee against Torture, including ten experts monitoring compliance with the Convention against Torture. None of these developments made any difference to the Bush administration.

The UN's Convention against Torture has defined it as "any act by which severe pain or suffering, whether physical or mental, is intentionally inflicted on a person for such purposes as obtaining from him . . . information or a confession."[16] The Bush administration defined torture as treatment that produced pain comparable to major organ failure (or, apparently, to vivisection). That definition ignored such minor considerations as the international criminalization of all cruel and degrading treatment.

In spite of all the standards, laws, and agencies established since World War II, the Bush administration acted far worse, on a greater scale, than the men who tortured Drechsler's killers. To be sure, this country has been suspicious of any international constraints on its freedom of action and slow to ratify such agencies as the International Criminal Court. It has also long ignored the first step toward creating new international standards, the principles set by the International Military Tribunal which tried the top Nazis. This enterprise, strongly sponsored by the United States at the time, was the first of many noble efforts to humanize modern war by punishing aggressors. Its judges defined a war crime as "a violation of the laws of war including, among other things, the murder or ill-treatment of prisoners of war . . . not justified by military necessity."[17] How shall one interpret this last phrase?

From the earliest military manuals in any Western country, the concept of military necessity has "legitimated every sort of destruction deemed 'unavoidable,'" although causing "suffering for the sake of suffering" was frowned upon. American troops used torture during their nasty suppression of the Filipino rebellion at the beginning of the twentieth century. After that, most versions of the American laws of war forbade using poisons, committing acts of perfidy, and using "torture to extract confessions." Then, although the United States had been the leading influence behind the Nuremberg War Crimes Trials,[18] it soon turned most of its principles into paper scraps.[19] In Vietnam, "the American practice of torturing prisoners of war finally stopped because it was unproductive, rather than from any sense of humanitarian outrage."[20] The American military law forbidding poisons was altered in 1976 to permit chemical and biological weapons. The term "collateral damage"—the deaths of innocent civilian bystanders—is now shocking only when used by the Oklahoma City bomber.

In every army, all attempts to define the laws of war have foundered on two unyielding principles: the doctrine of military necessity and the fact that reprisals are allowed. What the United States did in Vietnam broke every rule it established at Nuremberg. Therefore, there are no rules.

One of the most disillusioning aspects of the current situation, in my opinion, is the lack of moral outrage among people who should know better. Since 9/11, some commentators have said that torturing terrorists was justified, if it prevented the greater evil of terrorism itself. Some have said that the president, by virtue of his constitutional power as commander in chief, may set aside the Geneva Convention and all the other treaties and conventions outlawing cruel, inhuman, and degrading treatment of human beings, in spite of the fact that a treaty ratified by Congress is as much a fundamental law of the land as the Constitution itself. Some commentators assume that human rights are a function of American citizenship, not of human existence. Our Declaration of Independence voices this ideal of basic human rights but it has no legal standing. The Universal Declaration of Human Rights voices it also, and it has the force of international law.

On a practical level, the Bush administration defined the followers of Osama bin Laden as merely freelance, illegal combatants with no Geneva rights and, furthermore, no standing under the American Constitution's Bill of Rights because they were imprisoned on "foreign" soil at Guantánamo, Cuba, awaiting trial by (secret?) military tribunals. At least the Supreme Court shot down this theory.

Meanwhile, the scandal over Abu Ghraib prison has revealed that the United States was holding some prisoners secretly, unreported to the Red Cross. The Bush administration, in short, revealed what one observer has called "the hubris of moral exceptionalism," the notion that we United States citizens are so superior that "we don't need to abide by the rules we expect others to follow."[21]

One may detect some of the same attitudes in the American personnel who dealt with the Drechsler case. What is different today, aside from the scale of operations and the public scandal, and aside from the fact that now no one is accusing the Pentagon of coddling prisoners, is the apparent lack of concern about present or future retribution against American personnel in enemy hands. Common sense, it seems, should make a habitually warring country like the United States support the Geneva Convention.

A parting shot: The operations at Fort Hunt during World War II were meant to be secret forever. Perhaps they would have been, but for an alert National Parks Service employee. The Parks Service regained the Fort Hunt site, for it had once been part of George Washington's property. The land had also held a fort during the Spanish American War, an encampment for post-World War I bonus marchers, and a CCC camp during the depression. In 2006 a ranger was lecturing a tour group about this history when someone remarked: "My neighbor used to work here during World War II." The rangers tracked down that neighbor, who admitted that he had "worked at P.O. Box 1142 . . . and I'd love to tell you everything about it. . . . We did some great stuff there. . . . But I signed a secrecy agreement."[22]

Vincent Santucci, the chief ranger at George Washington Memorial Parkway, knew that government documents about P.O. Box 1142 had been declassified gradually since 1977, "but no one had told the vets that." Santucci and his fellow rangers "had to go to great lengths" to assure them that they were free to speak. They got the chief of Army counterintelligence to write them letters, encouraging them to share their stories with the Parks Service for the sake of history. Almost fifty veterans have now been interviewed, about ten years too late, Santucci says, because they are dying of old age. Now the U.S. Park Service is planning exhibits where visitors can don earphones and simulate the experience of eavesdropping on German POWs.

Nothing is secret forever.

Notes

Introduction

Editorial note: The umlaut (for the vowel combinations ae, oe, ue) has not been used in the names of German POWs (e.g., Kuelsen instead of Külsen). During World War II the umlaut was not available on military or government typewriters and thus does not appear in archival materials consulted for this book. However, for common German words the umlaut has been retained.

1. Regnery, Chicago, in 1971 (reissued by the Naval Institute Press, Annapolis, Maryland, in 1997). The quote is from his preface to the 1997 edition, viii.

2. Random House in 1978 (reissued by the Naval Institute Press, Annapolis, Maryland, in 2006).

3. Stein and Day, New York (reissued by the Naval Institute Press, Annapolis, Maryland, in 1991). See chapter 5, "Wrestling for the Tiller."

4. Published by Verlag Ulstein, GmbH, Frankfurt am Main, in 1980 (reissued in 1991).

5. Kenneth Knox, personal communication to author, July 1998.

6. Ibid. As the Los Angeles *Times* journalist David Lamb put it, these forgotten men lay segregated even from the 240 American convicts whose souls remained "forever tainted by some dishonorable deed that made this Godforsaken place their final outpost." "Prisoners of Silence," Nov. 30, 1990. Traditionally, graves face east in anticipation of the second coming of Christ and the resurrection from the dead.

7. Bernard Guffler headed State's SWPD. Brig. Gen. Blackshear M. Bryan, Assistant PMG, headed the PWD, assisted by Col. A. M. Tollefson.

8. Krammer, *Nazi Prisoners of War in America*, 153; also ch. 1, n. 1. See also U.S. War Department, U.S. Prisoner of War Operations Division, *Historical Monograph* (Washington: Office of the Provost Marshal General, 1945–1946), which contains microfilmed files "proving" that the PMGO always observed the Geneva Convention (hereafter cited as *POW Monograph).* See also Eleanor C. Flynn, "The

Geneva Convention on the Treatment of Prisoners of War," *George Washington Law Review* 11 (June 1943), 505–520.

9. *POW Monograph*, reel 1, 186 at 056. (Note: Since this collection lacks consecutive pagination, citations give the page of the document involved, if any, and the location, as measured by the inch counter on the microfilm reader from the beginning of the first typed page on the reel.)

10. Convention on July 27, 1929, Relative to the Treatment of War Prisoners, signed at Geneva, Article 7, in *Treaties and Other International Agreements of the United States of America, 1776–1949*, vol. 2, *Multilateral, 1918–1930*, U.S. Department of State Publication 8442 (1969), 932–964. Hereafter cited as Geneva Convention.

11. Geneva Convention, Article 2: Prisoners "must at all times be humanely treated and protected, particularly against acts of violence, insults and public curiosity."

12. Report of Conference at Headquarters, Eighth Service Command, on Prisoners of War and Prisoner of War Camps, 8 January 1944, p. 20, NA, RG 389, Entry 451 (hereafter Entry rendered E), box 1308 290/3495, file 337, General PW. This document also contains an address by the prosecutor, Lt. Col. Leon Jaworski, about the problems of investigating such cases. For the trial itself, see Court Martial Records, Court Martial 248793, "Record of Trial of Walter Beyer, 8WG-49588; Berthold Seidel, 8WG-49593; Hans Demer, 8WG-49597; Hans Schomer, 8WG-49620; and Willi Scholz, 8WG-49691; at Camp Gruber, Oklahoma, 17, 18, 19, 20, 21, 24, and 25 January, 1944," in 3 vols., numbered separately, General Services Administration, National Archives and Records Service, World War II Records Division, College Park, Maryland. Hereafter this source will be cited as B-CMR (for Beyer). (All court-martial materials are now housed at the Washington National Records Center, Suitland, Maryland.)

13. John Hammond Moore, "Getting Fritz to Talk," *Virginia Quarterly Review* 54, no. 2 (1978), 273. See also 268, 270, 274.

14. Statements by Bernhard Reyak, Heinrich Ludwig, and Helmuth Fischer to pretrial investigator, July 5, 1944. Court Martial Record No. 264108, The United States v. Helmut Fischer, ISN-10G-NA; Fritz Franke, ISN-10G-1083-NA; Guenther Kuelsen, ISN-AoG-1073-NA; Heinrich Ludwig, ISN-7G-132-NA; Bernhard Reyak, ISN-10G-1069-NA; Otto Stengel, ISN-6–112-NA; and Rolf Wizuy, ISN-10G-1072-NA, all in NA (National Archives), World War II Records Division (Dreschsler-Court Martial Records, 4 vols.), 1:216, 239–240, 190. Hereafter this source will be cited as D-CMR (D for Drechsler). Note: There are pagination problems with this source. The pages in vol. 4 have been rearranged so often that some have up to four sets of numbers; I have used the final set.

15. Geneva Convention, Article 61: "No prisoner may be obliged to admit himself guilty of the act of which he is accused." Article 62 did allow secret trials if "the interests of the safety of the State" were involved.

16. Col. Archibald King, Chief of the Judge Advocate General's Office's (JAGO) War Plans Division and expert in international law, to Asst. JAG for Military Affairs

Col. William A. Rounds, undated rough draft signed by King, late November 1944. D-CMR 2:136–137.

17. Five from Camp Gruber, Oklahoma (Walter Beyer, Berthold Seidel, Hans Demme, Willi Scholz, and Hans Schomer); two from an Aiken, South Carolina, branch camp (Erich Gauss and Rudolf Straub); seven from Papago Park, Arizona (Helmuth Fischer, Fritz Franke, Guenther Kuelsen, Heinrich Ludwig, Bernhard Reyak, Otto Stengel, and Rolf Wizuy); and one (Edgar Menschner) from Camp Chaffee, Arkansas, whose sentence was later commuted.

18. Bryan, Asst. Provost Marshal General, to SWPD, Dept. of State, NA, RG 59, box 2204, file 1, in reply to State's 711.62114/10344.

19. Michael McDonough, "2 Britons, Australian likely to face Tribunal," AP news release, *News-Leader* (Springfield, Mo.), July 5, 2003, 9A.

Chapter 1

1. Memorandum for Chief, Administrative Services, SOS, from the PMG, June 26, 1942, subject: Interrogation Centers, NA, RG 389, E 452, box 1393, folder 383.6, "Segregation, Screening"; ONI Commander John Riheldaffer to Lt. Cmdr. Howard C. Taylor at Byron Hot Springs, October 24 and November 25, 1942, both in NA, RG 38, Records of the Chief of Naval Operations, Office of Naval Intelligence, Special Activities Branch (OP 16-Z), subject file 1942–1944, box 3, folder "Byron Hot Springs (1)." Hereafter cited as RG 38 (OP 16-Z).

2. Moore, "Getting Fritz to Talk," 264, 279. The total came to 3,451 at Fort Hunt and 2,210 at Byron Hot Springs (5,661 out of 371,683 German, 50,273 Italian, and 3,975 Japanese prisoners). *POW Monograph*, reel 1, 251 at 074: "It is estimated that approximately 600" POWs per month went through these two installations "continuously, until the time they were repatriated."

3. Memo from PMG to Chief, Aliens Division, Jan. 20, 1942, NA, RG 38 (OP 16-Z), subject file 1942–1945, box 5, folder "Forts Hunt-Meade." See also the following items in NA, RG 389, E 452, box 1393, folder 383.6, "Segregation, Screening": Memo, AG to Commanding Generals, Eastern and Western Defense Commands and Third and Ninth Corps Areas (later renamed Service Commands), and to the PMG, May 16, 1942, Subject: "Joint Interrogation Centers"; Memo to Chief, Administrative Services, S.O.S. from Acting Assistant Chief of Staff, G-2, Subject: Responsibility of Chiefs, Interrogation Section No. 1, Military Intelligence Service at Fort Hunt, Virginia and Interrogation Section No. 2, Military Intelligence Service, at Byron Hot Springs, California," August 13, 1942; Memo to the Commanding Generals, Eastern and Western Defense Commands and the Third and Ninth Service Commands, August 22, 1942.

4. See secret memorandum by John L. Riheldaffer, July 30, 1942, setting up standing orders for the Naval Interrogation Section at Fort Hunt, NA, RG 38 (OP 16-Z), subject file 1942–1945, box 5, folder "Forts Hunt-Meade."

5. Standing Orders for the Interrogation Center, July 30, 1942, NA, RG 389, E 452, box 1393, folder 383.6, "Segregation and Screening"; Memo by Maj. Gen.

Strong, A.C. of S., G-2, "Joint Agreement Between the Assistant Chief of Staff, G-2, and Director of NI" Rear Admiral H. C. Train, May 6, 1943, NA, RG 38 (OP 16-Z), subject file 1942–1945, box 3, folder "Byron Hot Springs (1)"; Memo from Lt. I. R. Johnson, May 16, 1944, NA, RG 38 (OP 16-Z), subject file1942–1945, box 5, folder "Farm File." (The ONI often called Fort Hunt "the Farm.") Johnson had many complaints. When he argued for making prisoner processing "an Army-Navy affair," he "got 'the cold shoulder' more than once."

6. Ian Dear, *Escape and Evasion: POW Breakouts in World War Two* (London: Cassell, 1997), 70. The Military Intelligence Service had been formed in 1942. The Captured Personnel and Material Branch, housed at Fort Hunt, had two sections, one for interrogating enemies and one for encouraging Americans to escape.

7. Memo of Feb. 8, 1943, NA, RG 38 (OP 16-Z), subject file1942–1945, box 5, folder "Farm File." This file also contains Riheldaffer to Jones, Feb. 18, 1944, praising the army monitoring staff which listened to and recorded whatever its microphones picked up. Gheradi to Col. Walker, 24 August 1943, folder "Hunt-Meade."

8. Moore, "Getting Fritz to Talk," 265. See also pp. 263–264, and Moore, *The Faustball Tunnel*, 29–32.

9. Memorandum from the PMG to the Sec. of War, July, 1942, NA, RG 389, E 452, box 1393, folder 383.6, "Transfer of P/W, Procedures for." The PMG was responding to orders from the AG "by order of the Secretary of War." Memorandum from the PMG for the Chief of Staff, August 31, 1942, tab A, ibid.

10. Clarence Ferguson, *Kriegsgefangener 3074, Prisoner of War* (Waco, Texas: Texian Press, 1983), 47–95. Ferguson describes his long transit from Salerno, Italy to a camp in what was once western Poland. At the outset, when he complained of an infraction of the Convention, he was told (p. 54): "You are not a registered Prisoner-of-War and will not be registered until you get to Germany."

11. Moore, "Getting Fritz to Talk," 267.

12. Martin Tollefson, "Enemy Prisoners of War," *Iowa Law Review* 32 (1946), 53. Tollefson had been Director of the PMGO's POW Operations Division. Gullion had been the senior Army representative at Geneva.

13. Memo to Defense Commanders and Service Commanders, Aug. 22, 1942, NA, RG 389, E 452, box 1393, folder 383.6, "Segregation, Screening."

14. PMG Gullion to the Sec. of War, July 9, 1942; enclosure: Memo from Director of Naval Intelligence to A.C. of S., G-2, July 7, 1942; enclosure, Hull to Stimson, July 2, 1942; NA, RG 389, E 452, box 1393, folder 383.6, "Transfer of P/W, Procedures for."

15. PMG to AG, June 24, 1942, excerpted in enclosure to memo, PMG to Chief of Staff, August 31, 1942. See also memo from Director of Naval Intelligence to A.C. of S., G-2, July 7, 1942, subject: Naval POWs, both in NA, RG 389, E 452, box 1393, folder 383.6, "Transfer of P/W, Procedures for."

16. PMG to the Chief of Staff, Subject: Compliance with the Geneva Convention, Aug. 31, 1942, NA, RG 389, E 452, box 1393, folder 383.6, "Transfer of P/W, Procedures for."

17. This was done on Sept. 1, 1942. Memo for the Secretary, War Dept. General Staff, from the Acting Chief of Staff, Subject: Compliance with the Geneva convention, ibid.

18. Quoted in PMG Gullion to Chief, Administrative Services, Feb. 11, 1943, NA, RG 389, E 452, box 1389, folder 336.6, "General PW." See also box 1393, folder 383.6, "Transfer of P/W, Procedures for" with following documents.

19. Sept. 22, 1942, NA, RG 389, E 452, box 1393, folder 383.6, "Transfer of P/W, Procedures for." Geneva's Article 36 had to do with the POWs' right to correspond "by the shortest route," as rapidly as possible after capture.

20. On Oct. 23 Col. B. M. Bryan of the PMGO's Aliens Division reminded G-2's Asst. Chief of Staff that the Sec. of War required the PMGO to report all prisoners as soon as they reached a permanent camp. However, he pointed out the drawbacks (marginal note: "G-2 said OK, 11–6-42"). NA, RG 389, E 452, box 1393, folder 383.6, "Transfer of P/W, Procedures for."

21. Gen. Styer to Dep. Chief of Staff, G-2, Feb. 2, 1943, NA, RG 389, E 452, box 1389, folder 336.6, "Gen. P/W." It contained a draft letter addressed to Bernard Gufler, head of State's SWPD. The U-boat in question was commanded by Capt. Wattenberg, a prime troublemaker, who was "held in Army custody unreported for 60 days," according to PMG Gullion, Feb. 11, 1943, ibid.

22. Transcript of phone conversation with Gen. Pearson, Feb. 10, 1943, NA, RG 389, E 452, box 1389, folder 336.6, "Gen. P/W."

23. Ibid; Gullion to Chief, Administrative Services [later, the Army Service Forces, ASF], Feb. 11, 1943; both in NA, RG 389, E 452, box 1389, folder 336.6, "Gen. P/W." According to Moore, *The Faustball Tunnel Tunnel*, 33, Gullion was also "far from happy" when the Swiss complained that prisoners at Fort Hunt were not allowed the exercise mandated by Geneva. He "had no jurisdiction over the *inside* of that facility," he complained to the Deputy Chief of Staff.

24. Memo to Cmdr. Riheldaffer from Lt. Gheradi, Jan. 9, 1943, NA, RG 38 (OP 16-Z), subject file 1942–1945, box 5, folder "Forts Hunt-Meade."

25. Ibid.

26. Memo, July 21, 1943, "Interrogation Center at Fort Hunt," ibid. Gherardi credited G-2 with being generous in the room allocations, "despite very pressing demands" of its own. This file also contains a letter Gherardi wrote on Aug. 24 praising an alert G-2 monitor who had "overheard two Ps/W express suspicion of their roommate" and had told a naval officer, who removed the stool pigeon.

27. Draft dated Oct. 16, 1943, RG 38 (OP 16-Z), subject file1942–1945, box 2, folder "B.A.D." ONI also approached Adm. King through the Royal Navy liaison at Fort Hunt, with good results. Two months later Riheldaffer wrote a friend at Byron Hot Springs that "our German work has proven to be of such really great value that the high command here is now convinced of the possibilities of our work." He offered to share "the hot dope which we handle on an hourly basis . . . mostly of very high technical value." Riheldaffer to Lt. K. W. Dowie, P. O. box 651,

Tracy, California, Dec. 14, 1943, NA, RG 38 (OP 16-Z), subject file 1942–1945, box 3, folder "Byron Hot Springs (2)."

28. Memo of July 12, 1944, NA, RG 38 (OP 16-Z), subject file 1942–1945, box 5, folder "Forts Hunt-Meade." Canadian and English agents sometimes questioned prisoners at Fort Hunt.

29. Memo for Lt. Cmdr. R. G. Albrecht, Oct. 1, 1942. Ibid.

30. Moore, The *Faustball Tunnel*, 53. On the size of the mikes, see Heidi Ridgely, "WW II: The Lost Chapter. P.O. box 1142," *National Parks*, winter 2010, 46.

31. Subject: "Segregation of German Naval Prisoners of War at Fort Meade," Dec. 9, 1943, NA, RG 38 (OP 16-Z), subject file 1942–1945, box 5, folder "Forts Hunt-Meade."

32. Moore, The *Faustball Tunnel*, 102–103.

33. Interrogation of POW Wilhelm Taubert, pp. 580–581 of Military Intelligence Dossier X6042762: "Report of Board of Officers Appointed to Inquire into and Determine the Responsibility for the Death of Prisoner of War Werner Drechsler, ISN-5G-61-NA, Prisoner of War Camp, Papago Park, Arizona, Pursuant to Paragraph 78, Special Orders 77—Headquarters Ninth Service Command, Dated 27 March 1944." NA, RG 319, Records of the Army Staff of the Assistant Chief of Staff, G-3, Intelligence Records of the Investigative Repository, Security Classified Intelligence and Investigative Dossiers 1939–1976, box 338, Personal Name File Werner Drechsler. Hereafter this important document will be cited as BR (Board Report).
Note: There are pagination problems. The original typescript begins each part with a page 1 (alphabetical and chronological indexes, Summary of Evidence, Report of Proceedings—selected transcripts of prisoners' interrogations—and supporting documents such as photographs, maps, and photostats of prisoners' written statements with official translations). Someone in G-2 re-numbered them consecutively, so that page 1 of the Report of Proceedings is page 24 of the manuscript. Although the alphabetical index of witnesses uses the original page numbers, I have cited the consecutive numbers to avoid confusion.

34. Collective memo to Commandant, P/W Camp Indianola, Nebraska, Dec. 11, 1943, 10–12. RG 389, E 452, box 1363, folder 014.33 (Gen. P/W #1) April 1943–June 1944.

35. Moore, *The Faustball Tunnel*, 35–36.

36. Interrogation of Karl Preuss. BR 301.

37. Moore, *The Faustball Tunnel*, 45.

38. Ibid., 38. Moore's chapter on Fort Hunt routine, pp. 29–54, is based on raw intelligence reports. See also Moore, "Getting Fritz to Talk," 268–270.

39. Ridgley, "P.O. box 1142," 46.

40. Col. Russell H. Sweet, Executive, Military Intelligence Service to Lieutenant Kidd, U.S.N., Dec. 20, 1943, NA, RG 38 (OP 16-Z), subject file 1942–1945, box 5, folder "Farm File." This file, the first mention of SP rewards one has found, also contains ONI memos dated Dec. 21 and 29, apparently standard forms, listing five

naval SPs who had been "accorded special privileges" including Hans Wosnitzka from Werner Drechsler's boat. G-2 allowed such jaunts since "Navy . . . officers alone are in a position to judge their security."

41. OP 16-Z to OP 16-Z-P/W, Feb. 7, 1944, ibid. An attached routing lists names all the major ONI personnel at Fort Hunt.

42. Ibid.

43. Ibid., box 5, folder "Forts Hunt-Meade."

44. ONI kept "berthing lists" for Fort Hunt, some of which are charts showing which rooms were allocated to the Navy each day. Some show the specific room allocation of an SP and his companions. RG 38 (OP 16-Z), box 2, folder "Berthing Lists, 1944" (there were none for 1943). Box 10, folder "Log at Ft. Hunt (1944)," contains logs of which ONI agent interviewed which prisoner on any day in 1943, 1944, and 1945.

45. "Expenses for Maintenance of SPs," Dec. 30, 1944, NA, RG 38 (OP 16-Z), box 5, folder "Farm File." After paying SP Kelly's arrears, the weekly budget would be only $105.00.

46. William P. Woodward, Naval Unit, P.O. box 651, Tracy, Calif. to Cmdr. Riheldaffer, Dec. 26, 1944, NA, RG 38 (OP 16-Z), box 4, folder "Byron Hot Springs, 2 Jan. 1944-29 Dec. 1944."

47. See p. 9 of a collective memorandum these five wrote to the Camp Commandant, P/W Camp Indianola, Nebraska, Dec. 11, 1943, NA, RG 389, E 452, box 1363, folder 014.33 (Gen. P/W #1) April 1943-June 1944." For details, see chap. 2 .

48. Moore, *The Faustball Tunnel*, 98.

49. Brig. Gen. B. M. Bryan, Asst. PMG, to Commanding Generals, all Service Commands, March 17, 1943. NA, RG 389, E. 452, box 1395, folder 383.6, "Gen. P/W, April 1943-Oct. 1943." For details, see U.S. War Department, Headquarters, Army Service Forces, Office of the Provost Marshal General, *Programs of the Office of the Provost Marshal General in World War II* (Washington, 1946), 393.

50. After all, a war prisoner is still a member of his country's armed forces. See Ferguson, *Kriegsgefanger 3074*, 100, for a description of the limited self-government in Oflag 64.

51. Krammer, *Nazi Prisoners of War in America*, 149, 153, 161; Henry L. Ansbacher, "Attitudes of German Prisoners of War: A Study of the Dynamics of National-Socialist Followership," *Psychological Monographs* 62 (1948), 1–42; Martin K. Sorge, *The Other Price of Hitler's War: German Military Losses Resulting from World War II* (New York: Greenwood, 1986), 74.

52. On the sudden onset and sudden stoppage, see the account by the former director of the PMGO's POW Operations Division, Martin Tollefson, "Enemy Prisoners of War," *Iowa Law Review* 32 (1946), 58–59. The Canadians also shared this fear of camp terrorism. See John J. Kelley, "Intelligence and Counterintelligence in German Prisoner of War Camps in Canada during World War II," *Dalhousie Review* 58, no. 2 (1978), 285–294, covering a murder at Medicine Hat.

53. Krammer, *Nazi Prisoners of War in America*, 180. Archer L. Lerch, "The Army Report on Prisoners of War," *American Mercury* 58 (May 1945), 536–547. Brig. Gen. Lerch succeeded Gullion as PMG in June 1944.

54. Richard P. Walker, *The Lone Star and the Swastika: Prisoners of War in Texas* (Austin: Eakin Press, 2001), 98–103, details this "most serious breach of security in the entire United States prisoner of war program." Nazi workers at Camp Hearne sorted and forwarded all POW mail. However, this unit was not established until the month when Werner Drechsler died (March 1944). See Michael R. Waters, *Lone Star Stalag: German Prisoners of War at Camp Hearne* (College Station: Texas A&M University Press, 2004), 95–110.

55. Daniel Costelle, *Les Prisonniers* (Paris: Flammarion, 1975), 63; Krammer, *Nazi Prisoners of War in America*, 170; Address by PMG Lerch to the Military Affairs Committees of the Senate and the House of Representatives, February 1945, NA, RG 389, E 452, box 1388 (see chap 17); Tollefson, "Enemy Prisoners of War," 59; John Brown Mason, "German Prisoners of War in the United States," *American Journal of International Law* 39 (1945), 213, n. 37. Mason served in the Internees Section of State's SWPD. Near the end of the war, the PMG's Office made lists of every death, natural, accidental, or otherwise. NA, RG 389, E 467, box 151, file 4.14 "Violent Incidents among Prisoners of War to 3-1-45," and "to 4-21-45," "Monthly Death and Violence Report to 3-1-45."

56. See NA, RG 389, E 452, box 1395, folder 383.6 "Gen. P/W, April 1943-Oct. 1943" for two documents. G-2's Catesby ap C. Jones to Asst. PMG B. M. Bryan, Oct. 21, 1943, shows how authorities tried to identify Gestapo agents. A memo from the Chief of G-2's POW Branch to G-2's Acting Chief of Staff, Aug. 17, 1943, has two enclosures: The first enclosure, a memo from British Intelligence, warned that a convoy of German prisoners contained fifty-eight potential troublemakers. It listed fifty-two who were officers disguised as enlisted men, and six Gestapo agents who were "potential or past murderers." The second enclosure was a draft of a letter to be sent by the AG to all POW camp commandants repeating the British warning about German officers disguising themselves as enlisted men in order to "cause disturbances, plan escapes and sabotage and to pursue Nazi activities in Allied territory." The stated purpose of this letter was "to segregate dangerous prisoners of war and to safeguard the security of prisoners of war camps." Ibid.

57. Service Commands were supply and administrative branches of the Army Service Forces (ASF) in the continental United States. They had jurisdiction over POW camps, military police, the operation of disciplinary barracks, and the review of court martial cases and records. Geneva placed POWs under the same military laws as the soldiers of the Detaining Power. Each Service Command headquarters had a staff judge advocate and adjutant general, as well as a Security and Intelligence Division which reported directly to G-2 in Washington as well as handling duties under the jurisdiction of the PMG and of the Service Commander. Both the PMG and the AG were subordinate to the Commander of the

ASF. See John D. Millett, *The Organization and Role of the Army Service Forces* (Washington: Department of the Army, 1954), 105–106, 315, 316, 334, 461–462.

58. Circular dated June 25, 1943, NA, RG 389, E 452, box 1395, folder 383.6, "Gen. P/W, April 1943-Oct 1943." When an intelligence officer discovered a prisoner was willing to give information, he was immediately to send his name, background and a summary of "the information he is believed to possess, and his attitude toward divulging it" to the Chief of G-2's POW Branch.

59. Jones to Col. I. B. Summers, PMGO, Jan. 20, 1944. Forwarded to the PMG on Jan. 25. NA, RG 389, E 452, 1942–1946, box 1403, file 1.

60. Krammer, *Nazi Prisoners of War in America*, 170–171.

61. NA, RG 59, 711.62114/371. See also Wilma Parnell with Robert Taber, *The Killing of Corporal Kunze* (Secaucus, N..J.: Lyle Stuart, 1981). Parnell was the court reporter at the trial. See also Leon Jaworski's memoirs, *After Fifteen Years* (Houston, Texas: Gulf Publishing Co., 1961). The most recent study of this case is Vincent Green, *Extreme Justice* (New York: Pocket Books, 1995). Although Green has done archival research, he cites no sources and writes in an unscholarly style.

62. "Report of a Conference, 8 January 1944 at Headquarters, Eighth Service Command, on Prisoners of War and Prisoner of War Camps," NA, RG 389, E 451, box 1308 290/3495, file 337 "General PW," 18, 20.

63. For a particularly large collection, see NA, RG 389, E 452, 1942–1946, box 1403, files 1 and 2. Eighth Service Command included Arkansas, Louisiana, New Mexico, Oklahoma, and Texas.

64. Waters, *Lone Star* Stalag, 115–116, 120–134.

65. Report from Col. B. M. Bryan, Chief, Aliens Division, PMGO to Bernard Guffler of State's SWPD, for transmission to Swiss Legation, Jan. 17, 1944, NA, RG 389, E 452, 1942–1946, box 1403. An attached file 1 contains correspondence between the father, Mr. Henry Krauss, and the War Department; see also file 2.

66. Ibid., file 1. For more on the fate of Krauss's murderers, see ch. 18 in this book.

67. NA, RG 389, E 467, box 1518, folder 10, "Adjutant General (a) War Department Letters," Subject: POW Non-Commissioned Officers.

68. NA, RG 389, box 1395, folder 383.6, "Gen. P/W, April 1943-Oct 1943."

69. NA, RG 389, E 452, box 1403, file 1. On May 15, the PWD asked the general of the Eighth Service Command to report on the investigation to the PMG. Marginal comment: "Case sent to Ft. Meade File, RLP 24/8/44."

70. This PWD document went forward under the signature of Gen. B. M. Bryan, Assistant PMG. The Deputy Chief of Staff for Service Commands sent the draft to the Assistant Chief of Staff, G-1 (personnel), for his approval. NA, RG 389, E 452, box 1396, folder 383.6, "Gen. P/W, Nov. 1943-Sept. 1944."

Chapter 2

1. Quoted in Moore, *The Faustball Tunnel*, 96–97.

2. Collective memorandum to Camp Commandant, P/W Camp Indianola, Nebraska, Dec. 11, 1943, pp. 2–3, NA, RG 389, E 452, box 1363, folder 014.33 "Gen. P/W #1, April 1943-June 1944." Hereafter cited as Memo to Indianola Commandant.

3. Ibid., 1–2. Barthel was twenty-three and Linke twenty-nine.

4. Ibid., 3–4.

5. Ibid., 4–5.

6. Ibid., 5–6. Vogler, twenty-two, was the team's youngest.

7. Additional Statement of Ogefr. Albert Mueller, 23881 MI, NA RG 389, E 452, Decimal File 1941–1945, 253.5–253.6, box 1372, folder 253.6, "Escape and Apprehension of Ps of W from Indianola P/W Camp."

8. Petratschek was thirty. Statement and Additional Statement of O/Sold. Anton Petratschek, 21 June 1944, ibid.

9. Memorandum to Indianola Commandant, Dec. 11, 1943, 6–7.

10. Moore, *The Faustball Tunnel*, 98.

11. Memorandum to Camp Indianola Commandant, Dec. 11, 1943, 6–8; Moore, *The Faustball Tunnel*, 98.

12. Memorandum to Camp Indianola Commandant, Dec. 11, 1943, 8–9.

13. Ibid., 9.

14. Barthel asked for a bill which he "immediately recognized . . . as a lie. Two months' pay, twice $25; suit $28.50; shoes $3.95 (old shoes) etc. . . . drawn up in a peculiar way without date or signature." Ibid., 9–10.

15. Ibid., 10–11.

16. Ibid., 10–11. See Arnold Krammer, "American Treatment of German Generals During World War II," *Journal of Military History* 54 (Jan. 1990), 27–46.

17. Memorandum to Camp Indianola Commandant, Dec. 11, 1943, 11–12.

18. Ibid., 12–13.

19. Ibid., 13.

20. Memo, SAC (Special Agent in Charge): RE: Prisoners of War, internal security, alien enemy control, 100–18336–24, Jan. 11, 1944, FBI, San Francisco Division, Central Records, Prisoner of War file.

21. Memo, SAC, RE: Prisoner of War instructions in Event of Escape, 100–18336–24. Ibid.

22. Memorandum to Indianola Commandant, Dec. 11, 1943, 13–14.

23. Moore, *The Faustball Tunnel*, 99–100.

24. Memorandum to Indianola Commandant, Dec. 11, 1943, 7. Emphasis added.

25. Ibid., 14.

26. Additional statement of Soldat Karl Linke, 48598 MI, NA, RG 389, E 452, file 1942–45, box 1372, folder 253.6, "Escape and Apprehension of Prisoners of War from Indianola P/W Camp."

27. Statement of Infantry Major W. A. Erwin, July 7, 1944, ibid.; Moore, *The Faustball Tunnel*, 99; Brig. Gen. Blackshear M. "Babe" Bryan, Chief of the PMGO's Aliens Division, handled all POW issues. This former line coach at West Point would become PMG in Dec. 1945.

28. Side or satellite camps placed POWs close to farms or businesses that contracted their labor.

29. Letter from Lt. Col. Leonard R. Smith, Commanding, Prisoner of War Camp Atlanta, Nebraska to: Commanding Gen., 7th SC, ATTN: Prisoner of War Branch, "Transmittal of Reports of Escape and Apprehension of PWs," June 27, 1944. RG 389, E 452, box 1372, folder 253.6, "Escape and Apprehension of Ps/W from Indianola P/W Camp." Since the prisoners at Indianola were newly-captured, they must have learned about the five through the grapevine described in chap. 2. The exceptional treatment the five received must also have caused speculation.

30. Memorandum to Indianola Commandant, Dec. 11, 1943, 14.

31. Statement by Stockade Commander Erwin, "Report of the Escape and Apprehension of O/Sold. Marcel Barthel," etc., June 23, 1944, NA, RG 389, E 452, box 1372, folder 253.6 "Escape and Apprehension of Ps/W from Indianola P/W Camp."

32. Copy enclosed in NA, RG 389, E 452, box 1363, folder 014.33 (Gen. PW #1), April 1942–June 1944, Memo for Asst. C. of S, G-2, March 3, 1944. The newspaper clipping was dated Jan. 22, 1944. Secretary of the Treasury Morgenthau shamed Roosevelt into setting up this board to "forestall the plot of the Nazis to exterminate the Jews and other persecuted minorities in Europe" after discovering the depth of State Department anti-semitic obstructionism. See Arthur D. Morse, *While Six Million Died: A Chronicle of Apathy* (New York: Random House, 1968), 100, 327 ff.; and David S. Wyman, *The Abandonment of the Jews: America and the Holocaust, 1941–1945* (New York: Pantheon Books, 1984), 209–215, 285–287.

33. Memorandum for Asst. C. of S., G-2, March 13, 1944, NA, RG 389, E 452, box 1363, folder 014.33 "Gen. P/W #1, April 1942—June 1944," enclosures 1 and 2. Barthel's two notes were dated Feb. 4.

34. Catesby ap C. Jones, Asst. Exec., G-2 to POW Branch, G-2, March 30, 1944, ibid. The State Department code for Hull's letter was SWP 711.62114.499.

35. Ibid. On April 5, the PWD so ordered the Commander of the Seventh Service Command. The order to the commandant at Indianola confirmed the order which the commandant had taken the initiative to request.

36. NA, RG 38 (OP 16-Z), Reports on Interrogations, 1941–1945, box 1, folder "Report on Interrogation of Survivors from U-118."

37. Apparently Drechsler was better educated than most sailors. He spoke English and claimed to have attended a university in England. Testimony of Tech. 4 Fred R. Boronstein, BR 100–101, who drove Drechsler to Papago Park in his ambulance. According to Richard Whittingham, Drechsler had ten years of public school and one of trade school, studying mechanics. *Martial Justice*, 38, 41, 46. According to his dossier, he had some knowledge of English and French. By the time he left Ft. Hunt, he spoke fluently.

38. NA, RG 389, E 452, box 1378, folder 253.91 "(Fort Hunt) Gen." Copies went to the JAG (G-2's boss) and the Navy Department.

39. NCO Rudolf Wiemer, Drechsler's boat mate, saw this as a ploy to get him to talk, too. BR 369–370.

40. Moore, *The Faustball Tunnel*, 95–96.

41. NA, RG 38 (OP 16-Z), subject file 1942–1945, box 2, "Farm File," contains lists for 1942 and 1944, but unfortunately not for 1943. Drechsler left Fort Hunt on Jan. 8, 1944, having had only three "customers" that year, soldiers rather than sailors.

42. Ibid., box 25. In either typed or handwritten form, they cover August 1942 to March 1945.

43. "Contacts of Werner Drechsler at Fort Hunt (In Chronological Order)," ibid., box 5, folder "Farm File." The list contains only prisoners interned at Papago Park Camp, except for Wosnitzka. Wosnitzka (using the alias Eschelbacher) appears to have been much more productive than Drechsler, remaining at Fort Hunt longer. (One of Drechsler's future assassins, Helmuth Fischer, had been Wosnitzka's victim. He hated all spies. BR 828–829).

44. See interrogation of ex-roommates Frederick Murza, BR 504–506; Friedrich Wagenfuehr, 562; Heinz Taubert, 579–581; and Willi Peters, 789.

45. Interrogation of Heinrich Ludwig. BR 775.

46. Chief Warrant Officer Josef Gross. BR 436–437.

47. Interrogation of Peter Duer, his last naval "customer," BR 601–602, and of Heinz Taubert, 580.

48. BR 267. 315. 327. These were Gustav Behlke, the petty officer Josef Höller, and Werner Reinl, the chief NCO. The U-118 survivors remained at Stringtown from early July 1943 until their transfer to Papago Park in early January, 1944.

49. Testimony of Hans Siebert, the U-118's chief boatswain's mate, BR 341; Werner Reinl, its chief NCO, BR 331; and Klaus Preuss, BR 305–306.

50. BR 546–547. For Josef Gross's description of a similar encounter, see 433. Siegfried Elser, another Drechsler victim, also said that he considered Drechsler's absence to be proof enough. BR 555.

51. BR 319. Because of his job, Chief Radio Operator Josef Hoeller had been kept at Fort Hunt for six weeks. At Papago Park there had been lots of rumors about Drechsler, he said, but not about Wosnitzka.

52. BR 294.

53. BR 435.

54. Moore, *The Faustball Tunnel*, 67–68. The other camps were Blanding in Florida, McCain in Mississippi, and Beale in California. Naval prisoners were "about 2 percent" of German POWs in the United States.

55. Gross interrogation. BR, 433.

56. Testimony of Heinz Taubert. BR 583–584. The *Graf* men asked about a man named Globus. The Fort Hunt log mentions an SP named Clobes, alias Brandt.

57. BR 927–928. Drechsler's records show him arriving at Fort George G. Meade from Norfolk, Virginia, on June 30, 1943. After a blank line where his time at Fort

Hunt should have been listed, it noted his arrival at Fort Leonard Wood, Missouri, on Feb. 4, 1944, implying that he had spent eight months in a transit camp. *Programs of the PMGO*, 374–375.

58. BR 579–580. Heinz Taubert was at Fort Hunt from Nov. 17 to Dec. 19, 1943.

59. D-CMR 4:166.

60. Quoted by another killer, Wizuy's friend Fritz Franke. BR 806.

61. NA, RG 389, E 452, box 1374, folder 253.91, "Gen. P/W #2, Transfers of PWs." The same request was made for Hans Wosnitzka about the same time, although he continued to work at Fort Hunt for several more months. This seems to have been a routine request for POWs taken to Hunt immediately after capture.

62. The assistant director asked G-2 for his date of capture, which Col. Catesby ap C. Jones, assistant executive, provided on December 4. On December 28, an official of G-2's POW Branch, signing for the post commander, box 1142, Alexandria, Virginia, sent Cmdr. John L. Riheldaffer of NI's Interrogation Branch a receipt for $38.00 for Drechsler's account. NA, RG 38 (OP 16-Z), subject file 1942–1945, box 5, folder "Farm File."

63. Robert D. Billinger Jr., *Hitler's Soldiers in the Sunshine State: German POWs in Florida* (Galveston: University Press of Florida, 2000), 48, 50–59.

64. See form letters in NA, RG 389, E 452, box 1374, folder 253.91 "Gen. P/W #1."

65. Memorandum for Col. I. B. Summers, PMGO, of conversation between Lt. Pamplin, PMGO, and Major Parker. Marked secret. NA, RG 389, E 452, box 11378, folder 253.91 "(Ft. Hunt) Gen."

66. Memorandum for Col. I. B. Summers, PMGO, ibid. Marginal note: "transferred 28 Dec. '43" (the day his paycheck was cut). The penciled note continues: "this is an explanation to the letter of—(illegible) on specific directions from the asst. etc." At any rate, Jefferson Barracks, near St. Louis, did not have a POW branch camp until May 1944—two months after Drechsler's death. David Fiedler, *The Enemy among Us: POWs in Missouri During World War II* (Saint Louis: Missouri Historical Society Press, 2003), 311.

67. The protocol for moving prisoners between Forts Hunt and Meade had been set in July 1943 by high-level representatives of the PMGO, G-2 and Third Service Command: When security officials had "no further use of a P/W and would like to have him shipped to a permanent internment camp, the Commanding Officer . . . notifies the Chief, Provost Marshal Branch, Internal Security Division, Third Service Command, and the Office of the Provost Marshal General the name of each P/W that is being moved to . . . Fort Meade to await further orders." Any movement beyond Meade was to be arranged by Third Service Command's internal security office. Agreement between G-2, War Department and Third Service Command, NA, RG 319, E 47, Army Intelligence Dec. File 1941–48, box 941, folder 383.6 "7–1–43 to 8–31–43."

68. To Commanding Gen., Third Service Command. Subject: Transfer of German POW, 28 Dec. 1943. NA, RG 389, E 452, box 1378, folcer 253.91 (Ft. Hunt) Gen. Marked secret.

69. NA, RG 389, Enemy Information Bureau, Property Branch, box 2481, Camps Indianola to Maxey, file "Fort Leonard Wood." The PMGO letter of February 12 was coded SPMGA (58) 253.91 and the PMG's reply of March 2, SPMGA (47) 383.6.

70. Lt. Col. Frederick E. Whitten, Commanding Officer, Indianola, to Headquarters, Seventh Service Command, ASF, Omaha, Nebraska, March 4, 1944, Subject: "Transfer of Navy Prisoner of War Personnel"; and Whitten to PMG, March 6, 1944, in NA, RG 389, E 452, box 1374, folder 253.91 "Gen. P/W #1." It is interesting that Mueller, #23881 (UN 9529/4OS), did not have an obviously naval identification number because he had been transferred from British custody rather than captured by an American ship.

71. Col. Earl L. Edwards, Asst. Dir., Prisoner of War Division [of PMGO] to Commanding General, 7th SC, ibid. These documents may also be found in PMGO's Enemy POW Information Bureau, Reporting Branch, subject file 1942–1946, box 2481, folder "Indianola."

72. Testimony of Tech. 4 Fred R. Boronstein, camp medical department, BR 100–101.

73. Testimony of Otto Stengel to investigating board, BR 741. Prisoners at Papago Park were forbidden to wear anything but the regulation PW clothing common to all camps. Drechsler's wardrobe was puzzling as well as conspicuous.

74. Statement of Stockade Commander Erwin, NA, RG 389, E 452, Classified Dec. File 1941–1945, 253.5–253.6, box 1372, folder 253.6 "Escape and Apprehension." Screening teams went from camp to camp trying to identify Nazis and other non-cooperative elements in order to segregate them in special camps.

Chapter 3

1. *Quick*, no. 31 (July 1959), cited by Daniel Costelle, *Les Prisonniers* (Paris: Flammarion, 1975), 169.

2. Wolfgang Verhohr, U-175, cited by Costelle, ibid., 161.

3. Capt. D. L. Schweiger to PMG, March 6, 1944, quoted in Costelle, ibid., 162.

4. A month later, the State Department delivered the reply from the PMGO's POW Division (PWD): Only soap was now in short supply, and furniture was being made. Executive to Asst. PMG to SWPD, March 18, 1944; State to Swiss Legation, Feb. 19, 1944; NA, RG 59, file 711.62114/636. (Such letters went from the camp to the PWD, which then sent them, with justifying comments, to State's Special War Problems Division (SWPD), which delivered them to the Protecting Power. State Department files usually contain only notes from the War Department, from which State composed covering notes couched in diplomatic language. One must infer the complainant's message from these.

5. Wattenberg's complaints, dated March 13, 1944 (the day after Drechsler arrived), NA, RG 59, 711.62114/612; Acting Director, PWD, to SWPD, April 8, 1944, enclosing Col. Means' letter of March 22, denying the complaints, ibid.,

711.62114/737; Gen. McCoach's reprimand: PMGO to SWPD, 19 January, 1944, ibid., 711.62114/464.

6. Lt. H. T. Gheradi to OP-16-Z, Oct. 17, 1942, enclosed in John L. Riheldaffer to Commander W. S. Thomas, R.N., Oct. 19, 1942, NA, RG 38 (OP 16-Z), box 17, folder "Special Reports Issued by P/W Section."

7. Col. Catesby ap C. Jones, Chief of G-2's Prisoner of War Branch, to Brig. Gen. B. M. Bryan, PMGO, May 26, 1943, NA, RG 389, E 452, box 1381, folder 255 Gen. P/W, May 1943-Dec. 1944.

8. Letter from Crossville commandant, Sept. 4, 1943, NA, RG 389, E 452, box 1380, folder 253.91 "Transfers to/from Hospitalization." Dr. Lt. Herbrand also provided his captors with a bibliography of his medical publications. He was assigned to Halloran General Hospital, New York.

9. This is the subject of Moore, *The Faustball Tunnel.*

10. Testimony of Hermann Weidemann, U-118, June 16, 1944, at Papago Park, BR 906. See also testimony of Werner Reinl, BR 846, at Byron Hot Springs.

11. Otto Stengel testimony, BR 740; Peters testimony, BR 987. See also testimony of Rudi Stoessel, Byron Hot Springs, 799.

12. Testimony of seamen Gustav Behlke, BR 271, and Klaus Pruess, BR 304; testimony of NCOs Josef Hoeller (BR 318, 896–7), Werner Reinl (BR 329, 849), Hermann Weidemann (BR 906–7), and Werner Wilke (BR 904). Wilke thought Drechsler might have called out to Seaman Behlke.

13. Lothar Mandelkow testimony, BR 882; Elser, BR 751; Friedrich Murza, 691; Peter Duer, BR 602; Heinz Taubert, BR 581, 783.

14. Guenther Kuelsen interrogation at Byron Hot Springs, June 8, 1944, BR 813–814, and confession, D-CMR 4:126; Bernhard Reyak, BR 820–821; Helmut Fischer, BR 830 and D-CMR 4:103–104; Rolf Wizuy, D-CMR 4:195.

15. Stengel second confession, June 2, 1944, BR 740–741.

16. D-CMR 4:230. (Stengel confessed twice at Byron Hot Springs, then retold his story to a pretrial investigator and to a psychiatrist.)

17. Stengel first confession, June 1, 1944, BR 673.

18. Stengel second confession, June 2, 1944, BR 741.

19. Testimonies of Alfred Friedrich, BR 657, and Gerhard Richter, BR 646.

20. Otto Stengel's written confession, CMR 4:165. Compare confession of June 2, 1944, BR 741.

21. Stengel first confession, June 1, 1944, BR 671; Fischer, BR 833.

22. Stengel first confession, June 1, 1944, BR 675, 741.

23. D-CMR 4:165–166. Fort Leonard Wood, Missouri, had wooden bunks, not canvas cots. (In 1993, the post museum restored a barracks to celebrate a reunion for former prisoners and their wives.)

24. Stengel second confession, June 2, 1944, BR 742–743.

25. D-CMR 4:166.

26. D-CMR 4:165–166. Compare second confession, June 2, 1944, BR 742–743.

27. D-CMR 4:238.

28. Fischer, written confession, D-CMR 4:104. At Fort Hunt, Fischer had roomed with Wosnitzka, the other SP from Drechsler's boat. Either Kuelsen or Bleise had pointed Drechsler out to him. BR 828–830. Reyak interrogation, Byron Hot Springs, June 8, 1944, BR 820–821.

29. Fischer interrogation, BR 830.

30. Wizuy statement at Byron Hot Springs, June 3, 1944, BR 769, explaining his friends' motives. See also his written confession, D-CMR 4:195. Neither Kuelsen nor Bleise mentioned this conversation.

31. Fischer, written confession, D-CMR 4:104. Hans Franke remembered only himself and Wizuy being there, BR 806; D-CMR 4:116. Reyak remembered Bleise's presence, BR 821; D-CMR 4:135.

32. Fischer, D-CMR 4:104–105; Franke, BR 806.

33. Wizuy interrogation, Byron Hot Springs, June 3, 1844, BR 766; written confession, D-CMR 4:195.

34. D-CMR 4:127. Wizuy was in the Fort Meade hospital from Sept. 1 to 13, 1943. RG 38 (OP 16-Z), box 25. Berthing lists, daily room assignments.

35. Franke, BR 806; Reyak, BR 821.

36. Fischer, D-CMR 4:105; BR 831.

37. Stengel first confession, BR 679.

38. BR 688–690.

39. Heinrich Ludwig, June 3, 1944, BR 775–776; and Werner Reinl, June 9, 1994, BR 847, both at Byron Hot Springs.

40. BR 847–849.

41. BR 860–861 (interrogation at Byron Hot Springs), and 1093 (written statement). According to Reyak, Franz Hox also asked him if he knew Drechsler. D-CMR 4:135.

42. Bleise, BR 874.

43. Bleise, BR 874.

44. Only Ludwig, BR 780, said he definitely recalled seeing Reinl at Hox's meeting and afterward with two other NCO's, Murza and Elser. Murza thought Reinl might perhaps have been there and (erroneously) that Hermann Polowzyk, a U-118 seaman, definitely was. BR 693–694. The investigators kept trying to involve Drechsler's crew.

45. BR 882. Heinz Taubert and Peter Duer did not attend, either. A fifth, Paul Buchholz, refused to be sworn, even when threatened with court martial, and so left no record; but Elser remembered Buchholz corroborating his own testimony.

46. Murza, BR 695–696; Wizuy, D-CMR 4:196; Reyak, BR 821, D-CMR 4:135; Fischer, BR 832–833, D-CMR 4:104–105; Kuelsen, BR 814.

47. Hox interrogation, Byron Hot Springs, June 9, 1944, BR 858. Murza thought Hox had said: "Everything is understood now" or, in another statement, "Is everything clear?" Both Fischer and Reyak recalled: "Now everything is clear." Murza, BR 706 and 1015; Fischer, D-CMR 4:105; Reyak, D-CMR 4:135.

48. For example, see Fischer's interrogation, BR 833.

49. BR 859, 863.

50. Written confession, D-CMR 4:196.

51. BR 1093 (June 9, 1944). See also 863. As spokesman, Hox had an identity card that at least allowed him into compound 3. Officers were in compound 1. Possibly, Hox would have had to speak to Wattenberg in the presence of a German-speaking American. Unofficial contact "through the fence" would take time. Wattenberg had no formal power to discipline or remove Drechsler, but he could have made recommendations to the camp officials.

52. BR 833.

53. D-CMR 4:196.

54. Franke, BR 806–807, D-CMR 4:116. Ludwig recalled Hox saying that "he could do nothing as he did not know this man personally." D-CMR 4:182.

55. BR 814; compare D-CMR 4:127.

56. Siegfried Elser interrogation, BR 753. In his written statement, 1028, he said "Hox declared that he could not do anything about that, however we could beat up Drechsler."

57. Investigators' summary, BR 21.

58. Whittingham, *Martial Justice*, 86. See also 82–86.

59. Fischer, written confession, D-CMR 4:105. Fischer was twenty-one; Franke, Kuelsen, and Reyak, twenty; Wizuy twenty-two, and Ludwig twenty-four. The three NCOs: Elser, twenty-four; Murza, twenty-six, Hox, thirty-two.

60. Elser testimony, BR 753, 761; Murza testimony, BR 697, 707. Buchholz, Mandelkow and Wagenfeuer were possibly also in this first group.

61. Reyak, BR 822. He thought that everyone but Hox himself was in this group.

62. Wizuy written confession, D-CMR 4:197; interrogation, BR 769.

63. D-CMR 4:245.

64. Written confession, D-CMR 4:182–183.

65. Elser, written statement, BR 1028; Murza testimony, BR 707.

66. Written confession, D-CMR 4:182–183. Only Ludwig mentioned a call for volunteers. He could not remember whether it had been Reinl (who was not at the meeting), Elser or Murza who issued it. "Q. And what were these 6 men asked to volunteer to do? A. We didn't have any orders whatsoever. We just discussed what we should do with the man," hang him or beat him. BR, 776–777.

67. Report, BR 21.

68. Franke, BR 807. See also Kuelsen, BR 707.

69. Fischer written confession, D-CMR, 4:105 and interrogation, BR 833–834.

70. Ludwig interrogation, BR 777, and written confession, D-CMR 4:183; Reyak statement to pre-trial investigator, D-CMR 4:226 and interrogation, BR 822. The investigators emphasized gloves as evidence of premeditation.

71. Murza interrogation, BR 697–698, 707; Elser written confession, BR 1029.

72. Kuelsen interrogation, BR 815; confession, D-CMR 4:127.

73. Wizuy interrogation, BR 770; Elser interrogation, BR 753–754.

74. Reyak interrogation, BR 822.

75. Franke interrogation, BR 807; written confession, D-CMR 4:116–117.

76. Rudolf Wiemer interrogation at Papago Park, BR 376 (after the investigators had broken the case at Byron Hot Springs; none of Drechsler's NCOs had mentioned this visit until compelled to do so).

77. Hoeller interrogation at Papago Park, April 7, 1944, BR 318, and at Byron Hot Springs, June 14, 1944, BR 897–898.

78. Reinl interrogation, Byron Hot Springs, June 9, 1994, BR 849; written confession, 1103–1104.

79. Wiemer interrogation, Papago Park, BR 375–376, and Byron Hot Springs, June 13, 1944, BR 868–869, 871.

80. Polowzyk interrogation, BR, 288–289, 292, 878; Wiemer interrogation, Byron Hot Springs, BR 869.

81. Wizuy interrogation, BR 769; written confession, D-CMR 4:197; Franke interrogation, BR 807–808.

82. Ludwig interrogation, BR 777, and written confession, D-CMR 4:183 (he also thought Kuelsen merely wanted to eject Drechsler from camp); Kuelsen confession, D-CMR 4:127.

83. Reyak interrogation, BR 822, and written confession, D-CMR 4:136.

84. The following account is based on Polowzyk's second interrogation, BR 878–880, and on Wiemer's interrogation at Byron Hot Springs, BR 869–870. When pressed, Polowzyk admitted that he may also have seen Kuelsen, Fischer, and Ludwig. He definitely did not see Stengel, whom he knew.

85. Wiemer, BR 376; NCO Werner Wilke, BR 386; Seaman Karl Preuss, BR 307.

86. Murza interrogation, Byron Hot Springs, June 1, 1944, BR 708, 711; written confession, BR 1015.

87. Elser, Byron Hot Springs, June 2, BR 753–755; written confession, BR 1028–1030.

88. BR 676–677.

Chapter 4

1. Fischer to pretrial investigator: "I took part in the UNSCHÄDLICHMACHUNG (doing away with Drechsler) because I had to act as a German soldier." D-CMR 4:203.

2. Lothar Mandelkow, Drechsler victim, second interrogation, June 13, 1944, Papago Park, BR 882.

3. Reyak, BR 823.

4. Fischer, BR 834–835; Franke, 808; Reyak, BR 823; Kuelsen, BR 815 and D-CMR 4:127. The Investigating Board thought all six had entered the barracks. BR 22.

5. Fischer, D-CMR 4:106 and BR 835; Franke, BR 808; Kuelsen, BR 816 and D-CMR 4:127; Ludwig, D-CMR 4:183; Reyak, BR 823 and D-CMR 4:136, 223; Stengel, second confession, BR 746; Wizuy, D-CMR 4:197–198.

6. Murza, BR 701.

7. On June 1, BR 675–681. Stengel confessed to having been a bystander during the first attack, which was true, and also to merely witnessing the second, deadly foray, which was not.

8. BR 679–680.The Drechsler victim Walter Nieswand told a similar story. BR 888–889. The investigating board later questioned a Helmut Baden, BR 856, and a Helmut Soltek, BR 401, but found their testimony too insignificant to record.

9. Stengel interrogation, BR 743–748. Afterward, he would write a twenty-two-page statement. (Fischer would write twelve pages and the others between two and seven.)

10. Otto Behrens, four cots up across the aisle, who had shared Drechsler's ambulance ride into camp. BR 113–114, 117, 123. Many of Drechsler's unsympathetic barracks mates were not U-boatmen but merchant mariners and, in Stengel's words, "old soldiers of approximately 42–45 years of age." D-CMR 4:232.

11. Testimony of Otto Engler, BR 398, 400, 402. Emil Witt, sleeping directly across from Drechsler, told investigators he had never spoken to him "because I had my own comrades here." BR 128. Engler and Witt had arrived from Indianola.

12. Stengel written confession, D-CMR 4:167–168.

13. Franke interrogation, BR 808; Kuelsen, BR 816; Reyak interrogation, BR 823–824 and statement to pretrial investigator, D-CMR 4:223. Reyak knew Stengel only by sight. Wizuy, written confession, D-CMR 4:198, and interrogation, BR 770. Only Fischer believed that Stengel had joined them before the first attack, BR 834.

14. Stengel second confession, June 2, 1944, D-CMR 4:167.

15. Stengel written confession, D-CMR 4:169; oral confession, BR 746.

16. Reyak, BR 824; Kuelsen, BR 816 and D-CMR 4:127; Ludwig, BR 778.

17. Fischer, BR 836 and D-CMR 4:106; Ludwig, written confession, D-CMR 4:183; Kuelsen, BR 816–817 and D-CMR 4:127; Stengel, BR 744–746.

18. Franke, BR 809; Ludwig, BR 778; Stengel, D-CMR 4:170; Wizuy, D-CMR 4:198 and BR 772; Kuelsen, BR 816–817.

19. Reyak interrogation, BR 825 and written confession, D-CMR 4:137; statement to pretrial investigating officer, D-CMR 4: 224.

20. Stengel, BR 748; Franke, BR 810; Fischer, BR 837; Wizuy, BR 771.

21. Wizuy, BR 772; Stengel, second interrogation, BR 748, and written confession, D-CMR 4:170; Kuelsen, BR 817–818, D-CMR 4:128; Reyak, BR 825, D-CMR 4:137 and 225.

22. Elser written confession, BR 1030, said he was standing about fifteen meters away. He telescoped the two attacks into one. Murza, standing much farther away, told interrogators he recognized Wizuy, Ludwig, and (erroneously) Nieswand. Murza interrogation, BR 703–705, 708; written confession, BR 1015–1016.

23. Seaman Walter Nieswand (a Drechsler victim who had attended Murza's meeting), BR 889–890; Stengel, statement to pretrial investigating officer, D-CMR 4, 237; Murza interrogation, BR 703–705.

24. Taubert interrogation at Papago Park, April 22, 1944, BR 581–582; interrogation at Byron Hot Springs, June 3, 1944, BR 783–784.

25. Matzke interrogation, BR 795.

26. Reyak interrogation, BR 826; written confession, D-CMR 4:137; statement to pretrial investigation officer, D-CMR 4:225. Wizuy, BR 771.

27. Stengel second interrogation, BR 749; written confession, D-CMR 4:170–171; statement to pretrial investigating officer, D-CMR 4:237–238 (his most expansive version).

28. Alfred Friedrich would also be the first witness to be grilled at Byron Hot Springs. BR 630–633, 658, 660–661, 665. Gerhard Richter, another mate, would say he never heard anything about the other killers except that, according to Stengel and general opinion, "they were men who had met Drechsler at Fort Meade and knew that he was a traitor." BR 649.

29. Friedrich, BR 661; Stengel, second statement, D-CMR 4:171.

30. Stengel written confession, D-CMR 4:171. Punctuation slightly altered for clarity.

31. BR 791. Peters mentioned this again in his written statement, BR 987.

32. Fischer, statement to pretrial investigating officer, D-CMR 4:203. Rudi Stoessel, who had seen Drechsler carried out to the shower room, was washing up for the night when he heard some men talking about the gap between the episodes of screaming. "One said: 'The reason for the screaming is that the men got their gloves in between the two screams.'" Stoessel disapproved on two counts. He told them that this had not only "delayed and increased the torture of the man" but had been inefficient. "It would have been equally good if the men had worn no gloves and had just thoroughly washed their hands after the hanging." Interrogation, Byron Hot Springs, June 7, 1944, BR 801. He had gone next day to have another look at the corpse.

33. Comment overheard by Johann Matzke, written statement, Byron Hot Springs, June 6, 1944, BR 995–996. Peters interrogation at Byron Hot Springs, BR 788; written statement, BR 987.

34. Taubert interrogation, June 3, 1944, Byron Hot Springs, BR 784–785; written statement, June 6, 1944, BR 979–980. Taubert would be dragged to Byron Hot Springs because he was one of Drechsler's victims.

Chapter 5

1. BR 25, 29–32, 82–83, 640–643. Hebblethwaite's multiple tasks were not unusual. On Parshall, see BR 23–29, 33–34. Parshall's normal duty was to direct guards and prisoners outside camp. (Another captain had jurisdiction inside the wire.) Of German descent, he had been an American soldier, a Mexican general until he robbed a bank, an undercover agent in the Canal Zone, and a police detective in Wichita, Kansas. Moore interviewed the octogenarian Parshall, whom he admired. See Moore, *The Faustball Tunnel*, 25–27, 101.

2. Hebblethwaite testimony, BR 84–97.

3. Testimony of Capt. Claude C. Stafford, BR 51–57 and D-CMR 4:6, and Capt. Max Marks, BR 61–71 and D-CMR 4:10–12.

4. Rudi Stoessel, BR 801; Fischer, BR 837; Murza, BR 712–713; Willi Peters, BR 789; Johann Matzke, written statement, BR 996; the Drechsler victim Heinz Taubert, written statement, BR 979. Murza saw Fischer's maneuver; he probably knew about the injury, for he had watched some of the attackers wash out their gloves the night before. These facts came out at Byron Hot Springs.

5. At Byron Hot Springs, Seaman Alfred Friedrich would be compelled to describe Stengel's reaction to this news. BR 661–662.

6. D-CMR 4:212. Kuelsen was asking the pretrial investigator how he could possibly be punished under American rather than German law. The officer ignored both the question and the comment.

7. BR 163–164, 171–172.

8. Gabler's complaint to Protecting Power, March 24, 1944, NA, RG 389, E 452, box 1403, file 2.

9. File 2, ibid., also contains translated letters from four U-118 men (NCOs Werner Reinl and Hans Siebert and Seamen Hermann Polowzyk and Paul Reum) and from Josef Preuss and the new camp spokesman.

10. Ibid. Hans Siebert and Herman Polowzyk, who had similar experiences on March 15 and 17, repeated that phrase.

11. Ibid. His letter also deals with complaints relating to the Service Command's interrogations (see also chap. 6).

12. For this and other embarrassingly frequent escapes from Papago Park, see Moore, *The Faustball Tunnel.*

13. NA, RG 389, E 452, 1942–1946, box 1403, file 2, or RG 59, 711.62114/609 of March 15, 1944. The State Department's promise, dated Feb. 18, 1944, NA, RG 59, 711.62114/492, cited War Department policy as outlined in Prisoner of War Circular No. 5, Paragraph 2, of Nov. 2, 1943. The War Department's official notice informing State of Drechsler's death arrived on March 16. State sent it along to the Swiss Legation on March 29. NA, RG 59, 711.62114/610.

14. NA, RG 389, E 452, box 1403, file 2.

15. Chief of the POW Branch of the PMGO's Security and Intelligence Division to Commanding General, Army Service Forces, March 14, 1944: "It is suspected that this prisoner of war was murdered." Ibid.

16. Assistant Director, PWD, to Special War Problems Division, Department of State, April 12, 1944 (the Swiss protest was dated March 15). Ibid.

17. NA, RG 389, E 451, box 1312, folder 383.6 "General #5."

18. According to Krammer, *Nazi Prisoners of War in America*, 172, Geller angered his fellow prisoners by performing his work too well and being too friendly with his supervisor, adding that, after he got two men reassigned because their political activities were interfering with their work, he was tried and condemned by a "kangaroo court."

19. Report, Chief of the Intelligence Branch of the Eighth Service Command's Security and Intelligence Division to the Commanding General, Army Service Forces, May 4, 1944, NA, RG 389, E 452, box 1403, file 2.

20. PMG Gullion also recommended that the Adjutant General publish and distribute the ASF letter to all Service Commands. NA, RG 389, E 451, box 1312, folder 383.6 "General #5." See also NA, RG 407, Dec. File 383.6, box 2916. The policy would remain in effect from April 6, 1944 to March 14, 1945.

21. Director, PWD to State's SWPD, May 1, 1944, NA, RG389, E 452, 1942–1946, box 1403, file 1. According to Krammer, *Nazi Prisoners of War in America*, 172–173, Guenther was suspected of having "alerted the authorities to a pending prisoner work stoppage" and of liking jazz. He was "condemned by a midnight kangaroo court." Costelle, *Les Prisonniers*, 65, says that Guenther had favored Americans over fellow Germans when distributing milk.

22. Director, PWD to State's SWPD, May 6, 1944, NA, RG 389, E 452, box 1403, file 1. State relayed these bare facts to the Swiss Legation, along with Guenther's date of birth, next of kin, and burial site. The War Department intended this note to be the promised "further communication."

23. Geller's file, NA, RG 389, E 452, box 1403, file 2, also reveals lack of communication among the Pentagon bureaucracies. G-2 only learned of the incident when the Camp Chaffee public relations officer announced that an unnamed prisoner of war had been found dead in his bunk, "slain, apparently by fellow prisoners." On April 18, the Chief of the Counterintelligence Evaluation Branch asked the PWD for "further particulars" on behalf of G-2's Asst. Chief of Statff. PWD would not announce Geller's death to the Protecting Power until March 30. The legation had to ask, on May 13, if "further details are now available." On May 19, PWD directed State's SWPD to transmit the information it received on March 30.

24. POW Monograph, reel 2, at 011. As already noted, this microfilm of PMGO files has no consecutive pagination.

25. Transcript of phone call, March 24, 1944, NA, RG 389, E 451, box 1312, folder 383.6 "General #5." Bryan was talking about a speech which the commandant at Concordia, Kansas, proposed to give. Such speeches had to be pre-approved and censored.

26. On the reprimand, see chap. 3 and PMGO to State's SWPD, Jan. 19, 1944, NA, RG 59, 711.62114/464. Wattenberg had kept on making complaints.

27. Number WAR 16005, Office of the Commanding General, ASF, Deputy Chief of Staff for Service Commands, Correspondence File 1943–1945, NA, RG 160, E 13, box 45.

28. Each Service Command headquarters had seven staff divisions, including a Judge Advocate, an Adjutant General, and a Security and Intelligence Division that reported directly to G-2 in Washington as well as serving the PMG and the service commander. Ninth Service Command included Arizona, California, Idaho, Montana, Nevada, Oregon, Utah, and Washington with headquarters near Salt Lake City.

29. See Luther C. West, *They Call it Justice: Command Influence and the Court-Martial System* (New York: Viking, 1977). For the struggle to make command influence illegal, see Jonathan Lurie, *Arming Military Justice*, vol. 1: *The Origins of*

the United States Court of Military Appeals, 1775–1950 (Princeton, N.J.: Princeton University Press, 1993), especially chap. 10.

30. Telex SMPGA (36) 383.6, NA, RG 389, E 452, 1942–1946, box 1403, file 2.

31. The preliminary report to the Commander of the Army Service Forces, Military Intelligence Dossier No. X6042762, is cited as BR.

32. NA, RG 59, 711.62114/845.

33. Asst. Director, PWD, to Asst. PMG Bryan, May 10, 1944, NA, RG 389, E 452, box 1396, folder 383.6 "Gen P/W, Nov. 1943-Sept. 1944."

34. NA, RG 389, E 452, box 1398, folder 383.6 "Gen. P/W, Segregation." See also, in the same file, the response from the Director of the PWD to a request from the office of the Army's Commanding General for more information on segregation and re-education, dated May 20, 1944.

35. Memorandum for the Commanding General, U.S. Army Forces, from Director, PWD, May 20, 1944; Memorandum for the Adjutant General from Col. E. W. Gruhn, Deputy Director of Intelligence, ASF, May 30, 1944. Ibid.

Chapter 6

1. Until April 18, 1944, staff judge advocates and adjutants usually handled crimes. Since several Service Commanders had complained, G-2 had already taken an active interest in the deaths of Hans Geller on March 25 and Horst Guenther on April 5. Security and Intelligence divisions served both the Service Commander and G-2. See Millett, *Organization and Role of the Army Service Forces*, 334, 461–462; U.S. War Department, Headquarters, Army Service Forces, Office of the Provost Marshal General. *Programs of the Office of the Provost Marshal General in World War II* (Washington., 1946), 350–351.

2. Report of Conference, Jan. 8, 1944, HQ, 8th Service Command, on POW and POW camps (tabbed), p. 18, NA, RG 389, E 451, box 1308 290/34/9/5, file 337 General P/W. Jaworski's comments on how to investigate POW crimes, pp. 15–18, are very interesting.

3. BR 43.

4. Interrogation of Dr. Max Marks, BR 69.

5. Hebblethwaite, BR 78–79, 81–83, and 87–89 respectively.

6. *The Articles of War, Approved June 4, 1920* (Washington: Government Printing Office, 1920), 8.

7. Otto Behrens, BR 111–122.

8. Emil Watt, BR 128–132.

9. Arthur Bender, BR 141–151. The frustrated board read to Bender the list of men from the barracks who had arrived with him from his former camp in Colorado and asked, one by one, if he knew them. This name-reading technique would be used by the lie detector expert who arrived weeks later and re-interrogated the suspects. This and other small incidents make one suspect that this source con-

tains only final interrogations designed to get the most facts into the record in the least space, in anticipation of a court-martial.

10. Bender, BR 154.

11. Gerhard Richter, BR 159–175. The board also grilled Richter about some letter that the former head of the camp's personnel office had shown him. He denied reading it.

12. Paul Reum, BR 177–187.

13. Alfred Friedrich, BR 187–195.

14. Juergen Wattenberg, BR 198–212.

15. The Board Report only records this one interrogation of Wattenberg, but later it informed a protesting prisoner that even the captain had submitted to a lie detector examination. At Byron Hot Springs, the board would quiz the following men about him: Fischer, D-CMR 4:70; Bleise, BR 536–537; Elser, BR 557; Chief Quartermaster Hox, who had served on Wattenberg's boat, BR 858–860; and Murza, BR 512. At Papago Park: Nieswand, BR 575; Polowzyk, BR 295; Taubert, BR 585; Wagenfuer BR 567–568; and an anti-Nazi officer, H. C. Richter, BR 612–618. See also BR 453, 460, 470, 472–473, 478–479, 481–482, 496–497, 568, 603 (Duer).

16. Although these interviews allegedly began on April 5, they bear evidence of a technique used by the polygraph technician who arrived weeks later. Each of Drechsler's mates had to name all his own boatmates, usually by rank, sometimes more than once. The polygraph was supposed to detect guilty reactions.

17. Gustav Behlke, BR 266–278. Passages in Behlke's interrogation reveal that he had been questioned earlier. See particularly 275–276.

18. Erhardt Lenk, BR 281–282; Herman Polowzyk, BR 287–294. The board made Polowzyk recite the names of his crew, a useless drill unless it was for the benefit of the lie detector expert (who arrived some weeks later).

19. Klaus Preuss, BR 301–309.

20. Josef Hoeller, BR 315–322.

21. Werner Reinl, BR 326–334.

22. Memo for Brig. Gen. Bryan from Asst. Exec., G-2, March 29, 1944, subject: Photostats of P/W Mail, 3 enclosures, For the PMG: B. M. Bryan, Asst. PMG to Commanding General, Ninth Service Command, NA, RG 389, E 452, box 1403, file 2, to which is attached a handwritten memo to the PWD's legal department containing Bryan's comment and his order that the investigating board be informed that "these PWs who wrote the letters 'know something.'"

23. Bryan to Commander, Ninth Service Command, April 3, 1944, NA, RG 389, E 452, box 1403, file 2.

24. BR 414. The other letter read: "A few days ago a traitor to the cause" had been "put to death a few hours after his arrival in camp by his own friends. This dog was to live no longer as a German. Keep well." Bryan to Commander, Ninth Service Command, April 3, 1944, ibid.

25. They later installed "temporary laboratory coverage" at Papago Park "in view

of difficulties recently encountered in the conduct of an investigation there"; but by then Church's board had broken the case. Memo, Director, Personnel Security Division, May 23, 1944, NA, RG 389, E 467, box 1522, in POW Operations file.

26. NA, RG 389, E 452, box 1403, file 2.

27. Hans Siebert, BR 345; Walter Schiller, BR 355; Hermann Weidemann, BR 361, 363.

28. Wiemer, BR 370, 375–376.

29. Wilke, BR 386.

30. Reum, BR 393.

Chapter 7

1. Engler, BR 396–403; other sailors, 423–426.

2. Josef Gross, BR 429–433, 435–439.

3. BR 440–443.

4. Oskar Meyer, BR 449–455. Meyer had arrived at Papago Park on March 1 and been transferred on March 15.

5. Rolf Fitzner, BR 459–464.

6. John Neumair, BR 468–474. Neumair, a supporter of the late Austrian president Dolfuss, took fright when his compound spokesman called him to a meeting. Expecting a beating for repairing a GI's radio, he had appealed for protection.

7. Rudolph Wilhelmy, BR 478–482.

8. Herbert Wollenweber, BR 487–490.

9. Guenter Albert, BR 495–497. Albert and three others had been given refuge in Papago Park's guardhouse "about March 13." They had collaborated on a letter "to Washington," asking for a transfer to an anti-Nazi camp. Wollenweber, "very white and afraid," had come later.

10. Whittingham, *Martial Justice*, 106–107. Whittingham cites no sources.

11. Report of Investigating Board in the Case of Prisoner of War Werner Drechsler to Commanding General, Army Service Forces, Washington25, D.C. ATTENTION: The Provost Marshal General: Personal Attention: Col. Alton C. Miller, Director, Personnel Security Division, July 1, 1944, BR 18.

12. "Contacts of Werner Drechsler at Fort Hunt (In Chronological Order)," NA, RG 38 (OP 16-Z), subject file 1942–1945, box 5, folder "Farm File."

13. NA, RG 389, E 452, box 1403, file 2, dated April 26, 1944. It also pointed out that the Swiss Legation had complained.

14. D-CMR 1:24. This communication may have been sent in response to a telegram from the Provost Marshal General to the Commanding General, Ninth Service Command, asking for a report about "third degree methods" by Church's board. See D-CMR 2, 109.

15. Unnumbered page found among the supporting documents near the back of BR.

16. D-CMR 4:27; Whittingham, *Martial Justice*, 107. Church certainly applied the device to most of the seventy-four prisoners the report lists as having been questioned earlier.

17. Friedrich Murza, BR 504–512. The board always asked about Capt. Wattenberg's speech on the day Drechsler was hanged. Murza said he did not recall it.

18. Lothar Mandelkow, BR 516–523.

19. Guenther Bleise, BR 529–537. He would not be interrogated again until the board returned from Byron Hot Springs.

20. Paul Buchholz, BR 539.

21. Rolf Wizuy, BR 542–549.

22. Siegfried Elser, BR 553–557.

23. Friedrich Wagenfuehr, BR 561–563, 565–568.

24. Walter Nieswand, BR 572–575.

25. Heinz Taubert, BR 578–588.

26. Heinrich Ludwig and Peter Duer, BR 599–603.

27. Ludwig, BR 592–595.

28. Lt. Hermann Hans Carl Richter, Catholic son of a Finnish mother and an Austrian father, was raised in Czechoslovakia and had served in the Austrian merchant marine. BR 607–618.

29. On June 23, 1944, the Swiss Legation sent an inquiry to the State Department about Wattenberg's complaints to his Protecting Power. He had been removed, allegedly for abusing his position by inciting war prisoners "to take a non-cooperative attitude." He had been stripped of his officer's privileges and segregated, with eight others, in a small stockade. The legation commented that this seemed severe, since Wattenberg had not been court-martialed. Some officers viewed him as a martyr, but the camp commander described him as "a constant source of disturbance." American authorities might deem it wise to transfer him elsewhere. NA, RG 59, 711.62114/964. On July 1, State asked the PMG for guidance and on August 19 told the Swiss that the matter was receiving attention. 711.62114/8–1444.

30. Gerhard Richter, BR 619–627.

31. Alfred Friedrich, BR 628–633.

32. According to a protest by Capt. Paul Keller, Papago Park's new spokesman, to the Protecting Power, dated July 3, 1944, NA, RG 389, E 452, box 1403, file 2.

Chapter 8

1. NA, RG 389, E 452, box 1403, file 2.

2. Nieswand letter of June 23, 1944, ibid. Compare Schiller's letter of June 22, ibid., with his interrogation, BR 351–354.

3. Only there, according to BR 785–791, was Peters read his AW 24 (Articles of War) rights and sworn in as a first-time witness. His POW number reveals that Peters was a boatmate of Wizuy, Fischer, Franke, Reyak, and Kuelsen. He had

been assigned to Drechsler's barracks and had gone with Alfred Friedrich to see his body. His statement at Byron Hot Springs was a pitiful collection of rumors.

4. NA, RG 389, E 452, box 1403, file 2. Barber's note mentioned eight enclosures, which are not in the National Archives file, having been sent to the Swiss Legation. Some of these letters may have been among those forwarded much later by the camp spokesman Keller: those of Werner Reinl, Hans Siebert, Norbert Gabler, Hermann Polowzyk, Josef Preuss, and Paul Reum, which were written on March 23 and forwarded on July 7. (Those of Willi Peters, dated May 3, and Walter Nieswand, May 9, had been forwarded by Barber on May 12.) The Jaeger-Völker letter was dated May 11. Lothar Mandelkow, Josef Machenschalk, and Walter Schiller also wrote complaints on June 22 and 23. Ibid.

5. The transcript is filed with the letters in ibid.

6. The telex and the reply to it, dated May 26, are also filed with the letters.

7. Both replies were addressed to the Commanding General, Army Service Forces, attention the Provost Marshal General.

8. NA, RG 59, 711.62114/875, dated May 26, 1944.

9. June 17, 1944, ibid.

10. NA, RG 389, E 452, box 1403, file 2. This is a smudged carbon copy.

11. NA, RG 59, 711.62114/875. State delivered the letters. They are not included in its files.

12. NA, RG 389, E 452, box 1403, file 2. Capt. Keller wrote on June 17. Col. Barber's conveying note merely said: "1. This office disclaims knowledge of any pending action of this kind. 2. Forwarded without comment."

13. See chapter 3 in this book.

14. "Report of the Escape and Apprehension of O/Sold. Marcel Barthel, 35128-MI, Soldat Karl Linke, 48958-MI, O/Gefr. Albert Mueller, 23881-MI from Prisoner of War Camp Indianola, Nebraska," Statement by Maj. W. A. Erwin, June 23, 1944. NA, RG 389, E 452, classified dec. file 1941–1945, 253.5–253.6, box 1372, folder 253.6 "Escape and Apprehension of Ps/W."

15. "Additional Statement of Soldat Karl Linke," June 22, 1944. Ibid.

16. According to him, the commandant had asked the PMGO on May 18 for permission to transfer the five to Camp Atlanta. "The Commanding General, Seventh Service Command, by secret letter, dated 30 May 1944, directed that the prisoners be kept interned at this camp but their records may be transferred to Atlanta." This happened on June 7. (The five learned of it when their pay failed to arrive on time.) Ibid.

17. Statement of O/Sold. Marcel Barthel, June 23, 1944, and Linke additional statement, June 22. Ibid.

18. Barthel statement. Ibid.

19. Mueller statement, June 24; additional statement, June 22. Ibid.

20. Linke additional statement. Ibid.

21. Barthel statement; Linke, statement and additional statement; Mueller, additional statement. Ibid.

22. Typed copy of article in ibid.

23. "Report of the Escape and Apprehension of O/Sold. Anton Petratschek, ISN-35165-MI, O/Gefr. Herbert Vogler, 34255-MI from Prisoner of War Camp Indianola, Nebraska"; Statement by O/Sold. Anton Petratschek, June 21, 1944; Statement of O/Gefr. Herbert Vogler, June 21, 1944. Ibid.

24. Statement of Capt. Robert S. Keyes, June 19, 1944. Ibid.

25. Statement of First Lt. Ralph W. Wofford, June 23, 1944. Ibid.

26. Petratschek and Vogler wrote their statements on June 21, 1944. Barthel, Linke, and Mueller on June 22, Barthel on June 23, and the other two on June 24. Ibid.

27. Additional statements. NA, RG 389, E 452, box 1372, folder 253.6, "Escape and Apprehension of Ps/W."

28. Letter from Lt. Col. Leonard R. Smith, June 27, 1944; letter from Maj. W. L. Wolcott, June 28, 1944. Ibid.

29. Moore, *The Faustball Tunnel*, 100.

30. Barthel additional statement. NA, RG 389, E 452, box 1372, folder 253.6, "Escape and Apprehension of Ps/W."

Chapter 9

1. Glenda G. Carroll, "Angel Island State Park," *Travel-Holiday* 154 (Nov. 1980), 64. For a good prewar description, see *California: A Guide to the Golden State:* compiled and written by the Federal Writers Project of the Works Project Administration for the State of California, American Guide Series (New York: Hastings House, 1939), 297. Hereafter cited as Federal Writers Project, *California.*

2. NA, RG 389, box 2654, folder "PMGO Inspection Reports."

3. Federal Writers Project, *California*, 583.

4. Memorandum for the files, June 26, 1943; M.J.L. to Director-FBI RE: Internal Security, Alien Enemy Control, Aug. 13, 1943. See also Director to SAC, San Francisco, Oct. 16, 1943, RE: Camp Byron, California, Alien Enemy Control, Escaped Prisoners of War. On Jan. 28, 1944, Hoover demanded a report. SAC N. J. L. Pieper replied by air mail special delivery on Feb. 14, referring to Bureau File 100–164772. All materials in FBI, San Francisco Division Central Records, Prisoner of War file.

5. Memo for file, RE: prisoners of war, instructions in event of escape, by Agent Pieper, April 12, 1944. Ibid.

6. Memo from SAC RE: Prisoners of War, Event of escape, Nov. 7, 1943, 100–18336, ibid. Photographs and descriptions of escapees were obtainable from Angel Island. Two agents who interviewed its commandant, Maj. Chenoweth, described him as very "cozy" with his facts. Memorandum, SAC: RE: Prisoners of war, Internal Security, Alien Enemy Control, Dec. 28, 1943. Memo for the File by SAC Pieper RE: alien enemy control; escaped prisoners of war, April 12, 1944, warns that a recaptured POW immediately reverted to that status "and is entitled to be

treated as such." Geneva permitted searching him but shackles should be used very cautiously. G-2 would assume custody. Ibid.

7. BR 644. When Stengel confessed on June 1, 1944, Staff Sgt. Held was sworn in as the board's interpreter. BR 666. Held would replace Schmidt every time the board met at Byron Hot Springs except for the interrogation of Richter on May 30 and of Reyak on June 8. The board's own interpreter merely translated the prisoners' written confessions into English.

8. D-CMR 4:27, 35.

9. BR 644–653.

10. BR 654–665.

11. D-CMR 4:68.

12. BR 666–685. For the record, the board established that Stengel was twenty-five, had served five and a half years in the German Navy and two as a POW.

13. The board read the names of Drechsler's crew. Murza had to say "yes" if he knew them. (Predictably, he did not know the enlisted men.) This is a polygraph technique. Unless Byron Hot Springs had its own machine, this passage is a fragment of an earlier session with Dr. Keeler, hence more evidence of creative editing of the record. BR 688–689.

14. Murza, BR 686–714.

15. Ludwig had been in the shower room during the first attack. Stengel never knew he was involved.

16. Stengel, BR 739–749. Although Held's translation is clumsy, I believe it is substantially accurate since the note taker, Maj. Walsh, was a native German speaker. Later translations, Held's for a pretrial investigator and Schmidt's for the court-martial judges, are suspect.

17. Sworn testimony at court-martial. D-CMR 4:20.

18. BR 715–737 is a photostat of the German original.

19. Col. Catesby ap C. Jones, Chief, Prisoner of War Branch, War Department Military Intelligence Service, to Lt. Col. Bernays, C/O A. C. of S., G-1, Nov. 3, 1943, NA, RG 389, E 452 (1942–1946), 250.91, box 1371, OPS Operations Division—OPS Branch. Ironically, one of the other alleged German violations of Geneva was: "Letters to Protecting Power are tardy in arrival and sometimes never arrive."

20. D-CMR 4:67–68.

21. Elser testimony, BR 750–764.

22. D-CMR 4:71–72.

23. Tadeusz Wittlin, *Commissar: The Life and Death of Lavrenty Pavlovich Beria* (New York: Macmillan, 1972), 277. American personnel using the technique at places like Guantánamo, alleged that straining a person's "pressure points" is not torture.

24. Robert Conquest, *The Great Terror, Stalin's Purge of the Thirties* (New York: Macmillan, 1968), 138–140. Robinson O. Everett, *Military Justice in the Armed Forces of the United States* (Westport, Conn.: Greenwood, 1956), 87, cites a 1953 Supreme Court ruling that "a process of interrogation can be so prolonged and

unremitting, especially when accompanied by deprivation of refreshment, rest or relief, as to accomplish extortion of an involuntary confession." Stein v. N.Y. 346 US 156, 184.

25. D-CMR 4:71–72.

26. Wizuy, BR 765–773.

27. Ludwig named Elser, Murza, Nieswand, Reyak, Kuelsen, Franke, Wizuy, and Fischer.

28. BR 774–780.

29. Maj. Zabel, Sgt. Donohoe (the board's own interpreter), and sometimes Col. Church signed as witnesses. See D-CMR 4:101 (Fischer), 4:114 (Franke), 4:179–180 (Ludwig), 4:124 (Kuelsen), 4:133 (Reyak), 4:161–162 (Stengel), and 4:192–193 (Wizuy). There is no record of "certificates" signed by the others.

30. D-CMR 4:32.

31. BR 781.

32. D-CMR 1:25.

33. Taubert, BR 782–785; Stoessel, BR 796–802; Peters, 785–792 (Peters, although a Drechsler victim, had not attended Hox's meeting).

34. Matzke, BR 792–796, 838.

35. Franke, BR 803–810.

36. Kuelsen, BR 811–818.

37. Reyak, BR 818–826.

38. Fischer, BR 826–838.

39. D-CMR 4:70.

40. Ibid., 28–29.

41. BR 838–846. These confessions were marked as exhibits pending the court-martial.

42. Reinl, BR 846–852.

43. Hox, BR 852–866.

Chapter 10

1. Confidential orders prepared by Col. C. W. Wing, Director, 9th Serv. Cmd. Security and Intelligence (S & I), for Maj. Gen. McCoach's signature, June 7, 1944, D-CMR 1:25.

2. From Director, S & I, June 19, 1944, D-CMR 1:29.

3. S & I Director to Commanding Officer, POW Processing Station, Angel Island, California, June 16, 1944, D-CMR 1:26; Lt. Col. Archie L. Tower, Exec., Office of the Service Command JA to the PMG, July 11, 1944, D-CMR 1:89. The Service Commands had primary control over POW camps, named general hospitals, and military prisons. Ludwig went to DeWitt General Hospital, Menlo Park; Stengel (who had an appendectomy on June 5) to Dibble General Hospital, Auburn; and Wizuy to Hammond General Hospital, Modesto. Rehabilitation centers such as

Turlock were not intended for personnel convicted of murder or major crime. Millett, *Organization and Role of the Army Service Forces*, 106, 315.

4. June 20, 1944, D-CMR 1:27–28. In his July 3 letter to the Protecting Power (see n. 29), Papago Park's camp spokesman named eight men removed on June 17: Reinl, Bleise, Nieswand, Polowzyk, Wiedemann, Wiemer, Wilke, and one Edmund Staron. Weidman, Wilke, and Staron were not on the list of official witnesses (see n. 6).

5. BR 910–912.

6. The charge sheet, D-CMR 1:101–102, lists six Americans and ten POWs as witnesses: 1st. Lt. Cecil S. Parshall, Capt. Claude C. Stafford, Capt. Max Marks, Capt. Leland M. Hebblethwaite, Tec. 4 Fred Boronstein, and Gregg R. Irvine, a civilian engineer; and the POWs Otto Behrens, Gerhard Richter, Alfred Friedrich, Werner Reinl, and Franz Hox (listed as stationed at Angel Island), Heinz Richter, Walter Nieswand, Herman Polowzyk, Guenther Bleise, and Rudolph Wiemer. All the Americans on the list would testify at the trial. None of the Germans would do so. See also "Chronology of the Case . . . ," D-CMR 3:2.

7. D-CMR 1:94–103. His oath was attested by Maj. Francis T. Wade, asst. staff JA, who would later sit on the three-man board which reviewed and confirmed the death sentences.

8. Concurring Opinion to first review of sentence, Sept. 15, 1944, D-CMR 3:16.

9. It is worth noting that Edgar Menschner, another POW facing trial for murder, was investigated by a major, not a shavetail lieutenant. During World War II, pretrial investigations were so corrupt that the system had to be reformed after the war. See S. Sidney Ulmer, *Military Justice and the Right to Counsel* (Lexington: University of Kentucky Press, 1970), 46–49; and Everett, *Military Justice in the Armed Forces of the United States*, 70–74, 169–170. Everett had been a prosecutor and defense counselor, an investigating officer, and (after it was created in 1951) a commissioner of the U.S. Court of Military Appeals. The present-day Uniform Code of Military Justice requires pretrial investigators to be a field grade officer (above captain) or someone with legal training. It also allows the accused to have counsel during this investigation. An investigating officer today using a coerced, inadmissible confession could be prosecuted under the Civil Rights Act or subjected to a civil suit for damages to the accused. None of these rights applied before 1951.

10. Acting Serv. Cmd. JA to Commanding Officer, Prisoner of War Processing Station, Service Command Unit 1936, Angel Island, CA, June 29, 1944, D-CMR 1:94 and 3:178. The charge sheets, bearing the same date, 1:95–104. Angel Island's commandant appointed Baldwin on July 1, 1:93.

11. D-CMR 1:86.

12. Baldwin had signed for these documents on June 30. D-CMR 1:87. They also appeared in the Board Report, but that document was so secret that even Col. Church had to sign for it on July 10. D-CMR 1:88.

13. D-CMR 4:200, 205, 209, 214, 219, 227, and 241.

14. Stengel, D-CMR 4:228; Kuelsen, 210.

15. Kuelsen, D-CMR 4:210–212.

16. Wizuy, D-CMR 4:242, 244; Ludwig, 216; Reyak, 221.

17. "Summary of Evidence," BR 22–23.

18. Ludwig's statement, D-CMR 4:216–217, is the best and briefest. Wizuy's, D-CMR 245–246, is the most eloquent. See also Fischer, D-CMR 202–203; Stengel, 230–238; Kuelsen, 211–212; Reyak, 226.

19. The clearest copies of all interviews are found in D-CMR 4:100–247.

20. D-CMR 3:27–28. Baldwin submitted his report on July 8, 1944, through the commander of Angel Island, who also recommended trial: 1:92. Stengel statement, 4:240.

21. D-CMR 3:18, in a brief supporting the death penalty.

22. Office of Service Command JA, to [newly appointed] PMG, Archer L. Lerch, D-CMR 1:89–90. Lerch had telephoned to request a full copy of the final report. This could not be released until the AG had signed it. (Church had reported in his capacity as Chief, Intelligence Branch of the Command's Security and Intelligence Division.) D-CMR 1:78–80. Church final report: Report of Investigating Board in the Case of Prisoner of War Werner Drechsler; To: General, Army Service Forces, Washington 25, D.C.; Attention: The PMG: Personal Attention: Col. Alton C. Miller, Director, Personnel and Security Division. BR 18.

23. By way of contrast, when Edgar Menschner faced trial for the murder of Hans Geller, he wrote the Swiss Legation on June 1944 for help in obtaining the lawyer and interpreter Geneva allowed him. This request led to a discussion among PMG Lerch, his assistant Gen. Bryan, and Lt. Col. Leon Jaworski, who had prosecuted the Beyer case. Menschner's request made no difference. In March he allegedly accepted the defender provided by his prosecutors. NA, RG 389, E 452, box 1452, folder 1, file 2, containing POW Branch, Security and Intelligence Div., to PMG, June 23, 1944, and other documents.

24. At the very least, these officers were just as susceptible to "command influence" as Church's board had been. See Robert Sherrill, *Military Justice Is to Justice as Military Music Is to Music*, rev. ed. (New York: Harper and Row, 1970), 78–79; and West, *They Call It Justice*, 7–8. For the special orders appointing all court officials, see D-CMR 3:206.

25. July 11, 1944, D-CMR 1:76–77.

26. Why did the bilingual Gruenebaum occupy such a humble position? He told me that neither G-2 nor Western Defense Command had any use for him. Only an officer could do intelligence work, and he had been rejected for officer training because of his accent. He was on his way to register graves in China when the first German prisoners landed in San Francisco. From April 1944 to January 1946, he was a translator at Camp Stockton, California (near Byron Hot Springs). When he volunteered to parachute into Alsace, where he knew the local dialect

and had friends, G-2 asked him to jump over a part of Germany he did not know. He refused. Presumably G-2 remembered his name and recommended him to Walsh, for shortly afterward he was ordered to Arizona. See also Ilene Lelchuk, "Gruenebaum Served as an Interpreter in Nazi Trial," *Paradise* [California] *Post*, Dec. 26, 1992.

27. D-CMR 3:191–194. This report, dated July 13, 1944, also noted that Stengel had a history of gastrointestinal trouble since Feb. 1943, and had an appendectomy on June 5, 1944.

28. D-CMR 1:73–75, 77, and 3:182–184. The legation's acknowledgment was dated July 18, 1944.

29. D-CMR 2:124–127 and 1:72. The letter also requested the Ninth Service Command to inform the PMGO's POW Division of the sentences imposed and the action of the Reviewing Authority, "in order that the Protecting Power may be informed." However, Walsh would say on Aug. 17, 1944, that "by direction of the court the findings and sentence were not announced." D-CMR 1:69. When the command's review board confirmed the death sentences, Walsh would mark his Sept. 16 report secret. See D-CMR 1:36. The Protecting Power would not be informed of the sentences for a very long time.

30. These papers would become prosecution exhibits: D-CMR 4:248–261. Walsh mentioned Taylor's presence when he presented the documents in evidence. D–CMR 4:55.

31. PMGO to Ninth Service Command, dated July 29, 1944, signed by Col. A. M. Tollefson, Assistant Director, POW Division, D-CMR 1:71 and 3:185.

32. Francis E. Howard, Colonel, C.M.P. (military police), Director, PWD to State's SWPD, June 1, 1944, NA, RG 389, E 452, box 1403, file 2. This file also contains Keller's letter.

33. WPD to SWP, Aug. 8, 1944, ibid. The Swiss memo bears the legation code VIII-10 and the State Department note SWP 711.62114/7–1144.

34. Swiss Legation to State Department, March 24, 1944, NA, RG 59, 711.65114/451.

35. For the translations and the translators' comments, see NA, RG 389, E 452, box 1403, file 2. On July 22, 1944, Papago Park Commandant Barber also sent the Commanding General, Ninth Service Command, copies of the letters, in translation, and his own cover letter explaining them to the PMG. Ibid., box 1386, folder 330.14, May 1944-Sept. 1944.

36. The letters in the file are not the originals but translations, which Maj. Sullivan certified for accuracy on Aug. 3. This is the same officer who, on May 18, had telephoned Church for some explanations of alleged mistreatment. See chap. 8.

37. This is a (badly translated) reference to nine letters supposed to have been sent by the compound spokesmen Jaeger and Völker (see chap. 8). Possibly Keller himself had held them back, at Col. Barber's request, until the board's investigation was over. Keller's second letter had nine enclosures. Papago Park's Commandant

Barber had received these on July 3, but had not forwarded them until July 22. Barber's conveying letter lists notes from Werner Reinl, Hans Siebert, Hermann Polowzyk, and Paul Reum (all U-118 crewmen), Josef Preuss, and Norbert Gabler, all dated March 23, 1944; and from the Drechsler victim Lothar Mandelkow, the U-118 enlisted man Walter Schiller, and a Josef Machenschalk, dated June 22–23. Keller mentions a letter from the defendant Rolf Wizuy. One surmises that the Machenschalk letter, which is not in the file, was substituted for Wizuy's to make up the number nine.

38. NA, RG 389, E 452, box 1386, folder 330.14, May 1944-Sept. 1944.

39. Lt. Col. L. B. C. Jones to Commanding General, Army Service Forces, ATTENTION: The PMG, PWD. Ibid.

40. NA, RG 389, E. 452, box 1403, file 2.

41. Wattenberg cited Geneva Articles 4, 21, 45.2, 46.2, 47.1, 48.1 and 2, and 49.2 in his letter, marked CONFIDENTIAL. The same major who had translated Keller's correspondence, just as badly, wrote: "CONFIDENTIAL —(That's what *he* says)!" Wattenberg's complaint was sent by Col. A. M. Tollefson, Asst. Director, PWD to SWPD, State, Aug. 30, 1944, NA, RG 389, E 452, box 1384. folder 311.7 "Gen. P/W, June '44-August '44."

42. Holden's letter was dated Aug. 11, 1944, and Keller's on Aug. 16. Col. Tollefson, the PWD's assistant director, sent these letters to State's SWPD on Aug. 30, offering Holden's remark as proof that the United States was not violating Geneva Article 4. Ibid.

43. See Moore, *The Faustball Tunnel.*

44. "Prisoners of War Who Have Acted as Informants for American Intelligence." NA, RG 389, E 452, box 1396, folder 383.6 "Gen. P/W, Nov. 1943–Sept. 1944." The author was Second Lt. R. E. Guggenheim of the Military Police Corps, function unknown.

45. Asst. PMG Bryan to PWD, Legal Branch, July 28, 1944, ibid.

46. Col. Francis E. Howard, Director of the PWD, to Col. Russell H. Sweet, Chief of G-2's Captured Personnel and Material Branch, ibid.

47. Col. Howard wrote on Aug. 3, "For The Provost Marshal General" to "Assistant Chief of Staff, G-2, Attention of Col. Sweet, Chief, C.P.M. Branch, M.I.S." (Corps of Military Police, Military Intelligence Service). Ibid. Col. Sweet, when he replied on Aug. 9, wrote "For the Chief, Military Intelligence Service."

Chapter 11

1. A general from the Eighth Service Command, conducting a conference on POWs and POW camps, made this remark. Report of Conference, Jan. 8, 1944, 15, NA, RG 389, E 451, box 1308, 290/34/9/5, file 337 General PW.

2. Gruenebaum interview with the author, Magalia, California, June 1994; postcard in possession of Helen Gruenebaum. He insisted that this sergeant was

the court interpreter, "not that captain [Schmidt]. The captain was the one who testified." Actually, both would testify.

3. Gruenebaum interview, June 1994.

4. They were: Col. Clayton J. Herman, Infantry; Col. Bertram I. Lawrence, Infantry, Col. Callie H. Palmer, Cavalry; Col. Joseph H. Whiteley, Medical Corps; Lt. Col. William W. Wertz, Coast Artillery Corps; Maj. Robert R. Taylor. AUS (Army of United States); Maj. Curtis H. Wienker, Infantry; Capt. James C. Reilly, QMC (Quartermaster Corps); Capt. Norman W. Edwards, Ordinance Dept.; Capt. Ross J. Thomas, Jr., QMC; Capt. Clarence Evans, CMP (Corps of Military Police); and Capt. Thomas H. Carrick, CWS (Chemical Warfare Service). D-CMR 3:206.

5. Gruenebaum interview, June 1994. Taylor was an artillery officer from the Presidio. Gruenebaum does not recall the existence of Taylor's assistant, Maj. Furst. He also insists that someone from the Red Cross attended this secret trial, though the records do not mention him. "They introduced him, otherwise I would not have noticed."

6. D-CMR 4:5–6 (Stafford); 4:12 (Marks).

7. D-CMR 4:13–15. None of this dialogue appears in the interrogation transcripts in the Board Report.

8. D-CMR 4:20.

9. D-CMR 4:23.

10. D-CMR 4:24.

11. D-CMR 4:25.

12. D-CMR 4:27. Whittingham, *Martial Justice*, 107, says over 125 men were tested.

13. D-CMR 4:28.

14. D-CMR 4:70.

15. D-CMR 4:30–33.

16. D-CMR 4:34–35. Defense must limit cross-examination to those subjects which the prosecution raised.

17. D-CMR 4:36–40.

18. D-CMR 4:40–43.

19. D-CMR 4:44–55. Baldwin repeatedly named Sgt. Held as his translator.

20. D-CMR 4:56–57.

21. D-CMR 4:59.

22. D-CMR 4:60.

23. D-CMR 4:60–61.

24. D-CMR 4:61–62.

25. D-CMR 4:62–63.

26. D-CMR 4:64.

27. D-CMR 4:65.

28. Telford Taylor, *Anatomy of the Nuremberg Trials* (New York: Knopf, 1992), 534. The Nuremberg Trial charter allowed defendants to do both. Taylor was American chief prosecutor for the lesser Nuremberg trials.

29. Gruunbaum interview with author, June 1994. Gruenebaum had no idea if Taylor's decision was planned or spontaneous.

30. D-CMR 4:67. Mr. Gruenebaum did not recall this.

31. Ibid. For a fuller description of Stengel's statement, see chap. 8.

32. Mr. Gruenebaum never agreed that the prisoners were really tortured. "The Germans had better tortures than that." However, he also pointed out that Germans never use garlic. He agreed that Stengel's experience would have been like a gringo's first encounter with habanero peppers.

33. D-CMR 4:67–69.

34. If so, this interview is absent from the Board Record.

35. D-CMR 4:69.

36. Fischer testimony, D-CMR 4:69–72. For a full account of his testimony, see chap. 9.

37. Franke and Kuelsen had confessed on June 3, Fischer not until June 8.

38. D-CMR 4:70.

39. D-CMR 4:71–72.

40. *Manual for Courts-Martial*, 1928 edition, chapter 25, para. 3.

41. D-CMR 4:73–74.

42. D-CMR 4:74.

43. Here Taylor was quoting from p. 162 of the *Manual for Courts-Martial*, a discussion of AW 92.

44. D-CMR 4:74–75.

45. Gruenebaum interview, June 1994.

46. Walsh had already furnished the Law Member (Poust) with a Supreme Court ruling in a similar case: *Lyons v. State of Oklahoma*, 64 *Supreme Court Reporter* 1208.

47. William Winthrop, *Military Law and Precedents*, 2nd edition (Washington: Government Printing Office, 1920), 300.

48. D-CMR 4:75–77.

49. Gruenebaum interview, June 1994.

50. D-CMR 3:186–187.

51. Memo from Walsh to Col. Thomas J. White, Service Command Judge Advocate, Sept. 15, 1944, D-CMR 1:65–66. Prisoners' signed receipts, 199–205.

Chapter 12

1. The Vanderbilt Committee produced the Uniform Code of Military Justicc. Its report is quoted in Jonathan Lurie, *Arming Military Justice*, vol. I of *The Origins of the United States Court of Military Appeals, 1775–1950* (Princeton, N.J.: Princeton University Press, 1993), 1:137–138.

2. *Bulletin of the Judge Advocate General of the Army* 3, no. 6 (1944), 227–228. The reviewers cited Wharton's *Criminal Evidence*, 10th edition, sec. 601, pp. 998–1002.

3. Sherrill, *Military Justice Is to Justice as Military Music Is to Music*, 175. The author, a disillusioned veteran of the system says: "If the constitution carries little weight with the military, the U.S. Supreme Court has even less influence."

4. They were correct. See memo to JAG Cramer from Col. Rounds, Asst. JAG for Military Affairs, Dec. 7, 1944. D-CMR 2:115. White telexed a request for the records on May 9, 1944 and received them on Sept. 5, 1944. D-CMR 1:67, 118.

5. D-CMR 3:7–15. Lt. Col. John W. Cramer wrote the review, dated Sept. 15. One assistant was Maj. Francis T. Wade, who had attested the oath of the lieutenant who was the official accuser. D-CMR 1:64, 103.

6. D-CMR 3:9–10.

7. They were probably referring to a checklist prepared by Walsh, which contained such items as "were the witnesses sworn?" and "is the record properly authenticated?" D-CMR 3:3–4.

8. D-CMR 3:10.

9. D-CMR 3:11.

10. Manual for Courts-Martial, 1928 edition, p. 116, para. 114.

11. Wharton, *Criminal Evidence*, 10th edition, sec. 622L.

12. D-CMR 3:12. (Baldwin's report, part of the trial record, showed that he had falsely reported placing Reyak under oath and informing him of his AW 24 rights. D-CMR 3:146, 150.)

13. D-CMR 3:12–13.

14. Since Walsh had not introduced the Board Report into evidence, the reviewers did not know that Stengel had been compelled to confess twice to the board. Reviews are based on nothing but the written court record.

15. He had said that after collapsing unconscious from the garlic-and-gas mask torture, the captain had yelled, "Do you want any more of that stuff?" Stengel had said, "No, it is enough for me. I wanted to talk to the Major." See chaps. 8 and 11.

16. *Lyons v. State of Oklahoma*, 64 *Supreme Court Reporter* 1208, at 1212.

17. D-CMR 3:14.

18. D-CMR 3:15–20.

19. D-CMR 3:20.

20. D-CMR 4:83.

21. D-CMR 1:36. The review, the brief, and Shedd's "action" were sent to the PMGO on Sept. 15, 1944.

22. D-CMR 1:50.

23. Transcript of telephone conversation, Sept. 23, 1944, D-CMR 1:51–52.

24. Statement of Major Francis P. Walsh, JAGD, Sept. 25, 1944; Memo on Court-Martial of Seven Nazi Prisoners of War, to Col. Cassius Poust, Sept. 25, 1944. D-CMR 1:47–49.

25. Sherrill, *Military Justice Is to Justice as Military Music Is to Music*, 75.

26. U.S. War Department, *Annual Report of the Army Service Forces for the Fiscal Year 1945*; *Annual Report: Services of Supply for the Fiscal Year Ending June 30, 1942*, 265–266.

27. The forty-three days which Ninth Service Command had spent on the case was far longer than usual. It notified the JAG's Office: "It is believed that this Prisoner of War case should not be considered in computing processing time for this command as [thirty-five days of] the delays are the result of compliance with International Law." D-CMR 1:37 and 3:2.

28. Whittingham, *Martial Justice*, 222.

29. They used the command's description of Drechsler's body. D-CMR 2 contains two copies of the JAG review (pp. 2–14, which bear various notations, and pp. 77–99).

30. D-CMR 2:80.

31. King's memo for the files, Oct. 3, 1944, D-CMR 2:117. A copy went to Col. William A. Rounds, Asst. JAG for Military Affairs, the board's contact with the JAG himself.

32. D-CMR 2:79.

33. D-CMR 2:81–88.

34. D-CMR 2:88–90.

35. The first review had mentioned Held by name. D-CMR 3:10. He had been present at Fischer's interrogation.

36. D-CMR 2:93.

37. D-CMR 2:94.

38. D-CMR 2:95. Emphasis in the original.

39.D-CMR 2:98–99.

40. Col. Rounds to JAG Cramer, Dec. 7, 1944, D-CMR 2:115.

41. Undated rough draft, signed by King. D-CMR 2:128–138. The JAG's War Plans Division is not to be confused with the War Department's staff-level War Plans Division (renamed the Operations Division in 1942), which performed the highest strategic planning.

42. Moyse's reply to King, Nov. 29, 1944, signed by Col. Lyon, D-CMR 2:118–121; Rounds to JAG Cramer, Dec. 2, 1944, 115.

43. D-CMR 2:129–130.

44. D-CMR 2:130.

45. D-CMR 2:133.

46. According to *Black's Law Dictionary*, 5th edition, 409; *dicta* are a judge's remarks, not formal legal pronouncements.

47. D-CMR 2:132.

48. D-CMR 2:133.

49. D-CMR 2:134–135.

50. D-CMR 2:135.

51. D-CMR 2:136–137.

52. Rounds received it on Nov. 29, 1944. D-CMR 2:118–119.

53. D-CMR 2:121.

54. D-CMR 2:135.

Chapter 13

1. *Annual Report of the Army Service Forces for the Fiscal Year 1945* (Washington: Government Printing Office, 1946), 275 (hereafter cited as *ASF Report, 1945)*; Sidney B. Fay, "German Prisoners of War," *Current History* 8, no. 43 (1945), 194; Secretary of War Stimson in *New York Times*, Dec. 1, 1944,. 15:5 (p. 15, col. 5). See also New York Times, Dec. 7, 1944, 16:5.

2. *ASF Report, 1945*, 266.

3. See, for example, "750 Freed Soldiers Brought to Boston," *New York Times*, April 21, 1945, 5:2.

4. *ASF Report, 1945*, 276.

5. See several articles in the *New York Times*: Sidney Shalett, "Prisoner Coddling Is Denied by Army," May 7, 1944, 14:1; "Stimson Denies U.S. Going to Give Italian PW's Citizenship in Exchange for Loyalty," Aug. 30, 1944, 10:2. See also "How We Treat War Prisoners," *U.S. News and World Report*, July 7, 1944, 24, and "Are Prisoners Pampered?," *U.S. News and World Report*, Dec. 22, 1944, 22; *Newsweek*, Aug. 28, 1944, 40, and Oct. 10, 1944, 8.

6. The *New York Times* alone in 1944 reported protests by the Army and Navy Union (July 22, 17:2), the 101st Infantry Veterans' Association (July 25, 7:1), the New York Department of the American Legion (Aug. 13, 28:1), the Society of the War of 1812 (Sept. 24, 15:1), the New Jersey Department of the American Legion (Oct. 20, 5:2), and the National Executive Committee of the American Legion (Nov. 20, 10:4).

7. See, for example, "War Prisoner Troubles," *Newsweek*, Feb. 28, 1944, 15; "Captives 'Coddled' in U.S., Russia Says," *New York Times*, May 26, 1944, 3:5; and "French Complaints of U.S. Coddling [in European Camps]," *New York Times*, Nov. 23, 1944, 4:7; Nov. 27, 3:3; and Nov. 29, 5:4.

8. Report of Conference, Jan. 8, 1944, p. 1, NA, RG 389, E451, box 1308 290/34/9/5, file 337 "General PW." Another reference on pp. 27–28 reveals that Winchell had charged that a farmer had treated ten of his POW workers and their guards to a fish fry in a restaurant's private room while Americans waited in line. He also said that other POWs were "entertained by Louisiana socialites, and that prisoners had frequent acquaintance with women of questionable character." The issue "is still going on the Winchell Broadcast every Sunday." Command headquarters was still receiving "lots of telephone calls on one thing and another" (p. 37). See other examples of War Department reaction to coddling charges in NA, RG 389, E 452, box 1361, folder 000.7 "General PW," especially Dep. C. of S. for Service Commands to PMG, March 12, 1945, and Memorandum for the Commanding Gen., Army Service Forces, Subject: "Investigation of the Handling of German POWs by the War Department," March 21, 1945. The Inspector General had investigated allegations, including those made by Walter Winchell on March 4, 1945 and Feb. 11, 1945. See also Director, Security and Intelligence Div. to Cmd. Gen., ASF, Nov. 29, 1945 concerning Winchell's column in the New York *Daily Mirror* of Nov. 9, 1945.

9. Quoted in "Report of Investigation of Alleged Irregularities in the Administration of the Prisoner of War Camp, Camp Breckinridge, Kentucky," April 5, 1944, p. 8, NA, RG 389, E 452, box 1382, folder "Breckenridge, Gen. P/W."

10. Ibid., p. 7, Exhibit G-2, Testimony of Col. Peyton Winlock, March 10, 1944.

11. "Typescript of radio broadcast, Miss Dorothy Thompson," NA, RG 389, E 452, box 1361, folder 000.77 General P/W. She was, for a time, Sinclair Lewis's wife.

12. She was quoting Mrs. Dorothy Brombar Bromley of the New York *Herald Tribune*, "War Prisoners Include Nazis and Anti-Nazis," April 12, 1944.

13. Asst. PMG Bryan to Office of the Under Sec. of War, "Comments on Radio Broadcast, Miss Dorothy Thompson," May 6, 1944, NA, RG 389, E 452, box 1361, folder 000.77 General PW.

14. Ibid.

15. Gufler to Plitt, Jan. 22, 1945, NA, RG 59, box 3337, 711.62114/1–2545, confidential file.

16. "House Group Sifts Prisoner Coddling," *New York Times*, Aug. 20, 1944, 15:5. See also "House Military Affairs Committee Expected to Report Soon," Oct. 8, 1944, 14:1.

17. U.S. Congress, House of Representatives, Committee on Military Affairs, *Investigation of National War Effort, Relative to the Treatment of Prisoners of War in the United States and Abroad*, 78th Congress, 2nd session, Nov. 30, 1944, Report no. 1992; hereafter cited as House Report 1992. See also "Congressmen Deny Prisoner Pampering," *New York Times*, Dec. 10, 1944, 13:1.

18. One review of House Report 1992 ("House Committee Says Nazis Keep to Prisoner 'Code,'" *New York Times*, Dec. 1, 1944, 5:1) remarked that the committee was "now engaged in a survey of the situation from every angle, especially first hand observation." (Its second report would be issued on June 12, 1945.)

19. Ibid. See also "Germans Respected Geneva Convention," *U.S. News and World Report*, Jan. 6, 1945, 2, citing an International Red Cross prediction that 99 percent of American prisoners in German hands would survive due "entirely to Germany's observance of the Geneva Convention."

20. "14,000,000 Leaflets Dropped over France," *New York Times*, Aug. 17, 1944, 3:1.

21. Bryan to Guffler, Dec. 23, 1944, NA, RG 59, E 711.62114/12–2344, box 2205, folder 3.

22. John Mason Brown, "German Prisoners of War in the United States," *American Journal of International Law* 39 (1945), 198–215.

23. Russel Porter, *New York Times*, Jan. 16, 1945, 1:3, continued on 13:2.

24. Ibid., Jan. 17, 1945, 11:1.

25. Ibid., Jan. 18, 1945, 5:1.

26. Robert D. Billinger Jr., *Hitler's Soldiers in the Sunshine State: German POWs in Florida* (Gainesville: University Press of Florida, 2000), 120–121, gives several examples. The *ASF Report, 1945*, 277–278, mentioned "many newspaper and magazine articles" resulting from the PMG's "persistent efforts to present to the American public the true facts about the War Department's treatment of prisoners and the

contribution of these prisoners to national production. A continuing invitation was extended to all accredited [male!] newspaper writers and radio commentators to inspect prisoner of war camps and to obtain accurate information regarding prisoners of war."

27. Sidney B. Fay, "German Prisoners of War," *Current History* 8, no. 43 (1945), 193–200.

28. Report from the Chief of the Office of Technical Information, Dec. 30, 1944, NA, RG 389, E 452, box 1361, folder 000.77, General P/W.

29. Ibid., January 9, 1945, labeled "secret."

30. Hanson's visit had taken place on Dec. 2 and 4, 1944. The stockade officer's report, dated Jan. 19, 1945, was included in Col. Holden's reports to Service Command, Jan. 20 and 22, 1945.

31. *ASF Report, 1945*, 277. For example, see "Nazi Policy of Organized Murder Blackens Germany for All History," *Newsweek*, April 30, 1945, 56. This article, describing Buchenwald as "the biggest and worst," speaks in the same breath of the liberation of slave labor camps and death marches of allied prisoners. See also Abraham L. Sacher, *The Redemption of the Unwanted: From the Liberation of the Death Camps to the Founding of Israel* (New York: St. Martin's Press, 1983), 3–4, 10–11, 32, 40–41. For General Dwight Eisenhower's reaction, see *Crusade in Europe* (Garden City, N.Y.: Doubleday, 1948), 408–409.

32. "American Battle Casualties," *New York Times*, Feb. 9, 1945, 8:2, reported 764,584 casualties.

33. War Department press release for Jan. 22, 1945, NA, RG 165, Records of War Department General and Special Staffs, E 498, War Department Special Staff, Public Relations Division—News Branch, Press and Radio Releases 1921–1947, box 92. Not many American prisoners had been liberated yet. A few had escaped. There was a constant exchange, through the Red Cross, of seriously wounded or physically or mentally ill prisoners. Since the United States regarded merchant seamen as war prisoners and Germany did not, there were also at least two "man for man, skill for skill" exchanges. See urgent, confidential telegram 1704, State Department to Bern Legation, May 16, 1944, and telegram 4212, Dec. 14, 1944, NA, RG 38 (OP 16-Z), subject file 1942–1945, box 17, Special Reports Issued by PW Section, folder "Repatriation of Ps//W, 1945."

34. D-CMR 2:115.

35. *Military Laws of the United States*, 7th edition (1929), 293–294, para. 405. See also 295, 297–299.

36. D-CMR 2:136–137.

37. PMG to Rounds, D-CMR 2:116. (Ninth Service Command's Maj. Gen. Shedd, who favored mercy, would be responsible for the executions.) There had been an "administrative tangle" connected with moving Gauss and Straub from Leavenworth back to the Fourth Service Command, where they had killed a man at Aiken side camp, in South Carolina. Six more came from the Eighth Service

Command: the "Beyer Five" from Camp Tonkawa, Oklahoma, and Menschner from Camp Chaffee, Arkansas.

38. D-CMR 2:71–72.

39. Millett, *The Organization and Role of the Army Service Forces*, 106.

40. Henry Lewis Stimson, Diaries, vol. 47 (microfilm, reel 9), Manuscripts and Archives, Yale University Library, New Haven, Conn.

41. Stimson, Diaries, vol. 48, p. 2 of daily entry, Oct. 5, 1944 (microfilm, reel 9). Maj. Gen. Edwin M. "Pa" Watson kept the president's appointment book and served as liaison between him and the War Department. See James MacGregor Burns, *Roosevelt, the Soldier of Freedom* (New York: Harcourt, Brace, Jovanovich, 1970), 9, 61, 406, 475. The identity of Konenman is unknown.

42. D-CMR 2:128, 137–138.

43. PMG Lerch described the situation to Gen. Wilson, the Ninth Service Command's chief of staff, over the telephone. The transcript from Wilson's office is found in D-CMR 2:110–11, and the one from the PMG's office in 1:21–22. They spoke on Jan. 27, 1945, about a week after Stimson approved the death sentences.

44. D-CMR 1:23. This list is filed immediately after one of the telephone transcripts noted above.

45. D-CMR 1:24. The document also drew attention to the fact that the investigating board's report had "been forwarded to [Stimson's] office."

46. Phone call of Jan. 27, 1945, transcribed on Wilson's end. Col. White, "memorandum for files," D-CMR 1:22.

47. D-CMR 1:21–22 and 2:110–111.

48. D-CMR 1:21. The memo, signed T.J.W. (Thomas J. White) and dated Jan. 29, refers to a telegram, WD Code TWX, of Jan. 26, 1945, which I have not located in the National Archives. I found no trace of Church's visit in the Archives or the Stimson papers.

49. Memo for the JAG from Maj. Gen. Clayton Bissell, Assistant Chief of Staff, G-2, Feb. 1, 1945, subject: "Coercion in Connection with Confessions of Five [*sic*] Prisoners of War Charged with Murder." D-CMR 2:107–108.

50. Stimson, Diaries, vol. 50, p. 102 (reel 9). I found no trace of Weckerling's "thorough investigation" in the Archives.

51. D-CMR 2: 73–75. It had been written by two members of Review Board No. 2, Cols. Hermann Moyse and Terry Lyon, and approved by Col. William A. Rounds on Jan. 1, 1945. Such a letter to Maj. Gen. Watson accompanied all the Secretary of War's recommendations that the death sentences upon German war prisoners be confirmed.

52. D-CMR 2:68–70. Review Board No. 2 wrote this letter also. Its chairman, Col. Lyon, certified on the file copy that "all notes, rough drafts, etc." in connection with it had been destroyed.

53. NA, RG 389, E 467, box 1517, folder 8.4 "Habeas Corpus," Jan. 12, 1945 [last draft]. This draft is addressed to the Commanding Generals, First through Ninth

Service Commands, Italian Service Units, and the Military District of Washington. It concludes: "By command of Lieutenant General Stier: J. A. Ulio, Major General, The Adjutant General." According to the cover letter, the AG had already substantially approved the draft's contents and its intended use as a restricted letter to commanding generals and commandants of POW base camps. The JAG had given informal approval. The PMG described the document as essential and took "full responsibility for its accuracy and for clearance of the material with other agencies concerned:" The draft then went to the Chief of Staff, Army Service Forces for approval. One assumes it was actually issued. A covering note of Jan. 12, 1945, Memo for Asst. Chief of Staff, G-1 from the Chief of the Legal Branch, POW Ops Division, PMG's Office, shows the route of this proposal through the War Department. Bureaucracies before it was issued on Feb. 2.

Chapter 14

1. Notices were usually delivered by someone from the PMG's Office, accompanied by someone from State's SWPD. Col. Martin Tollefson, Director, Prisoner of War Operations Branch, to POW Operations Division, Legal Branch, NA, RG 389, E 467, box 1517, folder 8.

2. NA, RG 59, 711.62114/371. The riot occurred on Nov. 4, 1943, the notification on Jan. 12, 1944. The note is in B-CMR 1:191.

3. Swiss Memo VIII-G-5a PRZ of Sept. 13, 1944, NA, RG 59, box 2203, file 5, 711.62114/9–1344.

4. Ibid.

5. NA, RG 59, box 2204, file 1, 711.62114/10–344.

6. State memo of Oct. 26, 1944, NA, RG 389, E 467, box 1517, folder 8, which contains correspondence about Menschner's death sentence.

7. To reprise: the "Beyer Five" from Camp Gruber, Tonkawa, Oklahoma (Walter Beyer, Berthold Seidel, Hans Demme, Willi Scholz, and Hans Schomer); two from an Aiken, South Carolina branch camp (Erich Gauss and Rudolf Straub); the seven from Papago Park (Helmut Fischer, Fritz Franke, Guenther Kuelsen, Heinrich Ludwig, Bernhard Reyak, Otto Stengel, and Rolf Wizuy); and one (Edgar Menschner) from Camp Chaffee, Arkansas.

8. Memorandum for the Chief of Staff from Lt. Gen. Brehon Somervell, Commanding, Army Service Forces, Office of the Commanding General, Nov. 7, 1944. Subject: Executions of Prisoners of War, Stimson Safe File, NA, RG 107, E 74A, box 11, folder "Prisoners of War." This memo was composed after Secretary Stimson inquired into the status of the Beyer case.

9. Swiss Minister to Sec. of State, October 24, 1944, NA, RG 59, 711.62114/10–2444.

10. Ibid. The official American notification that the Beyer Five were going to

be tried had taken from Dec. 18, 1943 until Feb. 9, 1944 to reach Berlin, arriving nearly the same time as notice of the verdicts.

11. NA, RG 59, 711.62114/10–2844 (Swiss code VIII-G-5a/9). See also Memo from Legation to State, Oct. 31. 711.62114/10–3144.

12. It had been three months since the PMGO had notified the Legation of their death sentences (July 13, 1944). NA: RG 59, 711.62114/11–144), Swiss code VIII-G-5a/22, referring to War code PMGO SPMGA (75) 383.6. The War Department file contains a carbon of this notice with a handwritten note: "This is a secret document as far as all government agencies are concerned."

13. Ibid. Swiss codes VIII-G-5a-PRZ and VIII-G-5a-28.

14. On order of Asst. PMG Bryan. NA, RG 59, box 2204, file 4, 711.62114/1–844.

15. Ibid. (War Department code SPMGA (36) 383.6, Nov. 8, 1944). An enclosure indicated how and when the requirements of Geneva Articles 60–66 had been met. Under Article 62, provision for qualified counsel, it noted that "POW Frederick Opp was introduced by the prisoners and allowed to serve throughout the trial as assistant defense counsel" to an American Lt. Col. and a Major, "both Attorneys, [who] were appointed by convening power" in default (!) of counsel of prisoner's own choice. It also noted that the chief of the legation's Department of German Affairs, Mr. Weingaertner, attended the three-week Beyer trial "throughout, in company of State Department representative." (This reflects badly on the two-day Papago Park trial.)

16. The Swiss memos of Dec. 1, 1944 and State's reply of Dec. 9, NA, RG 59, 711.62114/12–144. State would be provided with the same reply to inquiries about the Papago Park seven and the Beyer Five.

17. The draft (NA, RG 59, 711.62114/11–144) is stamped Dec. 7, 1944. State's legal advisor approved its submission to War on Dec. 5. Someone from the SWPD had discussed the draft with Gen. Tollefson, who had taken it to Asst. PMG Bryan. NA, RG 59, box 2204, file 4, 711.62114/11–844, contains a letter from Bryan dated Nov. 8, adding legal details, particularly about compliance with Geneva, and considering what action was to be taken in the Beyer case.

18. The SWPD forwarded two copies of this note, dated Dec. 16, 1944, "informally to Col. Tollefson" the same day and "to War on the eighteenth." NA, RG 59, box 2205, file 2, 711.62114/12–1644 (Swiss code VIII-G-5a/O).

19. All these documents are located in NA, RG 59, box 2205, folder 3, 711.62114/12–2044. The SWPD's own working draft had been a modest six pages.

20. Pp. 8–9 of final draft, ibid. Emphasis added.

21. Ibid., 711.62114/12–2644 (Swiss codeVIII-G-5a/9).

22. Sec. of State to Sec. of War, Dec. 27, 1944, ibid., 711.62114/12–2644.

23. Ibid., 711.62114/12–2844 (Swiss code VIII-G-5a/PRZ, VIII-G-5a/9).

24. Tollefson to SWPD, Jan. 1, 1945, SPMGO (6) 250.45. State would not convey this cold reply to the legation until Jan. 11. NA, RG 59 box 3336, file 3, 711.62114/1–145. This file also contains SWPD to Tollefson, Feb. 11, 1945, conveying three Swiss

memoranda he had requested for his files: VIII-G-5a/35 of Oct. 31, 1945 concerning the "Fischer" (Papago Park) case; VIII-G-5a/PRZ/VIII-G-5a/28 of Nov. 1 concerning the Menschner case; and VIII-G-5a/11 of Nov. 1, concerning the Gauss case.

25. NA, RG 59, box 3336, 711.62114/1–245 (War Dept. code SPMGO (6) 383.6). Emphasis added.

26. Ibid., 711.62114/1–545 (Swiss code VIII-G-5a/PRZ; VIII-G-5a/9 of Jan. 5, 1945).

27. There was a handwritten notation on the memo to the legation: it had been "sent on because of urgency" in spite of an error in the diplomatic language. No time for retyping.

28. See covering note, Jan. 12, 1945, NA, RG 389, E 467, box 1517, folder 8.4 "Habeas Corpus."

29. D-CMR 2:113–114 (War code SPMGO (6) 250.45).

30. Cable 111, State to AMLEGATION, BERN, Jan. 6, plain, NA, RG 59, box 3348, 711.62114A/1–645.

31. Swiss Legation to State, Jan. 9, 1945; State to War, Jan. 13, 1945, NA, RG 59, box 3336, 711.62114/1–945 (Swiss code VIII-G-5a/Prz, VIII-G-5a/9).

32. NA, RG 59, box 3337, 711.62114/1–1045.

33. Ibid. Other supporting documents included a warning from the American ambassador in Bern, dated July 20, 1943, that the Germans might execute POWs escaping in civilian clothing or German uniform, on the ground that they were spies or *franc tireurs*; Secretary of State Hull's protest of Aug. 2; and three items from the *Rules of Land Warfare*: No. 349, War Rebels, No. 350, War Treason, and No. 351, Unauthorized Belligerents.

34. Stimson, Diaries, vol. 50, pp. 24–25 (reel 9). Under the provisions of the Geneva Convention, a Red Cross ship, the *Gripsholm*, criss-crossed the Atlantic throughout the war bearing prisoners with amputations, tuberculosis, mental illness, etc.; these prisoners were selected by Mixed Medical Commissions composed, in Germany, of two Swiss doctors and one German doctor. Col. Drake, WDGS-G3, had been repatriated for severe ulcers on Sept. 6, 1944. He had been camp spokesman at Oflag 64 and, according to Ferguson, *Kriegsgefangener 3074*, 101–102, 215–218, a very good one. He had received a Distinguished Medal of Honor in World War I. In captivity, his constant challenging of every slight infraction of Geneva attracted unwanted international interest and, Ferguson believed, was the real reason for his repatriation.

35. Stimson, Diaries, vol. 50, pp. 27, 48 (microfilm, reel 9).

36. Exhibit F, Documents appended to Inspector General's Report of February 8–21, 1945, NA, RG 159, E 26f, General correspondence 1939–1947, 333.9(2), box 64. Hereafter, this will be cited as IG Report File. This file contains another letter Drake wrote McCloy on the same day, Jan. 10. He had just learned that the Swiss had not reported on conditions at Oflag 64 since October. Furthermore, the American Red Cross had made no progress on launching a protest, at his request, against German confiscation and destruction of food packages, without

which "our prisoners . . . in their overcrowded condition . . . will sicken and die." He concluded: "I realize you are a very busy person but you and Mr. Stimson are the first men of importance in the Government to show interest in the condition of our prisoners. . . . You will be doing a great humanitarian service in any thing that you may do for them." Between these two letters, one finds Drake's undated report, "Starvation of American Prisoners of War," based on the letters of five POWs and "another source": For eight weeks in Nov. and Dec., 1944, American POWs in Germany had no Red Cross food parcels. Drake also related information which State provided on Jan. 12 about three American officers condemned to death: Lt. Col. William H. Schaefer and Lt. James R. Schmitz from Oflag 64, and Col. Spicer.

37. Urgent telegram no. 8167 from Bern Legation to State, Dec. 16, 1944, and Stettinius's reply, no. 93 of Jan. 5, 1945 (NA, RG 59, 711.62114/12–1644). Paraphrases are enclosures 1 and 2 in a secret War Department memo for Mr. Lauchlin Currie, dated Jan. 25, which in turn is Tab C of a memo to the Deputy Chief of Staff of the War Department General Staff from his Assistant Chief of Staff, Feb. 5. These are located in a file relating to a preliminary report of the Inspector General's investigation of Switzerland's performance as Protecting Power, conducted at Stimson's request. IG Report File.

38. Telegram 230, NA, RG 59, box 3348, 711.62114A/1–1245.

39. Telegram 234, ibid.

40. Telegram 232, ibid. Nicosia was held in Stalag II B.

41. Telegram 231, ibid. Huddle sent more details by airmail pouch; see Dispatch No. 10482, 711.62114A/1–545. This file also contains translations of the original German notice to the Swiss, dated Dec. 31, 1944, of the condemnations of Cosolet, J. Walsh, Martin, E. Walsh, Greyfield, and Davis.

42. Ambassador Hubble sent much longer reports in his airmailed diplomatic pouch. NA, RG 59, box 3348, 711.62114A/1–1245. These would reach State by Jan. 24, the SWPD on Jan. 27, and War (Asst. PMG Gen. Bryan and Lt. Col. M. C. Bernays, Chief of the Special Branch of G-1) on the Jan. 29. On Jan. 19, SHAEF (General Eisenhower's headquarters in Europe) requested that the Protecting Power be notified immediately that Schaefer, Schuts (Schmitz), and Spicer were to be shot on trivial grounds; NA, RG 59, 711.62114A/1–1945. Ambassador Winant in London also learned from repatriated British war prisoners that Schaefer and Schmitz were to be executed; n.d., 711.62114A/2–245.

43. NA, RG 59, DF 1945–9, box 3336, F.W. 711.62114/1–1745. Plitt also reminded Dunn of previous conversation about the matter. Attached file: Tollefson, PWD to SWP, Jan. 17, 1945 rejecting extension of time before Beyer Five hangings, War code SPMGO (6) 383.6. The "strong protest" Plitt mentioned was evidently the document which would be presented to the Swiss Legation on January 20. See later discussion.

44. Memorandum from Mr. Leverich to Mr. Dunn, Jan. 19, 1945. 711.62114/1–1745, ibid.

45. Ibid. (War code SPMGO (6) 383.6).

46. NA, RG 218, Central Decimal File 1942–1945, box 352, file CCS 383.6 (10-21-44), sec. 1. Secretary Stimson and Admiral Leahy would reject this proposal. See chap. 15.

47. NA, RG 59, box 3348, Telegram 310, 711.62114A/1-1245. The message was drafted by the SWPD.

48. These rights are enumerated in Article 42.

49. Letter to SWPD from Col. Francis E. Howard, Director, PWD, War code SPMGA (75) 383.6, Oct. 28, 1944; State to Swiss Legation, Nov. 4, 1944; State to PMGO, Nov. 7, 1944, asking for further information and sending along the Swiss memo. NA, RG 59, 711.62114/10-2844.

50. Swiss Legation to State Department, Oct. 30, 1944; State to War for the PMG, Nov. 20, 1944; both in NA, RG 59, 711.62114/10-3044. Tollefson, Asst. Director, PWD to SWPD, Nov. 24, 1944, NA, RG 59, 711.62114/11-2444 (War code SPMGA (75) 383.6).

51. NA, RG 59, 711.62114/11-644, Swiss code VIII-G-5a/35. Note handwritten at top: "12/13/44 memo to Swiss. Note to War."

52. The State file, NA, RG 59, 711.62114/12-1244 CS/D, contains Tollefson to SWPD, Dec. 12, 1944 (War file no. SPMGA (36) 383.6); memo of telephone call about missing letter; note conveying letter to SWPD, Dec. 18, 1944 (after it was located in the PWD's legal branch); memorandum forwarding Stengel's and Tollefson's letters to the Swiss Legation, Dec. 20, 1944. The file also contains an unaddressed draft that seems to be a letter of conveyance from State to the Swiss Legation.

53. At the Fort Leavenworth Disciplinary Barracks, at least, officials decided that same month to interpret Geneva Article 42 to mean that war prisoners could only complain about "the conditions of captivity to which they are [being] subjected" at the moment of writing, not in the past. Memorandum, "Instructions to Prisoners of War," Dec. 5, 1944, NA, RG 407, Army AG Dec. File 383.6 1940–45, box 2913.

54. Giles Romilly and Michael Alexander, *Hostages of Colditz* (New York: Praeger, 1954), 75. These men, the nephews of Winston Churchill and Field Marshal Alexander, were hardly among the worst treated prisoners in Germany.

55. NA, RG 59, 711.62114/12-2244.

56. Tollefson to SWPD (War code SPMGO (929) 383.6, responding to Swiss code VIII-G-5a/35). State conveyed part of this memo to the legation that same day. NA, RG 59, 711.62114/12-2244. Meanwhile, Tollefson had also forwarded, on Dec. 29, complaints from Walter Beyer (again), Edgar Menschner, and Erich Gauss. See chap. 16.

Chapter 15

1. Stimson Safe File, NA, RG 107, E 74A, box 13, folder "STATE DEPT." This letter was one of the documents provided to the Inspector General for his investigation of Swiss malfeasance.

2. Sent to Ambassador Hubble in Bern in an urgent ten-page cable, Telegram 326, NA, RG 59, box 3348, 711.62114A/1–1245.

3. Stettinius to Ambassador Hubble, Bern. Ibid.

4. Currie succeeded "through a skillful application of strength and tact" and "the threat to cut off American trade and the promise to replace German coal from Allied sources." Joseph E. Persico, *Roosevelt's Secret War: FDR and World War II Espionage* (New York: Random House, 2001), 369, 371, 441. (Fifty years later, the world learned how many Nazi millions Switzerland still hid.)

5. McCloy's letter to Currie is tab D of a document to the Deputy Chief of Staff, War Department, from his assistant, dated Feb. 5, 1945: NA, RG 159, IG Report File, E 26f, General Correspondence, 1939–1947, 333.9(2), box 64. Hereafter cited as IG Report File.

6. Grew's letter, dated Jan. 27, 1945, was stamped "Confidential File." NA, RG 59, box 3348, SWP 711.62114A/1–1945.

7. On Jan. 31, McCloy notified Stettinius that, in response to Grew's letter, an investigation of Swiss deficiencies had begun. McCloy would inform State of the results. Also, the subject had been "brought to the attention of Mr. Lauchlin Currie on 27 January." IG Report File. (McCloy delivered his memo to Gen. Handy that day—see later in this chapter.)

8. MacLeish, report, NA, RG 59, DF 1945–9, box 3336. 711.62114/1–2245.

9. NA, RG 59, 711.62114/1–2345, Swiss code VIII-G5a/9.

10. Marginal note on German cable, ibid. See also NA, RG 59, DF 1945–1949, box 3336, 711.62114/1–2645.

11. NA, RG 59, 711.62114/1–245, stamped "SECRET" and "Confidential File."

12. Secretary of State to Minister of Switzerland, Telegram 407 to Bern, Jan. 25, 1945, NA, RG 59, 711.62114A/1–2345. Bailey telephoned Weingaertner at the Swiss Legation, informing him of postponement "for a while," and asking him not to inform the Beyer Five because it was customary for the Detaining Power to announce such news.

13. Stimson, Diaries, vol. 50, p. 74 (microfilm, reel 9).

14. 711.62114/1–2645, NA, RG 59, DF 1945–9, box 3336, Swiss code VIII-G-5a/9.

15. Memorandum from Brig. Gen. R. W. Berry, Deputy Asst Chief of Staff, for Sec. of War, 29 Jan. 1945, Stimson Safe File, NA, RG 107, E 74A, box 11, folder "Prisoners of War."

16. Remarks of Lt. Archie W. Sornberger with regard to the case of Colonel J. S. Spicer, Jan. 26, 1945. Another repatriate confirmed his report, adding that two American officers had tried to contact Spicer by faking an escape, only to be

locked into a different jail. Statement by Lt. McNamara about Colonel J. S. Spicer at Walter Reed Hospital, Jan. 26, 1945. Stimson Safe File, NA, RG 107, E 74A, box 11, Folder "Prisoners of War."

17. Col. Nathaniel R. Hoskot, according to Oflag 64 survivor Herbert R. Garris. Letter to author, Feb. 2, 2003.

18. According to the newsletter of the survivors' association, the *Post Oflag 64 Item*, Winter 2000, p. 7, he was known as "King Kong" Schaefer.

19. According to his memoir, *Kriegsgefangener 3074*, 220–240, Capt. Clarence Ferguson did accompany them to Greniesen. (Thanks to an Oflag 64 survivor, Clarence R. Meltesen, for the citation.) According to an excerpt in the *Post Oflag 64 Item*, p. 9, Ferguson was allowed to question two German soldiers and to present the defense, after speaking to Schaefer for fifteen minutes.

20. Confirmed by the Oflag 64 survivor Irving J. Yarock, letter to author, Jan. 20, 2003. Although two Nazis kept other camp personnel in line with "constant threat[s] of sending them to the Russian front," Yarock said, the GIs developed a "rapport with some of the regular army people," who mentioned "rumors of an order to crack down on the camps and the Schaefer-Schmitz affair . . . was the first chance [to do so]. It was also rumored that the death sentence was ordered from higher up even before the trial. Many of us believed that they didn't want [former camp spokesman] Col. Drake around for the trial," and so repatriated him "for medical reasons." Yarock had a high opinion of Drake's leadership.

21. Memo from Brig. Gen. Berry to Sec. of War, 29 Jan., 1945, Stimson Safe File, NA, RG 107, E 74A, box 11, folder "Prisoners of War." On January 27, Acting Secretary of State Grew informed the American Legation in Bern that Goode had written a report to the Swiss Legation in Berlin, requesting a copy of it as soon as "the German authorities" delivered it. Telegram 471, NA, RG 59, box 3348, 711.62114A/1–1245. According to the Oflag 64 survivor Herbert L. Garris (letter to author, Feb. 2, 2003), the translator's name was Gottfried Dietze, and two ex-prisoners endorsed his application to emigrate to America after the war. He gained a Ph.D. in political science and taught at Johns Hopkins University. Dietze himself modestly assigns his part in the posting incident to "my good comrade Heise," whose name sounded similar to the prisoners' ears. Letter, Dietze to Col. Hoskot, March 2, 2003.

22. He added: "but in the confusion of the last two months of the war appeals to the different Swiss and German authorities never got disposed of, and Schaefer survived." Reinhold Eggers, *Colditz: The German Side of the Story* (New York: W. W. Norton, 1961), 9, 169.

23. *Ferguson, Kriegsgefangener 3074*, 211–214. When Col. Drake was to be repatriated for ill health, he declared he would not go if he were forced to march to the train station in the street. When threats of shooting did not move him, the Germans finally trucked him there (215–218).

24. Ibid., 222–238.

25. Telegram 666, NA, RG 59, box 3348, 711.62114A/1–3045.

26. Grew, Acting, to Bern, telegram 556, ibid.

27. The title, "Improvement in Our Efforts to Protect U.S. Prisoners of War in German Hands through the Protecting Power," would remain with the project all through the Inspector General's work. Tab A of Memorandum for the Deputy Chief of Staff, Feb. 5, 1945, IG Report File.

28. These were the Ground Forces, the Air Force, and the Services of Supply. Under the 1932 reorganization, the Deputy Chief of Staff also acted for the Chief of Staff in his absence and dealt with budgetary, legislative, and administrative matters. Ray S. Cline, *The War Department: Washington Command Post: The Operations Division* (Washington: Center of Military History, United States Army, 1951; reprint, 1990), 93–94 and n. 16. This is vol. 4, pt. 2, of the official *United States Army in World War II.*

29. When Eisenhower became Deputy Chief of Staff in Oct. 1944, Handy became the second man to command OPD, the largest, most vital unit of the War Department General Staff. It helped Marshall deal with 40 large commands and around 350 small ones, as well as "Joint and Combined [Anglo-American] military negotiations." Its main interests were strategic planning and control of overseas operations such as Torch, the invasion of North Africa, in which Handy had a part. OPD also chose members of the General Staff. Ibid., 120, 165–166, 180–181, 191–194, 202–203.

30. Gen. Handy reported this to McCloy on Feb. 7. See Memorandum of Feb. 5 and tabs E and F, IG Report File.

31. Memorandum for the Deputy Chief of Staff, War Department from Maj. Gen. Philip E. Brown, Deputy, The Inspector General, Feb. 21, 1945, conveys the Preliminary Report of Investigation and Exhibits A to G, Inclusive, also dated Feb. 21. IG Report File. Drake's Feb. 19 memo, Exhibit F, failed to mention the Americans under death sentence.

32. Preliminary Report, IG Report File.

33. "Final Report of Investigation and Exhibits A to E, Inclusive," IG Report File. It dealt mainly with what fifty repatriated GIs knew about Switzerland's responses to Geneva violations (hardly anything).

34. The War Department responded eventually. On April 8, AG Julio sent a memo to all commanding generals, "Improvements in Our Efforts to Protect U.S. POWs in German Hands," quoting the report's criticism that the average GI was ignorant of his Geneva rights. The War Department also organized a committee to set up "an agency of central record. "Memo by Lt. Col. G. B. Walker to CG, ASF (Attn: PMGO), 18 May 1945; Memo by Col. A. B. Johnson, Acting PMG, 25 May 1945, and other documents. See Final Report, IG Report File.

35. Final Report, IG Report File.

36. Stimson to Stettinius, March 19, 1945, IG Report File.

37. Leland Harrison, American Minister in Bern, to Secretary of State, March 23, 1945, conveying a memorandum dated March 19 from the Chief of the Division

of Foreign Interests of the Federal Political Department to His Excellency Max Petitpierre, Federal Councillor and Chief of the Federal Political Department, in reply to Lauchlin Currie's memo of Feb. 21, No. 11223, NA, RG 59, 711.6211fA/3–2345. It arrived on March 31.

38. See Ronald W. Zweig, "Feeding the Camps: Allied Blockade Policy and the Relief of Concentration Camps in Germany, 1944–1945," *Historical Journal* 41, no. 3. (1998), 825–851.

39. Stimson, Diaries, vol. 51, p. 55 (reel 9).

40. Ibid., vol. 50, p. 216 (reel 9).

41. Ibid., p. 74, Jan. 25, 1945. Further proof of War Dept. concern may be found in Memo of Conference with Under Sec. of War Patterson, 25 Apr. 1945. NA, RG 389, E 452, box 1389, folder 337, "Gen. PW."

42. Stimson and Forrestal made counter-proposals to the rejected JCs 1164/4: warning the German High Command that it would be held accountable, in hope of widening the breach between the army and the Nazi Party; and publicizing all atrocities and punishments in a way that would reach individual German and American soldiers and the Swiss government. Stimson and Forrestal to Adm. Leahy, Chief, JCS, Feb. 8, 1945. Stimson Safe File, NA, RG 107, E 74A, box 11, Folder "Prisoners of War." See box 13, Folder: "State Department" for British amendments. For JCS 1164/4 and its development, see NA, RG 218, Central Dec. file 1942–1945, box 352, file CCS 383.6 (10–21–44), sec. 1. The revised document, JCS 1164/6, was dated Feb. 16, 1945.

43. Stimson, Diary, vol. 50, pp. 122–124 (microfilm, reel 9), and various references between Feb. 19 and Mar. 16.

44. Krammer, *Nazi Prisoners of War in America*, 167–168, 294 n. 50. He cites a memo from March 9, 1945, to this effect from Lt. Col. John S. Meyers, CMP, Special Assistant to the PMG, to Maj. Gen. Lerch, Subject: Public Relations Problems of PW Special Projects Division, NA, RG 389. PMGO, Prisoner of War Operations, Administrative Branch, Decimal File, 1943–46, 383.6, General, MMB-NA. For many examples of the War Department's reaction to charges of coddling, see NA, RG 389, E 452, box 1370, folder 250.1, "Gen. PW," 21 March 1945.

45. "Presentation of Maj. Gen. Archer L. Lerch, U.S. Army, The PMG, to be given at conference requested by the War Dept." NA, RG 389, E 452, box 1388, folder 334, "General P/W."

46. Actually, this untypical group (including a doctor of economics who had represented the German Chamber of Commerce in Egypt) was discussing which movies the prisoners could view and what courses they might take as an "Intellectual Diversion Program." See Ron Robin, *The Barbed Wire College: Reeducating German POWs in the U.S. during World War II* (Princeton, N.J.: Princeton University Press, 1995).

47. That of Hugo Krause, at Hearne, Texas, on Dec. 23, 1943. See chap. 18.

48. Here and in the following quotations, all emphasis is original.

49. Lerch was quoting a story in the Washington, D.C., *Sunday Star* of Feb. 18, 1945.

50. James H. Powers in the *Atlantic Monthly*. See chap. 13.

51. NA, RG 389, E 452, box 1388, folder 334, "General P/W." Lerch's subordinates would use this speech to prepare an article to appear under his name as "Army Reports on Prisoners of War" in the *American Mercury, May 1945*, , 536–547. See chap. 17.

52. U.S. Congress, House of Representatives, Committee on Military Affairs, *Investigation of National War Effort, Relative to the Treatment of Prisoners of War in the United States and Abroad*, 79th Congress, 1st Session, June 12, 1945, House Report 728. The committee heard testimony from Brig. Gen. R. W. Berry, Deputy Assistant Chief of Staff, G-1, War Department General Staff; Edwin A. Plitt, of State's SWPD; Asst. PMG B. M. Bryan, who according to the report cleared up "many popular misconceptions of the Army's handling of enemy prisoners"; Maurice Pate, Director of the American Red Cross Prisoners of War Relief program; and William W. Bishop Jr., a State Department legal advisor.

Chapter 16

1. Stettinius to Stimson, Jan. 24, 1945; Stimson to Stettinius, Feb. 14; NA, RG 59, DF 45–9, box 3336A, 711.62114/2–1445. This was not a two-way street. When the Secretary of State attempted to have all communications "pursuant to Articles 60 to 67" of Geneva forwarded to his office, Stimson replied tartly that the War Department would continue to deal directly with the Swiss Legation about POW trials. He would, however, provide State with copies.

2. Swiss Legation to Stettinius, NA, RG 59, box 3348, 711.62114A/1–3145 (Swiss code VIII-A-21).

3. Exhibit F, dated Feb. 19, 1945, appended to IG Report of Feb. 8–21, 1945; Drake to Inspector General, "Factual Data Concerning Pro-Nazi Attitude of of International . . .," April 18, 1945, point 3. IG Report File, NA, RG 159, E 26f, box 64, Gen. Correspondence 1939–1947.

4. A memo from the supervisor of prisoners to the commandant lists war prisoners with money on deposit or receiving POW pay as of Jan. 18, 1945: 5 Italians and 79 Germans, including the Beyer Five (prison nos. 9304–9308), Gauss and Straub (no numbers), and Menschner (no. 10425). A list of POWs by name, offense, trade, work assignment, and location, dated Jan. 17, notes that six condemned men were isolated in the basement of wing B (Gauss and Straub were not mentioned). Other prisoners' offenses were assault with or without a deadly weapon, disorderly conduct or rioting, destruction of property, unlawfully entering a private dwelling, auto theft, larceny, and willful disobedience and disrespect. NA, RG 407, Army AG Dec. File 1940–1945, 383.6, box 2913.

5. See Asst. PMG Bryan to SWPD, Nov. 8, 1944, NA, RG 59, box 2204, file 4, 711.62114/11–844. He brags about War's scrupulous protection of this very right.

6. Memo from Capt. Glenn M. Bradley, Adjutant, to The AG, ATTN: Correction Division, re: "Status of Prisoners of War Sentenced to Confinement at the

Disciplinary Barracks," Dec. 8, 1944, NA, RG 407, Army AG Dec. File 1940–1945, 383.6, box 2913. The PMG also got a copy.

7. Col. Tollefson, Asst. Director of the PMGO's PWD, had explained to State that his agency was "in communication" with the AG's office" for this purpose. NA, RG 59, box 2205, folder 3, 711.62114/12–2944.

8. Feb. 3, 1945, NA, RG 59, DF 1945–9, box 3336A, 711.62114/2–345. Marginal notation: "Encl. sent to Swiss 2/7/45."

9. Memo to Asst. PMG Bryan from Maj. Farrand, PWD Legal Branch, Jan. 25, 1945, NA, RG 59, box 3337, Confidential File 711.62114/2–345. This file contains Bryan to SWPD, Nov. 17, 1944, announcing presidential confirmation of Gauss's and Straub's sentences; Bryan to Swiss Legation, same date, informing the legation, with "a statement in detail of the nature and circumstances" of Gauss's offense and a reminder that "the confirmation . . . is treated as secret"; and Bryan to Col. Bernays, G-1, Jan. 26, 1945, enclosing a copy of this memo and describing the steps taken to comply with Geneva Article 66.

10. Edwin A. Plitt to Bryan, Feb. 7, 1945, NA, RG 59, box 3336A, 711.62114/2–345. On Feb. 14, the PMG's Office cabled all Service Commands that "in order to prevent possible protests" they should distribute copies of the Articles of War and inform POWs of their liability. Copy to SWPD, ibid., 711.62114/2–1445. That same file contains a scathing note from the chief of War's legal branch of the POW Operations Division: Maj. Stephen Farrand to State's SWPD: How could German POWs profess ignorance of Geneva "in view of their often scholarly claims" to its protections, "made in other connections?" Also, ignorance was no excuse for criminality.

11. NA, RG 59, box 3336A, 711.62114/2–845, State sent his letter to the legation on Feb. 10, with the usual assurance that the matter was being investigated.

12. Menschner finally got his records on May 3. Its "secret" classification had to be canceled first. Court Martial 260781, "Trial of Menschner, Edgar, 58804, German Prisoner of War, Unteroffizier, Prisoner of War Camp Chaffee, Arkansas by General Court-Martial appointed by the Commanding General of the Eighth Service Command, ASF. Tried at Camp Gruber, Oklahoma 3–4–5 July, 1944." His court-martial is in 2 vols.; concerning his personal copy, see 1:172–178 (counting from the cover page). Hereafter cited as M-CMR.

13. This request had been inspired by a complaint from Guenther Kuelsen. Tollefson to SWPD, responding to Swiss Legation's VIII-G-5a/35; State to Legation. NA, RG 59, box 2205, folder 3, 711.62114/12–2244.

14. NA, RG 59, box 3336A, 711.62114/2–845. State parroted this message to the Swiss on Feb. 15, 1945: 711.62114/2–1045.

15. NA, RG 59, box 3336A, 711.62114/2–1045 (Swiss code XI-91, VIII-G-5a/35). I could not locate two documents that, according to a charge slip in the file, SWPD had removed: a Feb. 15 memo from the Swiss Legation to the Secretary of War concerning the treatment of these seven prisoners and a carbon copy of a Swiss memo dated Jan. 9 "in re. above matter."

16. Feb. 21, 1945, NA, RG 59, box 3336A, 711.62114/2–2145. Maj. Farrand had asked the SWPD two days earlier to inform the Swiss that their transfer there "has been completed." 711.62114/2–1345. State did so on Feb. 24. 711.62114/2–1045.

17. Memo, telephone conference among the executive officer to the Assistant PMG, Marcy of State's SWPD, and an officer from G-1, March 3, 1945. Marcy "discussed the advisability of raising the question" of allowing the Protecting Power to visit German prisoners under judicial sentence. Would the PMGO permit visits to Leavenworth and other penitentiaries? The answer was no, the PMGO "would rather not raise that question at this time." NA, RG 59, 711.62114 Mail/3–344. This was a change of policy. In Feb. 1944 Asst. PMG Bryan had specifically allowed Swiss inspectors access to the Beyer Five. NA, RG 389, E 452, 1942–1946, 250.91, box 1371.

18. Despatch No. 10810, NA, RG 59, box 3348, 711.62114A/2–745. The document from German Court of Division No. 402 is dated Nov. 22, 1944. The Swiss Foreign Office had sent it to the American Legation on Feb. 1, 1945. SWPD sent copies to Bryan and Bernays on March 5. Sgt. Nicosia, a prisoner at Stalag II B Hammerstein, was a professional soldier born on Feb. 20, 1917, at Bethlehem, Pa.

19. Enclosure 2 to Despatch No. 10810, ibid.

20. Enclosure 4 to Despatch No. 10810, and telegram 882, 711.62114A/2–845, NA, RG 59, box 3348. The lawyer had been requested by the "counsel of the American POWs" at Nicosia's camp, Stalag II B. "Man of confidence" means elected spokesman, the contact person between the prisoners, their Protecting Power, and the IRC.

21. Huddle to State, Feb. 8, 1945, telegram 906, 711.62114A/2–845, NA, RG 59, box 3348. The documents arrived later by air mail pouch. SWPD sent copies of the telegram to Bryan, Bernays and Sweet on Feb. 15 and of the documents (Despatch No. 10825) on March 6.

22. Enclosure 2 to Despatch No. 10825, NA, RG 59, box 3348. The petition was addressed to the Court of Division No. 404, Dresden.

23. Ibid.

24. Enclosure no. 6, ibid..

25. NA, RG 59, box 3349, folder 1, Despatch No. 10875, 711.62114A/2–1545, so SWPD sent copies to Bryan and Bernays on March 6, 1945. State finally received a copy of the poster on February 15, four months after requesting it. It had been displayed in all German camps containing American and British prisoners.

26. Telegram 671, 711.62114/2–845, NA, RG 59, box 3349, folder 1.

27. The request was made on Feb. 12 and the reply came on the Feb. 17. Telegram 1058, 711.62114A/2–1745, NA, RG 59, box 3349, folder 1. See also airmail pouch no. 10875, 711.62114A/2–1545.

28. SPMGO (6), State code 711.62114/2–2245, NA, RG 59, DF 1945–9, box 3336A. The legation received the requested information on Feb. 24. Farrand added that he enclosed copies of Gauss's petition for the Swiss and for State's files, but none was attached to this letter. On Col. Schaefer's appeal of his death sentence, see below, n. 41.

29. NA, RG 59, box 3337, Confidential File 711.62114/2–2245.

30. March 2, 1945, ibid.

31. NA, RG 59, box 3349, folder 2 (Swiss note VIII-G-5a/9, State code 711.62114A/3–145). See later in this chapter. See also Stimson to Stettinius, March 1, 1945, in folder 5.

32. Telegram 1367, received at 7:02 P.M., Secret File FW 711.62114A/3–245, NA, RG 59, box 3349, folder 2.

33. Gufler to Plitt, March 3, 1945, NA, RG 59, box 3349, folder 4. Charles "Chip" Bohlen was a State Department Russian expert who translated for Roosevelt and Truman. Eisenhower would make him ambassador to Moscow. This draft warning, begun in early February, was the counter-proposal to the Joint Chiefs of Staff's notion of taking reprisals on German prisoners. See chap. 15.

34. Urgent telegram 1312, ibid., folder 2, 711.62114A/2–2845. Copy sent to Bryan and Bernays on March 2.

35. Ibid., folder 4, 711.62114A/3–245. The SWPD received a copy on March 6.

36. NA, RG 59, box 3349, folder 4. The SWPD drafted the letter.

37. Confidential telegram 1343, NA, RG 59, box 3349, folder 4, 711.62114A/3–245. SWPD sent a paraphrase to Bryan and Bernays on March 13.

38. Telegram 1445, NA, RG 59, box 3349, folder 4, 711.62114A/3–745. A copy would be sent from SWPD to Bryan, Bernays, and Goff on March 10.

39. The document mentions four new names: Col. Henry R. Spicer, Capt. Wilbur E. McKee, Lt. John Rathbone, and Lt. George L. Durgin. On Rathbone and Durgin, see later in this chapter.

40. NA, RG 59, box 3349, folder 4, 711.62114A/1–545. This note was written at the bottom: "Cleared with Chief of Staff [Gen. Marshall] by Col. Bernays and with Mr. Stimson by Mr. McCloy." Also, copy for Amlegation, Bern, Telegram 996, 711.62114A/3–945.

41. Enclosure to Despatch No. 11068, dated March 7, 1945, from the American Legation, Bern, NA, RG 59, box 3349, folder 4, 711.62114A/3–745. The Swiss inspector also included a copy of the formal indictment. SWPD sent copies to Bryan, Bernays, and Goff on March 10. According to an excerpt from P. R. Reid, *Colditz: The Full Story* (New York: Macmillan, 1984), in *Post Oflag 64 Item*, p. 8, a British officer, "now Lord Campbell of Alloway," drafted an appeal for clemency for Lt. Col. Schaefer, "but it never appeared to get to its destination," Hitler.

42. Telegram 1605, March 15, 1945, NA, RG 59, box 3349, folder 3, 711.62114A/3–1545. SWPD sent a paraphrase to Bryan, Bernays, and G-2 on March 17. The note adds that the German government had been requested to cancel the sentences upon Schaefer and Schmitz. The Secretary of War got his copy on March 20.

43. NA, RG 59, box 3349, folder 3, 711.62114A/3–1745 (Swiss code VIII-G-5a/9; VIII-G-5a/22). State sent copies to Bernays and Bryan March 20.

44. Sec. of State to Minister of Switzerland, March 20, 1945, NA, RG 59, box 3349, folder 3, 711.62114A/3–1745.

45. Telegram 1728, NA, RG 59, box 3349, folder 3, 711.62114A/3–2245. When the airmail despatch, No. 11027, finally arrived it was given the code /3–2045. Copies were sent to Bryan and Bernays on April 11. There were two German notes dated March 12, D2346 and D2383, received by the Bern Legation on March 19 under cover of a note from the Swiss Foreign Office dated March 16.

46. Telegram 1207, NA, RG 59, box 3349, folder 3, 711.62114A/3–2245. There is a note written on the margin: "Substance cleared with Gen. Berry, G-1, War Department." The paraphrase prepared for the War Department contacts contained only the second paragraph.

47. 740.00115 EW/3–2745. Penciled in under the Americans' names is 740.00115 EW 1–1645.

48. Urgent telegram 1201, NA, RG 59, box 334, folder 3, 711.62114A/3–2245. This was written on the margin: Cleared with Gen. Berry, G-1 War Dept 3/24. ETB" (E. Tomlin Bailey of the SWPD, and Brig. Gen. R. W. Berry, Deputy Assistant Chief of Staff, G-1).

49. Stettinius to Minister of Switzerland and telegram 1277, RG 59, box 334, folder 3, 711.62114A/3–2245. On April 2, Gen. Berry of G-1 would write to Bailey of the SWPD to ask for a copy of this communication. He also confirmed "the information given you orally on 30 March, 1945 by Colonel M. C. Bernays of this Division to the effect that the proposed telegram from your Department to the American Legation, Bern . . . meets with the approval of the War Department." The copy was sent on April 9. See also box 3350, folder 1, 711.62114A/4–245.

50. Urgent telegram 2050, NA, RG 59, box 3350, folder 1, 711.62114A/4–745. Copies were sent to Bryan and Bernays on April 10.

51. This was a reference to the massacre of American soldiers by an SS unit during the Battle of the Bulge. Telegram 2116, NA, RG 59, box 3350, folder 2, 711.62114A/4–1045. Copies were sent to Bryan, Bernays, and Sweet on April 17.

52. NA, RG 59, box 3350, folder 2, 711.62114A/4–1045.

53. NA, RG 59, box 3350, folder 2, 711.62114A/4–1245. Copies were sent to Bryan and Bernays on April 15 (Swiss code VIII-G-5a/9; VIII-G-5a/22; VIII-G-5a/28; VIII-G-5a/35).

54. Stimson's diaries reveal that the issue preoccupied him from mid-February to mid-March. See vol. 50, pp. 122–124, 130, 133, 152–153, 158, 192 (reel 9). Pp. 152–153 recount how he told Col. Handy "I was sick of this business of fidgeting around so much about our prisoners without actually accomplishing anything." He inveighed against Stalin on April 2 (vol. 51, p. 2, reel 9) for his refusal "to let us send planes and officers behind their lines in Poland and eastern Germany in order to help collect and send home the American prisoners of war who are being uncovered by the Russian advance through Germany."

55. Memo to "EE Mr. Thompson," April 18, 1945, NA, RG 59, box 3337, 711.62114A/4–1845.

56. NA, RG 59, box 3350, folder 2, FW 711.62114A/4–1245. A handwritten note

at the end by E. T. Bailey says "Cleared by Major Brown, G-1, with Gen. Hamby, Deputy Chief of Staff, except last clause." The Bern Legation was notified on the same day by telegram 1604.

57. Emphasis added. Memo from JAG Cramer to Brig. Gen. Harry H. Vaughan, The White House, Washington, D.C., July 3, 1945, explaining the Papago Park case so that Vaughan could ask Truman for a second presidential confirmation. D-MCR 2:61–64. On p. 61, Cramer quoted the original order, citing War Department General Staff Disposition Form dated April 28, 1945, subject: Proposed exchange of condemned prisoners of war, file No. WPGAP 383.6 (7 Jan. 1945).

58. John Rathbone, telephone conversation with author, Jan. 17, 2003. Rathbone's fellow defendants were Seymor Bolten, Patrik Teel, and George Durgin. He kindly sent me a copy of his court record, a mere 4 pages, single spaced, in contrast to the multi-volume American court-martial records. He also sent a copy of a letter to him from the Oflag 67 translator Gottfried Diest, dated Dec. 19, 1979, describing how he learned of the plan to condemn as many Americans as possible. In Diest's opinion, none would have been executed as long as the regular army could keep control of the camps away from the SS.

59. The telegram, no. 2456, 711.62114A/4–2645, was not in the file. I have provided in this paragraph a summary of the document itself, German High Command 2 f 12.17 WR (III/10a), Nr. 82–85/44, which was sent in the next airmail pouch, Despatch No. 11597, NA, RG 59, box 3350, folder 2, 711.62114A/4–2748. The High Command also said it knew of no legal procedures pending against Captain Wilburg, one of three Americans inquired about in the American exchange proposal of March 9; the other two, Lt. Rathbone and Lt. Durgin, had been tried for disobedience but acquitted on Oct. 10, 1944.

60. Urgent telegram 2498, NA, RG 59, box 3350, folder 2, 711.62114A/4–2845. Copies were sent to Bryan and Bernays on May 1.

61. Urgent telegram 2533, ibid., 711.62114A/4–3045.

Chapter 17

1. Moore, *The Faustball Tunnel*, 45. Whittingham, *Martial Justice*, 237, 239.

2. William H. Radford, "Hang Seven Nazis," Kansas City *Star*, Aug. 25, 1945.

3. Note for G-2, for information, from G-1, May 7, 1945, Ninth Service Command. RG 319, E 47, box 940. Switzerland displayed no regret.

4. Brian Loring Villa, "The Diplomatic and Political Context of the POW Camps Tragedy," in Guenter Bischof and Stephen E. Ambrose, eds., *Eisenhower and the German POWs: Facts against Falsehood* (Baton Rouge: Louisiana State University Press, 1992), 63, also 58–66. This collection of essays critiques a book by the Canadian novelist James Bacque, *Other Losses: An Investigation into the Mass Deaths of German Prisoners at the Hands of the French and Americans after World War II*, 2nd rev. edition (Ontario: Little, Brown, 1999).

5. Villa, "The Diplomatic and Political Context," 66. See also Günter Bischof, "Bacque and Historical Evidence," in Bischof and Ambrose, eds., *Eisenhower and the German POWs,* 215, 217–218. He says that at one time there were "more than 5 million POWs/DEFs in Europe, in American hands, and "some 20 million DPs and refugees—not to mention the German civilian population" in the U.S. zone.

6. Whittingham, *Martial Justice*, chap. 14, "Death Cell," 237–256; quotation on p. 246. Whittingham's writing style makes it hard to discern whether he or someone else is providing the dialogue. One example will suffice: "Franke's mouth curled slightly downward as he muttered, more to himself than to Fischer, 'shit'" (240).

7. Ibid., 246, 253, 255–256.

8. *Military Laws of the United States*, 7th edition (1929), 293–294, para. 405. See also 295, 297–299.

9. Memo from the AG to the Asst. JAG, Through Acting Chief of Military Justice Group, Subject: "New Evidence in Connection with the Murder of POW Hans Geller," an undated draft from 1947 with handwritten corrections, sender unknown M-CMR, 1:126. See also Charge Sheet, April 25, 1944, 1:21–23. (Note: Except for the trial transcript and some lengthy memoranda, the pages of this record are not numbered. The author has counted them consecutively, beginning after the cover page.)

10. These definitions were appended to the Statement of PW Rudolf Neitzsch, Gefreiter . . . Relative to the Death of PW Keller [*sic*], Camp Chaffee, Ark," n.d., 1946. M-CMR 1:80.

11. Maj. John Fuller examined any witness Menschner requested, in his presence, allowing him "to examine and cross-examine witnesses as he wished." Fuller also scrutinized any witness "whose expected testimony was not fully and satisfactorily indicated in statements attached to the charges." In his summary, the investigator included "all the substantial evidence I have been able to find, for and against the accused." Report of Investigation of Charges, May 17, 1944. M-CMR 1:26.

12. M-CMR 2:272.

13. Opinion of the Board of Review, Lipscomb, O'Connor, and Golden, Judge Advocates, and Dissenting Opinion by Golden, both dated Oct. 31, 1944, M-CMR 1:129–143, 144–150. In the Papago Park case, two reviewers had supported life sentences while the third had insisted on death.

14. Rounds to Cramer, Subject "Unteroffizier Edgar Menschner," Nov. 7, 1944, M-CMR 1:191. He said the pro-death reviewers had acted upon "the theory of Federal and Military law," which holds anyone aiding, abetting, counseling, or inducing a crime" equally guilty. Though others battered Geller to death, Menschner was the "leader of this gang" and he had "expressed animosity" toward the victim.

15. JAG Cramer to Stimson, Jan. 3, 1945, M-CMR 1:186–187. Rounds was probably the author of his memorandum. Patterson to the President, 1:183–184.

16. M-CMR 1:168–169. Farrand's was comment no. 1 on the file SPMGO (6) 383.6, "Condemned German Prisoners of War."

17. G-1 to PMGO (Thru OCS—Office of Army Chief of Staff Gen. Marshall), June 19, 1945; comment No. 2, Major Brown. M-CMR 1:167.

18. Memorandum for the Deputy Chief of Staff, attention: Lt. Col. Thurman, Signed, for the Asst. Sec. of War, by Harrison A. Gerhardt, Col., GSC [his executive], M-CMR 1:170. This memo reveals that Angelo Nicosia had been liberated along with two others, Durgin and McKee. Despite a "persistent search in all US and British records," Lt. Greyfield remained unidentified. G-1 was still looking for "any possible news of Pfc. Snowden. In any event, G-1 believes it unlikely that he is held under German control or that there is possibility of reprisal against him." Col. Schaeffer was liberated from Colditz on April 14, 1945. *Post Oflag 64 Item*, winter 2000, 8.

19. Memorandum for the JAG, attention: Mil. Justice Division. Subject: "Death Sentences of Prisoners of War." Signed, Horatio R. Rogers, Lt. Col., CMP for Asst. PMG Bryan. M-CMR 1:171.

20. Memo from Col. William S. Eley, Commandant, U.S. Disciplinary Barracks, Ft. Leavenworth, Kansas to Commanding General, 7th Service Command, Omaha 2, Nebraska; enclosure 1, SO 131, 10 July 1945, NA, RG 407, AG Dec. File 1940–1945, 383.6, box 2910.

21. Such letters were standard procedure. (See a file copy of the one for Menschner's case, M-CMR 1:181, stamped Jan. 27, initialed by Rounds on Jan. 3.)

22. D-CMR 2:61–64. An identical process was performed for Edgar Menschner. M-CMR 1:180–181.

23. Whittingham, *Martial Justice*, 260. One cannot tell if he was quoting Father Towle or inventing the dialogue.

24. Ibid., 263.

25. D-CMR 2:76, scored across and marked "not used." Compare the one Roosevelt signed on Oct. 5, 1944, the Beyer court-martial, B-CMR 1:5.

26. The IRC had volunteered on June 6 to take over from Switzerland as neutral camp visitor, trial observer, and complaint receiver. Col. Tollefson of the PMG's POW OPS Division accepted the offer on June 14. After (not before) a POW was tried, the War Department would send "a full report" to IRC headquarters in Geneva. Tollefson shared this correspondence with State's SWPD. NA, RG59, box 3339, 711.62114/6–1445. Tollefson also told the IRC that "as in the past," POWs would be permitted "a reasonable choice in the matter of defense counsel," which would be an American officer. See also Edwin A. Plitt, Chief, SWPD, to The Hon. Charles Huber, Delegate, IRC Committee, July 14, 1945, ibid., 711.62114/6–1445; and Circular, PMG Cramer to a USDB commandant in Fifth Service Command, NA, RG 407, Army AG Dec. File 383.6, 1940–1945, box 2913.

27. Capt. Alwyn V. Freeman, Acting Chief, International Law Div., to Chief, Mil. Justice Div., D-CMR 2:60.

28. Gen. Myron C. Cramer to Under Sec. of War, D-CMR 2:56; Assistant Sec. Patterson's signed copy, D-CMR 2:66–67. The JAG sent a reminder to Vaughan four days later.

29. D-CMR 2:65.

30. GCMO 406, D-CMR 2:52–53. Telegram, Aug. 21, 1945, from Acting AG Witsell; Memo, Commandant Eley to the Adjutant General ATTN: Correction Division, Subject: General Court-Martial Orders, No. 406, War Department, Aug. 21, 1945; Memo, Eley to AG, ATTN: Correction Division, THROUGH Com. Gen., Ft. Leavenworth Kansas, Com. Gen. 7th SC, Omaha 2, Nebraska, Subject: Report of Executions, Aug. 25, 1945. NA, RG 407, E 360, box 2439, AG Classified 383.6 (4–2–45 to 7–31–45). This file also contains Cramer's memorandum and Patterson's letter, both of July 18.

31. Whittingham, *Martial Justice*, 263–272, based on his interview with Father Towle and on Guenther Kuelsen's last letter home; Radford, "Hang Seven Nazis."

32. SO 131, July 8, 1945, NA, RG 407, AG Dec. File 383.6, 1940–1945, box 2910. He was carrying out GCMO 262.

33. According to the Kansas City *Star*, July 10, 1945, Beyer stood about four feet from Col. Eley and about thirty feet from the gallows.

34. First Lt. Lawrence A. Ward, Adjutant, by order of Col. Eley, to: "All concerned." Eley first reported to the AG by telephone, then in writing, with copies for the PMG and the JAG, July 10, 1945. Beyer died at 0018 CWT, Seidel at 0050, Hans Demme at 0124, Hans Schomer at 0156, and Willi Scholz at 0225. SO 131, NA, RG 407, AG Dec. File 1940–1945, 383.6, box 2910. Their ages and equivalent American rank: Walter Beyer, thirty-two, first sergeant; Berthold Seidel, thirty, staff sergeant; Hans Demme, twenty-eight, sergeant; Hans Schomer, twenty-seven, sergeant, and Willi Scholz, twenty-two, corporal.

35. Leavenworth *Times*, July 10, 1945.

36. See "FIVE GERMAN WAR PRISONERS HANGED IN U. S., Convicted of Killing Comrade They Suspected of 'Treason' in Oklahoma Compound," St. Louis *Post-Dispatch*, July 10, 1945. The article began on p. 1. The *New York Times* had a practically identical piece on an inside page on July 11, "Five Nazis Hanged by Army in Kansas." Both papers used the term "fanatical Nazis" and said that the five men had only one request: to be buried in their German uniforms. Both articles listed the same "pertinent" provisions of the Geneva Convention which had been so scrupulously observed.

37. William H. Radford, "Hang Five Nazis," Kansas City *Star*, July 10, 1945. Other macabre details: The building, the oldest on the post, was normally used as a warehouse and the site of electrical and tailor shops. Prisoners in the tailor shop had woven and sewn the black hoods.

38. Eley's report to Washington on Aug. 23 was also identical. D-CMR 2:35–37. Fischer died at 00025 CWT, Franke at 0053, Kuelsen at 0120, Ludwig at 0144, Reyak at 0211, Stengel at 0238. Wizuy was the last, at 0300.

39. Whittingham, *Martial Justice*, 275.

40. Ibid., 478; Radford, "Hang Seven Nazis."

41. Whittingham, *Martial Justice*, 271. I found only one thorough article by William Radford, "Hang Seven Nazis," on the day after the hangings, August 25. The St. Louis paper was on strike. The Washington *Post* did not mention it,

though it must have made the wire services. Mr. Gruenebaum in California, who had a habit of reading space fillers, learned thereby that the men for whom he had translated had been hanged. He was shocked. Personal communication to author, June 1994. Curiously, one finds no mention of the Gauss and Straub executions in the St. Louis, Kansas City, or Washington papers.

42. Quoted in Whittingham, *Martial Justice*, 281.

43. Sgt. Ken Knox, a former MP, says he read this in a file from the DB public affairs office.

44. Archer L. Lerch, "Army Reports on Prisoners of War," American Mercury, May 1945, 536, 537, 538.

Chapter 18

1. Michael R. Waters, *Lone Star Stalag: German Prisoners of War at Camp Hearne* (College Station: Texas A&M University Press, 2004), 128. See 120–134 for an excellent view of the crime. Waters has interviewed the German chaplain and quotes Miesel's affidavit sworn on Oct. 19, 1945. For the court-martial, see *U.S. v. German POWs Boehmer et. al.* (CM 312330), Court-Martial Records, Archives of the Clerk of Court. U.S. Army Judiciary. (These are now housed at the Washington National Records Center, Suitland, Maryland.) For more documentation, see NA, RG 389, E 452, box 1371, folder 250.45 "General PW."

2. Krammer, *Nazi Prisoners of War in America*, 197, quoting PMGO, "Story of the PW Re-education Program" (Washington: Office of the Chief of Military History, March 5, 1946), 3. For more on this crash course to democratize the twenty-five thousand most "salvageable" German prisoners, see pp. 194–202, 221–223 and 226–227; and Robin, *The Barbed Wire College*. From the German viewpoint, see Hermann Jung, *Die deutschen Kriegsgefangenen in amerikanischer Hand: USA*, vol. 10, part 1, of Erich Maschke, ed., *Zur Geschichte der deutschen Kriegsgefangenen des zweiten Weltkrieges* (Munich: Verlag Ernst und Werner Gieseking, 1972), 232–238.

3. "New Evidence in Connection with the Murder of Prisoner of War Hans Geller," September 30, 1946, M-CMR 1:125–126.

4. M-CMR 1:120–123; emphasis added. The commander's reply is quoted in an unsigned draft with handwritten corrections, "Memo to the Asst. JAG Thru Acting Chief, Military Justice Group, Subject: "New Evidence in . . . the Murder of POW Hans Geller."

5. M-CMR 1:154.

6. Waters, *Lone Star Stalag*, 134.

7. David Lamb, "Prisoners of Silence, in a Small Kansas Cemetery, the Graves of 14 German POWs Represent One of the Last Untold Stories of World War II," Los Angeles *Times*, Nov. 30, 1990. Edgar Beyer was then manager of a Hamburg bank.

8. Rudiger Overmans, "German Historiography, the War Losses, and the Prisoners of War," in Bischof and Ambrose, eds., *Eisenhower and the German POWs*, 134, 167.

9. The original request, April 16, 1957, and the reply, June 4, are found in D-CMR 2:25–31; subsequent communications in 1:5–18.

10. Officer of Justice Santen, personal communication with author, Sept. 22, 1998.

11. Paul Carell and Günter Böddeker, *Die Gefangenen, Leben und Überleben deutscher Soldaten hinter Stacheldraht* (Frankfurt am Main: Verlag Ulstein, 1980), 91.

12. Ken Knox, personal communication with author, 1998.

13. David Lamb's interview with Knox, "Prisoners of Silence.".

14. Green, *Extreme Justice.*

15. Lamb, "Prisoners of Silence."

16. United Nations, Convention against Torture, part I, article 1. It came into effect on June 26, 1987, after ratification by twenty states. As of September 2010, it had 147 signatories. June 26 is now the International Day of Support for Torture Victims.

17. Quoted in Eugene Davidson, *The Trial of the Germans: An Account of the Twenty-two Defendants before the International Military Tribunal at Nuremberg* (New York: Macmillan, 1966), 19.

18. Bradley F. Smith, *The Road to Nuremberg* (New York: Basic Books, 1981); Telford Taylor, *The Anatomy of the Nuremberg Trials: A Personal Memoir* (New York: Alfred A. Knopf, 1992).

19. Telford Taylor, *Nuremberg and Vietnam: An American Tragedy* (Chicago: Quadrangle Books, 1970). Taylor was U.S. chief counsel at Nuremberg and taught law at Columbia.

20. Donald A. Wells, *War Crimes and Laws of War* (Lanham, Md.: University Press of America, 1984), 55–56, 68–69. The quote, on pp. 107–108, was uttered by Maj. Gorson Livingstone, Class of 1960 at West Point. (Wells cites *The Citizens Commission of Inquiry—The Dellums Committee Hearings on War Crimes in Vietnam* [New York: Random House, 1972], 33.)

21. David L. Miller, editorial, *The Lutheran,* July 2004, 58.

22. Heidi Ridgley, "WWII: The Lost Chapter: P.O. Box 1142," *National Parks,* winter 2010, 44.

Bibliography

Primary Sources

The Articles of War, Approved June 4, 1920. Washington: Government Printing Office, 1920.

BR (Board Report): Military Intelligence Dossier X6042762: Report of Board of Officers Pursuant to Paragraph 78, Special Orders 77—Headquarters Ninth Service Command, Dated 27 March 1944, subtitled Report of Proceedings of a Board of Officers Appointed to Inquire into and Determine the Responsibility for the Death of Prisoner of War Werner Drechsler, ISN-5G-61-NA, Prisoner of War Camp, Papago Park, Arizona. 4 vols., numbered consecutively. NA, RG 319, Records of the Army Staff of the Assistant Chief of Staff, G-3, Intelligence Records of the Investigative Repository, Security Classified Intelligence and Investigative Dossiers 1939–1976, box 338, Personal Name File Werner Drechsler.

Bulletin of the Judge Advocate General of the Army 3, no. 6 (1944).

Convention of July 27, 1929, Relative to the Treatment of Prisoners of War. *Treaties and Other International Agreements of the United States of America, 1776–1949*. Vol. 2, *Multilateral*, 932–964. Ed. Charles I. Bevans. Department of State Publication 8441. 1969.

Court Martial Records (B-CMR, D-CMR, M-CMR). General Services Administration, National Archives and Records Service, World War II Records Division, College Park, Maryland. (These are now housed at the Washington National Records Center, Suitland, Maryland.)

B-CMR: Court Martial 248793, "Record of Trial of Walter Beyer, 8WG-49588; Berthold Seidel, 8WG-49593; Hans Demer, 8WG-49597; Hans Schomer, 8WG-49620; and Willi Scholz, 8WG-49691; at Camp Gruber, Oklahoma, Jan. 17, 18, 19, 20, 21, 24, and 25, 1944." 3 vols., numbered separately.

D-CMR: Court Martial 264108, The United States v. Helmut Fischer, ISN-10-G-NA; Fritz Franke, ISN-10G-1083-NA; Guenther Kuelsen, ISN-10G-1073-NA;

Heinrich Ludwig, ISN-7G-132-NA; Bernhard Reyak, ISN-10G-1069-NA; Otto Stengel, ISN-6-112-NA; and Rolf Wizuy, ISN-10G-1072-NA. 4 vols., numbered consecutively.

M-MCR: Court Martial 260781, "Trial of Menschner, Edgar - 58804, German Prisoner of War, Unteroffizier, Prisoner of War Camp Chaffee, Arkansas by General Court-Martial appointed by the Commanding General of the Eighth Service Command, ASF. Tried at Camp Gruber, Oklahoma 3–4-5 July, 1944." 2 vols.

United States v. German POWs Boehmer et al. (CM 312330). Tried at Camp Swift, Texas, Jan. 22–30, 1946.

Eggers, Reinhold. *Colditz: The German Side of the Story*. New York: W. W. Norton, 1961.

FBI (Federal Bureau of Investigation). San Francisco Division. Central Records. Prisoner of War file.

Ferguson, Clarence. *Kriegsgefangener 3074, Prisoner of War*. Waco, Texas: Texian Press, 1983. (Memoir of a lawyer imprisoned at Oflag 64 [officer's camp]. He defended several of the American POWs who were condemned to death.)

Gruenebaum, Erwin J. Interview by Meredith L. Adams. June 1994. Magalia, California. (He was the prisoners' interpreter at the court martial of the Papago Park seven.)

Jaworski, Leon. *After Fifteen Years*. Houston: Gulf Publishing, 1961. (Memoir of the American officer who prosecuted the Beyer case.)

Lerch, Archer L. "The Army Report on Prisoners of War." *American Mercury*, May 1945, 536–547. (Lerch was Provost Marshal General.)

Military Laws of the United States. 7th edition (1929). Washington: Government Printing Office, 1929.

NA (National Archives of the United States). College Park, Maryland.

RG 38. Records of the Chief of Naval Operations, Office of Naval Intelligence, Special Activities Branch (OP 16-Z).

RG 59. Records of the Department of State.

RG 107. Records of the Secretary of War.

RG 159. Records of the Office of the Inspector General.

RG 165. Records of War Department General and Special Staffs. E 498, War Department Special Staff, Public Relations Division—News Branch, Press and Radio Releases, 1921–1947.

RG 319. Records of the Army Staff of the Assistant Chief of Staff, G-3.

RG 389. Records of the Office of the Provost Marshal General.

RG 407. Records of the Adjutant General's Office.

Parnell, Wilma, with Robert Taber. *The Killing of Corporal Kunze*. Secaucus, N.J.: Lyle Stuart, 1981. (Parnell was the court reporter at the trial of the "Beyer Five.")

Report of Conference at Headquarters, Eighth Service Command, on Prisoners of War and Prisoner of War Camps, Jan. 8, 1944. NA, RG 389, Entry 451, box 1308 290/3495, file 337 General PW.

Romilly, Giles, and Michael Alexander. *Hostages of Colditz*. New York: Praeger, 1954. (Memoir by British veterans of this maximum security prison.)

Stimson, Henry Lewis. Diaries and Papers. Manuscripts and Archives Collection, Yale University Library, New Haven, Conn. Microfilm.

Tollefson, Martin. "Enemy Prisoners of War." *Iowa Law Review* 32 (1946), 51–77. (Tollefson had been director of the POW Operations Division of the Provost Marshal General's Office.)

U.S. Congress. House of Representatives. Committee on Military Affairs. *Investigation of National War Effort, Relative to the Treatment of Prisoners of War in the United States and Abroad*. 78th Congress, 2nd Session, Nov. 30, 1944, Report no. 1992. Washington: Government Printing Office, 1944.

———. *Investigation of National War Effort, Relative to the Treatment of Prisoners of War in the United States and Abroad*. 79th Congress, 1st Session, June 12, 1945, Report no. 728. Washington: Government Printing Office, 1945.

U.S. War Department. *Annual Report: Services of Supply for the Fiscal Year Ending June 30, 1942*. Washington: Government Printing Office, 1942.

———. *Annual Report of the Army Service Forces for the Fiscal Year 1945*. Washington: Government Printing Office, 1946.

———. Headquarters, Army Service Forces. Office of the Provost Marshal General. *Programs of the Office of the Provost Marshal General in World War II*. Washington, 1946.

———. United States Prisoner of War Operations Division. *Historical Monograph*. Washington: Office of the Provost Marshal General, 1945–1946. Microfilm. (Cited as *POW Monograph*.)

Secondary Sources

Ansbacher, Henry L. "Attitudes of German Prisoners of War: A Study of the Dynamics of National-Socialist Followership." *Psychological Monographs* 62 (1948), 1–42.

Billinger, Robert D., Jr. *Hitler's Soldiers in the Sunshine State: German POWs in Florida*. Galveston: University Press of Florida, 2000.

Bischof, Günter, and Stephen E. Ambrose, eds. *Eisenhower and the German POWs: Facts against Falsehood*. Baton Rouge: Louisiana State University Press, 1992.

Carell, Paul, and Günter Böddeker. *Die Gefangenen, Leben und Überleben deutscher Soldaten hinter Stacheldraht*. Frankfurt am Main: Verlag Ulstein, 1980.

Cassidy, Henry C. "What to Do with German Prisoners: The Russian Solution." *Atlantic Monthly*, November 1944, 43–45.

Cline, Ray S. *The War Department: Washington Command Post: The Operations Division*. Washington: Center of Military History, United States Army, 1990. (This is vol. 4, part 2, of the official *United States Army in World War II*.)

Conquest, Robert. *The Great Terror: Stalin's Purge of the Thirties*. New York: Macmillan, 1968.

Costelle, Daniel. *Les Prisonniers*. Paris: Flammarion, 1975.

Dear, Ian. *Escape and Evasion: POW Breakouts in World War Two*. London: Cassell, 1997.

Everett, Robinson O. *Military Justice in the Armed Forces of the United States*. Westport, Conn.: Greenwood, 1956.

Fay, Sidney B. "German Prisoners of War." *Current History* 8, no. 43 (1945), 193–200.

Fiedler, David. *The Enemy Among Us: POWs in Missouri During World War II*. Saint Louis: Missouri Historical Society Press, 2003.

Flynn, Eleanor C. "The Geneva Convention on the Treatment of Prisoners of War." *George Washington Law Review* 11 (June 1943), 505–520.

Gansburg, Judith M. *Stalag, USA: The Remarkable Story of German POWs in America*. New York: Crowell, 1977.

Green, Vincent. *Extreme Justice*. New York: Pocket Books, 1995.

Jung, Hermann. *Die deutschen Kriegsgefangenen in amerikanischer Hand: USA*. Vol. 10, part 1, of Erich Maschke, ed., *Zur Gesichte der deutschen Kriegsgefangenen des zweiten Weltkrieges*. Munich: Verlag Ernst und Werner Geiseking, 1972.

Kelley, John J. "Intelligence and Counterintelligence in German Prisoner of War Camps in Canada During World War II." *Dalhousie Review* 58, no. 2 (1978), 285–294.

Krammer, Arnold. "American Treatment of German Generals During World War II." *Journal of Military History* 54 (January 1990), 27–46.

———. "German Prisoners of War in the United States." *Military Affairs* 40, no. 2 (1976), 68–73.

———. *Nazi Prisoners of War in America*. New York: Stein and Day, 1979; reprint, Lanham, Md.: Scarborough House, 1991.

Lurie, Jonathan. *Arming Military Justice*. Vol. 1, *The Origins of the United States Court of Military Appeals, 1775–1950*. Princeton, N.J.: Princeton University Press, 1993.

Mason, John Brown. "German Prisoners of War in the United States." *American Journal of International Law* 39 (1945), 198–215. (Mason had worked in the Internees Section of the State Department's Special War Problems Division.)

Millett, John D. *The Organization and Role of the Army Service Forces*. Washington: Department of the Army, 1954.

Moore, John Hammond. *The Faustball Tunnel: German Prisoners of War in America and Their Great Escape*. New York: Random House, 1978; reprint, Annapolis, Md.: Naval Institute Press, 2006.

———. "Getting Fritz to Talk." *Virginia Quarterly Review* 54, no. 2 (1978), 263–280.

Persico, Joseph E. *Roosevelt's Secret War: FDR and World War II Espionage*. New York: Random House, 2001.

Porter, Russell. "Ex-Yorkville Man Slain as Prisoner." *New York Times*, Jan. 17, 1945, 11:1.

———. "Prison Camps Rid of Nazi Terrorism. War Department Lifts Secrecy Now that Gestapo Activities Have Been Stamped Out." *New York Times*, Jan. 16, 1945, 1:3, continued 13:2.

——— "Violence Is Ended in Prisoner Camps." *New York Times*, Jan. 18, 1945, 5:1.

Post Oflag 64 Item. Winter 2000. (Publication of American survivors of German Oflag 64.)

Powers, James H. "What to Do with German Prisoners: The American Muddle." *Atlantic Monthly*, November 1944, 46–50.

Radford, William. "Hang Five Nazis." Kansas City *Star*, July 10, 1945.

Reid, P. R. *Colditz, The Full Story*. New York: Macmillan, 1984.

Robin, Ron. *The Barbed Wire College: Reeducating German POWs in the U.S. during World War II*. Princeton, N.J.: Princeton University Press, 1995.

Sherrill, Robert. *Military Justice Is to Justice as Military Music Is to Music*. Rev. ed. New York: Harper and Row, 1970.

Sorge, Martin K. *The Other Price of Hitler's War: German Military Losses Resulting from World War II*. New York: Greenwood, 1986.

Spidle, Jake W. "Axis Prisoners of War in the United States, 1942–1946: A Bibliographical Essay." *Military Affairs* 39, no. 2 (1975), 61–66.

Taylor, Telford. *Anatomy of the Nuremberg Trials*. New York: Knopf, 1992.

Ulmer, S. Sidney. *Military Justice and the Right to Counsel*. Lexington: University of Kentucky Press, 1970.

Villa, Brian Loring. "The Diplomatic and Political Context of the POW Camps Tragedy." In Günter Bischof and Stephen E. Ambrose, eds., *Eisenhower and the German POWs: Facts against Falsehood*. Baton Rouge: Louisiana State University Press, 1992.

Walker, Richard P. *The Lone Star and the Swastika: Prisoners of War in Texas*. Austin, Texas: Eakin Press, 2001.

Waters, Michael R. *Lone Star Stalag: German Prisoners of War at Camp Hearne*. College Station: Texas A and M Press, 2004.

Whittingham, Richard. *Martial Justice: The Last Mass Execution in the United States*. Chicago: Regnery, 1971; reprint, Annapolis, Md.: Naval Institute Press, 1997.

Wells, Donald A. *War Crimes and Laws of War*. Lanham, Md.: University Press of America, 1984.

West, Luther C. *They Call it Justice: Command Influence and the Court-Martial System*. New York: Viking, 1977.

Wittlin, Tadeusz. *Commissar: The Life and Death of Lavrenty Pavlovich Beria*. New York: Macmillan, 1972.

Zweig, Ronald W. "Feeding the Camps: Allied Blockade Policy and the Relief of Concentration Camps in Germany, 1944–1945." *Historical Journal* 41, no. 3 (1998), 825–851.

Index